Macedonia

Also by HARVEY PEKAR

(PUBLISHED BY BALLANTINE BOOKS)

AMERICAN SPLENDOR

OUR MOVIE YEAR

BEST OF AMERICAN SPLENDOR

EGO & HUBRIS: THE MICHAEL MALICE STORY

Macedonia

HARVEY PEKAR

AND

HEATHER ROBERSON

ILLUSTRATED BY

ED PISKOR

VILLARD | NEW YORK

Macedonia is a work of nonfiction.
Some names and identifying details
have been changed.

Published in the United States by Villard Books,
an imprint of The Random House Publishing Group,
a division of Random House, Inc., New York.

Villard and "V" Circled Design are registered
trademarks of Random House, Inc.

ISBN 978-0-345-49899-1

Printed in the United States of America

www.villard.com

2 4 6 8 9 7 5 3 1

First Edition

Macedonia

Macedonia

STORY BY: HARVEY PEKAR AND HEATHER ROBERSON
ART BY: ED PISKOR
WWW.EDPISKOR.COM

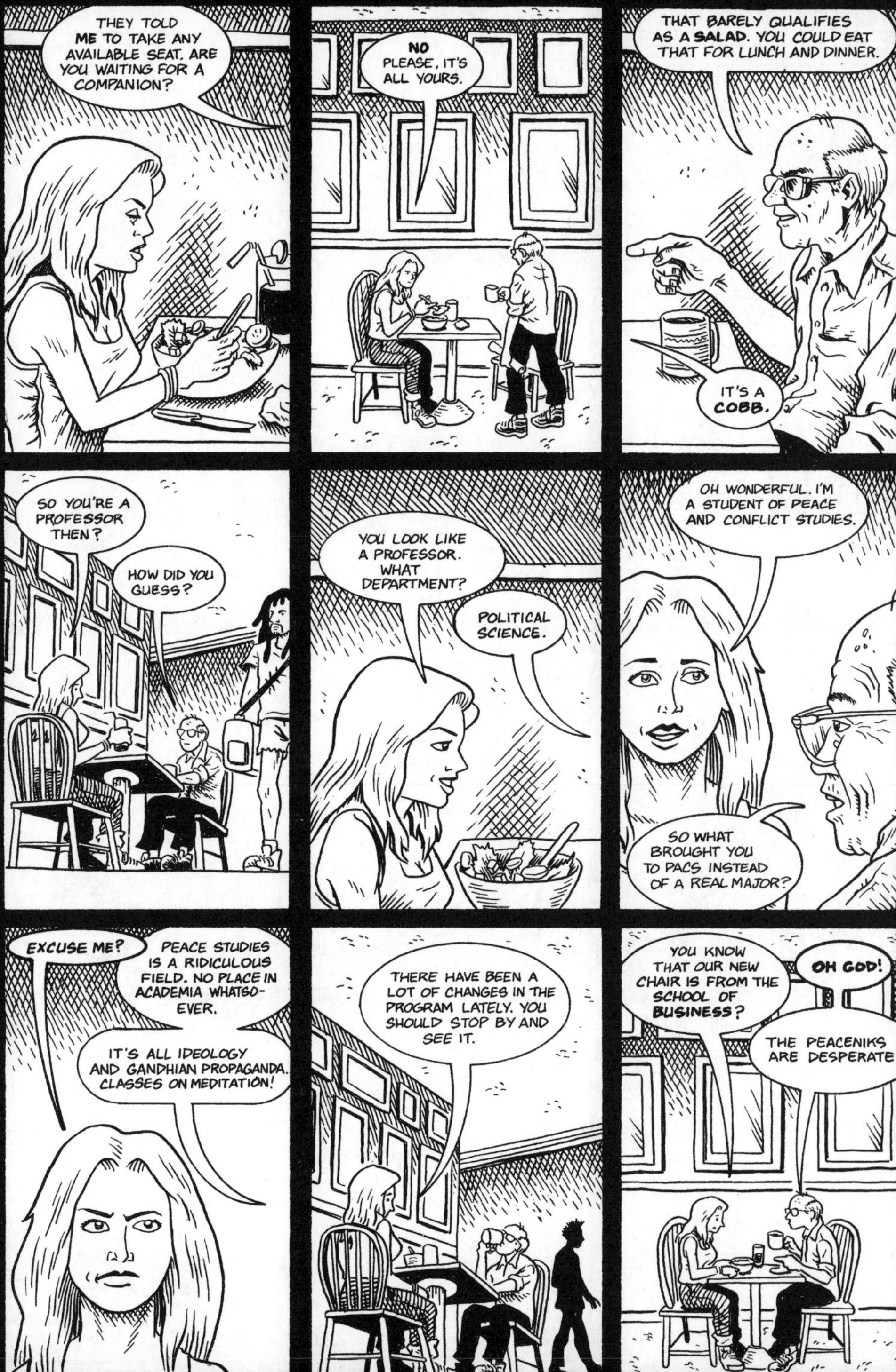
THEY TOLD ME TO TAKE ANY AVAILABLE SEAT. ARE YOU WAITING FOR A COMPANION?
NO PLEASE, IT'S ALL YOURS.
THAT BARELY QUALIFIES AS A SALAD. YOU COULD EAT THAT FOR LUNCH AND DINNER.
IT'S A COBB.
SO YOU'RE A PROFESSOR THEN?
HOW DID YOU GUESS?
YOU LOOK LIKE A PROFESSOR. WHAT DEPARTMENT?
POLITICAL SCIENCE.
OH WONDERFUL. I'M A STUDENT OF PEACE AND CONFLICT STUDIES.
SO WHAT BROUGHT YOU TO PACS INSTEAD OF A REAL MAJOR?
EXCUSE ME?
PEACE STUDIES IS A RIDICULOUS FIELD. NO PLACE IN ACADEMIA WHATSO-EVER.
IT'S ALL IDEOLOGY AND GANDHIAN PROPAGANDA. CLASSES ON MEDITATION!
THERE HAVE BEEN A LOT OF CHANGES IN THE PROGRAM LATELY. YOU SHOULD STOP BY AND SEE IT.
YOU KNOW THAT OUR NEW CHAIR IS FROM THE SCHOOL OF BUSINESS?
OH GOD!
THE PEACENIKS ARE DESPERATE.

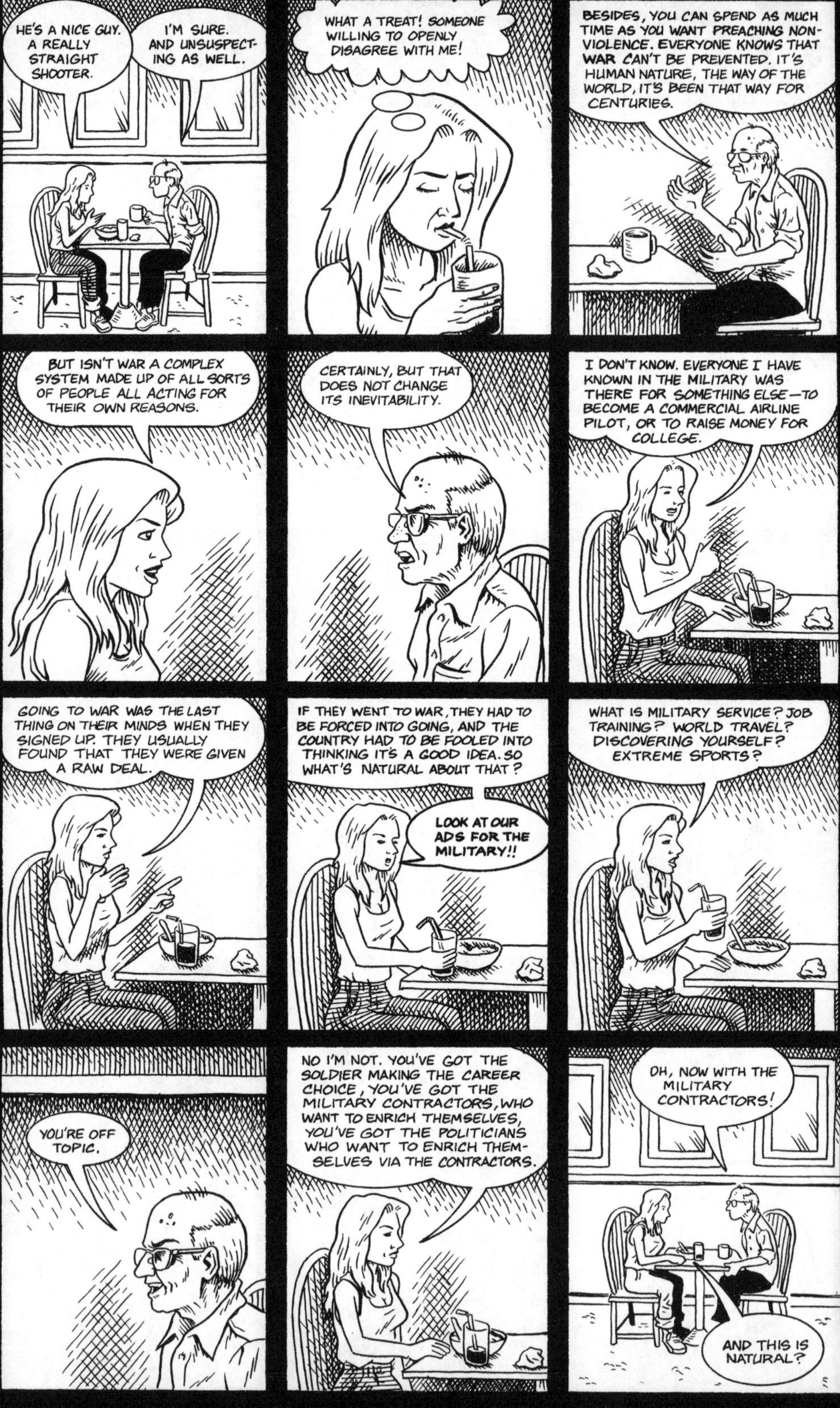
HE'S A NICE GUY. A REALLY STRAIGHT SHOOTER.
I'M SURE. AND UNSUSPECTING AS WELL.
WHAT A TREAT! SOMEONE WILLING TO OPENLY DISAGREE WITH ME!
BESIDES, YOU CAN SPEND AS MUCH TIME AS YOU WANT PREACHING NON-VIOLENCE. EVERYONE KNOWS THAT WAR CAN'T BE PREVENTED. IT'S HUMAN NATURE, THE WAY OF THE WORLD, IT'S BEEN THAT WAY FOR CENTURIES.
BUT ISN'T WAR A COMPLEX SYSTEM MADE UP OF ALL SORTS OF PEOPLE ALL ACTING FOR THEIR OWN REASONS.
CERTAINLY, BUT THAT DOES NOT CHANGE ITS INEVITABILITY.
I DON'T KNOW. EVERYONE I HAVE KNOWN IN THE MILITARY WAS THERE FOR SOMETHING ELSE—TO BECOME A COMMERCIAL AIRLINE PILOT, OR TO RAISE MONEY FOR COLLEGE.
GOING TO WAR WAS THE LAST THING ON THEIR MINDS WHEN THEY SIGNED UP. THEY USUALLY FOUND THAT THEY WERE GIVEN A RAW DEAL.
IF THEY WENT TO WAR, THEY HAD TO BE FORCED INTO GOING, AND THE COUNTRY HAD TO BE FOOLED INTO THINKING IT'S A GOOD IDEA. SO WHAT'S NATURAL ABOUT THAT?
LOOK AT OUR ADS FOR THE MILITARY!!
WHAT IS MILITARY SERVICE? JOB TRAINING? WORLD TRAVEL? DISCOVERING YOURSELF? EXTREME SPORTS?
YOU'RE OFF TOPIC.
NO I'M NOT. YOU'VE GOT THE SOLDIER MAKING THE CAREER CHOICE, YOU'VE GOT THE MILITARY CONTRACTORS, WHO WANT TO ENRICH THEMSELVES, YOU'VE GOT THE POLITICIANS WHO WANT TO ENRICH THEMSELVES VIA THE CONTRACTORS.
OH, NOW WITH THE MILITARY CONTRACTORS!
AND THIS IS NATURAL?

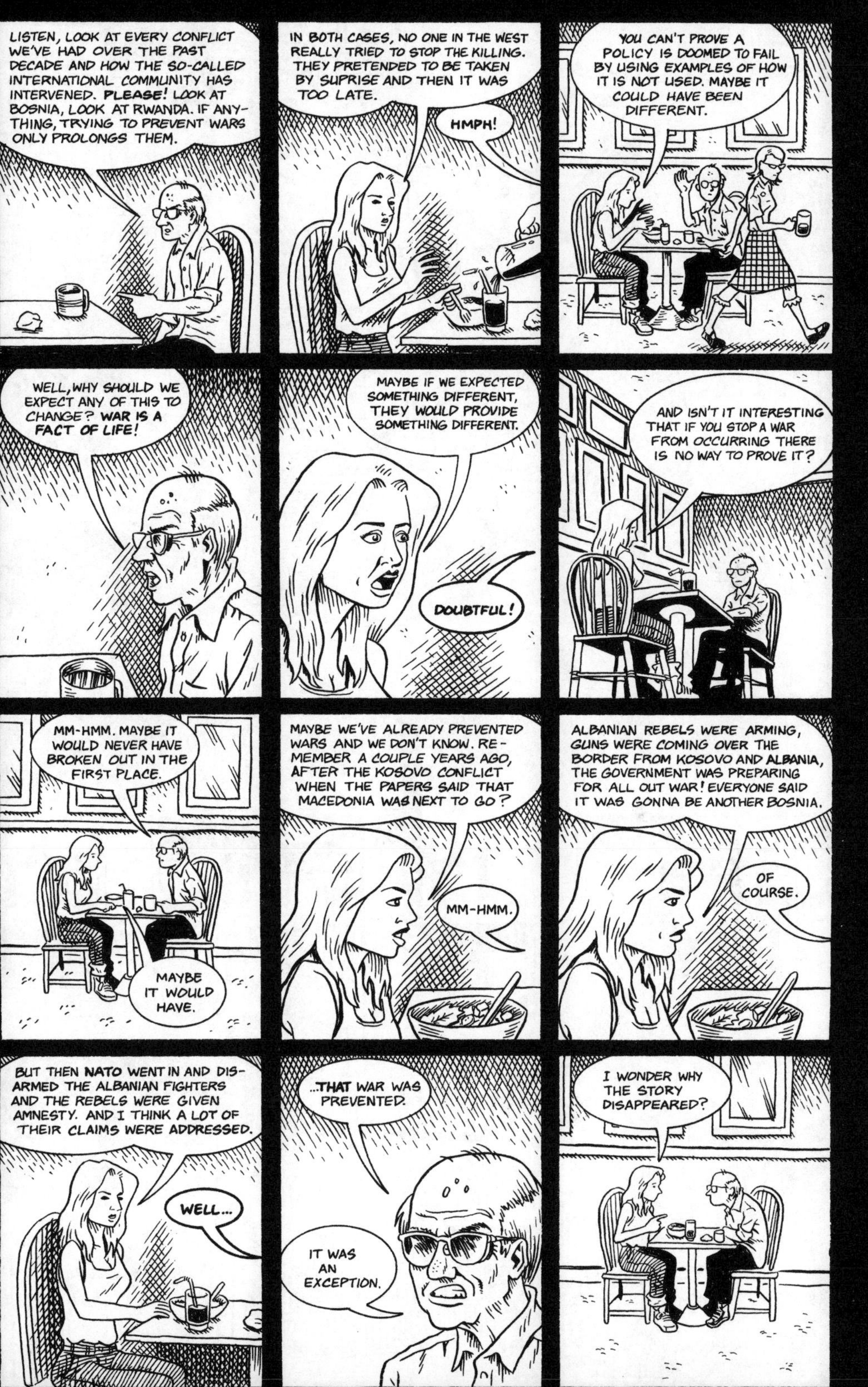
LISTEN, LOOK AT EVERY CONFLICT WE'VE HAD OVER THE PAST DECADE AND HOW THE SO-CALLED INTERNATIONAL COMMUNITY HAS INTERVENED. PLEASE! LOOK AT BOSNIA, LOOK AT RWANDA. IF ANYTHING, TRYING TO PREVENT WARS ONLY PROLONGS THEM.
IN BOTH CASES, NO ONE IN THE WEST REALLY TRIED TO STOP THE KILLING. THEY PRETENDED TO BE TAKEN BY SUPRISE AND THEN IT WAS TOO LATE.
HMPH!
YOU CAN'T PROVE A POLICY IS DOOMED TO FAIL BY USING EXAMPLES OF HOW IT IS NOT USED. MAYBE IT COULD HAVE BEEN DIFFERENT.
WELL, WHY SHOULD WE EXPECT ANY OF THIS TO CHANGE? WAR IS A FACT OF LIFE!
MAYBE IF WE EXPECTED SOMETHING DIFFERENT, THEY WOULD PROVIDE SOMETHING DIFFERENT.
DOUBTFUL!
AND ISN'T IT INTERESTING THAT IF YOU STOP A WAR FROM OCCURRING THERE IS NO WAY TO PROVE IT?
MM-HMM. MAYBE IT WOULD NEVER HAVE BROKEN OUT IN THE FIRST PLACE.
MAYBE IT WOULD HAVE.
MAYBE WE'VE ALREADY PREVENTED WARS AND WE DON'T KNOW. REMEMBER A COUPLE YEARS AGO, AFTER THE KOSOVO CONFLICT WHEN THE PAPERS SAID THAT MACEDONIA WAS NEXT TO GO?
MM-HMM.
ALBANIAN REBELS WERE ARMING, GUNS WERE COMING OVER THE BORDER FROM KOSOVO AND ALBANIA, THE GOVERNMENT WAS PREPARING FOR ALL OUT WAR! EVERYONE SAID IT WAS GONNA BE ANOTHER BOSNIA.
OF COURSE.
BUT THEN NATO WENT IN AND DISARMED THE ALBANIAN FIGHTERS AND THE REBELS WERE GIVEN AMNESTY. AND I THINK A LOT OF THEIR CLAIMS WERE ADDRESSED.
WELL...
...THAT WAR WAS PREVENTED.
IT WAS AN EXCEPTION.
I WONDER WHY THE STORY DISAPPEARED?

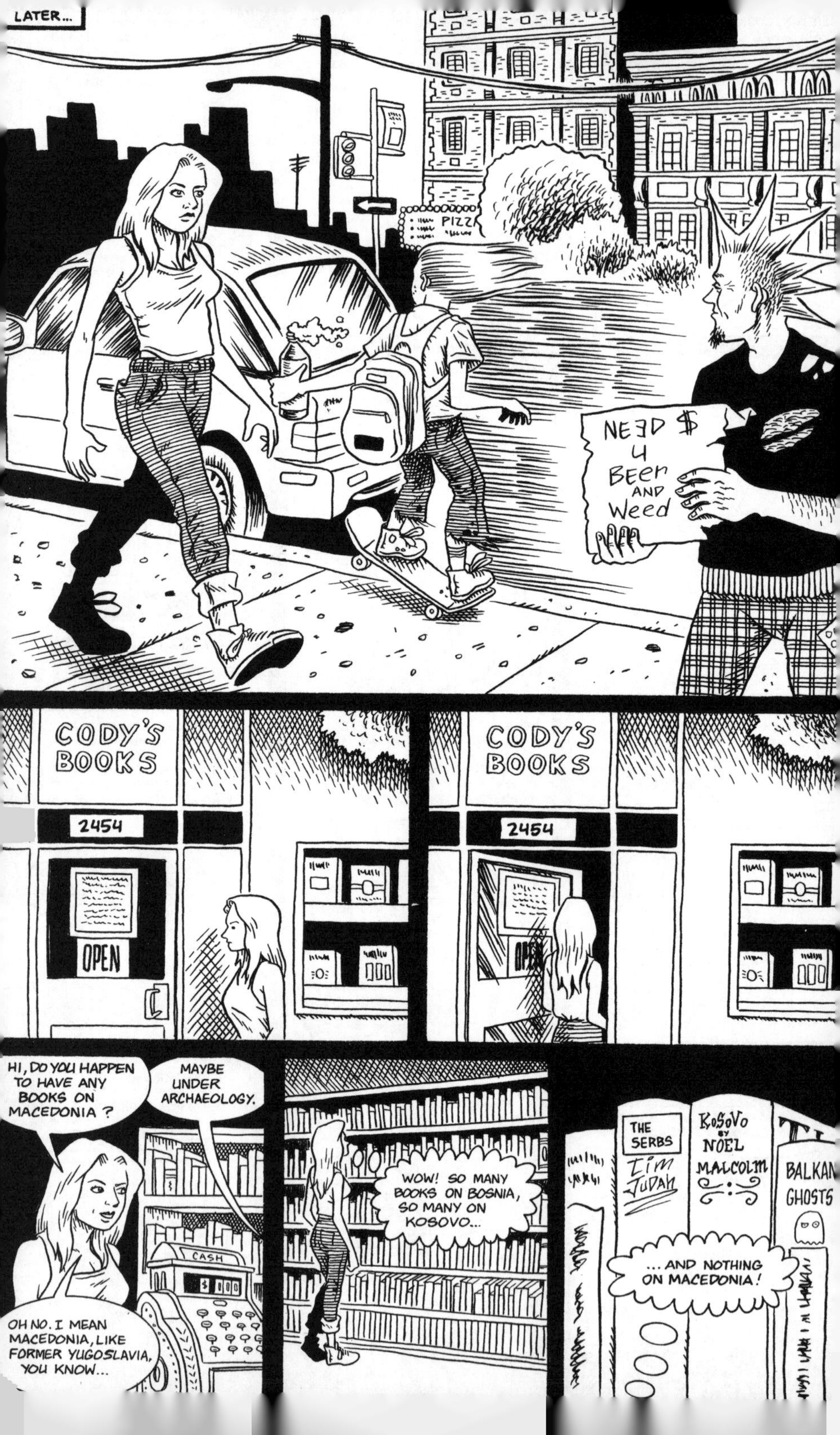
LATER...
PIZZ
NEED $ 4 Beer AND Weed
CODY'S BOOKS
2454
OPEN
CODY'S BOOKS
2454
HI, DO YOU HAPPEN TO HAVE ANY BOOKS ON MACEDONIA ?
MAYBE UNDER ARCHAEOLOGY.
OH NO. I MEAN MACEDONIA, LIKE FORMER YUGOSLAVIA, YOU KNOW...
CASH
WOW! SO MANY BOOKS ON BOSNIA, SO MANY ON KOSOVO...
THE SERBS
Tim Judah
KOSOVO BY NOEL MALCOLM
BALKAN GHOSTS
... AND NOTHING ON MACEDONIA!

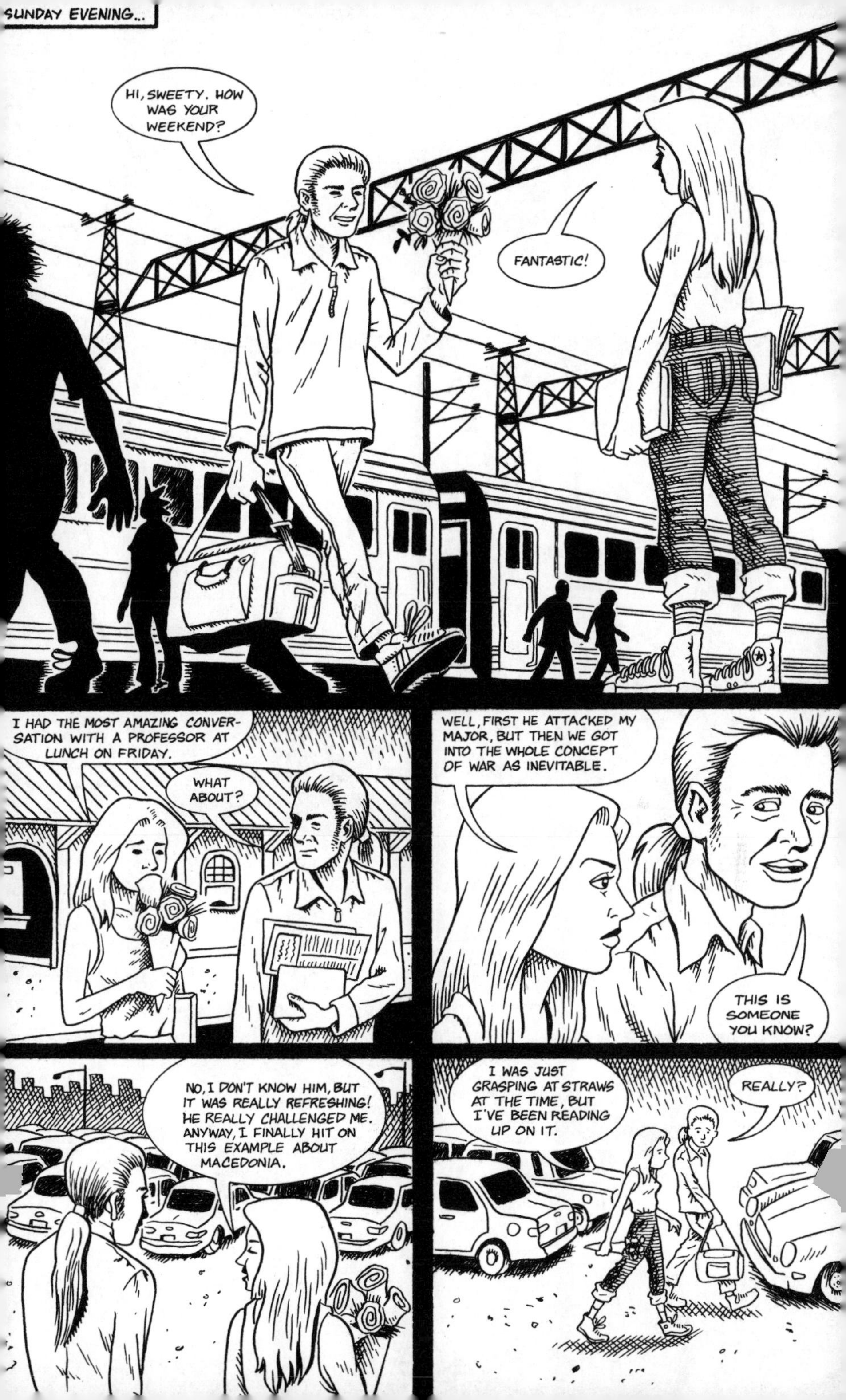
SUNDAY EVENING...
HI, SWEETY. HOW WAS YOUR WEEKEND?
FANTASTIC!
I HAD THE MOST AMAZING CONVERSATION WITH A PROFESSOR AT LUNCH ON FRIDAY.
WHAT ABOUT?
WELL, FIRST HE ATTACKED MY MAJOR, BUT THEN WE GOT INTO THE WHOLE CONCEPT OF WAR AS INEVITABLE.
THIS IS SOMEONE YOU KNOW?
NO, I DON'T KNOW HIM, BUT IT WAS REALLY REFRESHING! HE REALLY CHALLENGED ME. ANYWAY, I FINALLY HIT ON THIS EXAMPLE ABOUT MACEDONIA.
I WAS JUST GRASPING AT STRAWS AT THE TIME, BUT I'VE BEEN READING UP ON IT.
REALLY?

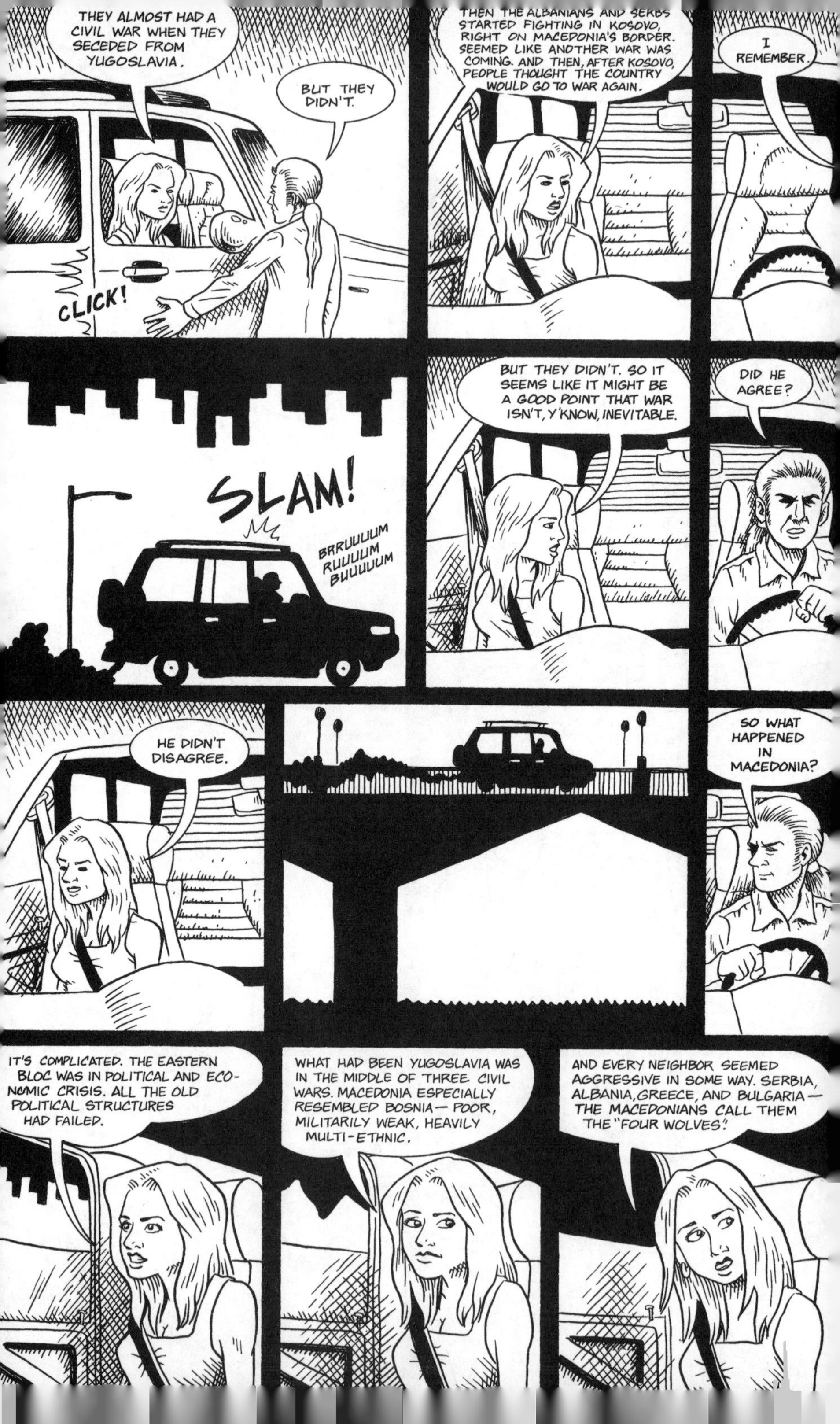
THEY ALMOST HAD A CIVIL WAR WHEN THEY SECEDED FROM YUGOSLAVIA.
BUT THEY DIDN'T.
CLICK!
THEN THE ALBANIANS AND SERBS STARTED FIGHTING IN KOSOVO, RIGHT ON MACEDONIA'S BORDER. SEEMED LIKE ANOTHER WAR WAS COMING. AND THEN, AFTER KOSOVO, PEOPLE THOUGHT THE COUNTRY WOULD GO TO WAR AGAIN.
I REMEMBER.
SLAM!
BRRUUUUM RUUUUM BUUUUUM
BUT THEY DIDN'T. SO IT SEEMS LIKE IT MIGHT BE A GOOD POINT THAT WAR ISN'T, Y'KNOW, INEVITABLE.
DID HE AGREE?
HE DIDN'T DISAGREE.
SO WHAT HAPPENED IN MACEDONIA?
IT'S COMPLICATED. THE EASTERN BLOC WAS IN POLITICAL AND ECO-NOMIC CRISIS. ALL THE OLD POLITICAL STRUCTURES HAD FAILED.
WHAT HAD BEEN YUGOSLAVIA WAS IN THE MIDDLE OF THREE CIVIL WARS. MACEDONIA ESPECIALLY RESEMBLED BOSNIA— POOR, MILITARILY WEAK, HEAVILY MULTI-ETHNIC.
AND EVERY NEIGHBOR SEEMED AGGRESSIVE IN SOME WAY. SERBIA, ALBANIA, GREECE, AND BULGARIA— THE MACEDONIANS CALL THEM THE "FOUR WOLVES".

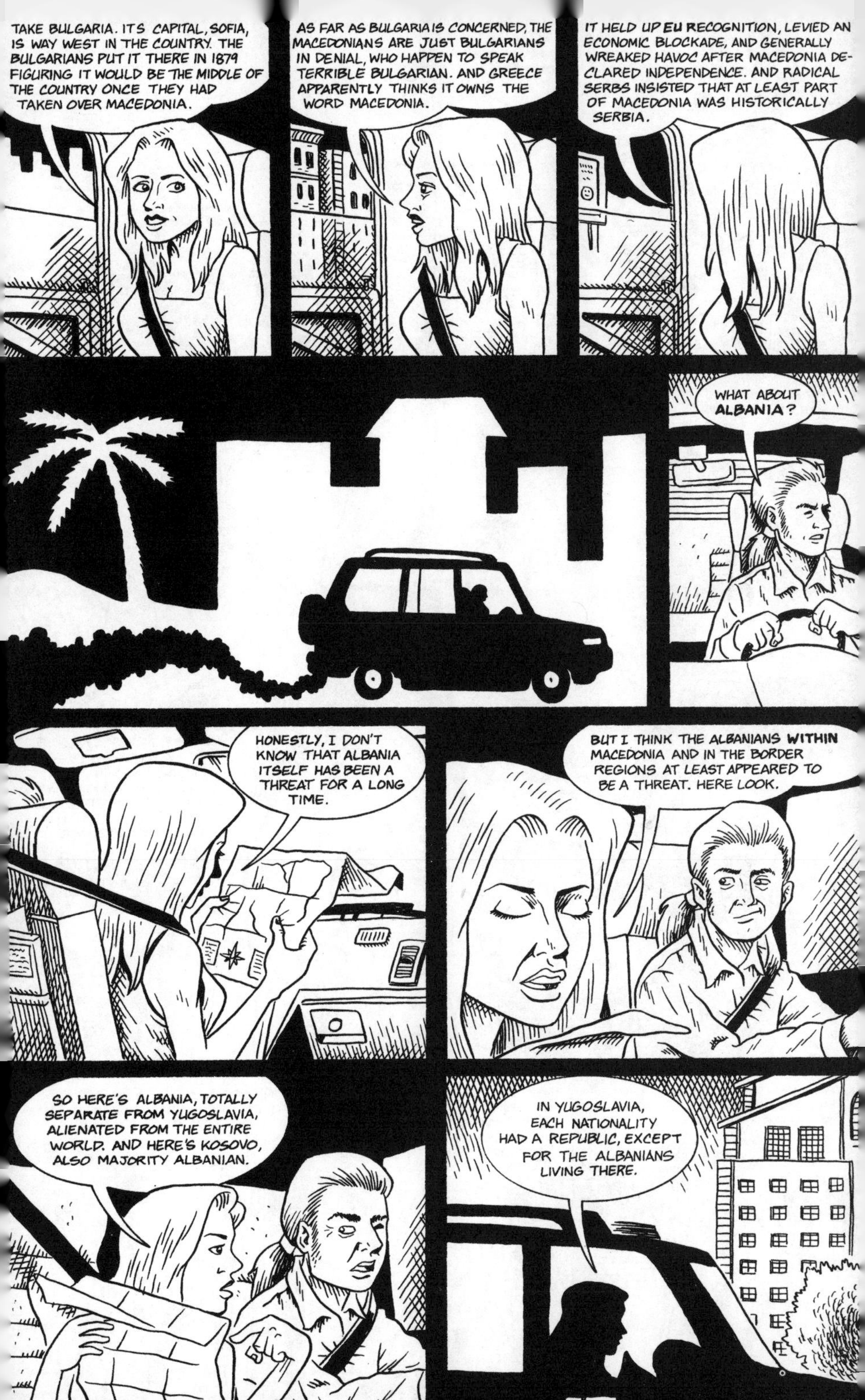
TAKE BULGARIA. ITS CAPITAL, SOFIA, IS WAY WEST IN THE COUNTRY. THE BULGARIANS PUT IT THERE IN 1879 FIGURING IT WOULD BE THE MIDDLE OF THE COUNTRY ONCE THEY HAD TAKEN OVER MACEDONIA.
AS FAR AS BULGARIA IS CONCERNED, THE MACEDONIANS ARE JUST BULGARIANS IN DENIAL, WHO HAPPEN TO SPEAK TERRIBLE BULGARIAN. AND GREECE APPARENTLY THINKS IT OWNS THE WORD MACEDONIA.
IT HELD UP EU RECOGNITION, LEVIED AN ECONOMIC BLOCKADE, AND GENERALLY WREAKED HAVOC AFTER MACEDONIA DECLARED INDEPENDENCE. AND RADICAL SERBS INSISTED THAT AT LEAST PART OF MACEDONIA WAS HISTORICALLY SERBIA.
WHAT ABOUT ALBANIA?
HONESTLY, I DON'T KNOW THAT ALBANIA ITSELF HAS BEEN A THREAT FOR A LONG TIME.
BUT I THINK THE ALBANIANS WITHIN MACEDONIA AND IN THE BORDER REGIONS AT LEAST APPEARED TO BE A THREAT. HERE LOOK.
SO HERE'S ALBANIA, TOTALLY SEPARATE FROM YUGOSLAVIA, ALIENATED FROM THE ENTIRE WORLD. AND HERE'S KOSOVO, ALSO MAJORITY ALBANIAN.
IN YUGOSLAVIA, EACH NATIONALITY HAD A REPUBLIC, EXCEPT FOR THE ALBANIANS LIVING THERE.

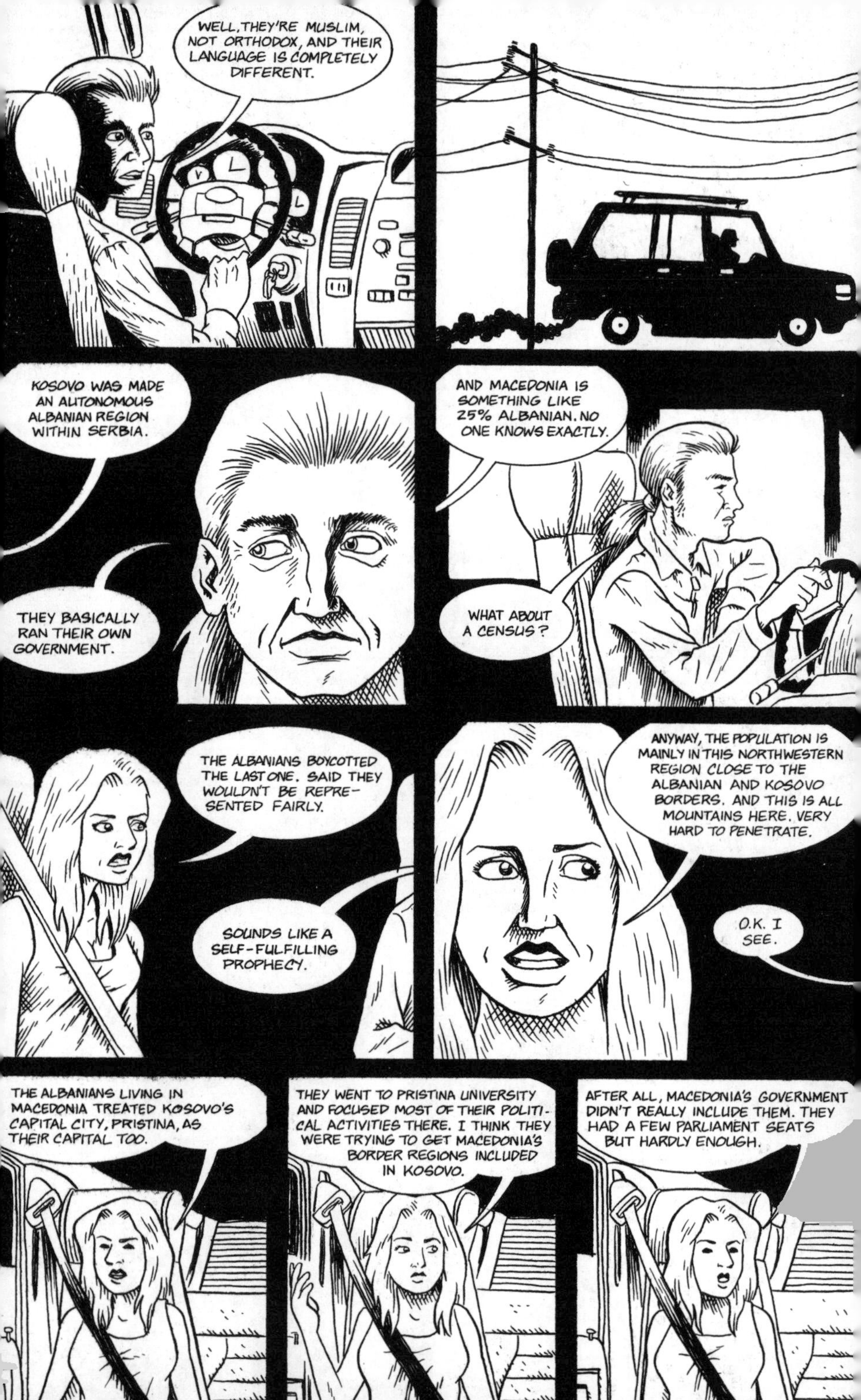
WELL, THEY'RE MUSLIM, NOT ORTHODOX, AND THEIR LANGUAGE IS COMPLETELY DIFFERENT.
KOSOVO WAS MADE AN AUTONOMOUS ALBANIAN REGION WITHIN SERBIA.
THEY BASICALLY RAN THEIR OWN GOVERNMENT.
AND MACEDONIA IS SOMETHING LIKE 25% ALBANIAN. NO ONE KNOWS EXACTLY.
WHAT ABOUT A CENSUS?
THE ALBANIANS BOYCOTTED THE LAST ONE. SAID THEY WOULDN'T BE REPRESENTED FAIRLY.
SOUNDS LIKE A SELF-FULFILLING PROPHECY.
ANYWAY, THE POPULATION IS MAINLY IN THIS NORTHWESTERN REGION CLOSE TO THE ALBANIAN AND KOSOVO BORDERS. AND THIS IS ALL MOUNTAINS HERE. VERY HARD TO PENETRATE.
O.K. I SEE.
THE ALBANIANS LIVING IN MACEDONIA TREATED KOSOVO'S CAPITAL CITY, PRISTINA, AS THEIR CAPITAL TOO.
THEY WENT TO PRISTINA UNIVERSITY AND FOCUSED MOST OF THEIR POLITICAL ACTIVITIES THERE. I THINK THEY WERE TRYING TO GET MACEDONIA'S BORDER REGIONS INCLUDED IN KOSOVO.
AFTER ALL, MACEDONIA'S GOVERNMENT DIDN'T REALLY INCLUDE THEM. THEY HAD A FEW PARLIAMENT SEATS BUT HARDLY ENOUGH.

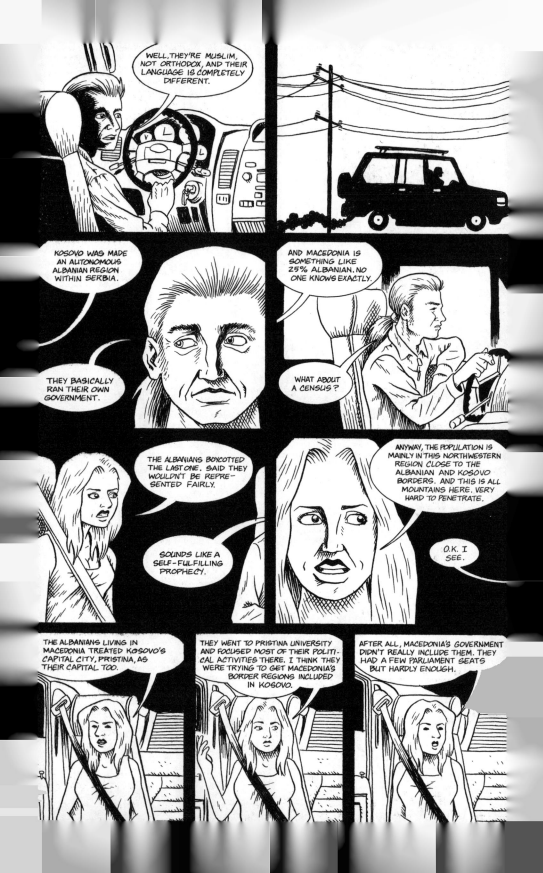

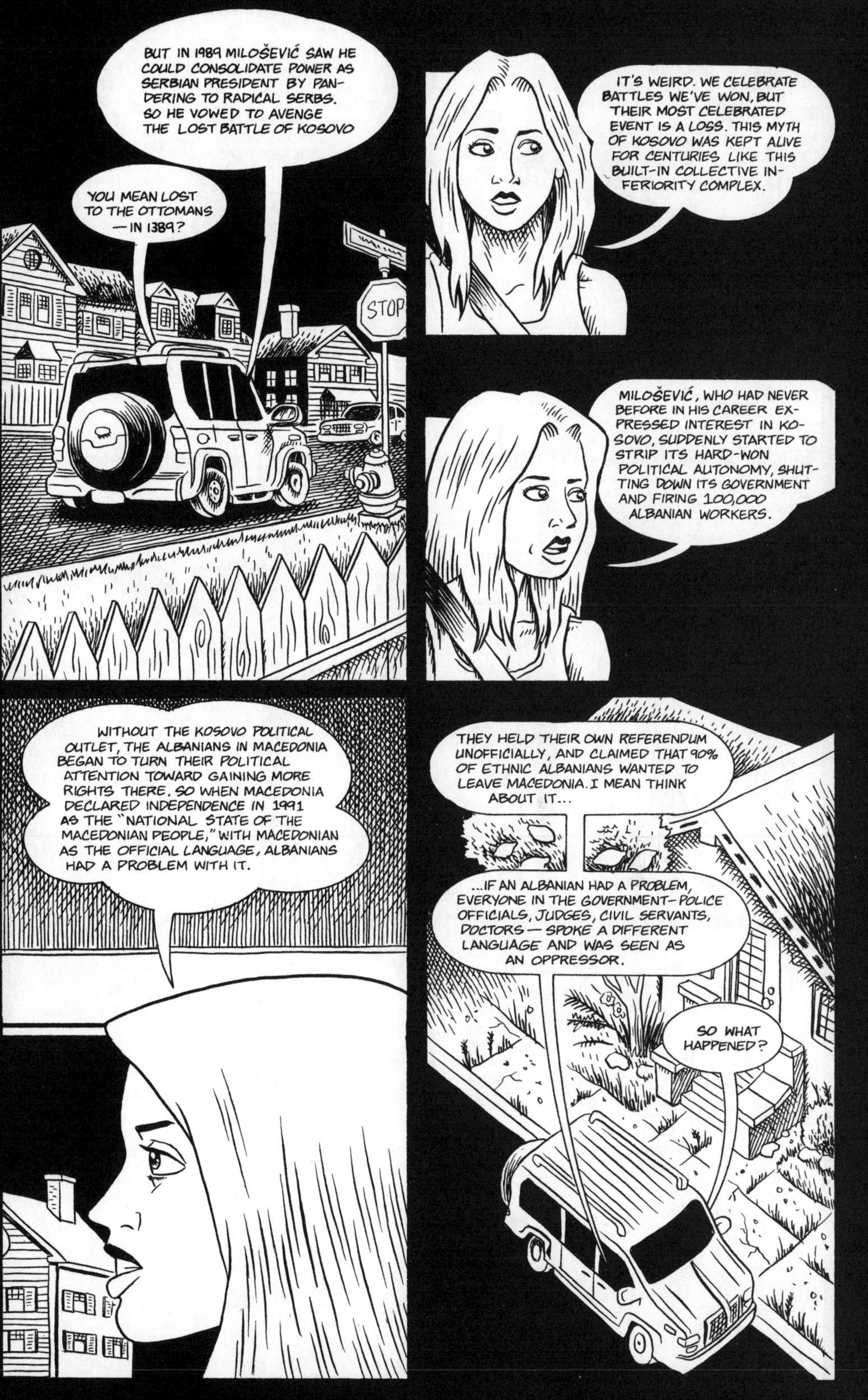
BUT IN 1989 MILOŠEVIĆ SAW HE COULD CONSOLIDATE POWER AS SERBIAN PRESIDENT BY PANDERING TO RADICAL SERBS. SO HE VOWED TO AVENGE THE LOST BATTLE OF KOSOVO
YOU MEAN LOST TO THE OTTOMANS —IN 1389?
STOP
IT'S WEIRD. WE CELEBRATE BATTLES WE'VE WON, BUT THEIR MOST CELEBRATED EVENT IS A LOSS. THIS MYTH OF KOSOVO WAS KEPT ALIVE FOR CENTURIES LIKE THIS BUILT-IN COLLECTIVE INFERIORITY COMPLEX.
MILOŠEVIĆ, WHO HAD NEVER BEFORE IN HIS CAREER EXPRESSED INTEREST IN KOSOVO, SUDDENLY STARTED TO STRIP ITS HARD-WON POLITICAL AUTONOMY, SHUTTING DOWN ITS GOVERNMENT AND FIRING 100,000 ALBANIAN WORKERS.
WITHOUT THE KOSOVO POLITICAL OUTLET, THE ALBANIANS IN MACEDONIA BEGAN TO TURN THEIR POLITICAL ATTENTION TOWARD GAINING MORE RIGHTS THERE. SO WHEN MACEDONIA DECLARED INDEPENDENCE IN 1991 AS THE "NATIONAL STATE OF THE MACEDONIAN PEOPLE," WITH MACEDONIAN AS THE OFFICIAL LANGUAGE, ALBANIANS HAD A PROBLEM WITH IT.
THEY HELD THEIR OWN REFERENDUM UNOFFICIALLY, AND CLAIMED THAT 90% OF ETHNIC ALBANIANS WANTED TO LEAVE MACEDONIA. I MEAN THINK ABOUT IT...
...IF AN ALBANIAN HAD A PROBLEM, EVERYONE IN THE GOVERNMENT—POLICE OFFICIALS, JUDGES, CIVIL SERVANTS, DOCTORS—SPOKE A DIFFERENT LANGUAGE AND WAS SEEN AS AN OPPRESSOR.
SO WHAT HAPPENED?

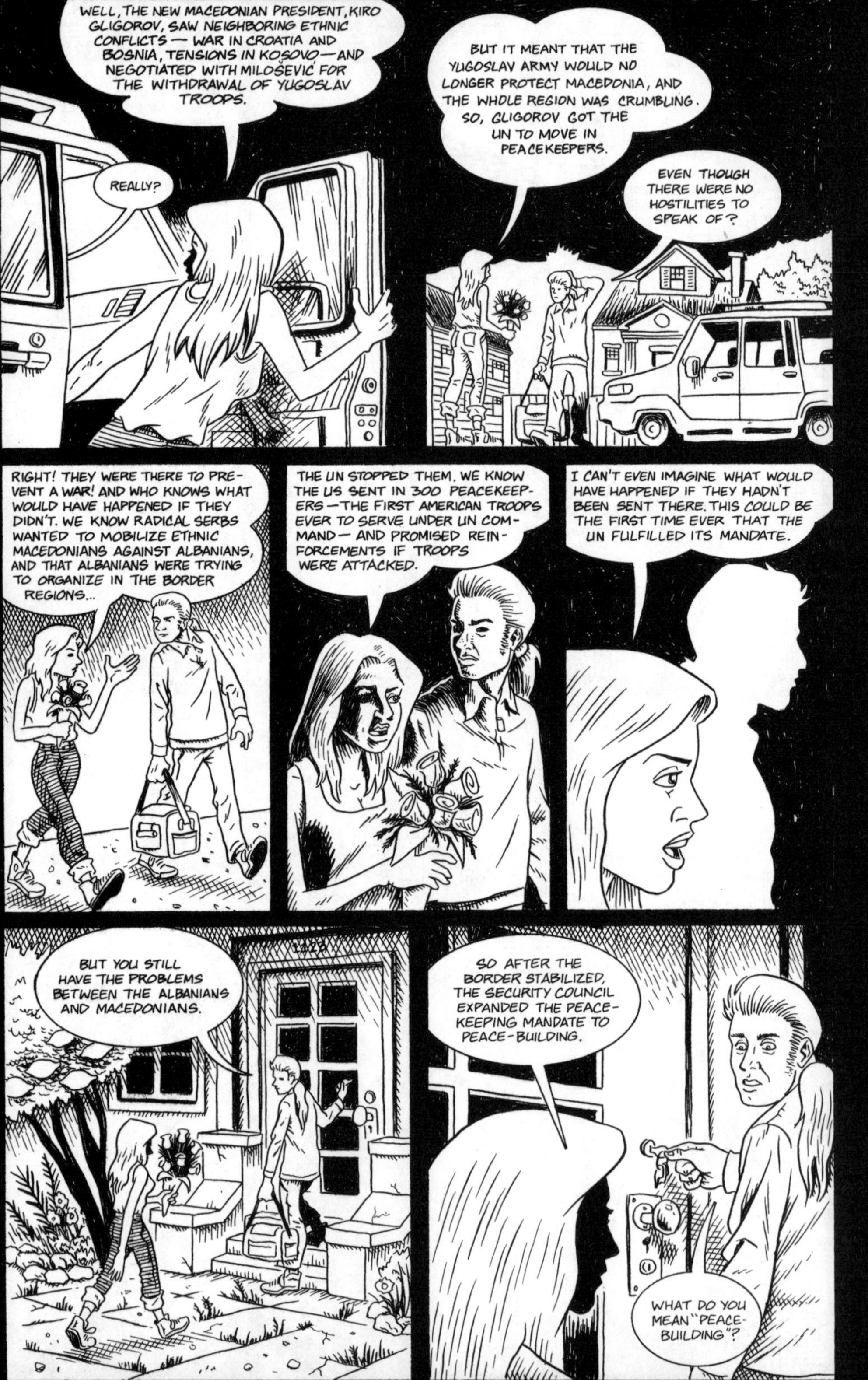
WELL, THE NEW MACEDONIAN PRESIDENT, KIRO GLIGOROV, SAW NEIGHBORING ETHNIC CONFLICTS — WAR IN CROATIA AND BOSNIA, TENSIONS IN KOSOVO — AND NEGOTIATED WITH MILOŠEVIĆ FOR THE WITHDRAWAL OF YUGOSLAV TROOPS.
REALLY?
BUT IT MEANT THAT THE YUGOSLAV ARMY WOULD NO LONGER PROTECT MACEDONIA, AND THE WHOLE REGION WAS CRUMBLING. SO, GLIGOROV GOT THE UN TO MOVE IN PEACEKEEPERS.
EVEN THOUGH THERE WERE NO HOSTILITIES TO SPEAK OF?
RIGHT! THEY WERE THERE TO PREVENT A WAR! AND WHO KNOWS WHAT WOULD HAVE HAPPENED IF THEY DIDN'T. WE KNOW RADICAL SERBS WANTED TO MOBILIZE ETHNIC MACEDONIANS AGAINST ALBANIANS, AND THAT ALBANIANS WERE TRYING TO ORGANIZE IN THE BORDER REGIONS...
THE UN STOPPED THEM. WE KNOW THE US SENT IN 300 PEACEKEEPERS — THE FIRST AMERICAN TROOPS EVER TO SERVE UNDER UN COMMAND — AND PROMISED REINFORCEMENTS IF TROOPS WERE ATTACKED.
I CAN'T EVEN IMAGINE WHAT WOULD HAVE HAPPENED IF THEY HADN'T BEEN SENT THERE. THIS COULD BE THE FIRST TIME EVER THAT THE UN FULFILLED ITS MANDATE.
BUT YOU STILL HAVE THE PROBLEMS BETWEEN THE ALBANIANS AND MACEDONIANS.
SO AFTER THE BORDER STABILIZED, THE SECURITY COUNCIL EXPANDED THE PEACEKEEPING MANDATE TO PEACE-BUILDING.
WHAT DO YOU MEAN "PEACE-BUILDING"?

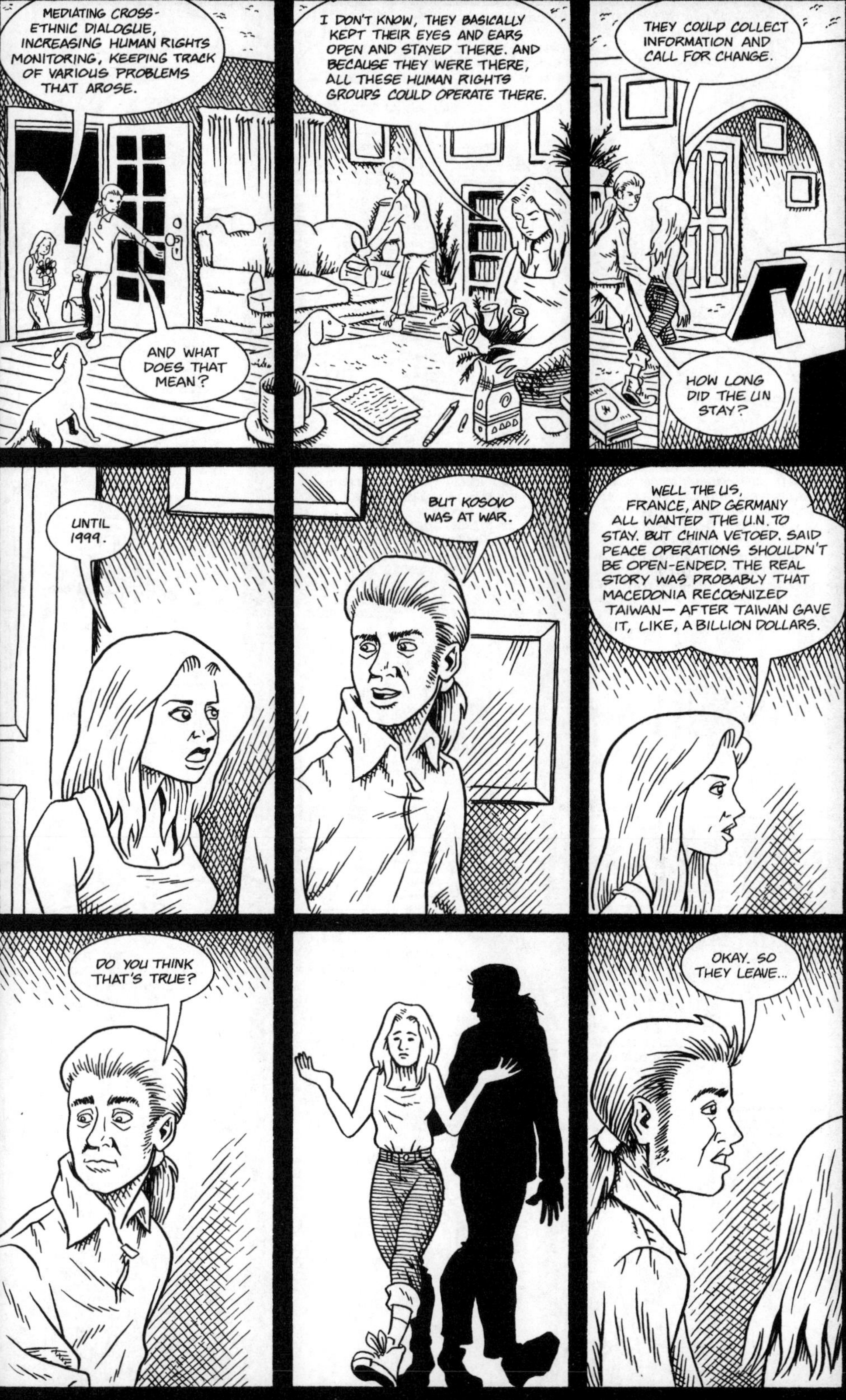
MEDIATING CROSS-ETHNIC DIALOGUE, INCREASING HUMAN RIGHTS MONITORING, KEEPING TRACK OF VARIOUS PROBLEMS THAT AROSE.
AND WHAT DOES THAT MEAN?
I DON'T KNOW, THEY BASICALLY KEPT THEIR EYES AND EARS OPEN AND STAYED THERE. AND BECAUSE THEY WERE THERE, ALL THESE HUMAN RIGHTS GROUPS COULD OPERATE THERE.
THEY COULD COLLECT INFORMATION AND CALL FOR CHANGE.
HOW LONG DID THE UN STAY?
UNTIL 1999.
BUT KOSOVO WAS AT WAR.
WELL THE US, FRANCE, AND GERMANY ALL WANTED THE U.N. TO STAY. BUT CHINA VETOED. SAID PEACE OPERATIONS SHOULDN'T BE OPEN-ENDED. THE REAL STORY WAS PROBABLY THAT MACEDONIA RECOGNIZED TAIWAN— AFTER TAIWAN GAVE IT, LIKE, A BILLION DOLLARS.
DO YOU THINK THAT'S TRUE?
OKAY. SO THEY LEAVE...

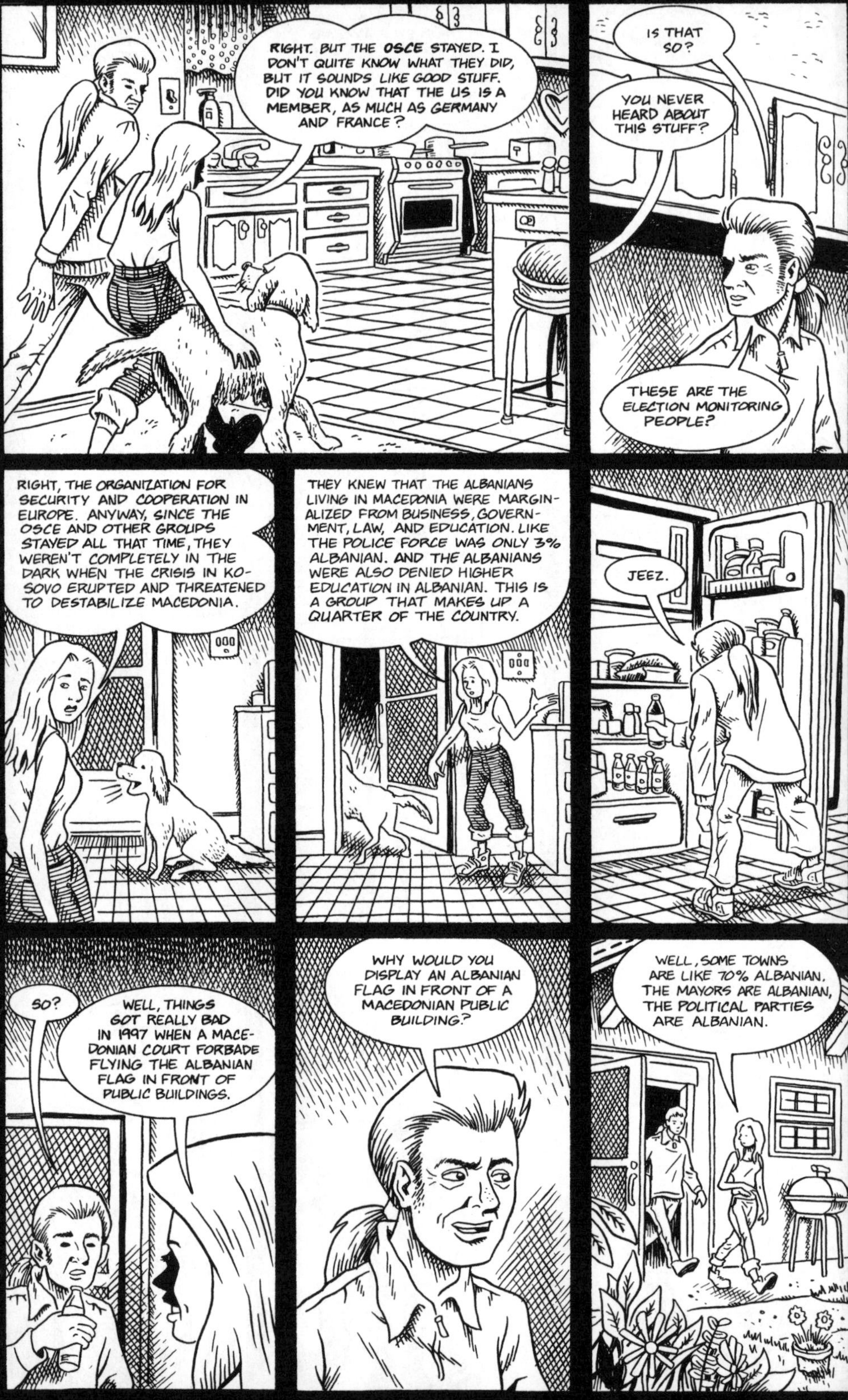
RIGHT. BUT THE OSCE STAYED. I DON'T QUITE KNOW WHAT THEY DID, BUT IT SOUNDS LIKE GOOD STUFF. DID YOU KNOW THAT THE US IS A MEMBER, AS MUCH AS GERMANY AND FRANCE?
IS THAT SO?
YOU NEVER HEARD ABOUT THIS STUFF?
THESE ARE THE ELECTION MONITORING PEOPLE?
RIGHT, THE ORGANIZATION FOR SECURITY AND COOPERATION IN EUROPE. ANYWAY, SINCE THE OSCE AND OTHER GROUPS STAYED ALL THAT TIME, THEY WEREN'T COMPLETELY IN THE DARK WHEN THE CRISIS IN KOSOVO ERUPTED AND THREATENED TO DESTABILIZE MACEDONIA.
THEY KNEW THAT THE ALBANIANS LIVING IN MACEDONIA WERE MARGINALIZED FROM BUSINESS, GOVERNMENT, LAW, AND EDUCATION. LIKE THE POLICE FORCE WAS ONLY 3% ALBANIAN. AND THE ALBANIANS WERE ALSO DENIED HIGHER EDUCATION IN ALBANIAN. THIS IS A GROUP THAT MAKES UP A QUARTER OF THE COUNTRY.
JEEZ.
SO?
WELL, THINGS GOT REALLY BAD IN 1997 WHEN A MACEDONIAN COURT FORBADE FLYING THE ALBANIAN FLAG IN FRONT OF PUBLIC BUILDINGS.
WHY WOULD YOU DISPLAY AN ALBANIAN FLAG IN FRONT OF A MACEDONIAN PUBLIC BUILDING?
WELL, SOME TOWNS ARE LIKE 70% ALBANIAN. THE MAYORS ARE ALBANIAN, THE POLITICAL PARTIES ARE ALBANIAN.

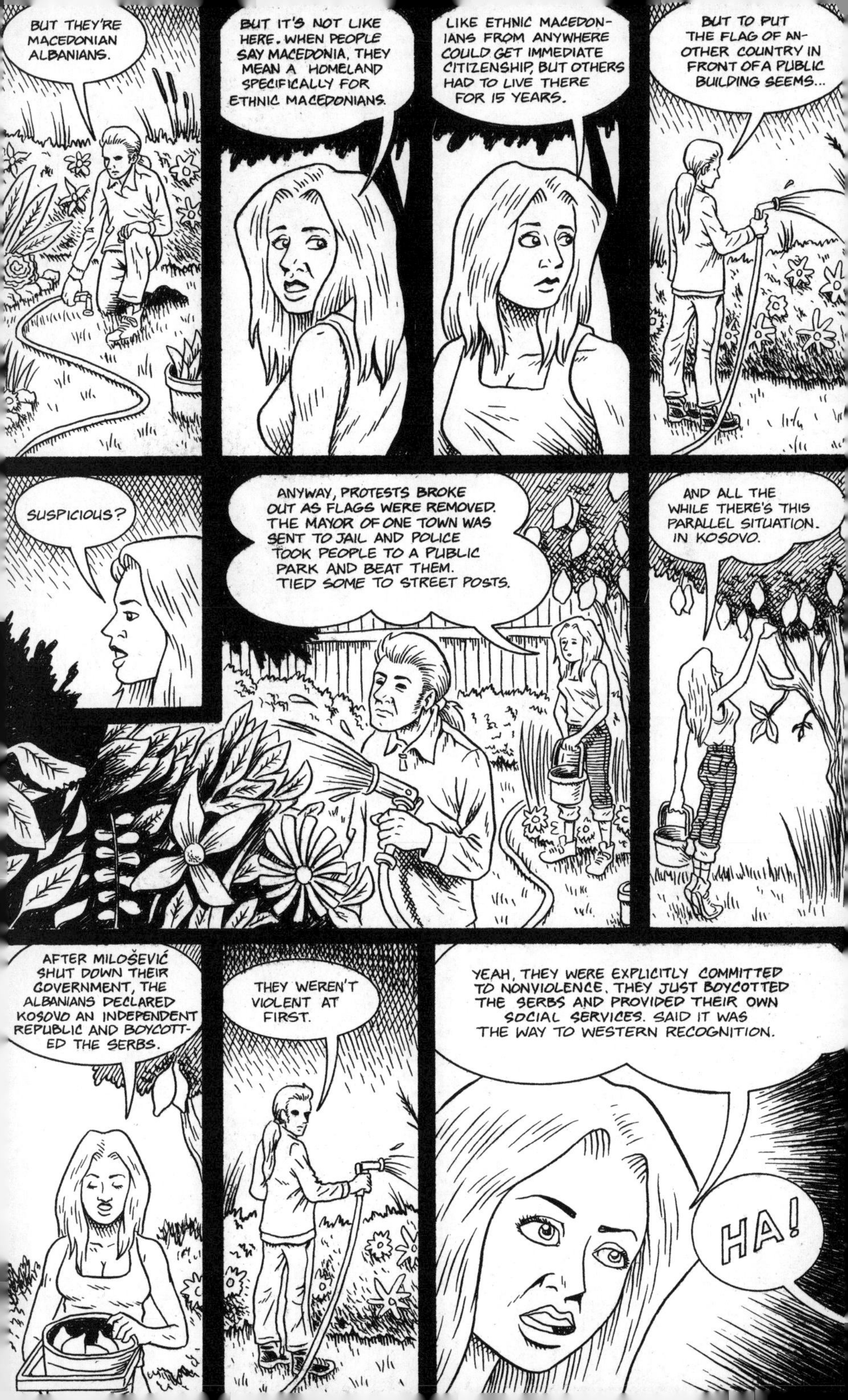
BUT THEY'RE MACEDONIAN ALBANIANS.
BUT IT'S NOT LIKE HERE. WHEN PEOPLE SAY MACEDONIA, THEY MEAN A HOMELAND SPECIFICALLY FOR ETHNIC MACEDONIANS.
LIKE ETHNIC MACEDONIANS FROM ANYWHERE COULD GET IMMEDIATE CITIZENSHIP, BUT OTHERS HAD TO LIVE THERE FOR 15 YEARS.
BUT TO PUT THE FLAG OF ANOTHER COUNTRY IN FRONT OF A PUBLIC BUILDING SEEMS...
SUSPICIOUS?
ANYWAY, PROTESTS BROKE OUT AS FLAGS WERE REMOVED. THE MAYOR OF ONE TOWN WAS SENT TO JAIL AND POLICE TOOK PEOPLE TO A PUBLIC PARK AND BEAT THEM. TIED SOME TO STREET POSTS.
AND ALL THE WHILE THERE'S THIS PARALLEL SITUATION IN KOSOVO.
AFTER MILOŠEVIĆ SHUT DOWN THEIR GOVERNMENT, THE ALBANIANS DECLARED KOSOVO AN INDEPENDENT REPUBLIC AND BOYCOTTED THE SERBS.
THEY WEREN'T VIOLENT AT FIRST.
YEAH, THEY WERE EXPLICITLY COMMITTED TO NONVIOLENCE. THEY JUST BOYCOTTED THE SERBS AND PROVIDED THEIR OWN SOCIAL SERVICES. SAID IT WAS THE WAY TO WESTERN RECOGNITION.
HA!

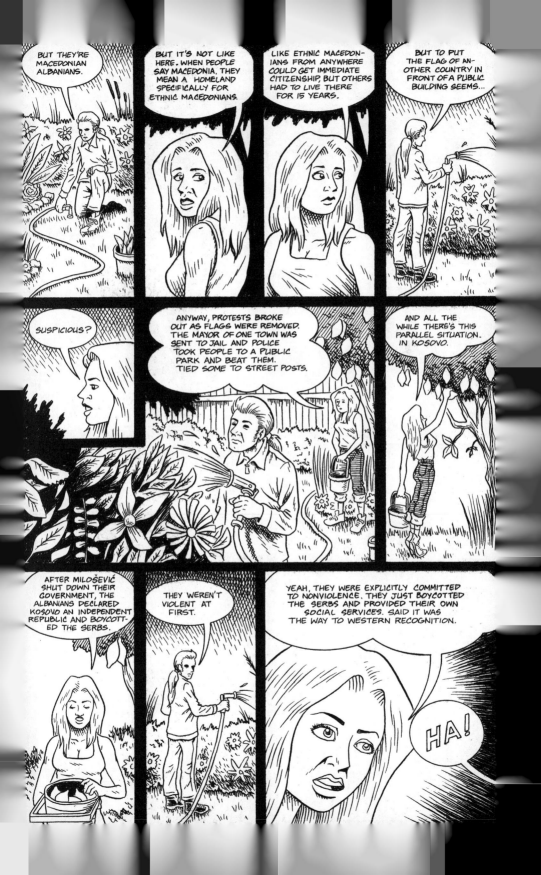

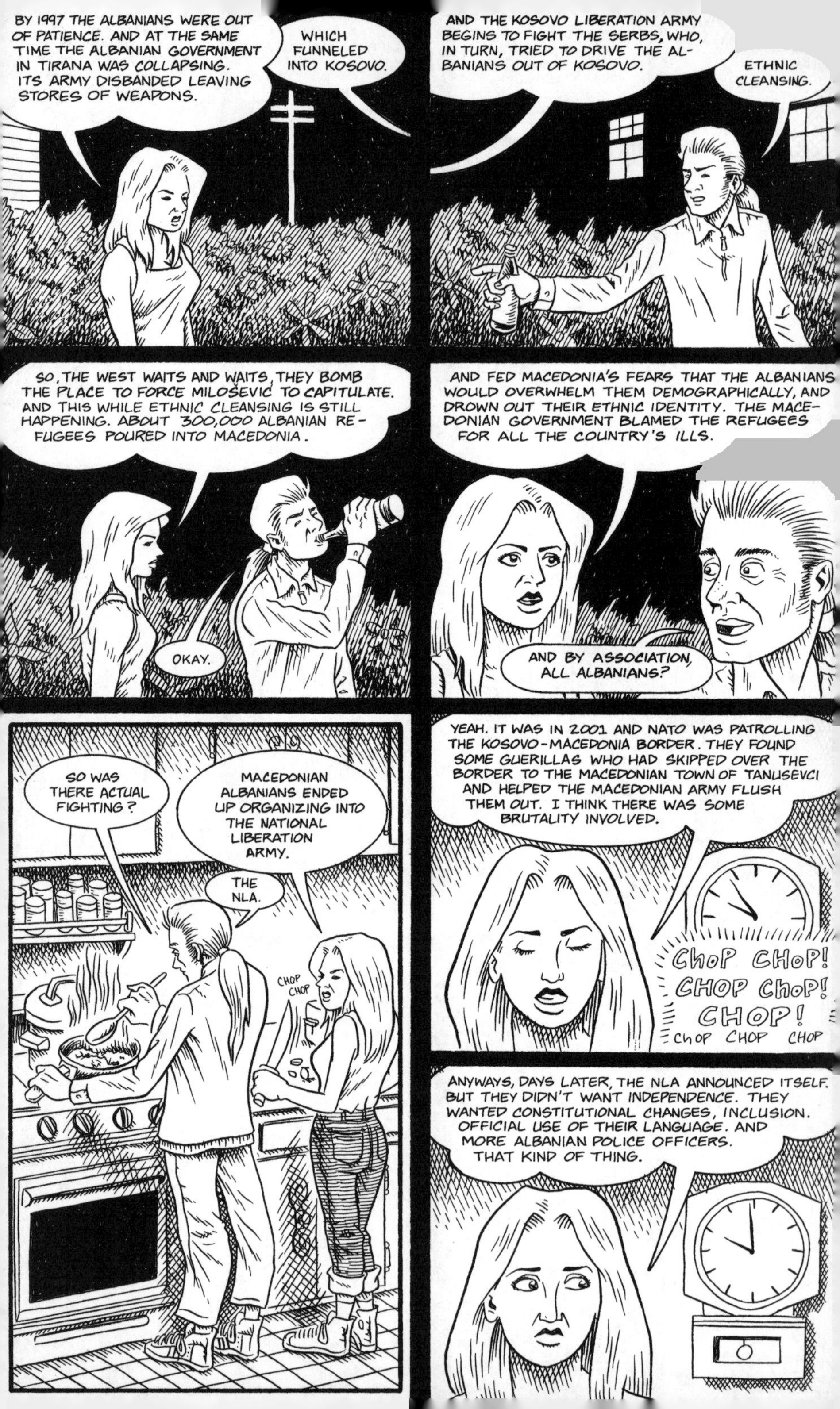
BY 1997 THE ALBANIANS WERE OUT OF PATIENCE. AND AT THE SAME TIME THE ALBANIAN GOVERNMENT IN TIRANA WAS COLLAPSING. ITS ARMY DISBANDED LEAVING STORES OF WEAPONS.
WHICH FUNNELED INTO KOSOVO.
AND THE KOSOVO LIBERATION ARMY BEGINS TO FIGHT THE SERBS, WHO, IN TURN, TRIED TO DRIVE THE ALBANIANS OUT OF KOSOVO.
ETHNIC CLEANSING.
SO, THE WEST WAITS AND WAITS, THEY BOMB THE PLACE TO FORCE MILOŠEVIĆ TO CAPITULATE. AND THIS WHILE ETHNIC CLEANSING IS STILL HAPPENING. ABOUT 300,000 ALBANIAN REFUGEES POURED INTO MACEDONIA.
OKAY.
AND FED MACEDONIA'S FEARS THAT THE ALBANIANS WOULD OVERWHELM THEM DEMOGRAPHICALLY, AND DROWN OUT THEIR ETHNIC IDENTITY. THE MACEDONIAN GOVERNMENT BLAMED THE REFUGEES FOR ALL THE COUNTRY'S ILLS.
AND BY ASSOCIATION, ALL ALBANIANS?
SO WAS THERE ACTUAL FIGHTING?
MACEDONIAN ALBANIANS ENDED UP ORGANIZING INTO THE NATIONAL LIBERATION ARMY.
THE NLA.
CHOP CHOP
YEAH. IT WAS IN 2001 AND NATO WAS PATROLLING THE KOSOVO-MACEDONIA BORDER. THEY FOUND SOME GUERILLAS WHO HAD SKIPPED OVER THE BORDER TO THE MACEDONIAN TOWN OF TANUSEVCI AND HELPED THE MACEDONIAN ARMY FLUSH THEM OUT. I THINK THERE WAS SOME BRUTALITY INVOLVED.
CHOP CHOP! CHOP CHOP! CHOP!
CHOP CHOP CHOP
ANYWAYS, DAYS LATER, THE NLA ANNOUNCED ITSELF. BUT THEY DIDN'T WANT INDEPENDENCE. THEY WANTED CONSTITUTIONAL CHANGES, INCLUSION. OFFICIAL USE OF THEIR LANGUAGE. AND MORE ALBANIAN POLICE OFFICERS. THAT KIND OF THING.

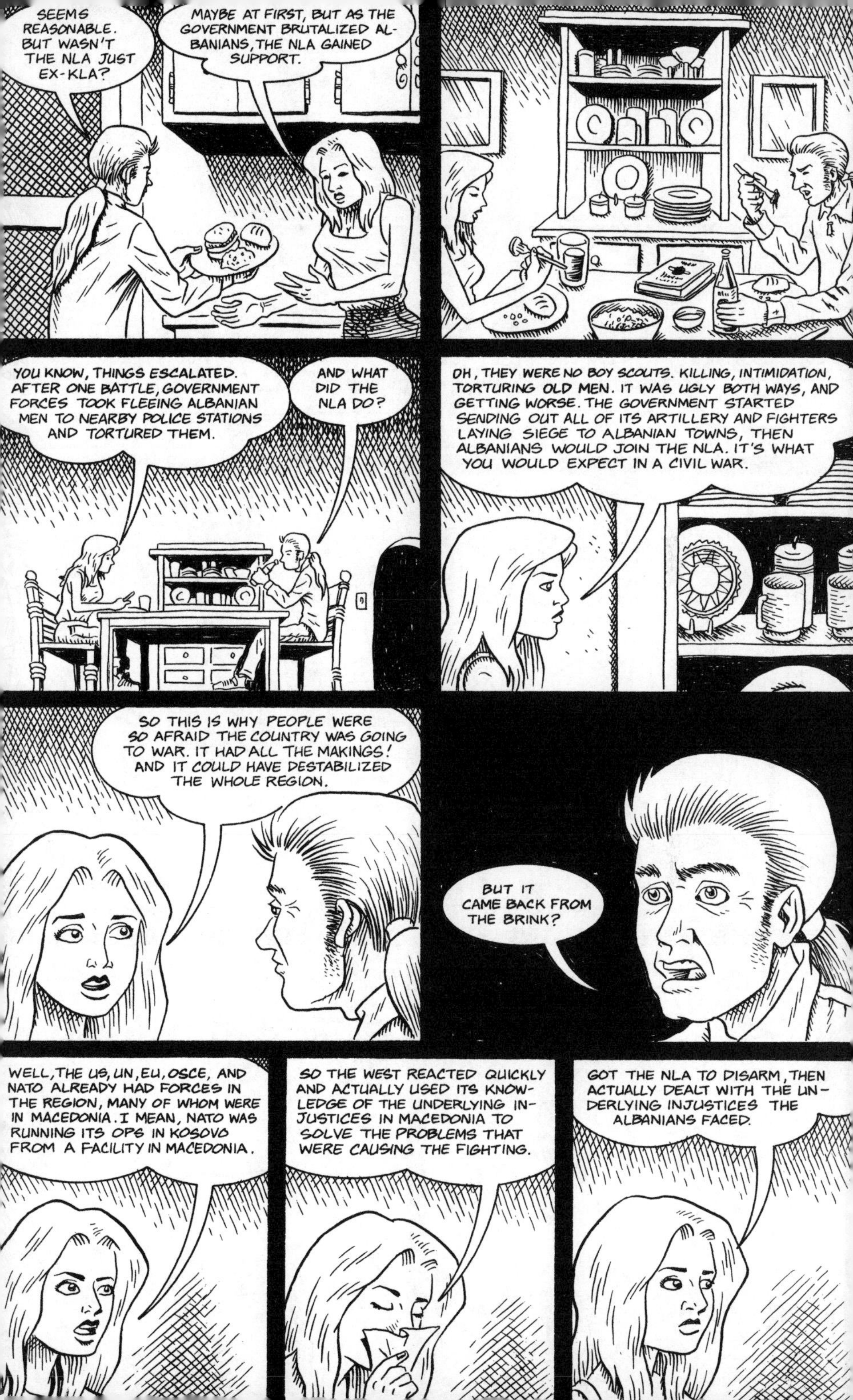
SEEMS REASONABLE. BUT WASN'T THE NLA JUST EX-KLA?
MAYBE AT FIRST, BUT AS THE GOVERNMENT BRUTALIZED ALBANIANS, THE NLA GAINED SUPPORT.
YOU KNOW, THINGS ESCALATED. AFTER ONE BATTLE, GOVERNMENT FORCES TOOK FLEEING ALBANIAN MEN TO NEARBY POLICE STATIONS AND TORTURED THEM.
AND WHAT DID THE NLA DO?
OH, THEY WERE NO BOY SCOUTS. KILLING, INTIMIDATION, TORTURING OLD MEN. IT WAS UGLY BOTH WAYS, AND GETTING WORSE. THE GOVERNMENT STARTED SENDING OUT ALL OF ITS ARTILLERY AND FIGHTERS LAYING SIEGE TO ALBANIAN TOWNS, THEN ALBANIANS WOULD JOIN THE NLA. IT'S WHAT YOU WOULD EXPECT IN A CIVIL WAR.
SO THIS IS WHY PEOPLE WERE SO AFRAID THE COUNTRY WAS GOING TO WAR. IT HAD ALL THE MAKINGS! AND IT COULD HAVE DESTABILIZED THE WHOLE REGION.
BUT IT CAME BACK FROM THE BRINK?
WELL, THE US, UN, EU, OSCE, AND NATO ALREADY HAD FORCES IN THE REGION, MANY OF WHOM WERE IN MACEDONIA. I MEAN, NATO WAS RUNNING ITS OPS IN KOSOVO FROM A FACILITY IN MACEDONIA.
SO THE WEST REACTED QUICKLY AND ACTUALLY USED ITS KNOWLEDGE OF THE UNDERLYING INJUSTICES IN MACEDONIA TO SOLVE THE PROBLEMS THAT WERE CAUSING THE FIGHTING.
GOT THE NLA TO DISARM, THEN ACTUALLY DEALT WITH THE UNDERLYING INJUSTICES THE ALBANIANS FACED.

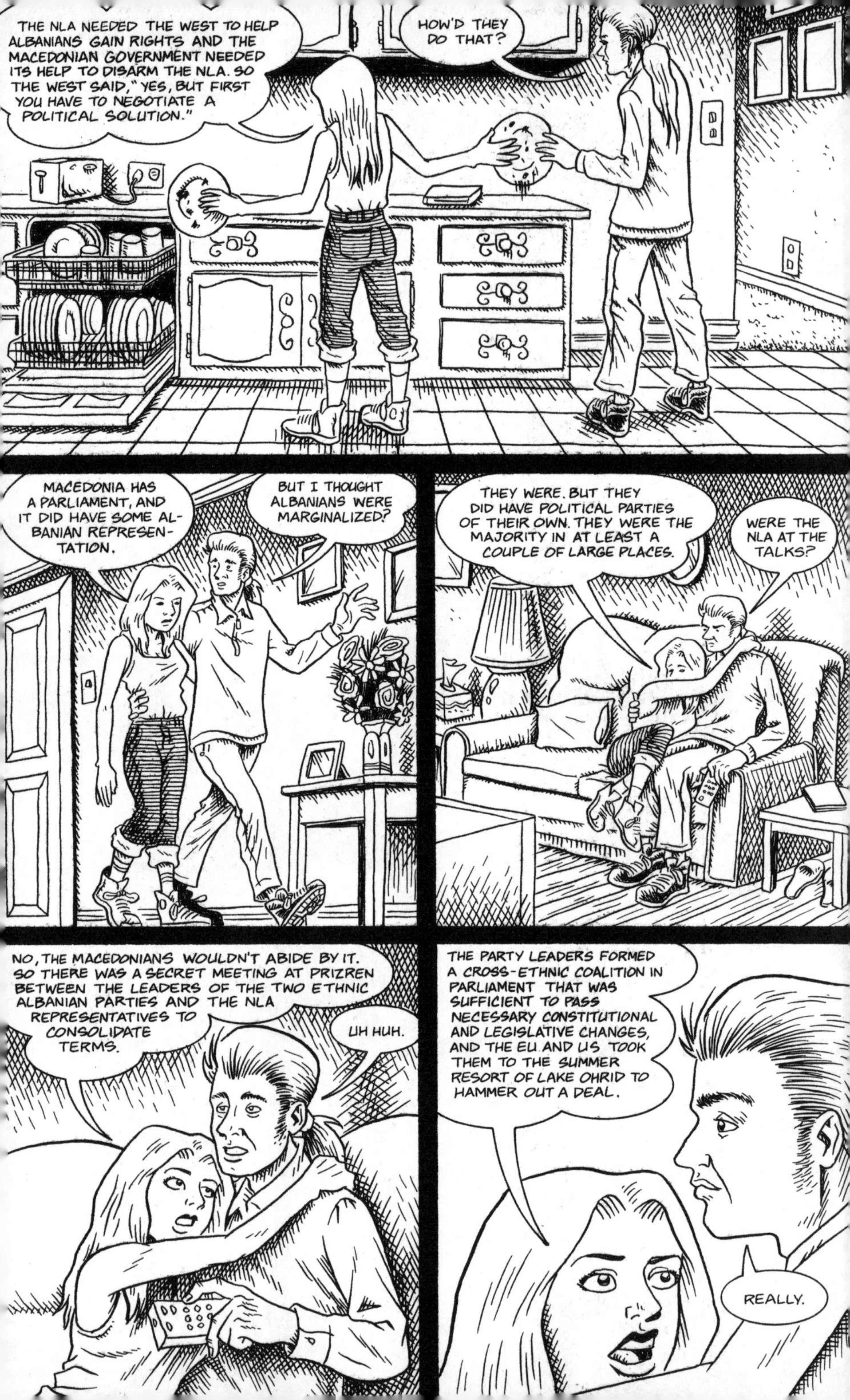

THE NLA NEEDED THE WEST TO HELP ALBANIANS GAIN RIGHTS AND THE MACEDONIAN GOVERNMENT NEEDED ITS HELP TO DISARM THE NLA. SO THE WEST SAID, "YES, BUT FIRST YOU HAVE TO NEGOTIATE A POLITICAL SOLUTION."
HOW'D THEY DO THAT?
MACEDONIA HAS A PARLIAMENT, AND IT DID HAVE SOME ALBANIAN REPRESENTATION.
BUT I THOUGHT ALBANIANS WERE MARGINALIZED?
THEY WERE. BUT THEY DID HAVE POLITICAL PARTIES OF THEIR OWN. THEY WERE THE MAJORITY IN AT LEAST A COUPLE OF LARGE PLACES.
WERE THE NLA AT THE TALKS?
NO, THE MACEDONIANS WOULDN'T ABIDE BY IT. SO THERE WAS A SECRET MEETING AT PRIZREN BETWEEN THE LEADERS OF THE TWO ETHNIC ALBANIAN PARTIES AND THE NLA REPRESENTATIVES TO CONSOLIDATE TERMS.
UH HUH.
THE PARTY LEADERS FORMED A CROSS-ETHNIC COALITION IN PARLIAMENT THAT WAS SUFFICIENT TO PASS NECESSARY CONSTITUTIONAL AND LEGISLATIVE CHANGES, AND THE EU AND US TOOK THEM TO THE SUMMER RESORT OF LAKE OHRID TO HAMMER OUT A DEAL.
REALLY.

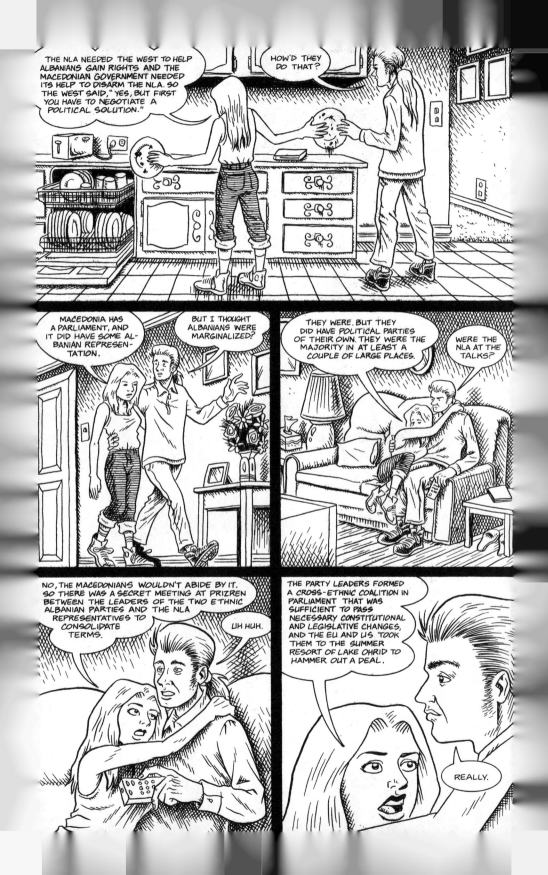

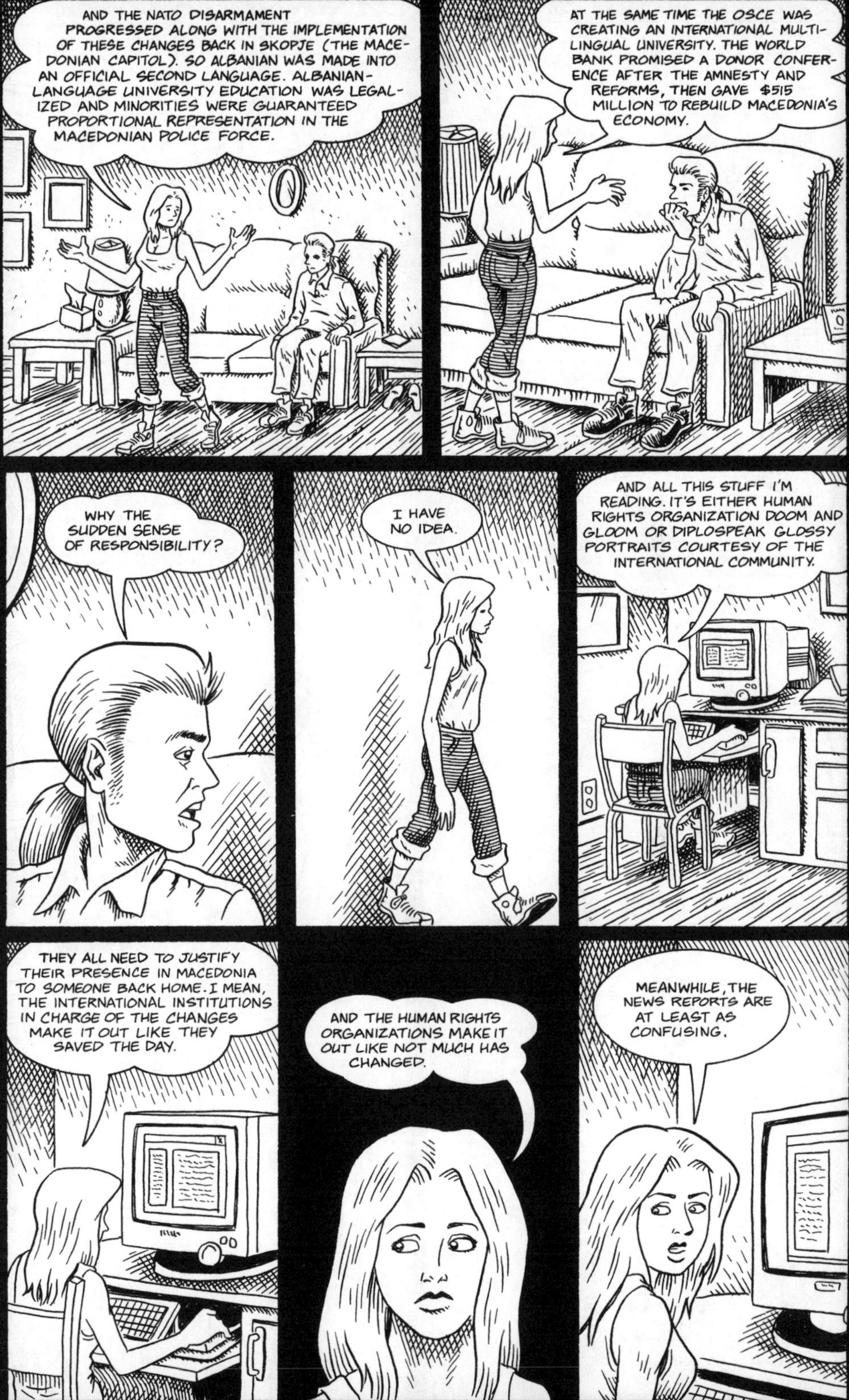
AND THE NATO DISARMAMENT PROGRESSED ALONG WITH THE IMPLEMENTATION OF THESE CHANGES BACK IN SKOPJE (THE MACEDONIAN CAPITOL). SO ALBANIAN WAS MADE INTO AN OFFICIAL SECOND LANGUAGE. ALBANIAN-LANGUAGE UNIVERSITY EDUCATION WAS LEGALIZED AND MINORITIES WERE GUARANTEED PROPORTIONAL REPRESENTATION IN THE MACEDONIAN POLICE FORCE.
AT THE SAME TIME THE OSCE WAS CREATING AN INTERNATIONAL MULTI-LINGUAL UNIVERSITY. THE WORLD BANK PROMISED A DONOR CONFERENCE AFTER THE AMNESTY AND REFORMS, THEN GAVE $515 MILLION TO REBUILD MACEDONIA'S ECONOMY.
WHY THE SUDDEN SENSE OF RESPONSIBILITY?
I HAVE NO IDEA.
AND ALL THIS STUFF I'M READING. IT'S EITHER HUMAN RIGHTS ORGANIZATION DOOM AND GLOOM OR DIPLOSPEAK GLOSSY PORTRAITS COURTESY OF THE INTERNATIONAL COMMUNITY.
THEY ALL NEED TO JUSTIFY THEIR PRESENCE IN MACEDONIA TO SOMEONE BACK HOME. I MEAN, THE INTERNATIONAL INSTITUTIONS IN CHARGE OF THE CHANGES MAKE IT OUT LIKE THEY SAVED THE DAY.
AND THE HUMAN RIGHTS ORGANIZATIONS MAKE IT OUT LIKE NOT MUCH HAS CHANGED.
MEANWHILE, THE NEWS REPORTS ARE AT LEAST AS CONFUSING.

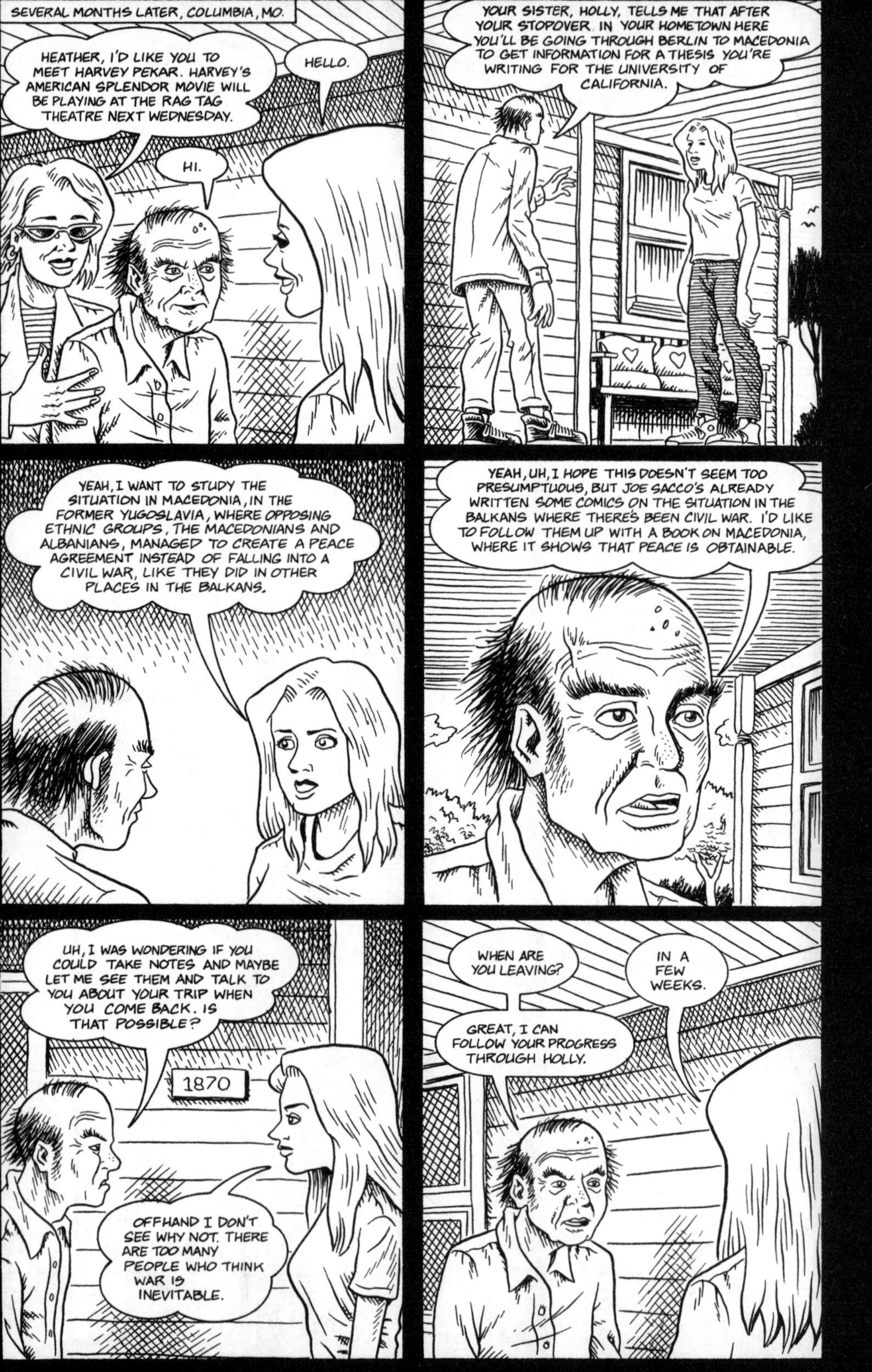
SEVERAL MONTHS LATER, COLUMBIA, MO.
HEATHER, I'D LIKE YOU TO MEET HARVEY PEKAR. HARVEY'S AMERICAN SPLENDOR MOVIE WILL BE PLAYING AT THE RAG TAG THEATRE NEXT WEDNESDAY.
HELLO.
HI.
YOUR SISTER, HOLLY, TELLS ME THAT AFTER YOUR STOPOVER IN YOUR HOMETOWN HERE YOU'LL BE GOING THROUGH BERLIN TO MACEDONIA TO GET INFORMATION FOR A THESIS YOU'RE WRITING FOR THE UNIVERSITY OF CALIFORNIA.
YEAH, I WANT TO STUDY THE SITUATION IN MACEDONIA, IN THE FORMER YUGOSLAVIA, WHERE OPPOSING ETHNIC GROUPS, THE MACEDONIANS AND ALBANIANS, MANAGED TO CREATE A PEACE AGREEMENT INSTEAD OF FALLING INTO A CIVIL WAR, LIKE THEY DID IN OTHER PLACES IN THE BALKANS.
YEAH, UH, I HOPE THIS DOESN'T SEEM TOO PRESUMPTUOUS, BUT JOE SACCO'S ALREADY WRITTEN SOME COMICS ON THE SITUATION IN THE BALKANS WHERE THERE'S BEEN CIVIL WAR. I'D LIKE TO FOLLOW THEM UP WITH A BOOK ON MACEDONIA, WHERE IT SHOWS THAT PEACE IS OBTAINABLE.
UH, I WAS WONDERING IF YOU COULD TAKE NOTES AND MAYBE LET ME SEE THEM AND TALK TO YOU ABOUT YOUR TRIP WHEN YOU COME BACK. IS THAT POSSIBLE?
1870
OFFHAND I DON'T SEE WHY NOT. THERE ARE TOO MANY PEOPLE WHO THINK WAR IS INEVITABLE.
WHEN ARE YOU LEAVING?
IN A FEW WEEKS.
GREAT, I CAN FOLLOW YOUR PROGRESS THROUGH HOLLY.

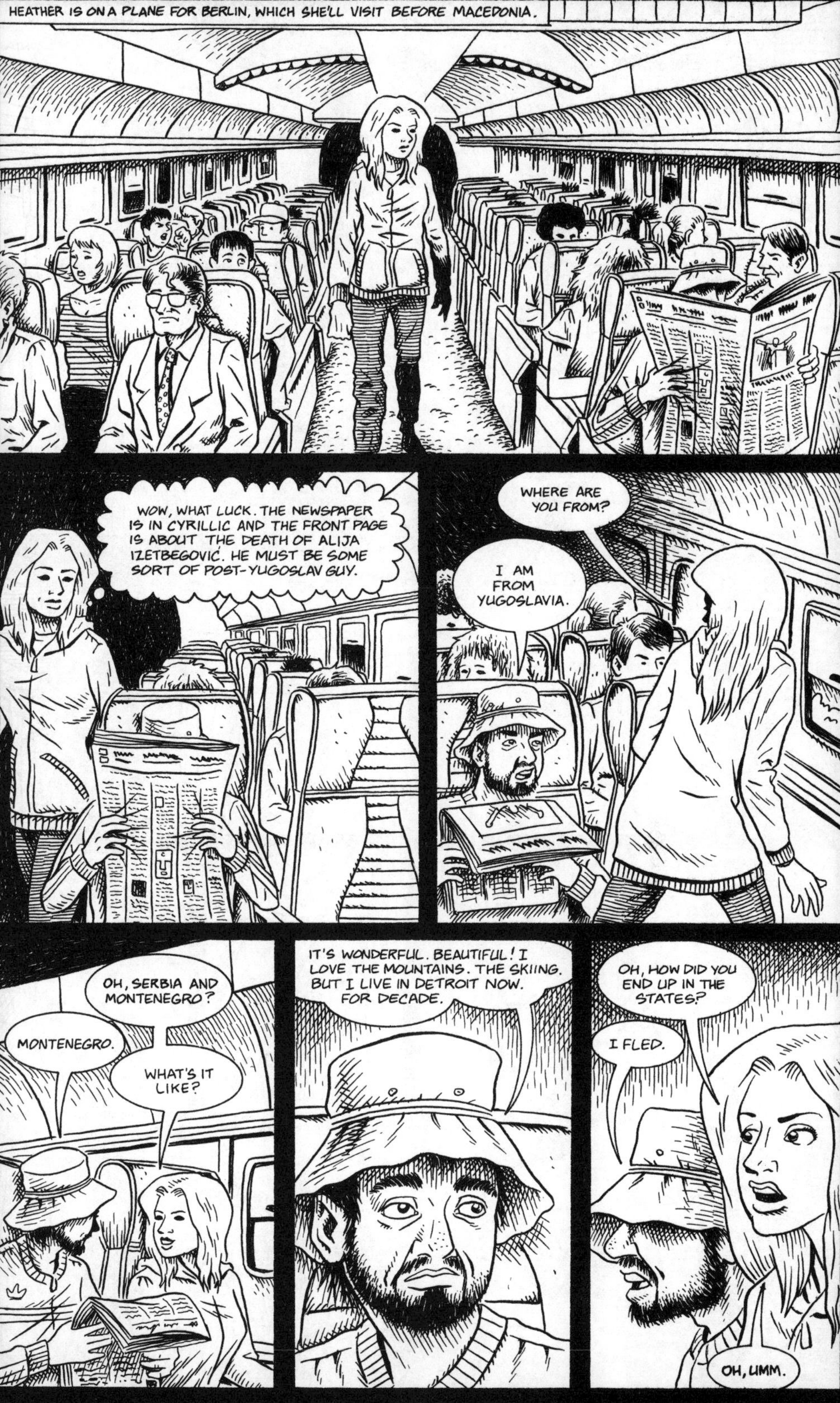

HEATHER IS ON A PLANE FOR BERLIN, WHICH SHE'LL VISIT BEFORE MACEDONIA.
WOW, WHAT LUCK. THE NEWSPAPER IS IN CYRILLIC AND THE FRONT PAGE IS ABOUT THE DEATH OF ALIJA IZETBEGOVIĆ. HE MUST BE SOME SORT OF POST-YUGOSLAV GUY.
WHERE ARE YOU FROM?
I AM FROM YUGOSLAVIA.
OH, SERBIA AND MONTENEGRO?
MONTENEGRO.
WHAT'S IT LIKE?
IT'S WONDERFUL. BEAUTIFUL! I LOVE THE MOUNTAINS. THE SKIING. BUT I LIVE IN DETROIT NOW. FOR DECADE.
OH, HOW DID YOU END UP IN THE STATES?
I FLED.
OH, UMM.

THEY TRIED TO RECRUIT ME. MY BROTHER AND I RAN.

OH.

WE KNEW MUSLIMS AND CROATS. WE DIDN'T WANT TO FIGHT.

WHAT DID YOU DO BEFORE THAT?

WE WERE SMUGGLERS.

DID KNOWING THE SMUGGLING ROUTES HELP YOU ESCAPE?

EVERYTHING WE KNEW HELPED US TO ESCAPE.

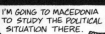
I'M GOING TO MACEDONIA TO STUDY THE POLITICAL SITUATION THERE.

YOU CAN STAY FOR SIX MONTHS, STAY FOR A YEAR. THEN MAYBE YOU WILL BEGIN TO SEE THE TRUTH.

I WOULDN'T PRESUME, I...

YOU COULDN'T KNOW, PEOPLE'S HEADS USED AS SOCCER BALLS FOR PLAY!

WE'LL BOTH HAVE WINE.

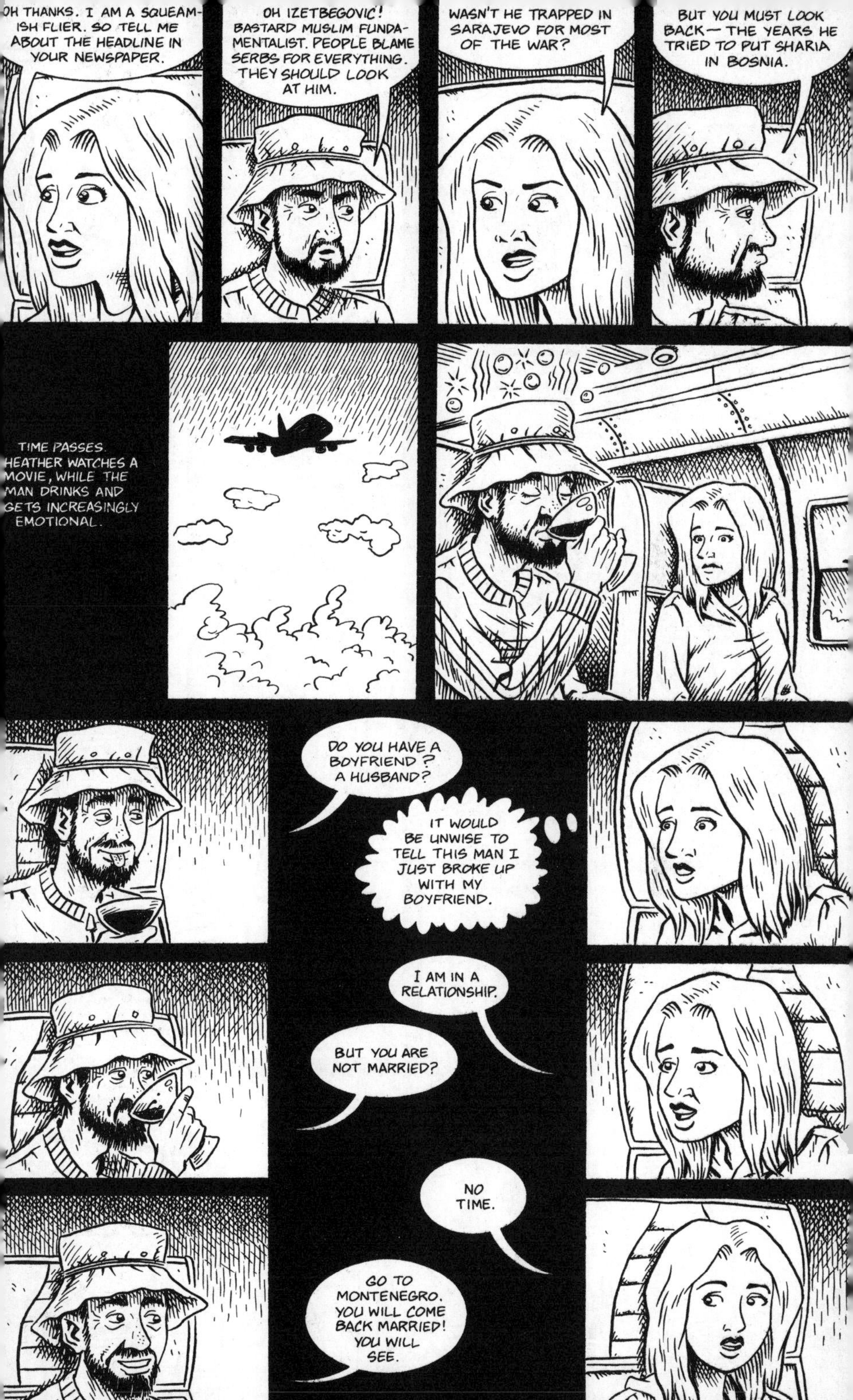
OH THANKS. I AM A SQUEAMISH FLIER. SO TELL ME ABOUT THE HEADLINE IN YOUR NEWSPAPER.
OH IZETBEGOVIC! BASTARD MUSLIM FUNDAMENTALIST. PEOPLE BLAME SERBS FOR EVERYTHING. THEY SHOULD LOOK AT HIM.
WASN'T HE TRAPPED IN SARAJEVO FOR MOST OF THE WAR?
BUT YOU MUST LOOK BACK — THE YEARS HE TRIED TO PUT SHARIA IN BOSNIA.
TIME PASSES. HEATHER WATCHES A MOVIE, WHILE THE MAN DRINKS AND GETS INCREASINGLY EMOTIONAL.
DO YOU HAVE A BOYFRIEND? A HUSBAND?
IT WOULD BE UNWISE TO TELL THIS MAN I JUST BROKE UP WITH MY BOYFRIEND.
I AM IN A RELATIONSHIP.
BUT YOU ARE NOT MARRIED?
NO TIME.
GO TO MONTENEGRO. YOU WILL COME BACK MARRIED! YOU WILL SEE.

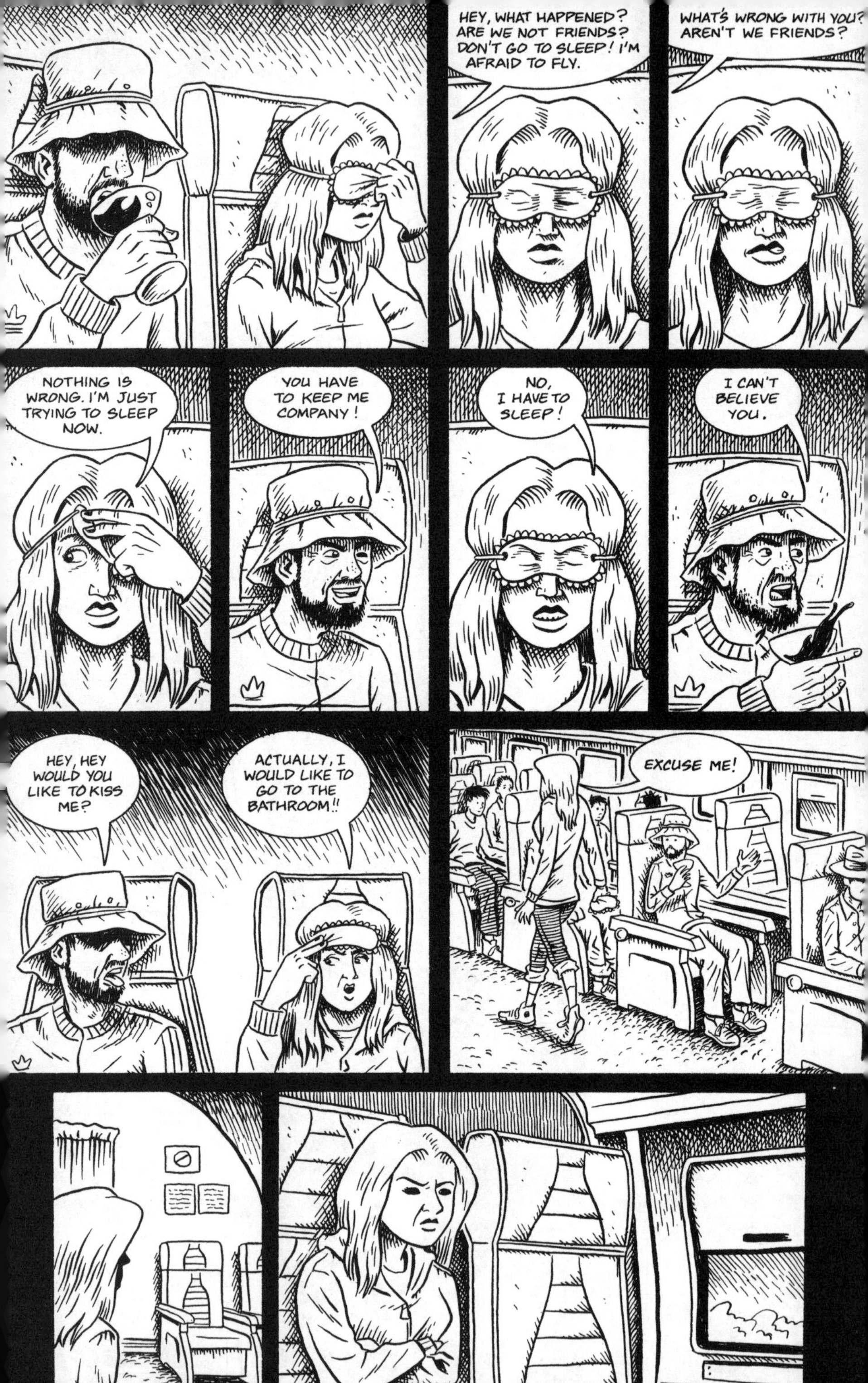
HEY, WHAT HAPPENED? ARE WE NOT FRIENDS? DON'T GO TO SLEEP! I'M AFRAID TO FLY.
WHAT'S WRONG WITH YOU? AREN'T WE FRIENDS?
NOTHING IS WRONG. I'M JUST TRYING TO SLEEP NOW.
YOU HAVE TO KEEP ME COMPANY!
NO, I HAVE TO SLEEP!
I CAN'T BELIEVE YOU.
HEY, HEY WOULD YOU LIKE TO KISS ME?
ACTUALLY, I WOULD LIKE TO GO TO THE BATHROOM!!
EXCUSE ME!

WOKE UP GROGGILY. LYING THERE ON THE ... SEAT, I THOUGHT OF WHAT MACEDONIA WOULD B
BALKANS WOULD BE LIKE. THE WHOLE IDEA OF THE BALKANS IS ONLY PARTLY GEOGRAPHIC. WHEN THE T
IT IN THE 1800S, IT WAS MEANT TO DESCRIBE OTTOMAN HOLDINGS IN EUROPE. EVERYTHING WEST O
PHORUS STRAIT, WHICH CONNECTS THE BLACK SEA TO THE MEDITERRANEAN. AS FOR WHAT IT CON
N, THATS MORE COMPLEX. BOSNIA AND CROATIA HAVEN'T BEEN OTTOMAN SINCE 1878 WHEN THE A
GARIAN EMPIRE CLAIMED THEM. NEITHER HAVE SERBIA, ROMANIA, OR MONTENEGRO, WHICH BECAME IN
BULGARIA, WHICH STAYED UNDER RUSSIAN INFLUENCE, NOR GREECE. ONLY MACEDONIA AND ALBA
AINED UNDER THE OTTOMANS.

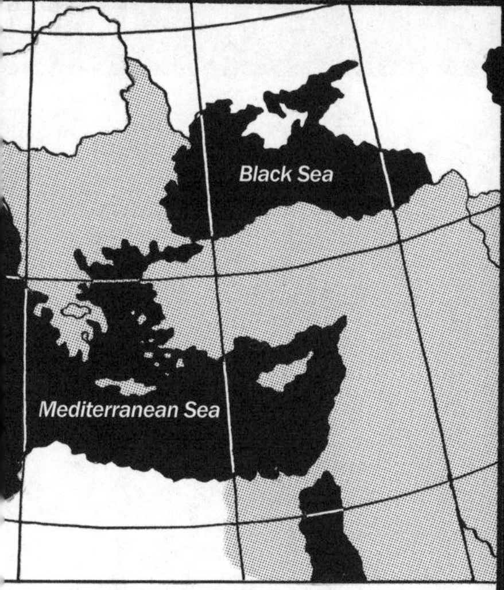
Black Sea
Mediterranean Sea

Ottoman territory during the early 1800s

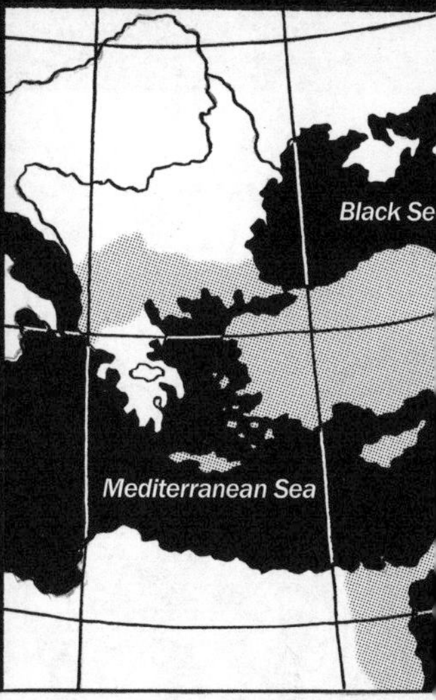
Black Se
Mediterranean Sea

Ottoman holdings afte the Treaty of Berlin (187

BALKANS! IS IT JUST A LAZY CATCH-ALL FOR A COMPLICATED REGION? AND WHAT PEOPLE R
AT IT'S FULL OF DISHONEST THUGS! NOT QUITE ASIAN AND NOT QUITE EUROPEAN. BECAUS
SISTS THAT ONCE A PLACE IS BALKAN, IT WILL ALWAYS BE BALKAN. AS IF THE PLACE SOMEH
TS ON ITS INHABITANTS A GENETIC DESTINY — ONE OF WAR, FRAGMENTATION, AND DECEIT.
D 'BALKAN' IS SCARY. BALKAN MENTALITY! BALKANIZATION! THE BALKANS! A FRACTIOUS, DE
S LAND! IF A STRONG NATION-STATE CAN IMPOSE ORDER ON IT, IT IS ONLY TEMPORAR
ITSELF AND ITS PEOPLE ARE UNAMENDABLE TO SELF-GOVERNMENT, PROGRESS, OR CIVILIZ
VIEW CRYSTALLIZED AROUND THE TURN OF THE CENTURY WHEN GREECE, SERBIA, BULGAR
TENEGRO — THE BALKAN LEAGUE — JOINED TO SUCCESSFULLY DRIVE THE OTTOMANS OU
EDONIA.

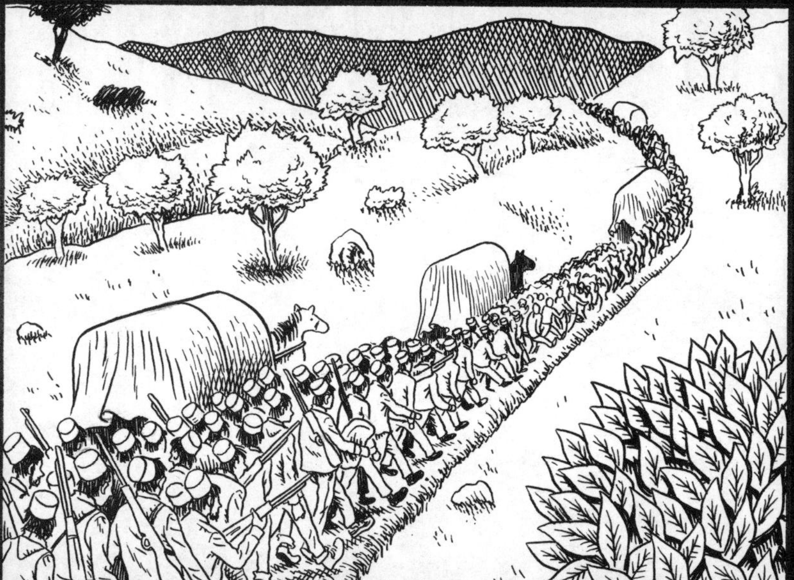

BUT BULGARIA TOOK MOST OF MACEDONIA. SO, SERBIA -- THE DAY AFTER THE TREATY WAS SIGNED -- MADE AN ALLIANCE WITH GREECE TO FIGHT BULGARIA. MONTENEGRO, ROMANIA, AND THE OTTOMANS SOON JOINED IN ON THE SIDE OF SERBIA AND GREECE AND THUS BEGAN THE SECOND BALKAN WAR. AT WAR'S END, GREECE TOOK HALF OF MACEDONIA, SERBIA GOT 40%, AND BULGARIA GOT THE REST. THE WORLD WAS AGHAST. HOW COULD THE BALKAN PEOPLE DIE BY THE THOUSANDS TO FIGHT OTTOMAN OPPRESSION ONLY TO TURN AROUND AND WAGE WAR ON EACH OTHER? THE CARNEGIE ENDOWMENT FOR INTERNATIONAL PEACE LAMENTED THAT THE WAR FOR MACEDONIAN LIBERATION HAD UNLEASHED "THE INHERITED REVENGES OF CENTURIES."

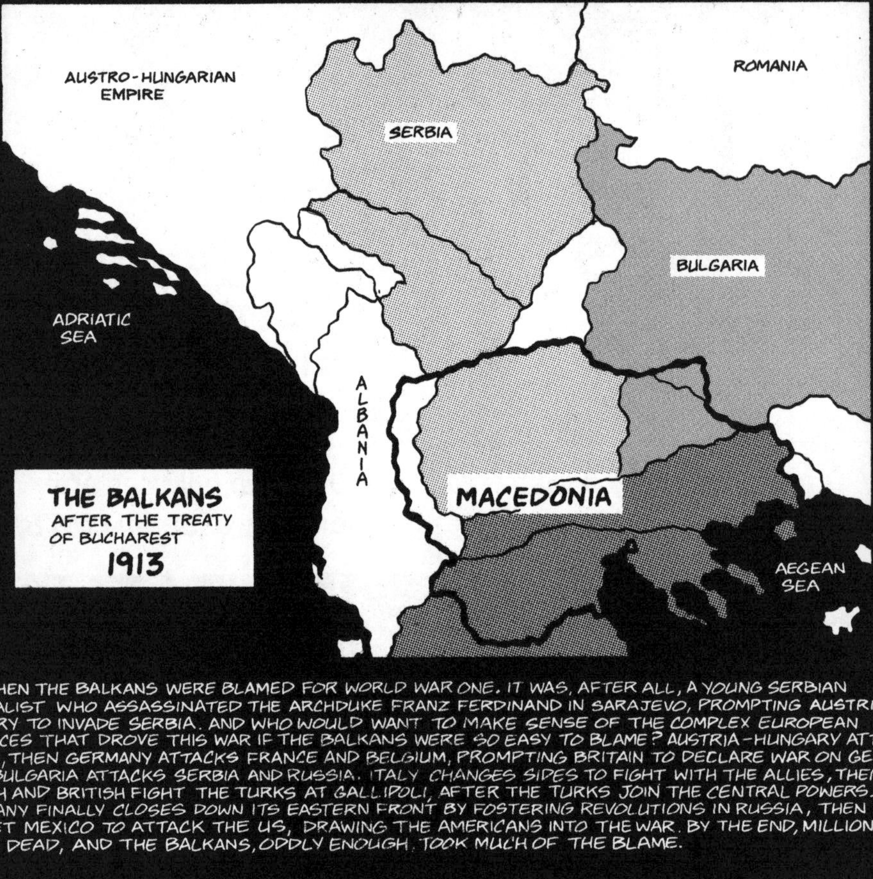
AUSTRO-HUNGARIAN EMPIRE
ROMANIA
SERBIA
BULGARIA
ADRIATIC SEA
ALBANIA
MACEDONIA
AEGEAN SEA
THE BALKANS
AFTER THE TREATY OF BUCHAREST
1913

AND THEN THE BALKANS WERE BLAMED FOR WORLD WAR ONE. IT WAS, AFTER ALL, A YOUNG SERBIAN NATIONALIST WHO ASSASSINATED THE ARCHDUKE FRANZ FERDINAND IN SARAJEVO, PROMPTING AUSTRIA-HUNGARY TO INVADE SERBIA. AND WHO WOULD WANT TO MAKE SENSE OF THE COMPLEX EUROPEAN ALLIANCES THAT DROVE THIS WAR IF THE BALKANS WERE SO EASY TO BLAME? AUSTRIA-HUNGARY ATTACKS SERBIA, THEN GERMANY ATTACKS FRANCE AND BELGIUM, PROMPTING BRITAIN TO DECLARE WAR ON GERMANY. THEN BULGARIA ATTACKS SERBIA AND RUSSIA. ITALY CHANGES SIDES TO FIGHT WITH THE ALLIES, THEN THE FRENCH AND BRITISH FIGHT THE TURKS AT GALLIPOLI, AFTER THE TURKS JOIN THE CENTRAL POWERS. GERMANY FINALLY CLOSES DOWN ITS EASTERN FRONT BY FOSTERING REVOLUTIONS IN RUSSIA, THEN TRIES TO GET MEXICO TO ATTACK THE US, DRAWING THE AMERICANS INTO THE WAR. BY THE END, MILLIONS WERE DEAD, AND THE BALKANS, ODDLY ENOUGH, TOOK MUCH OF THE BLAME.

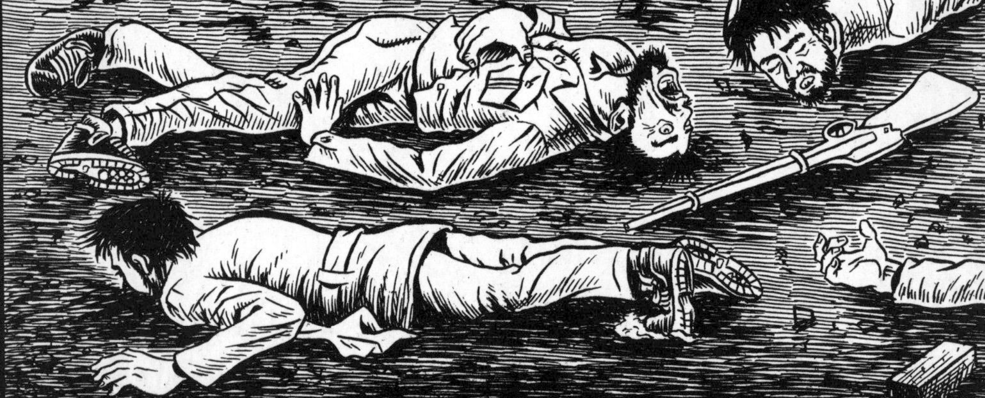

WAR ONE, THE SERBS TRIED TO GAIN CONTROL BY CREATING THE KINGDOM O
THE SLOVENES. THE IDEA WAS THAT SOUTH SLAVS WERE BASICALLY THE SAME, B
MES. IN 1929 THE NAME CHANGES TO "KINGDOM OF YUGOSLAVIA," YUGO MEANIN
ERMANS AND ITALIANS CAME INTO YUGOSLAVIA TO GAIN ACCESS TO THE AEGEA
HE ROYAL YUGOSLAV ARMY IN NO TIME. MOST OF WESTERN AND NORTHWESTER
ND KOSOVO WERE TAKEN AS PARTS OF ALBANIA, A CLIENT STATE OF ITALY. AN
T UP A CLIENT "USTASE" STATE IN CROATIA, WHICH GREW TO INCLUDE SLAVONIA
OVINA AS WELL.

CONTROLLED SERBIA DIRECTLY, OR AT LEAST TRIED TO. BUT A NUMBER OF YU
STREATED TO THE MOUNTAINS OF BOSNIA, MONTENEGRO, AND SERBIA TO BEGI
USTASES WERE FAMOUSLY BRUTAL FASCISTS, BENT ON EXTERMINATING SER
HERZEGOVINA AND, AS ORDINARY SERBS SAW IT, THEY HAD NO CHOICE BU
EITHER WITH THE EX-ROYAL YUGOSLAV ARMY, THE CETNIKS, OR WITH A BAND
BY JOSIP "TITO" BROZ, THE PARTIZANS. THE PARTIZANS PROVED MORE MOE
VE. YOU HAD TO BE A YUGOSLAV TO JOIN THE CETNIKS, BUT ANYONE COULD

AFTER THE WAR, TITO WAS A NATIONAL HERO. HE USED THIS RECOGNITION, IN 1946, TO ESTABLISH A PAN-SLAV POLITICAL SYSTEM. HE SET UP SIX REPUBLICS AND RECOGNIZED FIVE YUGOSLAV NATIONALITIES — THE SERBS, CROATS, SLOVENES, MACEDONIANS, AND MONTENEGRINS. HE PREACHED "BROTHERHOOD AND UNITY" FOR THE SLAVS. ETHNIC NATIONALISM, HE SAID, WAS ANTI-YUGOSLAV. YUGOSLAVS ENJOYED A HIGH STANDARD OF LIVING AND THE MOST DEMOCRATIC SYSTEM IN THE SOCIALIST WORLD. AND THEN, IN 1948, TITO AMAZED THE WORLD BY BREAKING TIES WITH STALIN! HE REFUSED TO JOIN WITH THE WEST OR THE EAST, STARTING THE NONALIGNED MOVEMENT DURING THE COLD WAR. HE GAVE THE SLAVS SOMETHING TO BE PROUD OF.

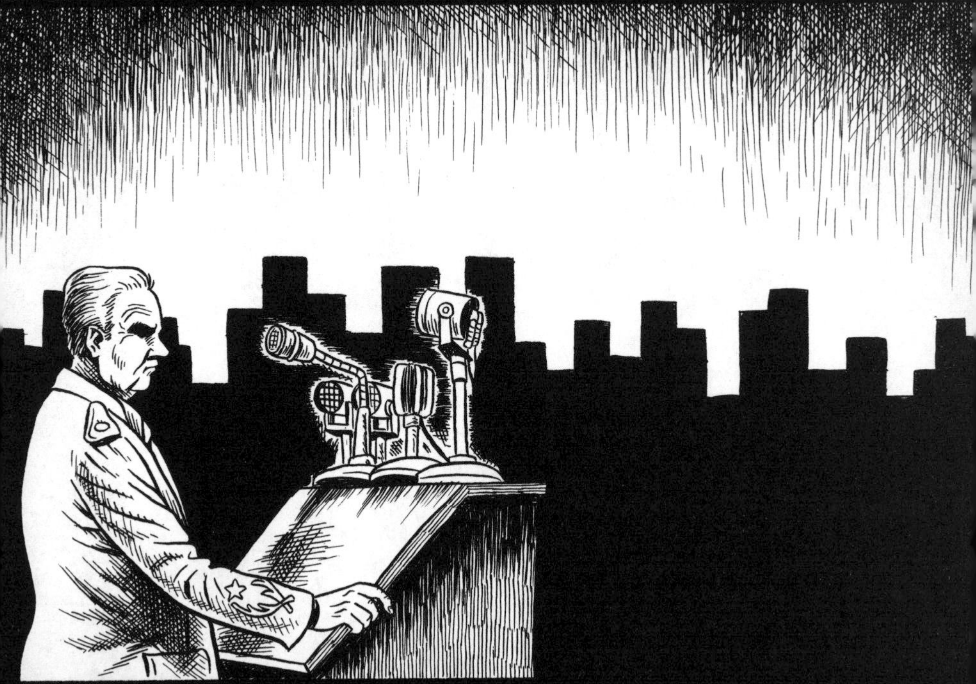

TITO ESTABLISHED MACEDONIA AS A SIXTH REPUBLIC TO CONTAIN THE SERBS FROM SPREADING AND TO ENSURE THAT MACEDONIANS WOULDN'T MISTAKE THEMSELVES FOR NEIGHBORING BULGARIANS OR GREEKS — TO MAKE SURE MACEDONIA HAD A STRONG EXTERNAL BORDER. AND HE ACCOMMODATED THE ALBANIANS, BUT HE DIDN'T WANT THEM TO GET TOO STRONG EITHER. RIGHT NEXT DOOR THERE WAS ALBANIA PROPER — ISOLATED, UNDERDEVELOPED, ITS CITIZENS FORCED TO LIVE UNDER A XENOPHOBIC, TOTALITARIAN REGIME, WHICH ENGAGED IN NEAR-CONTINUOUS PURGES OF SUPPOSED TITO COLLABORATORS AND OTHER CONSPIRATORS AGAINST THE ALBANIAN STATE. THIS STATE OF AFFAIRS INFORMED THE PREJUDICE AGAINST ALBANIANS AS A BACKWARD, BARBAROUS PEOPLE.

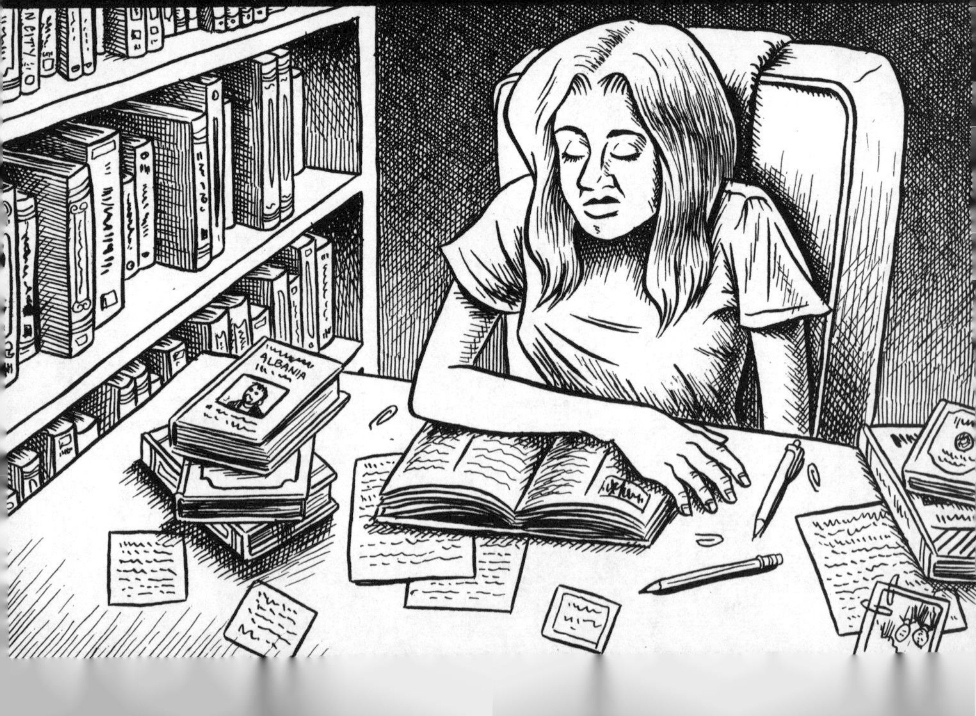
ALBANIA

PEOPLE SAID TITO WAS JUST KEEPING THE LID ON ETHNIC TENSIONS AND THAT WITHOUT HIS IRON FIST, THE PEOPLE OF THE BALKANS WOULD HAVE FOUGHT AMONGST THEMSELVES CONTINUALLY. AND SO, IN MANY WAYS, YUGOSLAVIA'S VIOLENT COLLAPSE — EVEN IF IT WAS NINE YEARS AFTER TITO'S DEATH — CONFIRMED THE CONVENTIONAL WISDOM: GIVEN THE OPPORTUNITY TO GOVERN THEMSELVES, THE BALKAN PEOPLES WOULD FALL PREY TO "ETHNIC HATREDS" AND STUMBLE INEVITABLY TOWARD WAR.

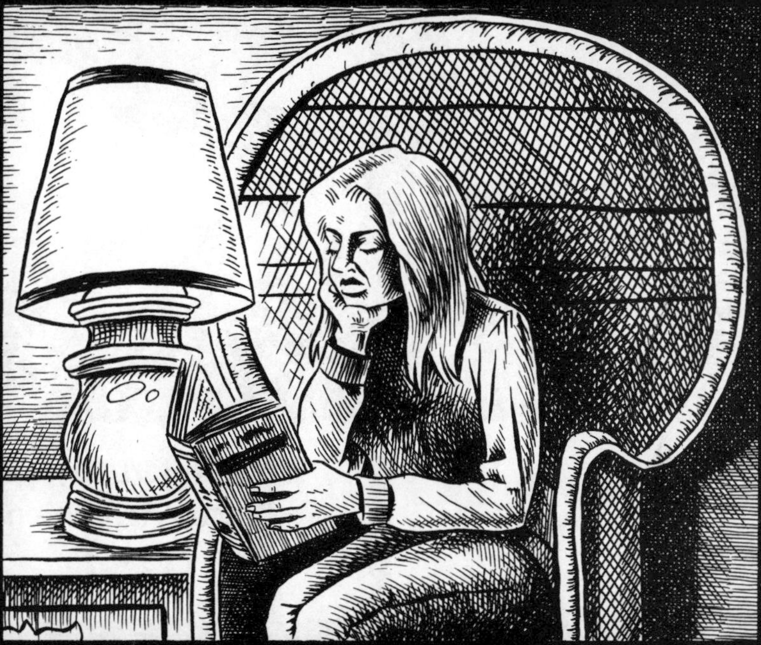

IN 1991, CROATIA AND SLOVENIA SECEDED. BOTH HAD STRONG EXPORT ECONOMIES AND CLOSE TIES TO CENTRAL EUROPE. SLOVENIA ESCAPED LARGELY UNSCATHED — OWING TO ETHNIC HOMOGENEITY, ALPINE LOCATION, AND PROXIMITY TO AUSTRIA AND ITALY. BUT CROATIA WAS QUICKLY PLUNGED INTO WAR. ITS NEW PRESIDENT, FRANJO TUDJMAN, HAD DECLARED AN ETHNIC STATE AND PLEDGED TO "DE-SERBIANIZE" ALL STATE INSTITUTIONS, WHILE ALSO RESTORING THE SYMBOLS AND FLAGS OF THE USTASE STATE.

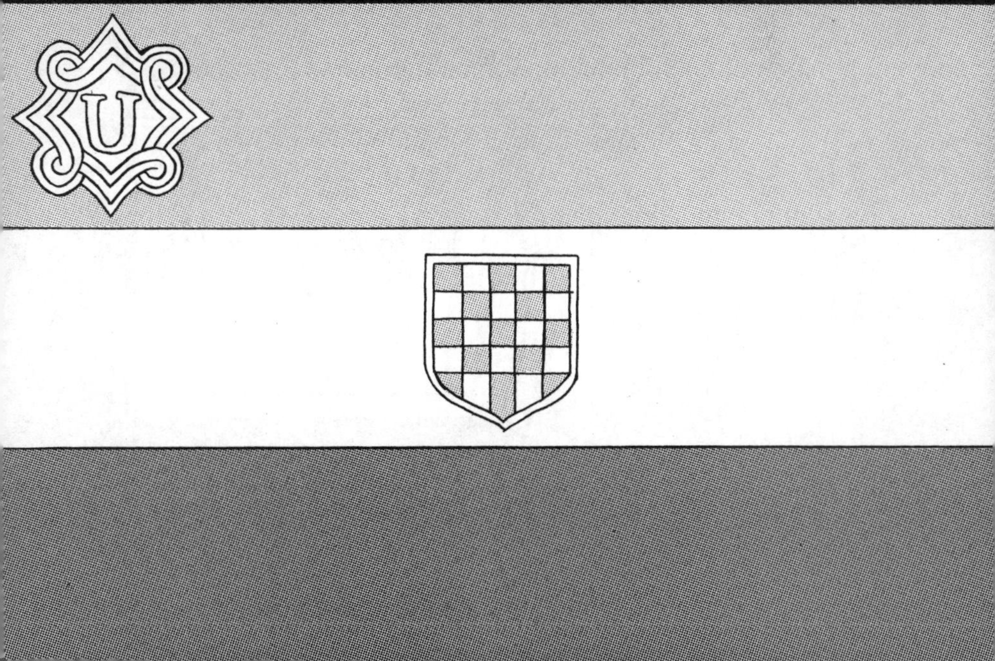
U

THE SERBS, IN TURN, WENT TO WAR TO LIBERATE AREAS THAT WERE HEAVILY SERB, PARTICULAR
AND BY THE END OF 1991, THEY CONTROLLED A THIRD OF CROATIA. FUELED BY THIS SUCCESS, SERB
DEPENDENT BOSNIA REBELLED AND QUICKLY CARVED OUT SEVENTY PERCENT OF ITS TERRITOR
JOINED WITH THEM TO LINK THE SERBIAN POPULATIONS OF CROATIA AND SERBIA THROUGH THE N
REGION OF BOSNIA. TUDJMAN AND THE BOSNIAN CROATS NOW WANTED BOSNIA'S EASTERN HER
GION, WHICH BORDERED CROATIA. BY THE TIME A MEANINGFUL CEASE-FIRE WAS REACHED, E
WAS COMPLETE. THE WEST COULD ONLY SOLIDIFY IT.

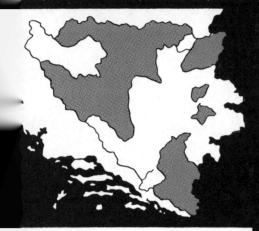

*Serbian lands
(around 1991)*

*Serbian territory, p
Dayton Agreeme
(1995)*

AND THEN THE MESS IN KOSOVO, WITH SERBS TRYING TO PUT DOWN A REBELLION OF ALBANIA
LARGE MAJORITY OF THE POPULATION IN THIS PROVINCE OF SERBIA, SO IT SEEMED THAT
RIGHT! THE BALKANS WERE DOOMED! BUT MACEDONIA WAS DIFFERENT. WHY? IT WAS THE
WITH THE WEAKEST SECURITY STRUCTURES, AND THE MOST HIGHLY CONTESTED NATIONAL
YET IT DIDN'T FOLLOW BOSNIA AND KOSOVO INTO WAR. SO ISN'T IT WORTH EXPLORING WH
MIGHT SAY ABOUT THE PEOPLE WHO LIVE THERE? ISN'T IT WORTH EXPLORING HOW PREV
IS ACCOMPLISHED? IT SEEMS NATURAL THAT WHEN A PERSON COMES HOME FROM WAR AND
MIRROR. THEY SEE SOMEONE DIFFERENT FROM THE PERSON WHO LEFT. BUT WHAT ABOUT T
KNOWS HIS COUNTRY WAS ALMOST ENGULFED IN WAR AND MANAGED NOT TO BE? ISN'T T
CHANGED AS WELL?

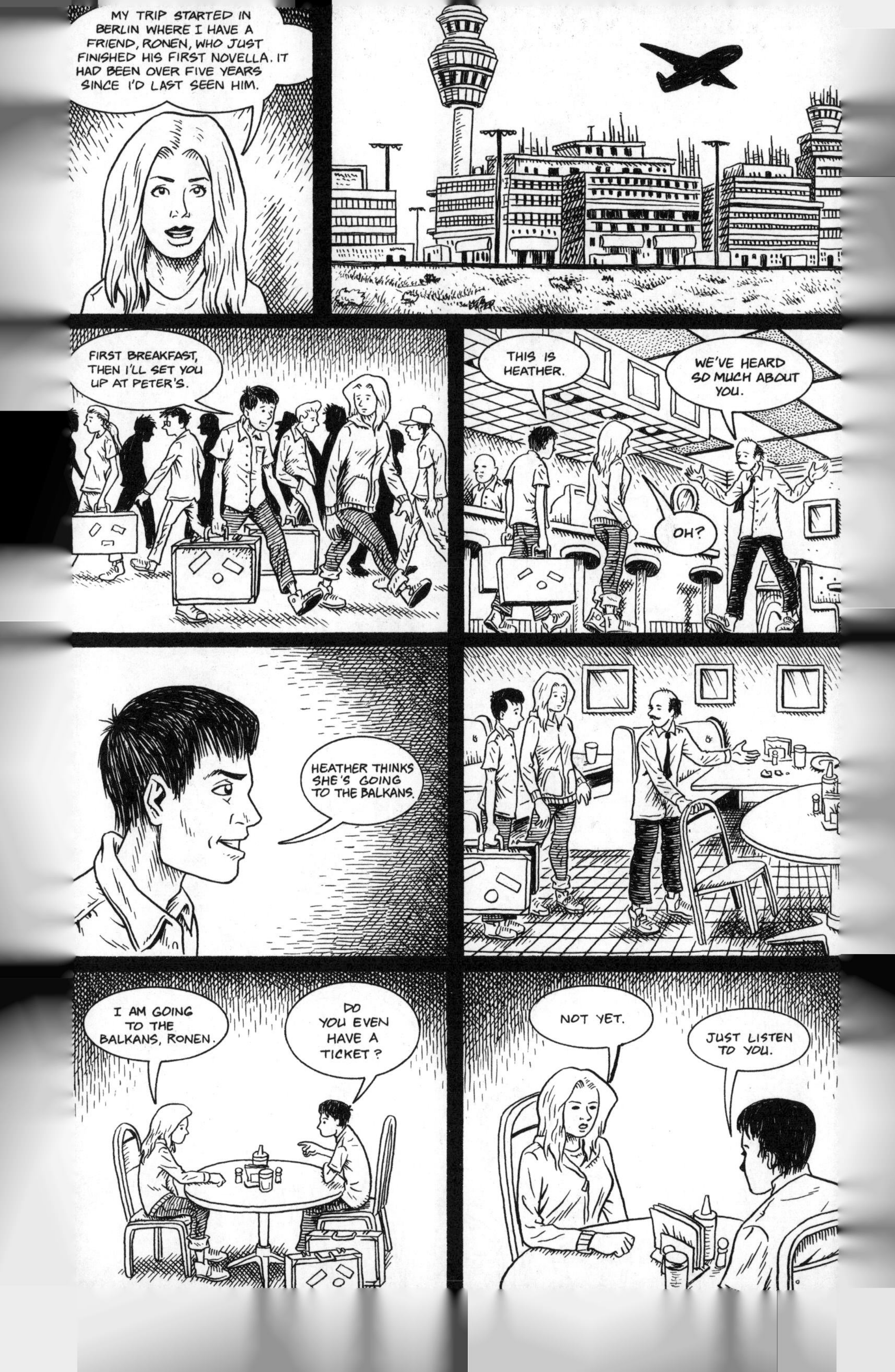
MY TRIP STARTED IN BERLIN WHERE I HAVE A FRIEND, RONEN, WHO JUST FINISHED HIS FIRST NOVELLA. IT HAD BEEN OVER FIVE YEARS SINCE I'D LAST SEEN HIM.
FIRST BREAKFAST, THEN I'LL SET YOU UP AT PETER'S.
THIS IS HEATHER.
WE'VE HEARD SO MUCH ABOUT YOU.
OH?
HEATHER THINKS SHE'S GOING TO THE BALKANS.
I AM GOING TO THE BALKANS, RONEN.
DO YOU EVEN HAVE A TICKET?
NOT YET.
JUST LISTEN TO YOU.

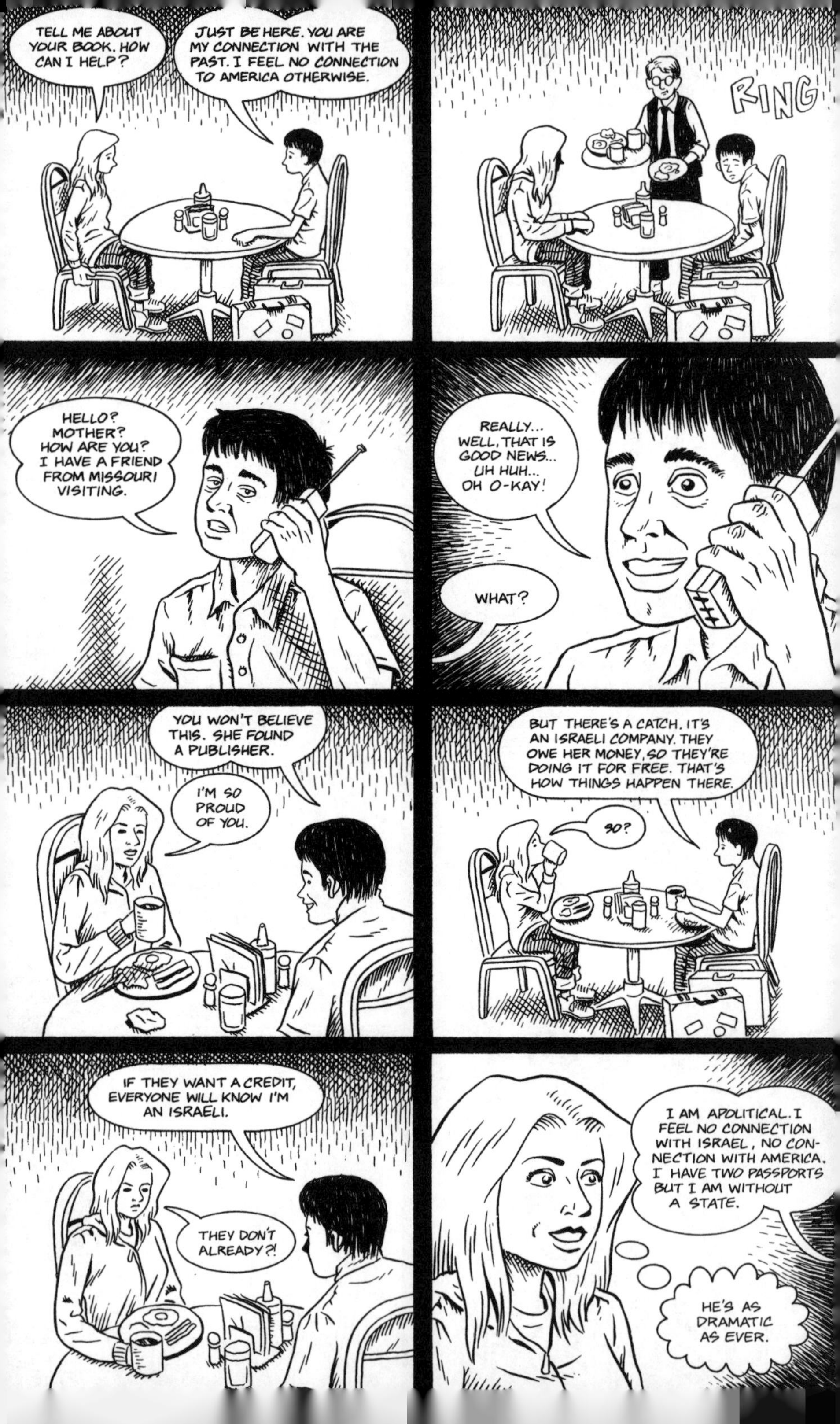
TELL ME ABOUT YOUR BOOK. HOW CAN I HELP?
JUST BE HERE. YOU ARE MY CONNECTION WITH THE PAST. I FEEL NO CONNECTION TO AMERICA OTHERWISE.
RING
HELLO? MOTHER? HOW ARE YOU? I HAVE A FRIEND FROM MISSOURI VISITING.
REALLY... WELL, THAT IS GOOD NEWS... UH HUH... OH O-KAY!
WHAT?
YOU WON'T BELIEVE THIS. SHE FOUND A PUBLISHER.
I'M SO PROUD OF YOU.
BUT THERE'S A CATCH. IT'S AN ISRAELI COMPANY. THEY OWE HER MONEY, SO THEY'RE DOING IT FOR FREE. THAT'S HOW THINGS HAPPEN THERE.
SO?
IF THEY WANT A CREDIT, EVERYONE WILL KNOW I'M AN ISRAELI.
THEY DON'T ALREADY?!
I AM APOLITICAL. I FEEL NO CONNECTION WITH ISRAEL, NO CONNECTION WITH AMERICA. I HAVE TWO PASSPORTS BUT I AM WITHOUT A STATE.
HE'S AS DRAMATIC AS EVER.

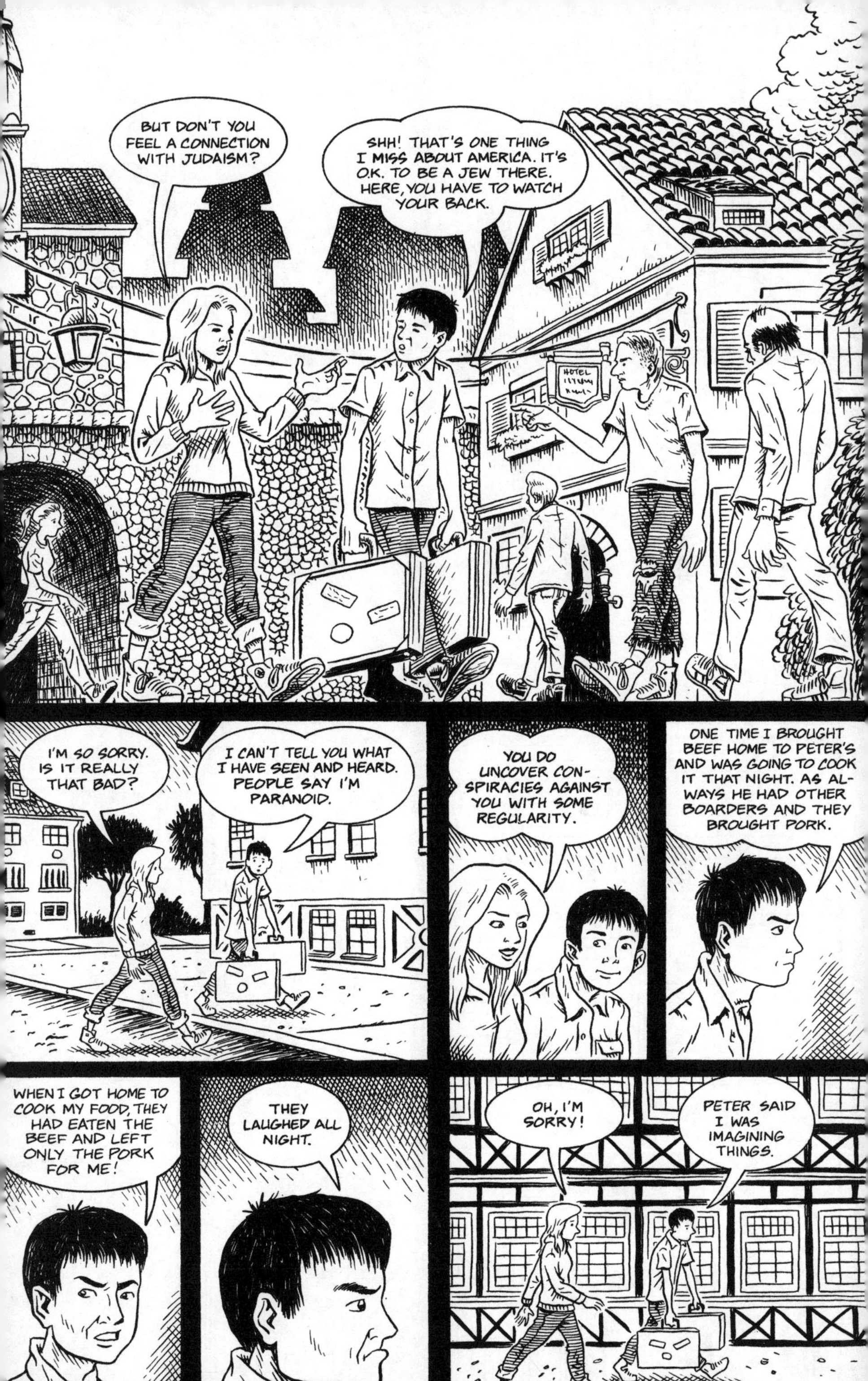
BUT DON'T YOU FEEL A CONNECTION WITH JUDAISM?
SHH! THAT'S ONE THING I MISS ABOUT AMERICA. IT'S O.K. TO BE A JEW THERE. HERE, YOU HAVE TO WATCH YOUR BACK.
HOTEL
I'M SO SORRY. IS IT REALLY THAT BAD?
I CAN'T TELL YOU WHAT I HAVE SEEN AND HEARD. PEOPLE SAY I'M PARANOID.
YOU DO UNCOVER CON-SPIRACIES AGAINST YOU WITH SOME REGULARITY.
ONE TIME I BROUGHT BEEF HOME TO PETER'S AND WAS GOING TO COOK IT THAT NIGHT. AS AL-WAYS HE HAD OTHER BOARDERS AND THEY BROUGHT PORK.
WHEN I GOT HOME TO COOK MY FOOD, THEY HAD EATEN THE BEEF AND LEFT ONLY THE PORK FOR ME!
THEY LAUGHED ALL NIGHT.
OH, I'M SORRY!
PETER SAID I WAS IMAGINING THINGS.

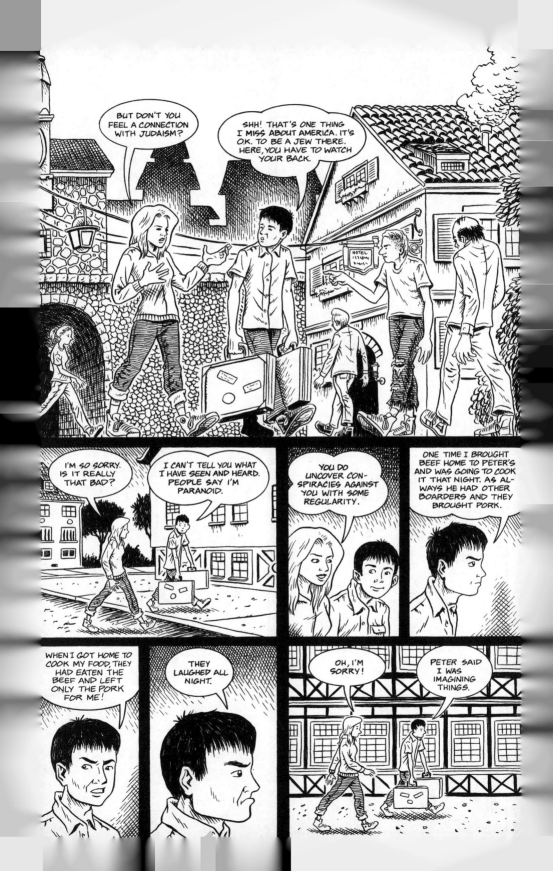

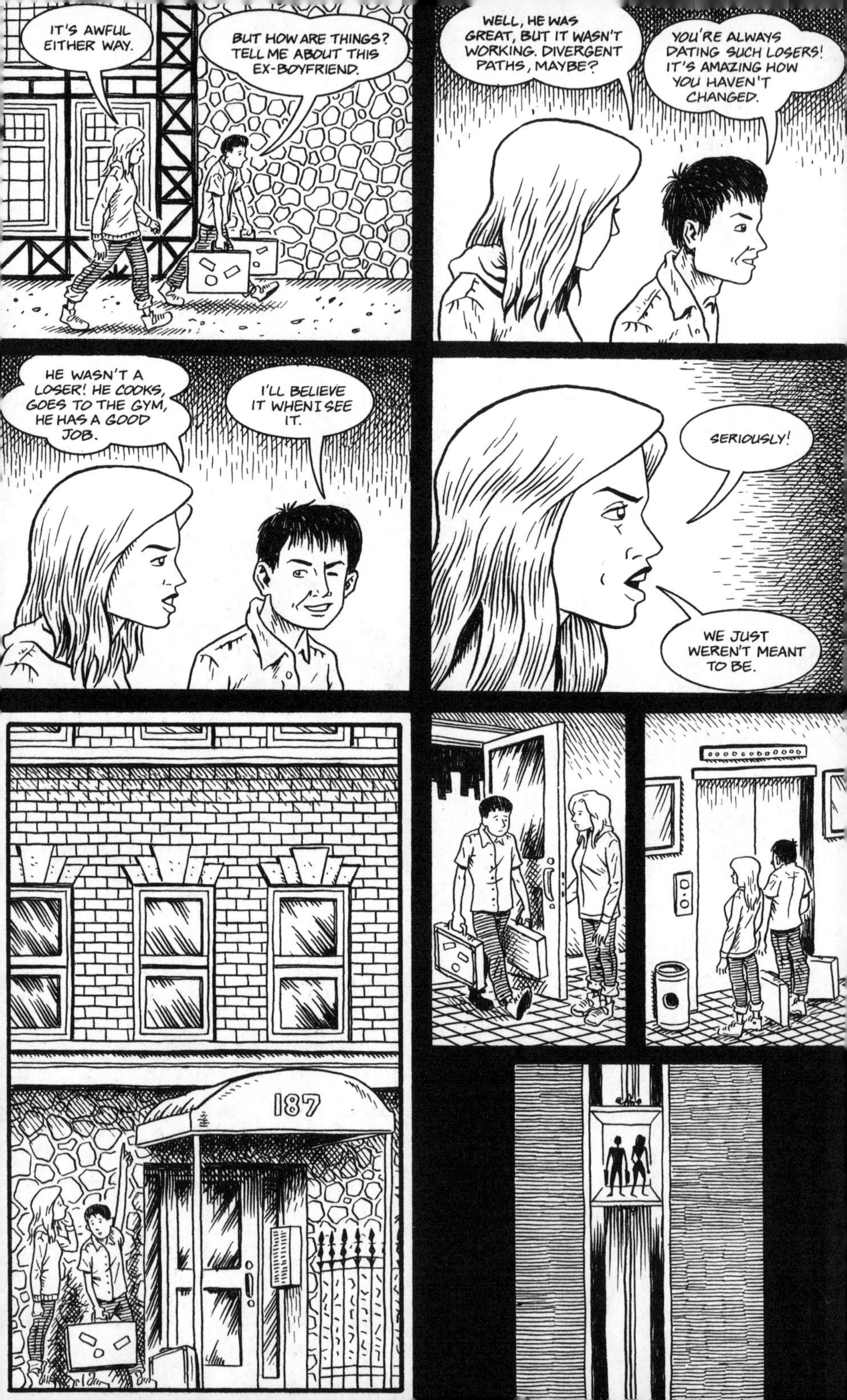
IT'S AWFUL EITHER WAY.
BUT HOW ARE THINGS? TELL ME ABOUT THIS EX-BOYFRIEND.
WELL, HE WAS GREAT, BUT IT WASN'T WORKING. DIVERGENT PATHS, MAYBE?
YOU'RE ALWAYS DATING SUCH LOSERS! IT'S AMAZING HOW YOU HAVEN'T CHANGED.
HE WASN'T A LOSER! HE COOKS, GOES TO THE GYM, HE HAS A GOOD JOB.
I'LL BELIEVE IT WHEN I SEE IT.
SERIOUSLY!
WE JUST WEREN'T MEANT TO BE.
187

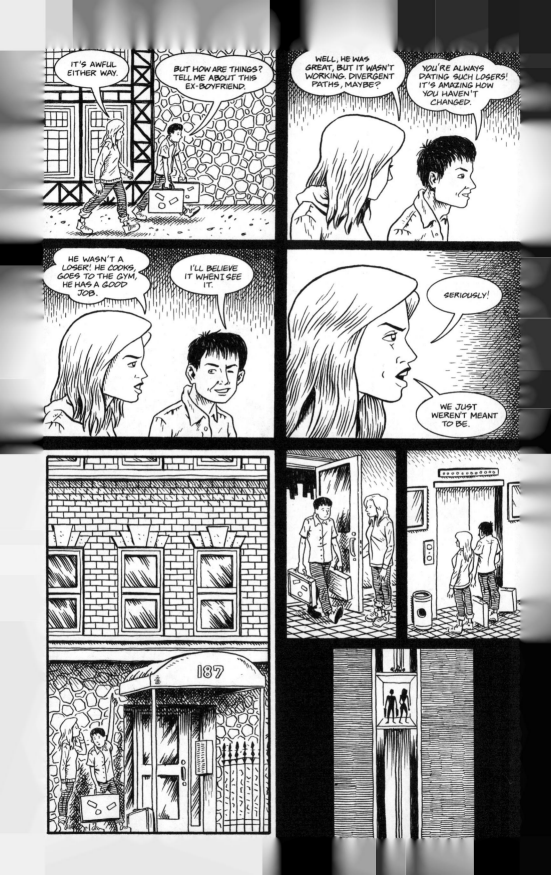

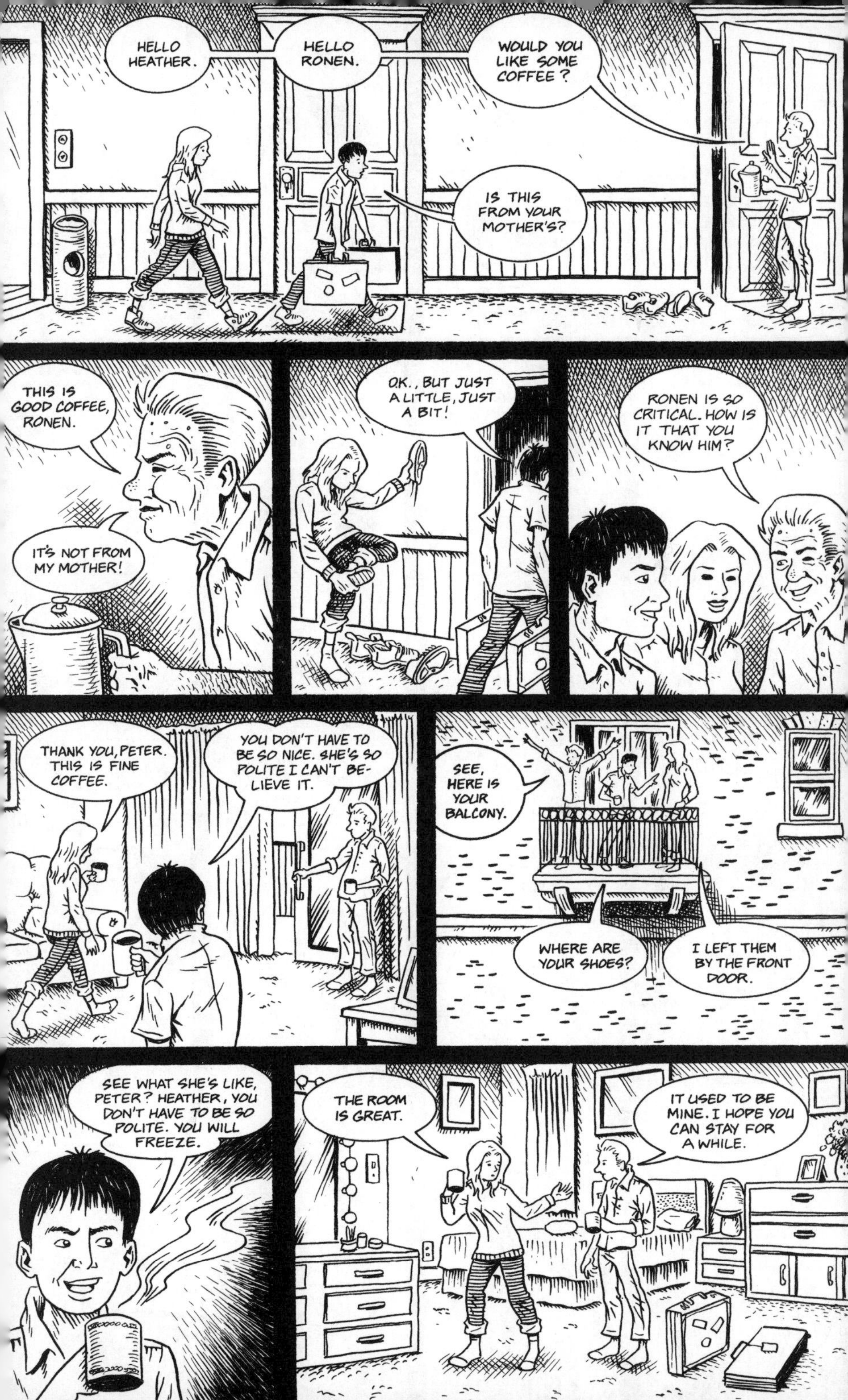
HELLO HEATHER.
HELLO RONEN.
WOULD YOU LIKE SOME COFFEE?
IS THIS FROM YOUR MOTHER'S?
THIS IS GOOD COFFEE, RONEN.
IT'S NOT FROM MY MOTHER!
O.K., BUT JUST A LITTLE, JUST A BIT!
RONEN IS SO CRITICAL. HOW IS IT THAT YOU KNOW HIM?
THANK YOU, PETER. THIS IS FINE COFFEE.
YOU DON'T HAVE TO BE SO NICE. SHE'S SO POLITE I CAN'T BE-LIEVE IT.
SEE, HERE IS YOUR BALCONY.
WHERE ARE YOUR SHOES?
I LEFT THEM BY THE FRONT DOOR.
SEE WHAT SHE'S LIKE, PETER? HEATHER, YOU DON'T HAVE TO BE SO POLITE. YOU WILL FREEZE.
THE ROOM IS GREAT.
IT USED TO BE MINE. I HOPE YOU CAN STAY FOR A WHILE.

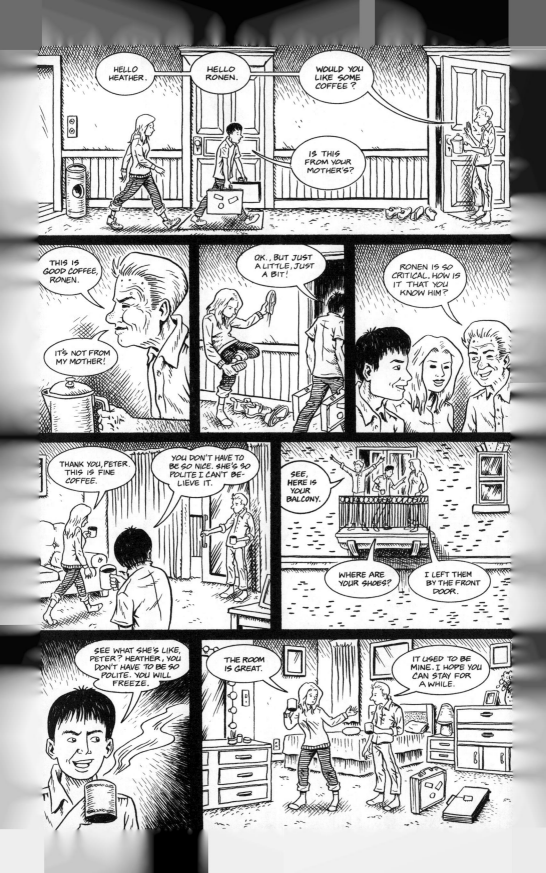

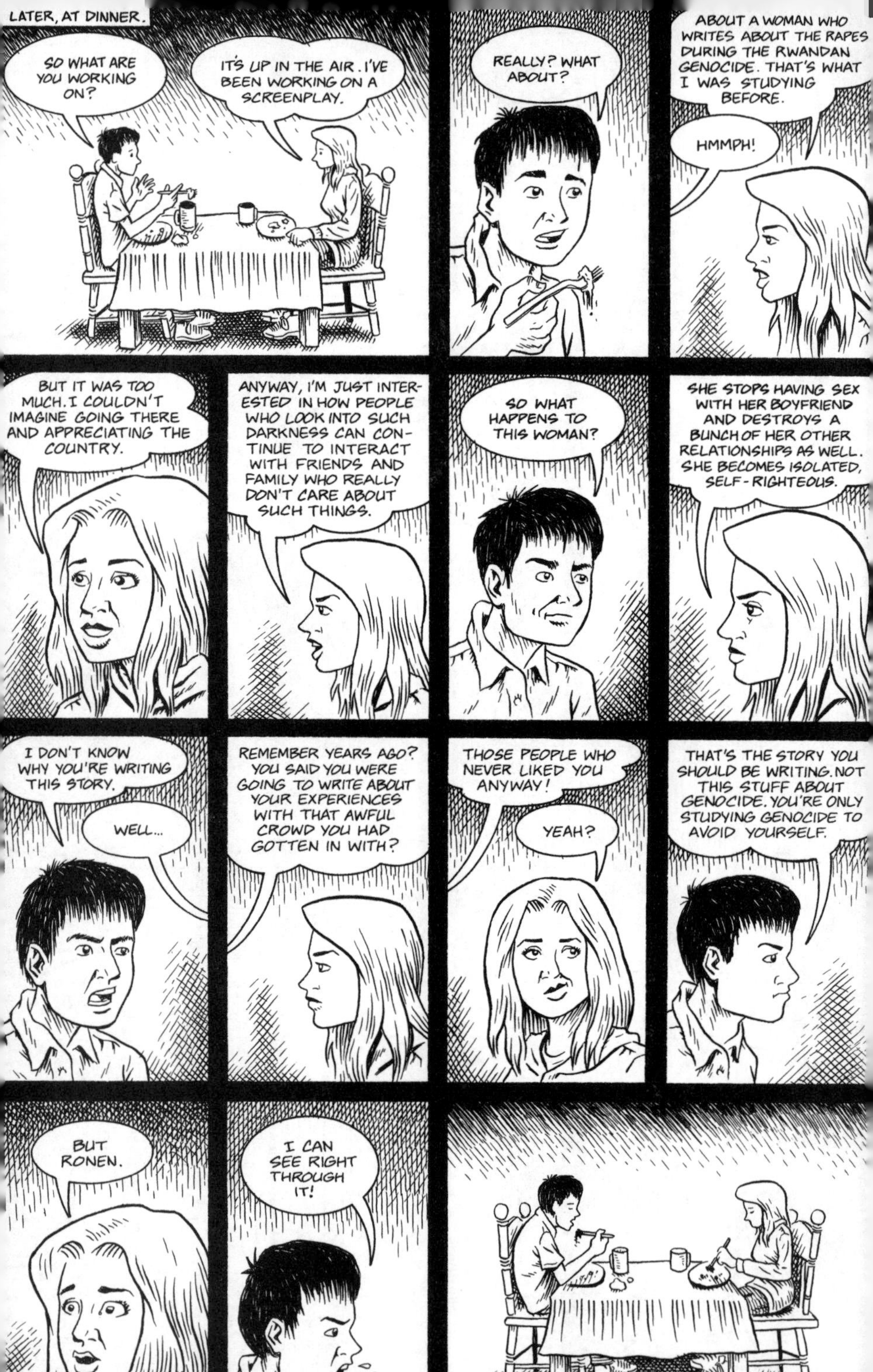
LATER, AT DINNER.
SO WHAT ARE YOU WORKING ON?
IT'S UP IN THE AIR. I'VE BEEN WORKING ON A SCREENPLAY.
REALLY? WHAT ABOUT?
ABOUT A WOMAN WHO WRITES ABOUT THE RAPES DURING THE RWANDAN GENOCIDE. THAT'S WHAT I WAS STUDYING BEFORE.
HMMPH!
BUT IT WAS TOO MUCH. I COULDN'T IMAGINE GOING THERE AND APPRECIATING THE COUNTRY.
ANYWAY, I'M JUST INTERESTED IN HOW PEOPLE WHO LOOK INTO SUCH DARKNESS CAN CONTINUE TO INTERACT WITH FRIENDS AND FAMILY WHO REALLY DON'T CARE ABOUT SUCH THINGS.
SO WHAT HAPPENS TO THIS WOMAN?
SHE STOPS HAVING SEX WITH HER BOYFRIEND AND DESTROYS A BUNCH OF HER OTHER RELATIONSHIPS AS WELL. SHE BECOMES ISOLATED, SELF-RIGHTEOUS.
I DON'T KNOW WHY YOU'RE WRITING THIS STORY.
WELL...
REMEMBER YEARS AGO? YOU SAID YOU WERE GOING TO WRITE ABOUT YOUR EXPERIENCES WITH THAT AWFUL CROWD YOU HAD GOTTEN IN WITH?
THOSE PEOPLE WHO NEVER LIKED YOU ANYWAY!
YEAH?
THAT'S THE STORY YOU SHOULD BE WRITING. NOT THIS STUFF ABOUT GENOCIDE. YOU'RE ONLY STUDYING GENOCIDE TO AVOID YOURSELF.
BUT RONEN.
I CAN SEE RIGHT THROUGH IT!

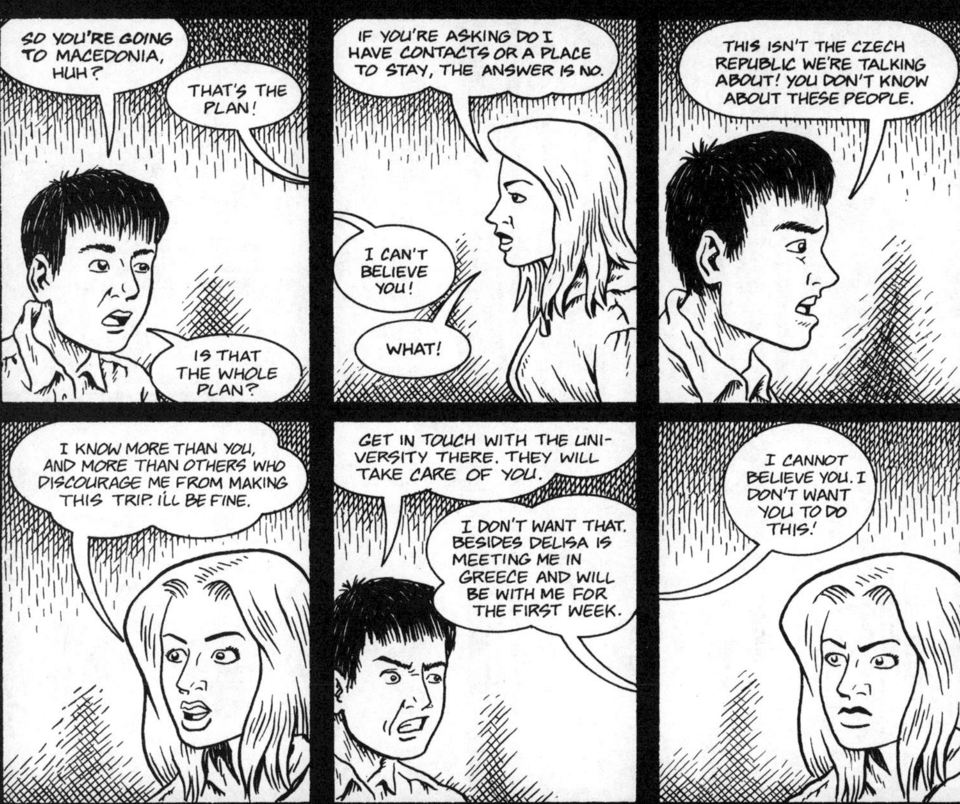
SO YOU'RE GOING TO MACEDONIA, HUH?
THAT'S THE PLAN!
IS THAT THE WHOLE PLAN?
IF YOU'RE ASKING DO I HAVE CONTACTS OR A PLACE TO STAY, THE ANSWER IS NO.
I CAN'T BELIEVE YOU!
WHAT!
THIS ISN'T THE CZECH REPUBLIC WE'RE TALKING ABOUT! YOU DON'T KNOW ABOUT THESE PEOPLE.
I KNOW MORE THAN YOU, AND MORE THAN OTHERS WHO DISCOURAGE ME FROM MAKING THIS TRIP. I'LL BE FINE.
GET IN TOUCH WITH THE UNIVERSITY THERE. THEY WILL TAKE CARE OF YOU.
I DON'T WANT THAT. BESIDES DELISA IS MEETING ME IN GREECE AND WILL BE WITH ME FOR THE FIRST WEEK.
I CANNOT BELIEVE YOU. I DON'T WANT YOU TO DO THIS!

WHILE I WAS WITH RONEN I BARELY THOUGHT OF THE MAN ON THE PLANE. I DIDN'T EVEN CONSIDER TELLING RONEN ABOUT IT, KNOWING IT WOULD ONLY LEAD TO A LECTURE, AND REALLY, WHAT COULD BE DONE ABOUT IT? BUT IT'S WHEN I LIE DOWN IN BED THAT THE INTERNAL DIALOGUE ALWAYS BEGINS. SOMETIMES I GIVE MYSELF A HEADACHE. TONIGHT I THINK "AM I CRAZY? CAN I DO THIS ALONE?"

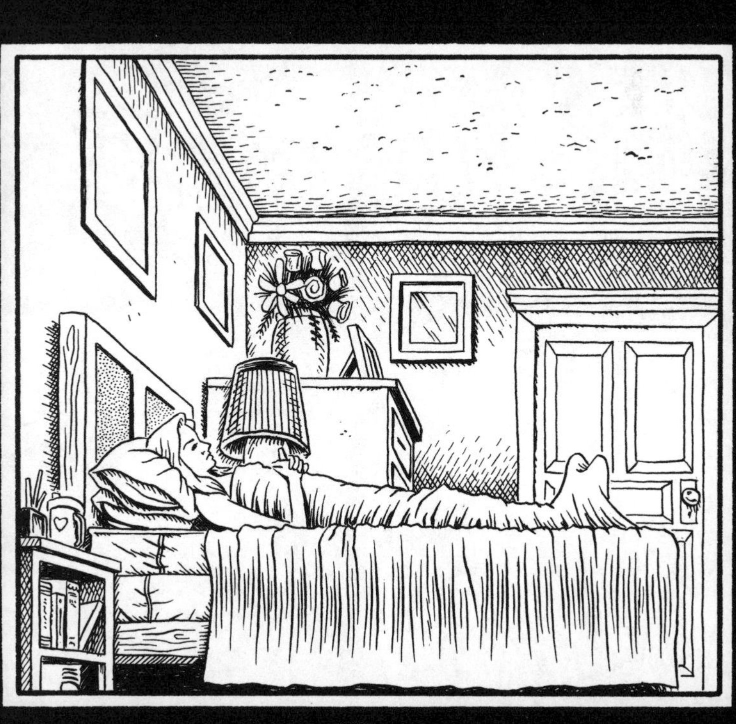

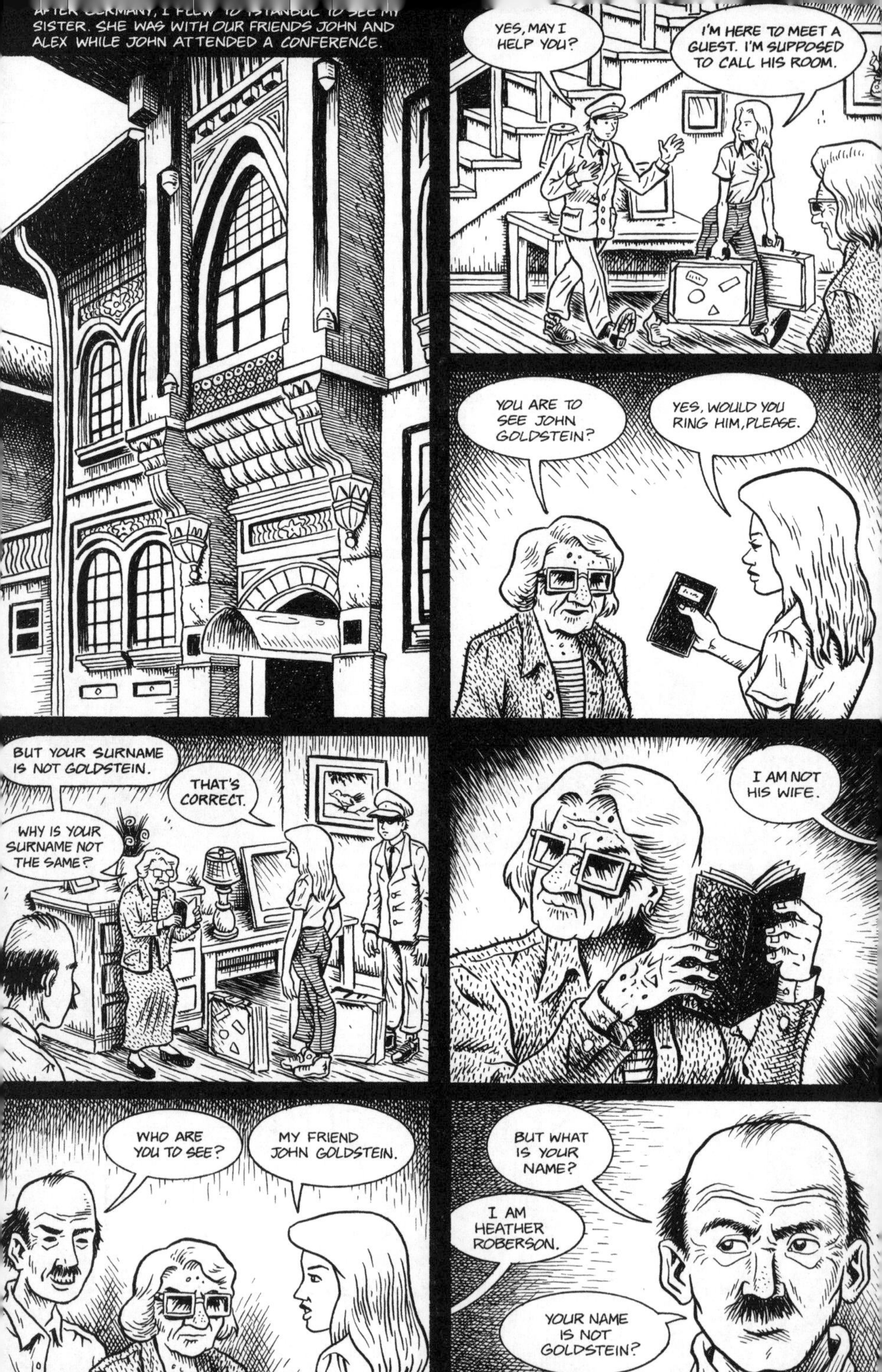

AFTER GERMANY, I FLEW TO ISTANBUL TO SEE MY SISTER. SHE WAS WITH OUR FRIENDS JOHN AND ALEX WHILE JOHN ATTENDED A CONFERENCE.
YES, MAY I HELP YOU?
I'M HERE TO MEET A GUEST. I'M SUPPOSED TO CALL HIS ROOM.
YOU ARE TO SEE JOHN GOLDSTEIN?
YES, WOULD YOU RING HIM, PLEASE.
BUT YOUR SURNAME IS NOT GOLDSTEIN.
THAT'S CORRECT.
WHY IS YOUR SURNAME NOT THE SAME?
I AM NOT HIS WIFE.
WHO ARE YOU TO SEE?
MY FRIEND JOHN GOLDSTEIN.
BUT WHAT IS YOUR NAME?
I AM HEATHER ROBERSON.
YOUR NAME IS NOT GOLDSTEIN?

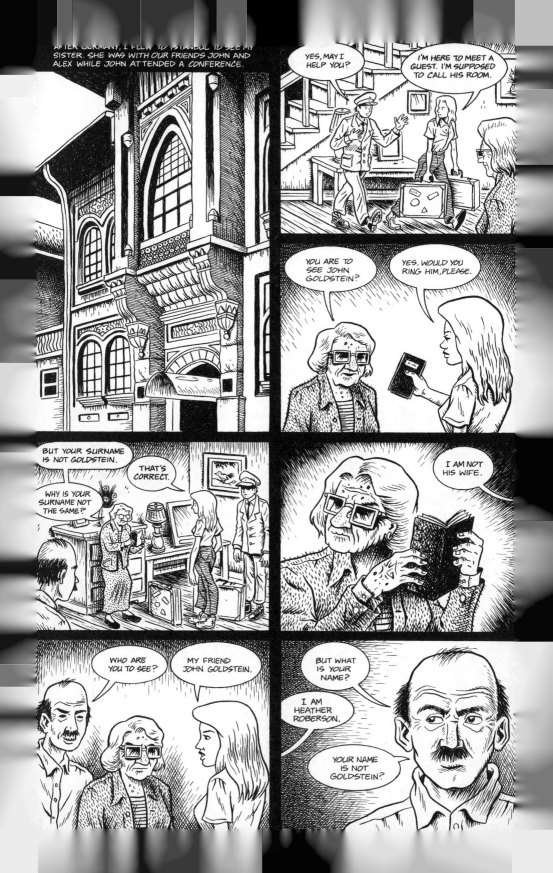

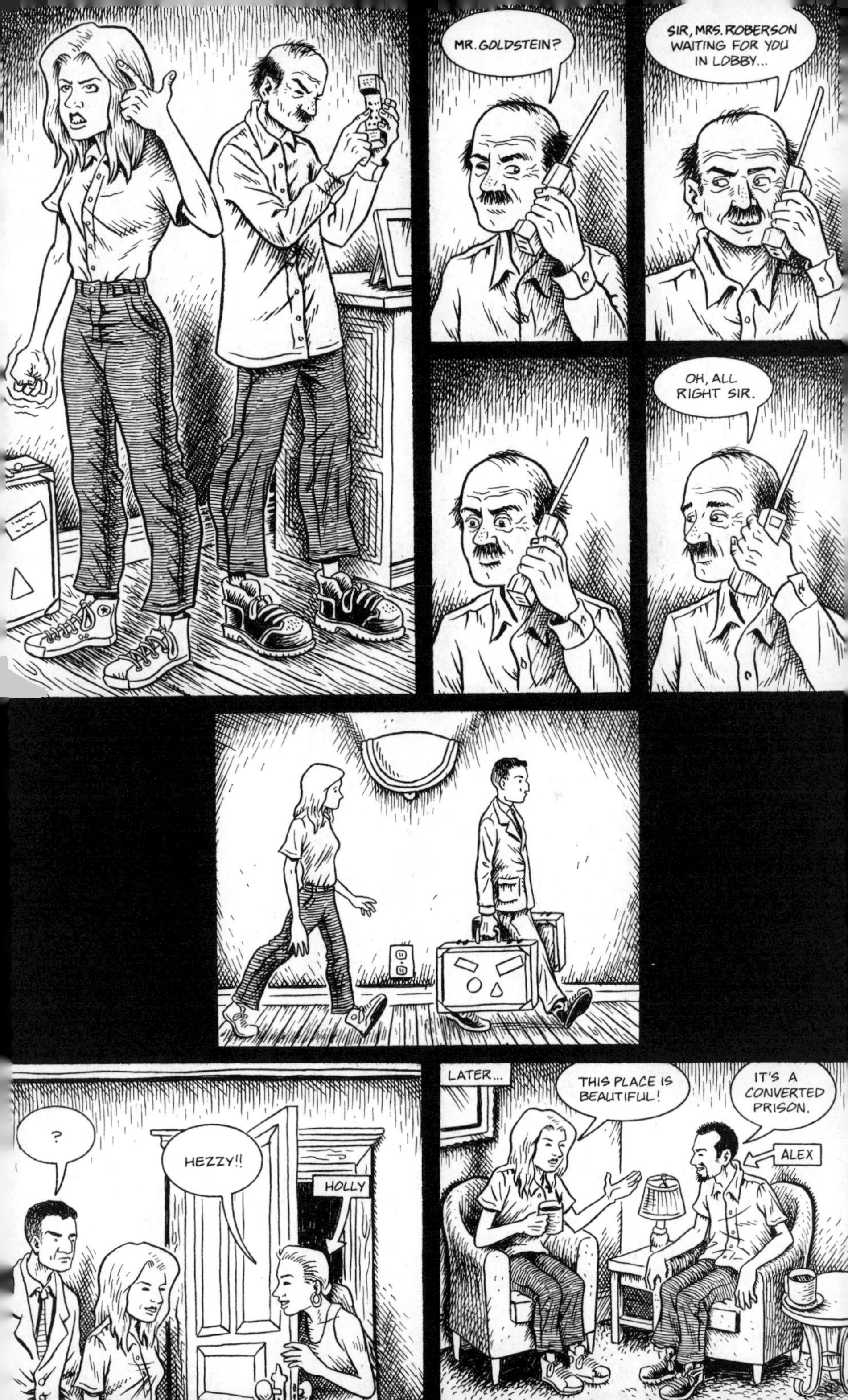
MR. GOLDSTEIN?
SIR, MRS. ROBERSON WAITING FOR YOU IN LOBBY...
OH, ALL RIGHT SIR.
?
HEZZY!!
HOLLY
LATER...
THIS PLACE IS BEAUTIFUL!
IT'S A CONVERTED PRISON.
ALEX

NIGHT HEATHER, HOLLY, JOHN, AND [illegible] DANCE IN THE BASEMENT OF THE ORIENT YOUTH HOSTEL.

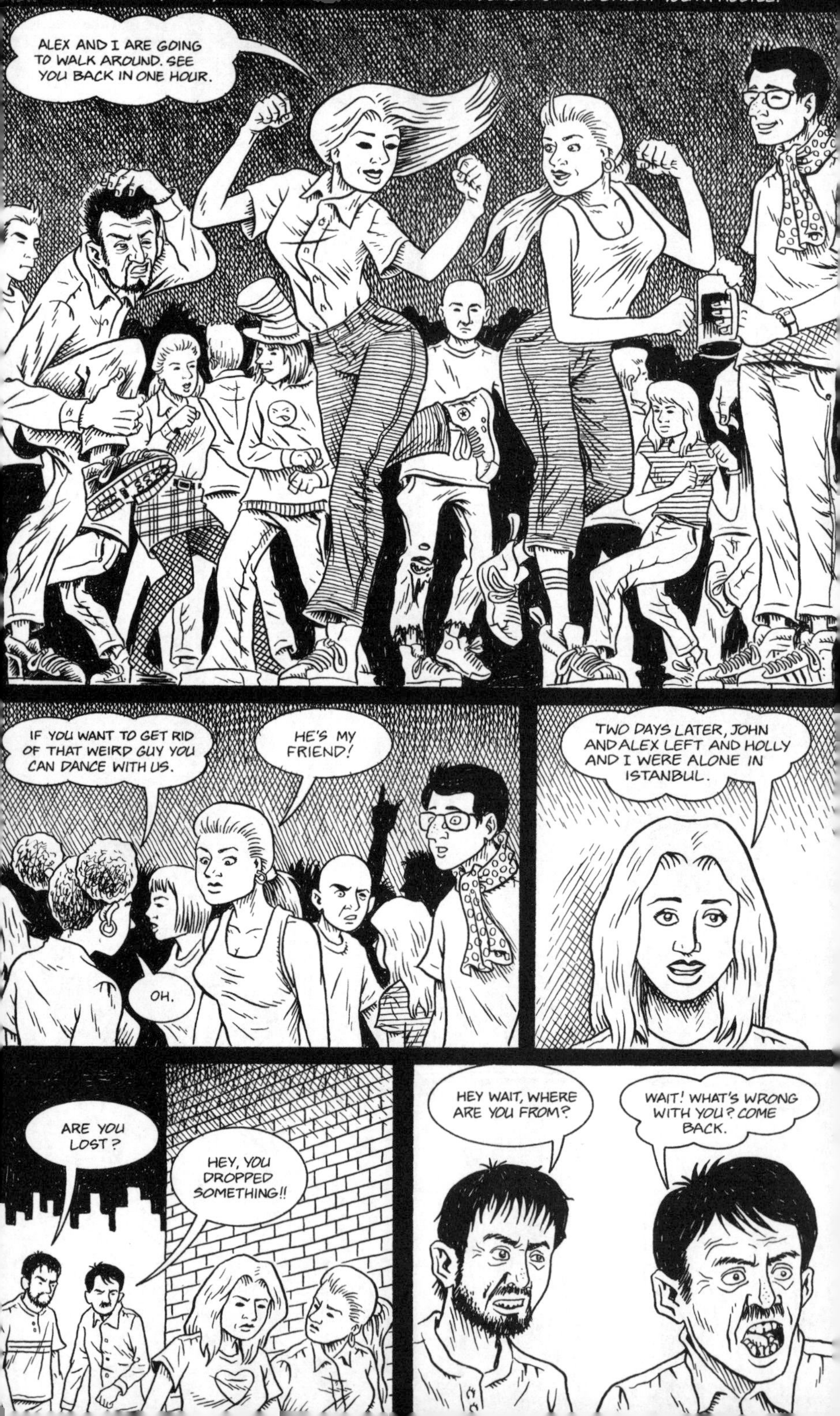

ALEX AND I ARE GOING TO WALK AROUND. SEE YOU BACK IN ONE HOUR.
IF YOU WANT TO GET RID OF THAT WEIRD GUY YOU CAN DANCE WITH US.
HE'S MY FRIEND!
OH.
TWO DAYS LATER, JOHN AND ALEX LEFT AND HOLLY AND I WERE ALONE IN ISTANBUL.
ARE YOU LOST?
HEY, YOU DROPPED SOMETHING!!
HEY WAIT, WHERE ARE YOU FROM?
WAIT! WHAT'S WRONG WITH YOU? COME BACK.

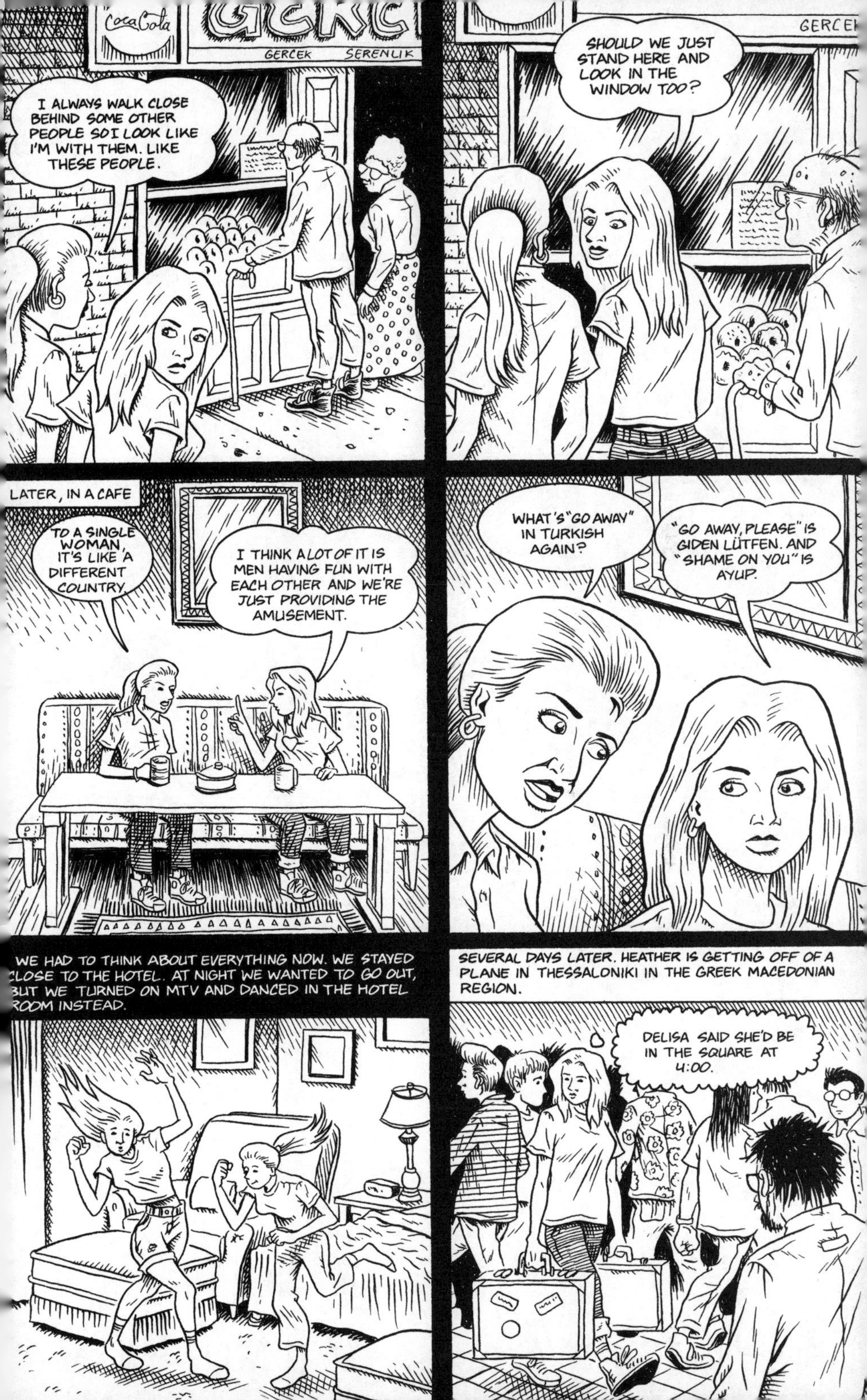

Coca-Cola
GERCEK SERENLIK
I ALWAYS WALK CLOSE BEHIND SOME OTHER PEOPLE SO I LOOK LIKE I'M WITH THEM. LIKE THESE PEOPLE.
GERCEK
SHOULD WE JUST STAND HERE AND LOOK IN THE WINDOW TOO?
LATER, IN A CAFE
TO A SINGLE WOMAN, IT'S LIKE A DIFFERENT COUNTRY.
I THINK A LOT OF IT IS MEN HAVING FUN WITH EACH OTHER AND WE'RE JUST PROVIDING THE AMUSEMENT.
WHAT'S "GO AWAY" IN TURKISH AGAIN?
"GO AWAY, PLEASE" IS GIDEN LÜTFEN. AND "SHAME ON YOU" IS AYUP.
WE HAD TO THINK ABOUT EVERYTHING NOW. WE STAYED CLOSE TO THE HOTEL. AT NIGHT WE WANTED TO GO OUT, BUT WE TURNED ON MTV AND DANCED IN THE HOTEL ROOM INSTEAD.
SEVERAL DAYS LATER. HEATHER IS GETTING OFF OF A PLANE IN THESSALONIKI IN THE GREEK MACEDONIAN REGION.
DELISA SAID SHE'D BE IN THE SQUARE AT 4:00.

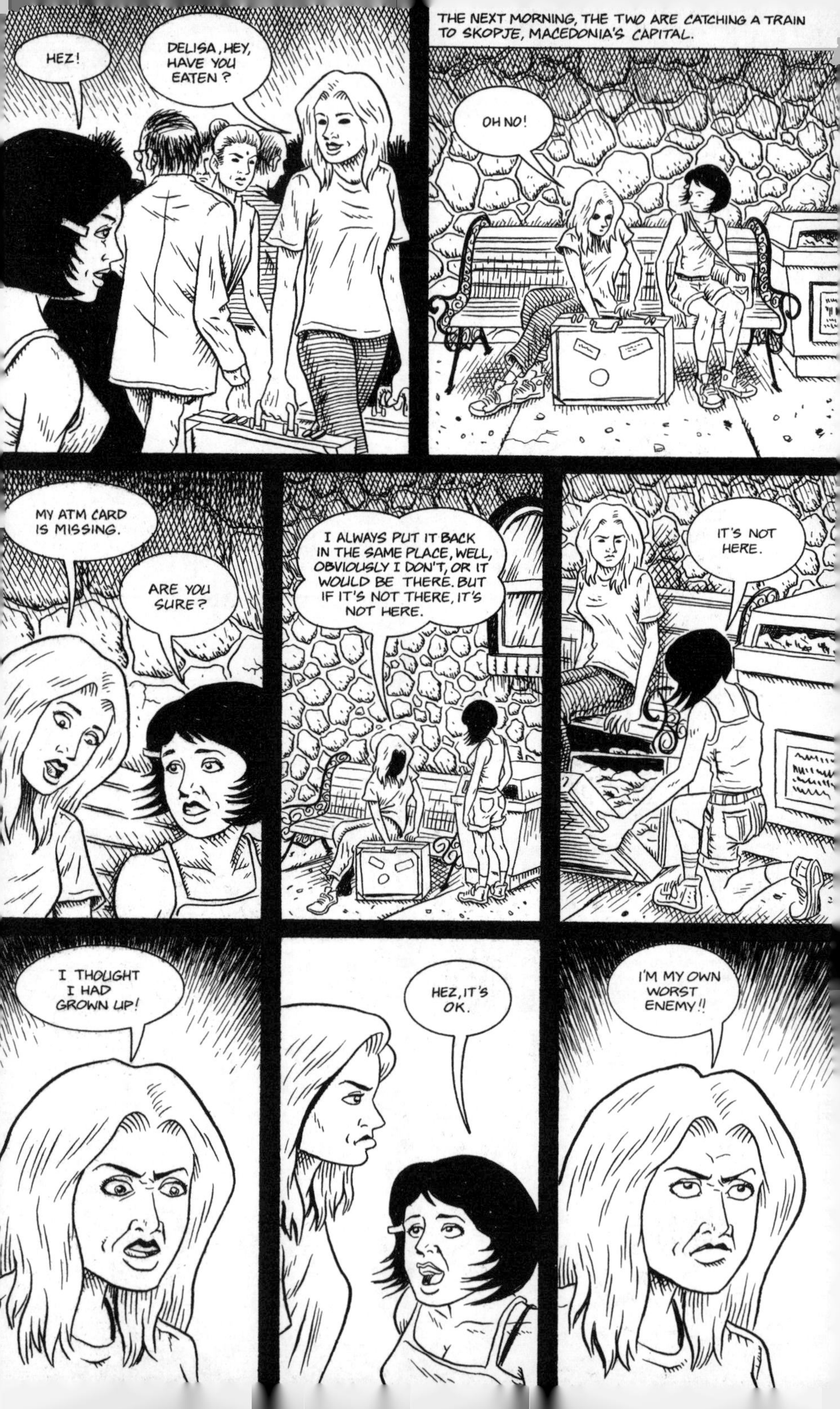
HEZ!
DELISA, HEY, HAVE YOU EATEN?
THE NEXT MORNING, THE TWO ARE CATCHING A TRAIN TO SKOPJE, MACEDONIA'S CAPITAL.
OH NO!
MY ATM CARD IS MISSING.
ARE YOU SURE?
I ALWAYS PUT IT BACK IN THE SAME PLACE, WELL, OBVIOUSLY I DON'T, OR IT WOULD BE THERE. BUT IF IT'S NOT THERE, IT'S NOT HERE.
IT'S NOT HERE.
I THOUGHT I HAD GROWN UP!
HEZ, IT'S OK.
I'M MY OWN WORST ENEMY!!

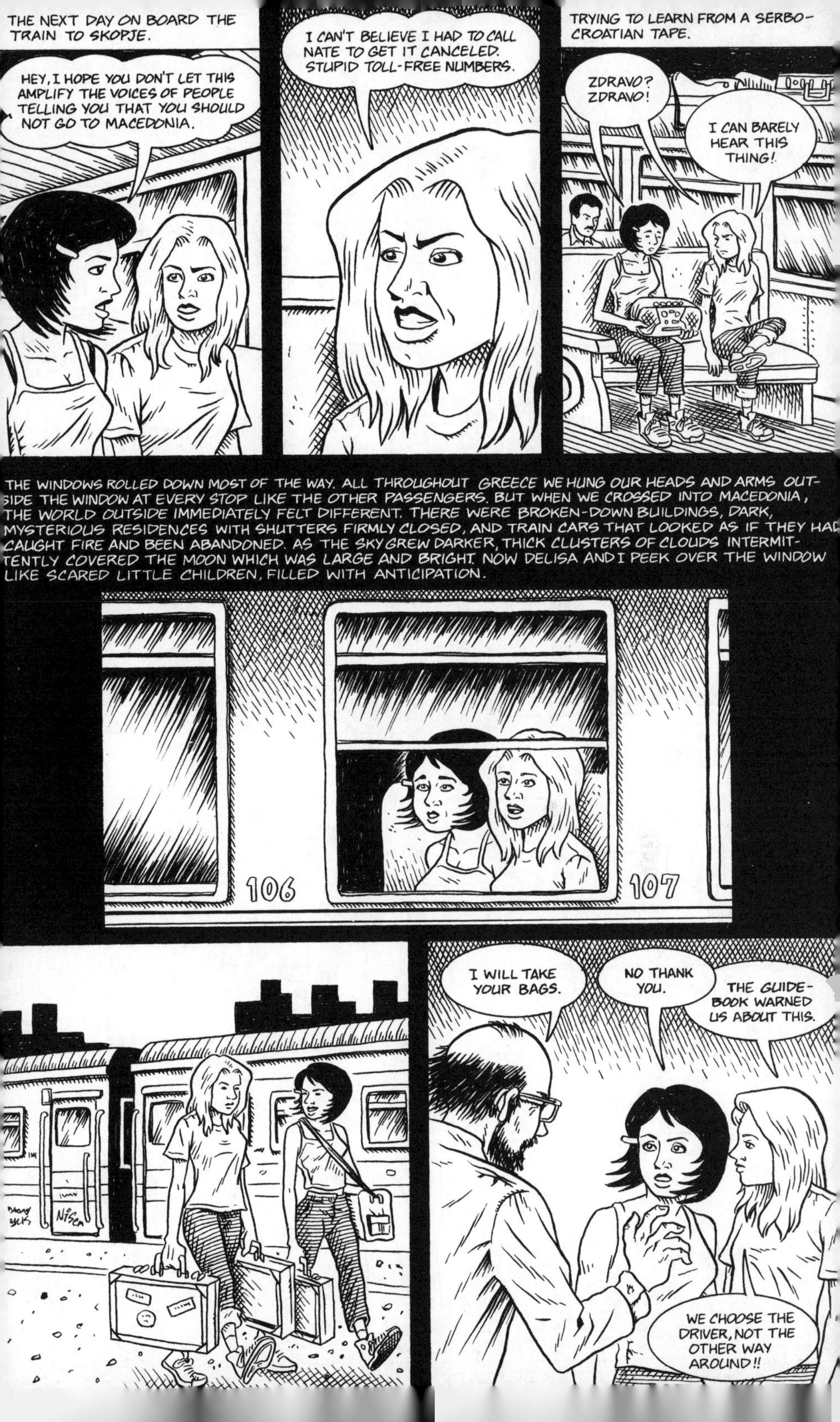
THE NEXT DAY ON BOARD THE TRAIN TO SKOPJE.
HEY, I HOPE YOU DON'T LET THIS AMPLIFY THE VOICES OF PEOPLE TELLING YOU THAT YOU SHOULD NOT GO TO MACEDONIA.
I CAN'T BELIEVE I HAD TO CALL NATE TO GET IT CANCELED. STUPID TOLL-FREE NUMBERS.
TRYING TO LEARN FROM A SERBO-CROATIAN TAPE.
ZDRAVO? ZDRAVO!
I CAN BARELY HEAR THIS THING!
THE WINDOWS ROLLED DOWN MOST OF THE WAY. ALL THROUGHOUT GREECE WE HUNG OUR HEADS AND ARMS OUTSIDE THE WINDOW AT EVERY STOP LIKE THE OTHER PASSENGERS. BUT WHEN WE CROSSED INTO MACEDONIA, THE WORLD OUTSIDE IMMEDIATELY FELT DIFFERENT. THERE WERE BROKEN-DOWN BUILDINGS, DARK, MYSTERIOUS RESIDENCES WITH SHUTTERS FIRMLY CLOSED, AND TRAIN CARS THAT LOOKED AS IF THEY HAD CAUGHT FIRE AND BEEN ABANDONED. AS THE SKY GREW DARKER, THICK CLUSTERS OF CLOUDS INTERMITTENTLY COVERED THE MOON WHICH WAS LARGE AND BRIGHT. NOW DELISA AND I PEEK OVER THE WINDOW LIKE SCARED LITTLE CHILDREN, FILLED WITH ANTICIPATION.
106
107
I WILL TAKE YOUR BAGS.
NO THANK YOU.
THE GUIDE-BOOK WARNED US ABOUT THIS.
WE CHOOSE THE DRIVER, NOT THE OTHER WAY AROUND!!

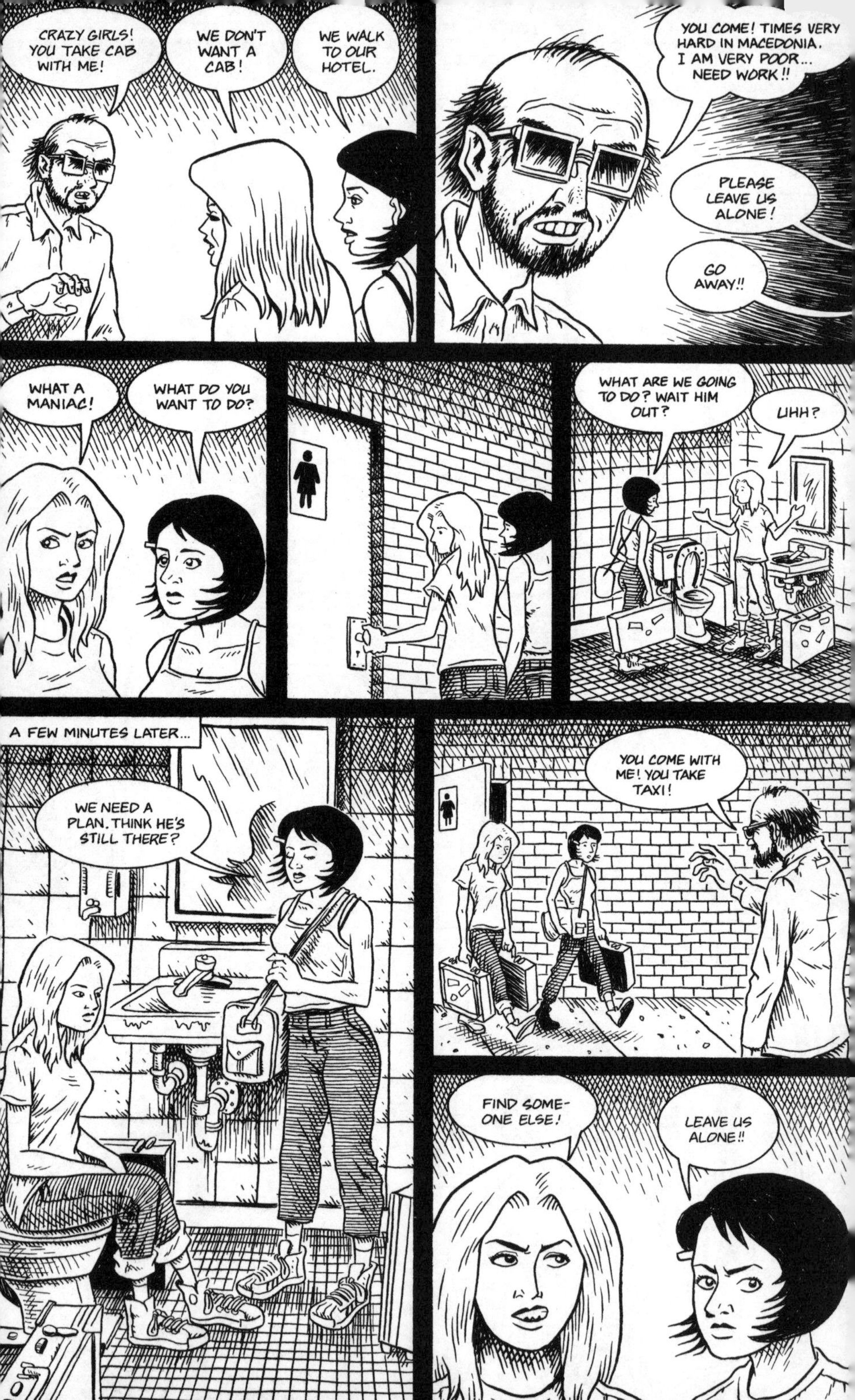
CRAZY GIRLS! YOU TAKE CAB WITH ME!
WE DON'T WANT A CAB!
WE WALK TO OUR HOTEL.
YOU COME! TIMES VERY HARD IN MACEDONIA. I AM VERY POOR... NEED WORK!!
PLEASE LEAVE US ALONE!
GO AWAY!!
WHAT A MANIAC!
WHAT DO YOU WANT TO DO?
WHAT ARE WE GOING TO DO? WAIT HIM OUT?
UHH?
A FEW MINUTES LATER...
WE NEED A PLAN. THINK HE'S STILL THERE?
YOU COME WITH ME! YOU TAKE TAXI!
FIND SOME-ONE ELSE!
LEAVE US ALONE!!

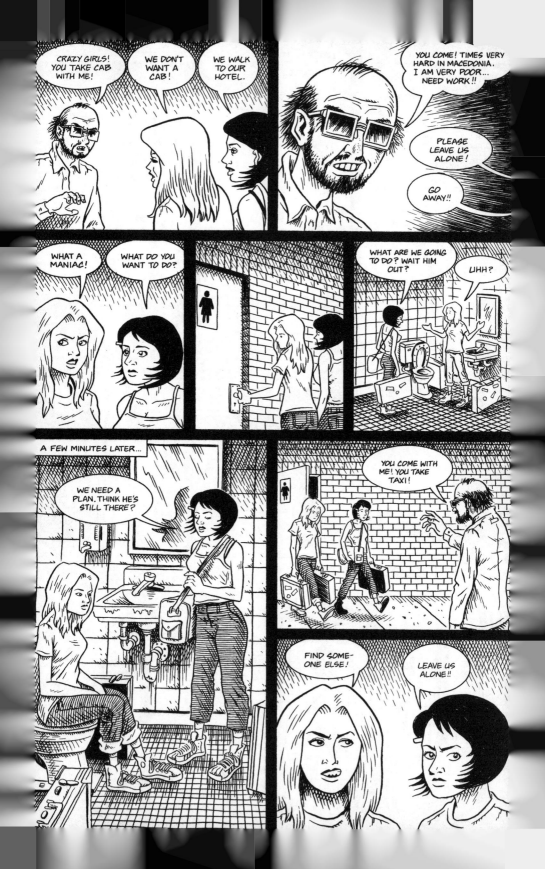

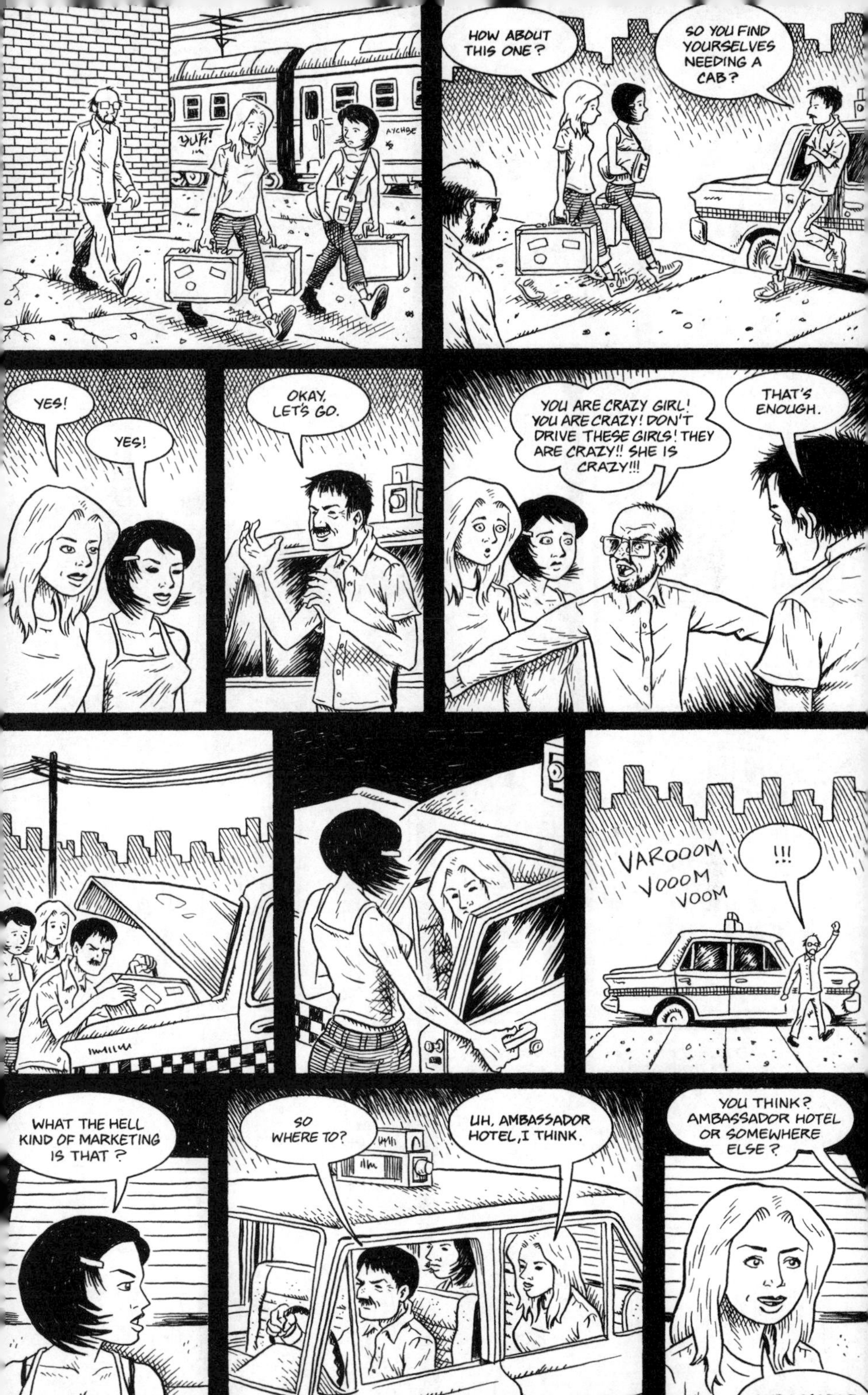
HOW ABOUT THIS ONE?
SO YOU FIND YOURSELVES NEEDING A CAB?
YES!
YES!
OKAY, LET'S GO.
YOU ARE CRAZY GIRL! YOU ARE CRAZY! DON'T DRIVE THESE GIRLS! THEY ARE CRAZY!! SHE IS CRAZY!!!
THAT'S ENOUGH.
VAROOOM VOOOM VOOM
!!!
WHAT THE HELL KIND OF MARKETING IS THAT?
SO WHERE TO?
UH, AMBASSADOR HOTEL, I THINK.
YOU THINK? AMBASSADOR HOTEL OR SOMEWHERE ELSE?
AMBASSADOR IS FINE.

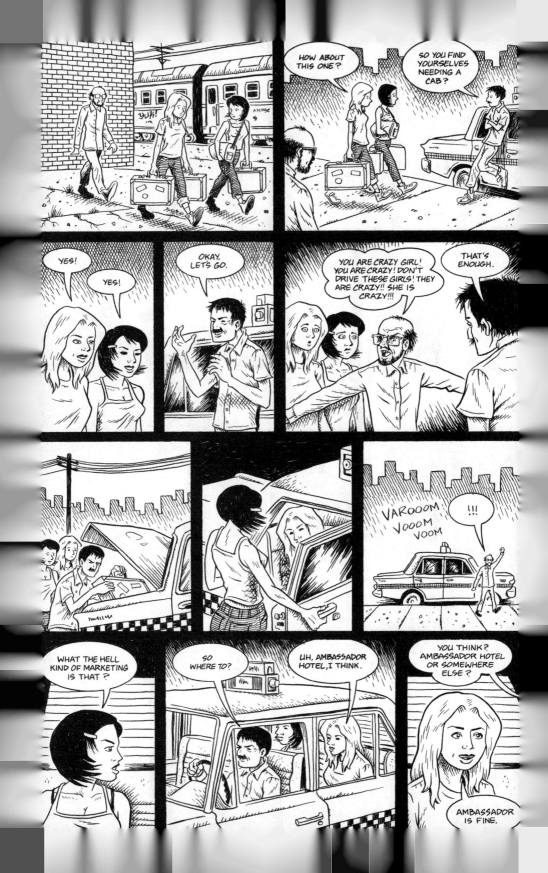

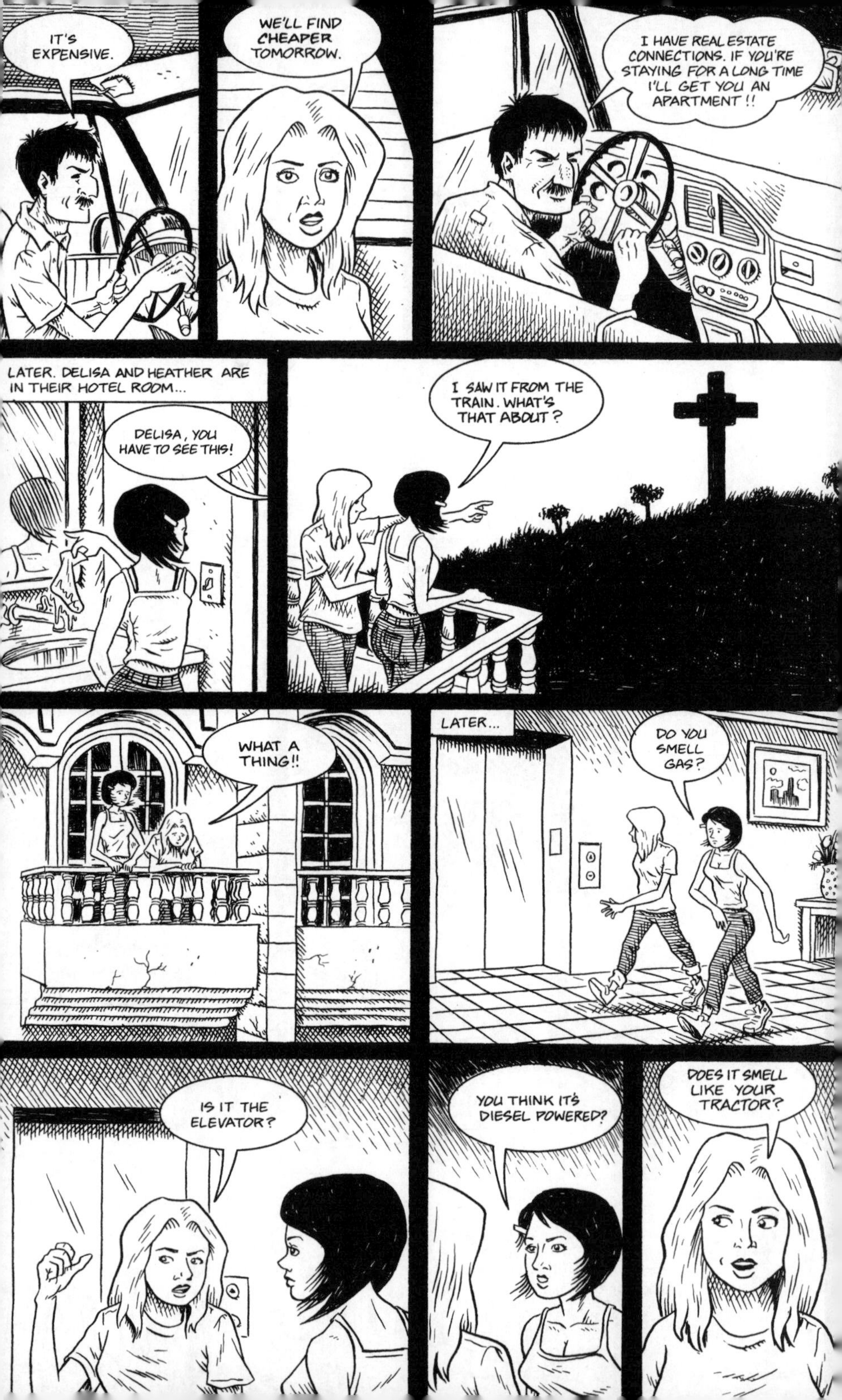
IT'S EXPENSIVE.
WE'LL FIND CHEAPER TOMORROW.
I HAVE REAL ESTATE CONNECTIONS. IF YOU'RE STAYING FOR A LONG TIME I'LL GET YOU AN APARTMENT !!
LATER. DELISA AND HEATHER ARE IN THEIR HOTEL ROOM...
DELISA, YOU HAVE TO SEE THIS!
I SAW IT FROM THE TRAIN. WHAT'S THAT ABOUT ?
WHAT A THING!!
LATER...
DO YOU SMELL GAS?
IS IT THE ELEVATOR?
YOU THINK IT'S DIESEL POWERED?
DOES IT SMELL LIKE YOUR TRACTOR?

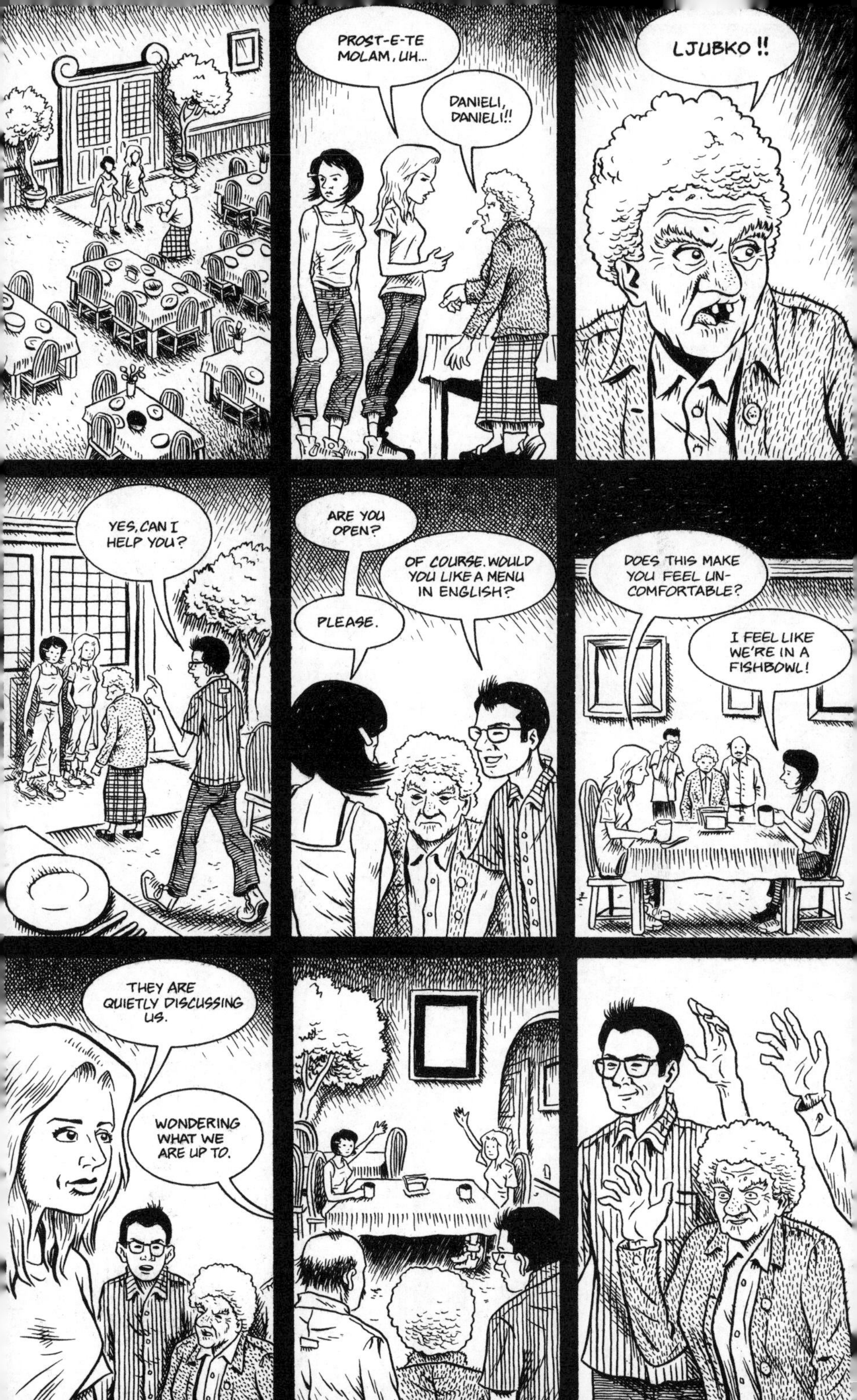
PROST-E-TE MOLAM, UH...
DANIELI, DANIELI!!
LJUBKO!!
YES, CAN I HELP YOU?
ARE YOU OPEN?
OF COURSE. WOULD YOU LIKE A MENU IN ENGLISH?
PLEASE.
DOES THIS MAKE YOU FEEL UN-COMFORTABLE?
I FEEL LIKE WE'RE IN A FISHBOWL!
THEY ARE QUIETLY DISCUSSING US.
WONDERING WHAT WE ARE UP TO.

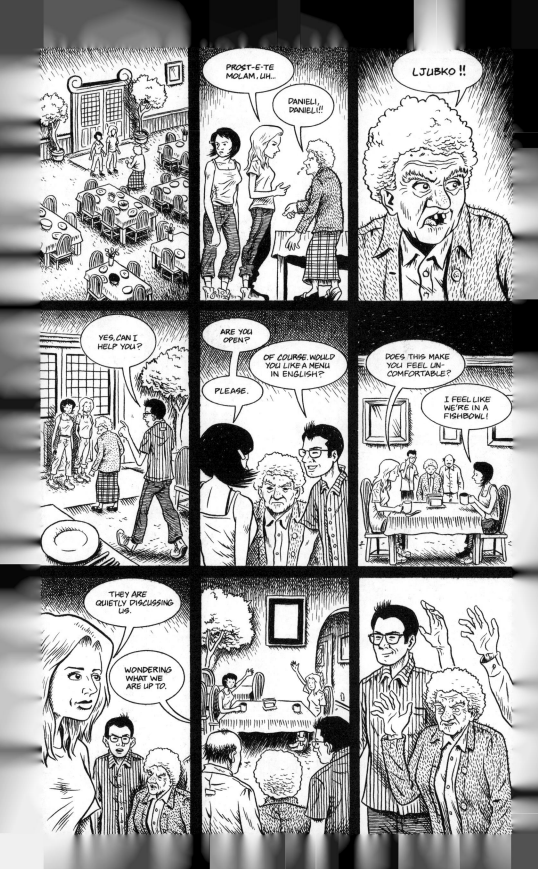

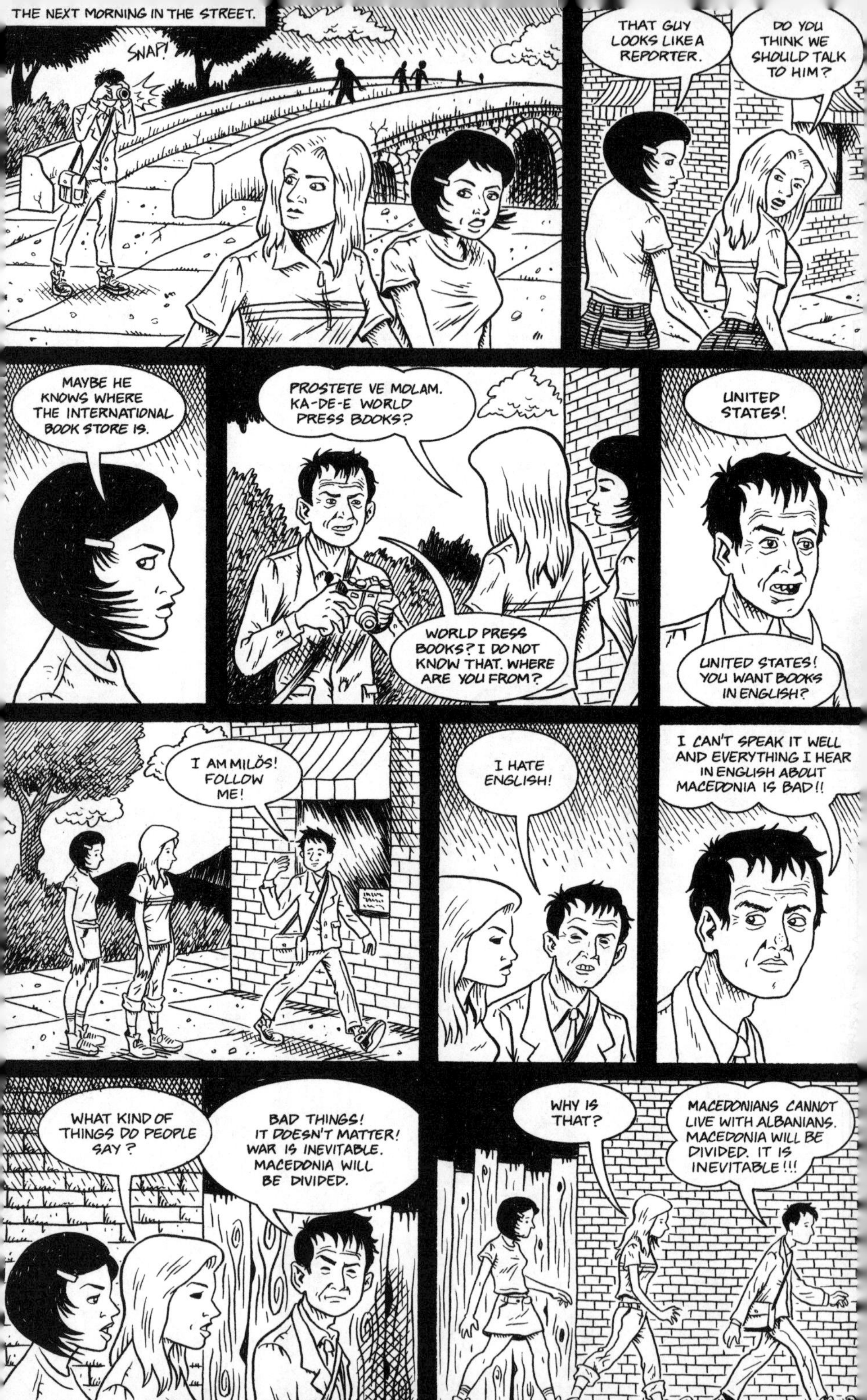
THE NEXT MORNING IN THE STREET.
SNAP!
THAT GUY LOOKS LIKE A REPORTER.
DO YOU THINK WE SHOULD TALK TO HIM?
MAYBE HE KNOWS WHERE THE INTERNATIONAL BOOK STORE IS.
PROSTETE VE MOLAM. KA-DE-E WORLD PRESS BOOKS?
WORLD PRESS BOOKS? I DO NOT KNOW THAT. WHERE ARE YOU FROM?
UNITED STATES!
UNITED STATES! YOU WANT BOOKS IN ENGLISH?
I AM MILÔS! FOLLOW ME!
I HATE ENGLISH!
I CAN'T SPEAK IT WELL AND EVERYTHING I HEAR IN ENGLISH ABOUT MACEDONIA IS BAD!!
WHAT KIND OF THINGS DO PEOPLE SAY?
BAD THINGS! IT DOESN'T MATTER! WAR IS INEVITABLE. MACEDONIA WILL BE DIVIDED.
WHY IS THAT?
MACEDONIANS CANNOT LIVE WITH ALBANIANS. MACEDONIA WILL BE DIVIDED. IT IS INEVITABLE!!!

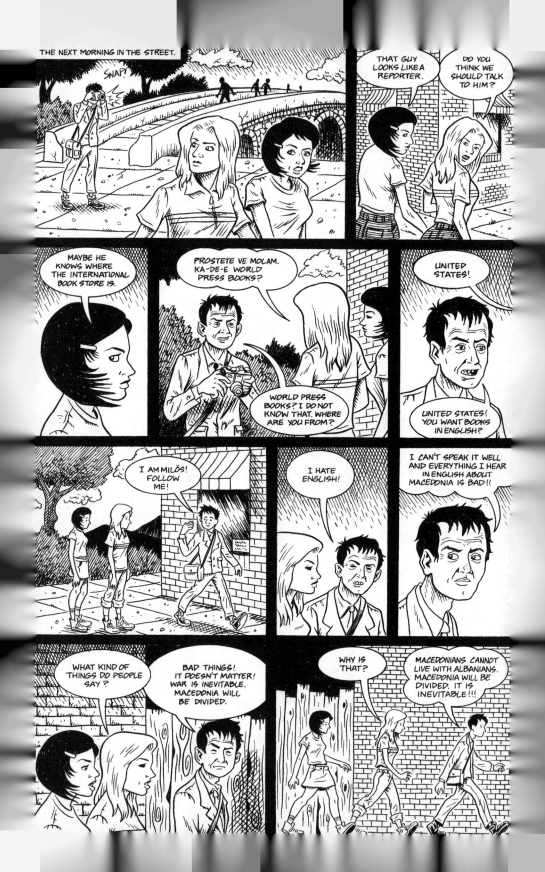

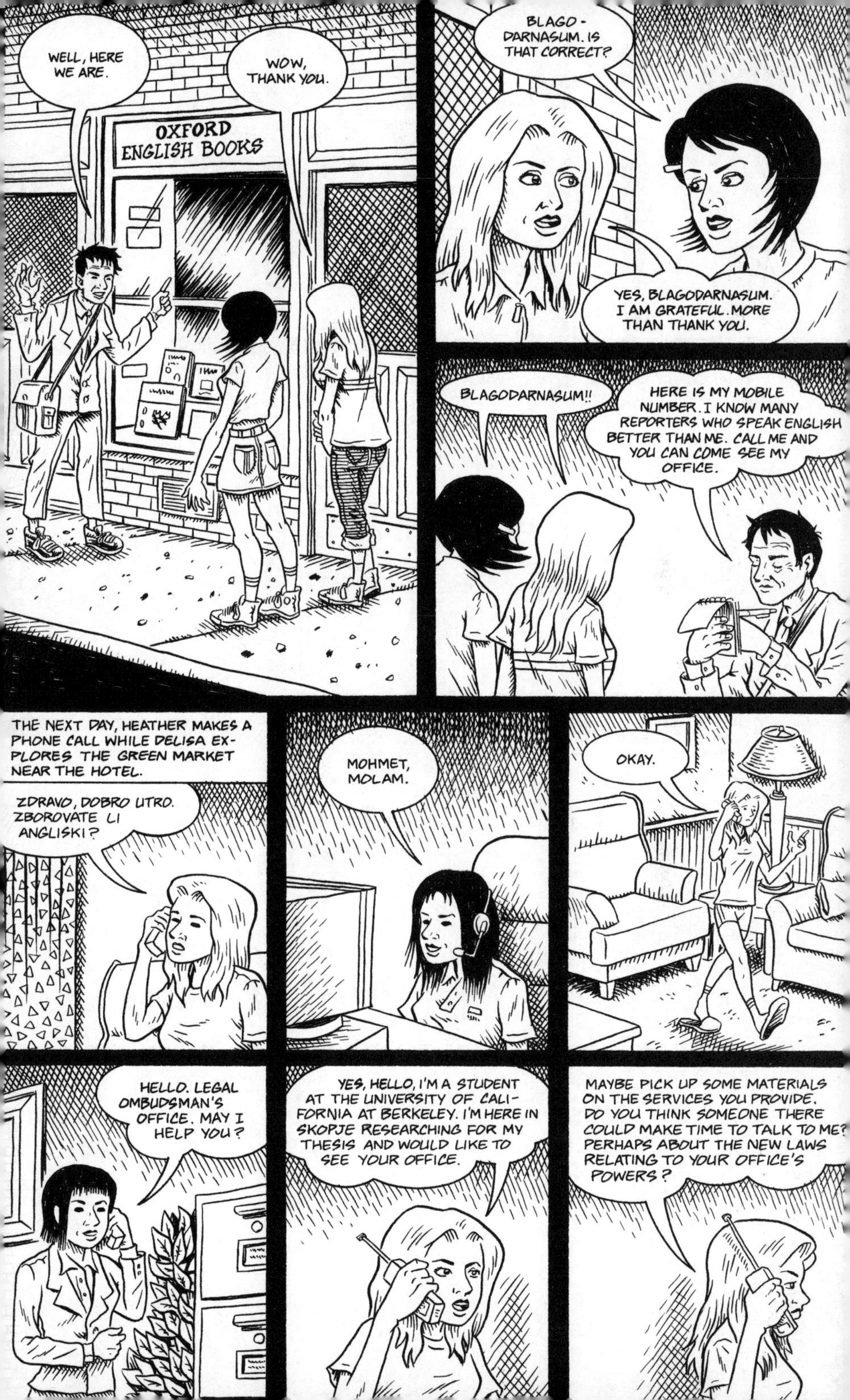
WELL, HERE WE ARE.
WOW, THANK YOU.
OXFORD ENGLISH BOOKS
BLAGO-DARNASUM. IS THAT CORRECT?
YES, BLAGODARNASUM. I AM GRATEFUL. MORE THAN THANK YOU.
BLAGODARNASUM!!
HERE IS MY MOBILE NUMBER. I KNOW MANY REPORTERS WHO SPEAK ENGLISH BETTER THAN ME. CALL ME AND YOU CAN COME SEE MY OFFICE.
THE NEXT DAY, HEATHER MAKES A PHONE CALL WHILE DELISA EXPLORES THE GREEN MARKET NEAR THE HOTEL.
ZDRAVO, DOBRO UTRO. ZBOROVATE LI ANGLISKI?
MOHMET, MOLAM.
OKAY.
HELLO. LEGAL OMBUDSMAN'S OFFICE. MAY I HELP YOU?
YES, HELLO, I'M A STUDENT AT THE UNIVERSITY OF CALIFORNIA AT BERKELEY. I'M HERE IN SKOPJE RESEARCHING FOR MY THESIS AND WOULD LIKE TO SEE YOUR OFFICE.
MAYBE PICK UP SOME MATERIALS ON THE SERVICES YOU PROVIDE. DO YOU THINK SOMEONE THERE COULD MAKE TIME TO TALK TO ME? PERHAPS ABOUT THE NEW LAWS RELATING TO YOUR OFFICE'S POWERS?

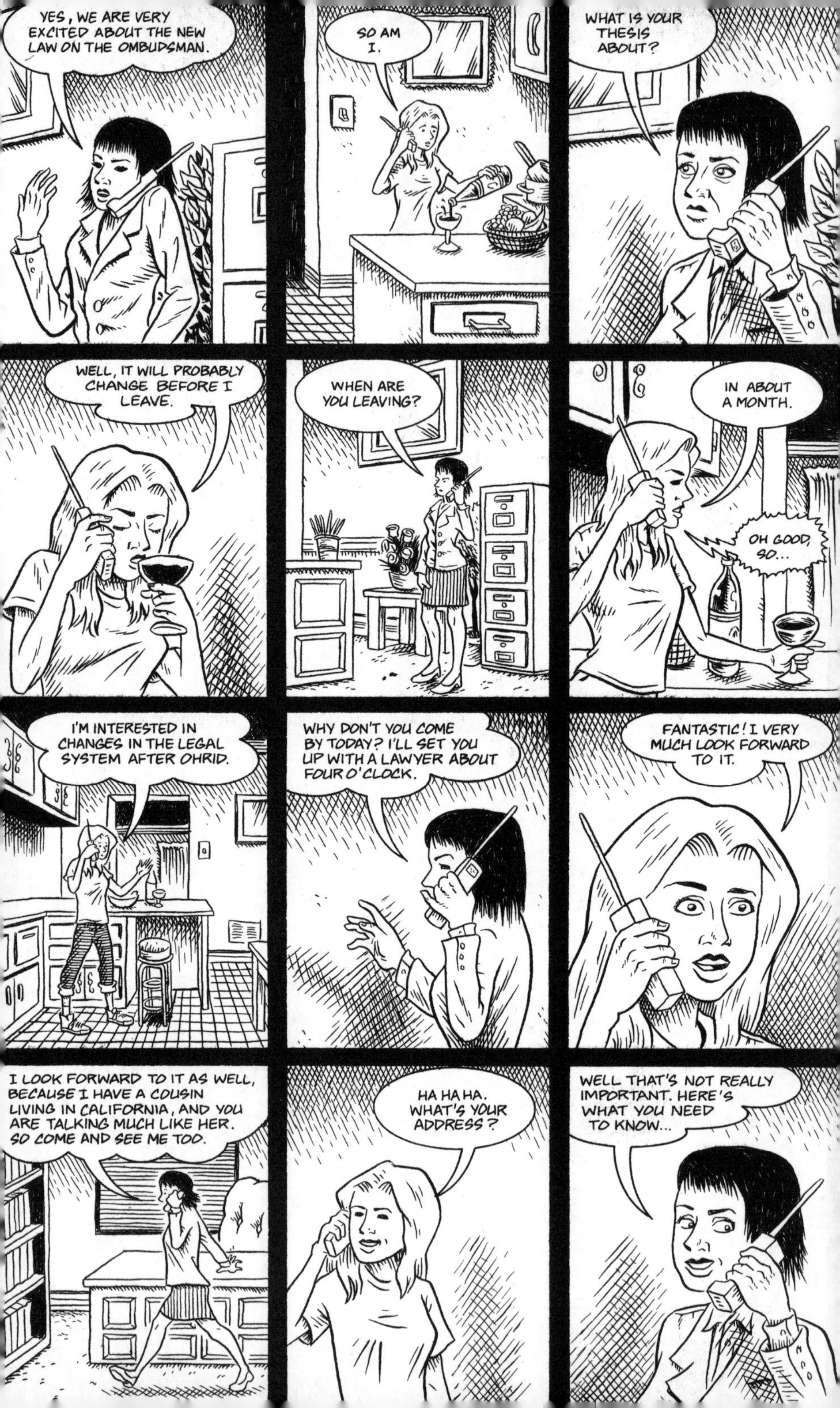

YES, WE ARE VERY EXCITED ABOUT THE NEW LAW ON THE OMBUDSMAN.
SO AM I.
WHAT IS YOUR THESIS ABOUT?
WELL, IT WILL PROBABLY CHANGE BEFORE I LEAVE.
WHEN ARE YOU LEAVING?
IN ABOUT A MONTH.
OH GOOD, SO...
I'M INTERESTED IN CHANGES IN THE LEGAL SYSTEM AFTER OHRID.
WHY DON'T YOU COME BY TODAY? I'LL SET YOU UP WITH A LAWYER ABOUT FOUR O'CLOCK.
FANTASTIC! I VERY MUCH LOOK FORWARD TO IT.
I LOOK FORWARD TO IT AS WELL, BECAUSE I HAVE A COUSIN LIVING IN CALIFORNIA, AND YOU ARE TALKING MUCH LIKE HER. SO COME AND SEE ME TOO.
HA HA HA. WHAT'S YOUR ADDRESS?
WELL THAT'S NOT REALLY IMPORTANT. HERE'S WHAT YOU NEED TO KNOW...

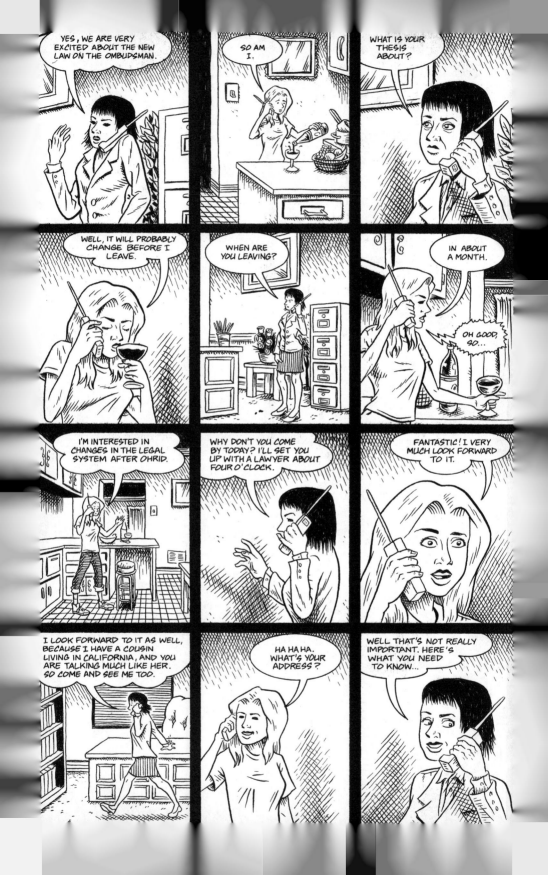

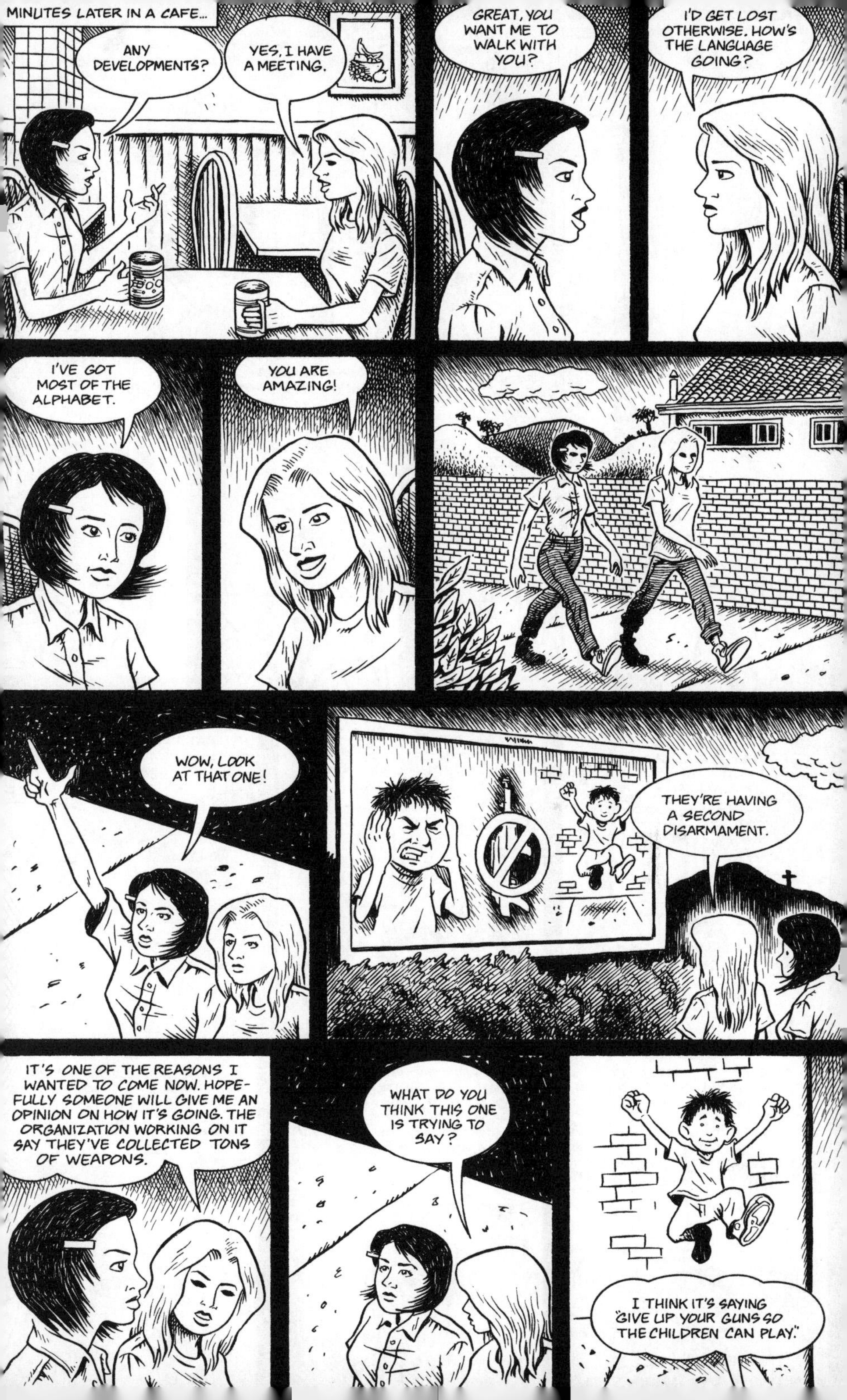
MINUTES LATER IN A CAFE...
ANY DEVELOPMENTS?
YES, I HAVE A MEETING.
GREAT, YOU WANT ME TO WALK WITH YOU?
I'D GET LOST OTHERWISE. HOW'S THE LANGUAGE GOING?
I'VE GOT MOST OF THE ALPHABET.
YOU ARE AMAZING!
WOW, LOOK AT THAT ONE!
THEY'RE HAVING A SECOND DISARMAMENT.
IT'S ONE OF THE REASONS I WANTED TO COME NOW. HOPE-FULLY SOMEONE WILL GIVE ME AN OPINION ON HOW IT'S GOING. THE ORGANIZATION WORKING ON IT SAY THEY'VE COLLECTED TONS OF WEAPONS.
WHAT DO YOU THINK THIS ONE IS TRYING TO SAY?
I THINK IT'S SAYING "GIVE UP YOUR GUNS SO THE CHILDREN CAN PLAY."

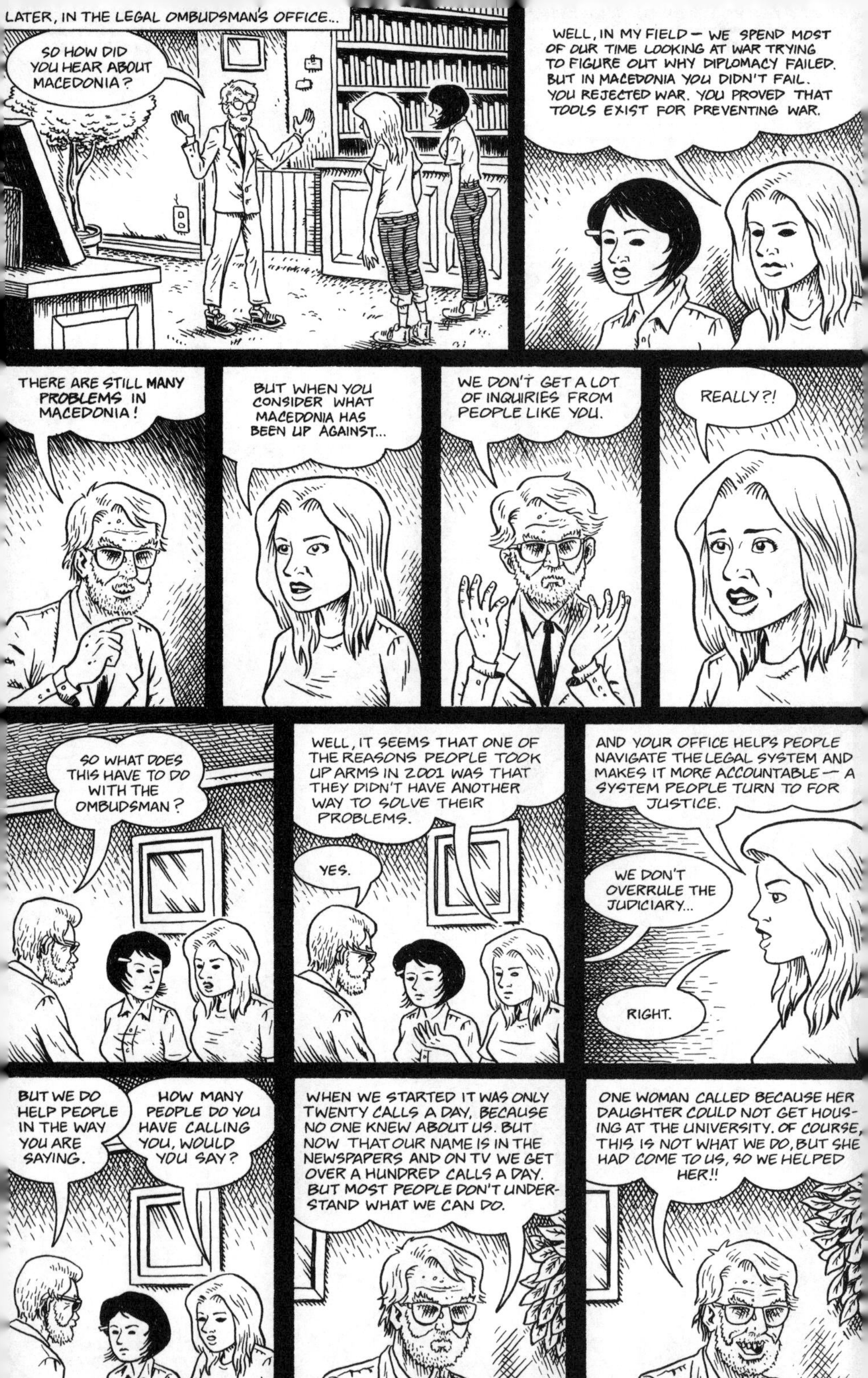
LATER, IN THE LEGAL OMBUDSMAN'S OFFICE...
SO HOW DID YOU HEAR ABOUT MACEDONIA?
WELL, IN MY FIELD — WE SPEND MOST OF OUR TIME LOOKING AT WAR TRYING TO FIGURE OUT WHY DIPLOMACY FAILED. BUT IN MACEDONIA YOU DIDN'T FAIL. YOU REJECTED WAR. YOU PROVED THAT TOOLS EXIST FOR PREVENTING WAR.
THERE ARE STILL MANY PROBLEMS IN MACEDONIA!
BUT WHEN YOU CONSIDER WHAT MACEDONIA HAS BEEN UP AGAINST...
WE DON'T GET A LOT OF INQUIRIES FROM PEOPLE LIKE YOU.
REALLY?!
SO WHAT DOES THIS HAVE TO DO WITH THE OMBUDSMAN?
WELL, IT SEEMS THAT ONE OF THE REASONS PEOPLE TOOK UP ARMS IN 2001 WAS THAT THEY DIDN'T HAVE ANOTHER WAY TO SOLVE THEIR PROBLEMS.
YES.
AND YOUR OFFICE HELPS PEOPLE NAVIGATE THE LEGAL SYSTEM AND MAKES IT MORE ACCOUNTABLE — A SYSTEM PEOPLE TURN TO FOR JUSTICE.
WE DON'T OVERRULE THE JUDICIARY...
RIGHT.
BUT WE DO HELP PEOPLE IN THE WAY YOU ARE SAYING.
HOW MANY PEOPLE DO YOU HAVE CALLING YOU, WOULD YOU SAY?
WHEN WE STARTED IT WAS ONLY TWENTY CALLS A DAY, BECAUSE NO ONE KNEW ABOUT US. BUT NOW THAT OUR NAME IS IN THE NEWSPAPERS AND ON TV WE GET OVER A HUNDRED CALLS A DAY. BUT MOST PEOPLE DON'T UNDERSTAND WHAT WE CAN DO.
ONE WOMAN CALLED BECAUSE HER DAUGHTER COULD NOT GET HOUSING AT THE UNIVERSITY. OF COURSE, THIS IS NOT WHAT WE DO, BUT SHE HAD COME TO US, SO WE HELPED HER!!

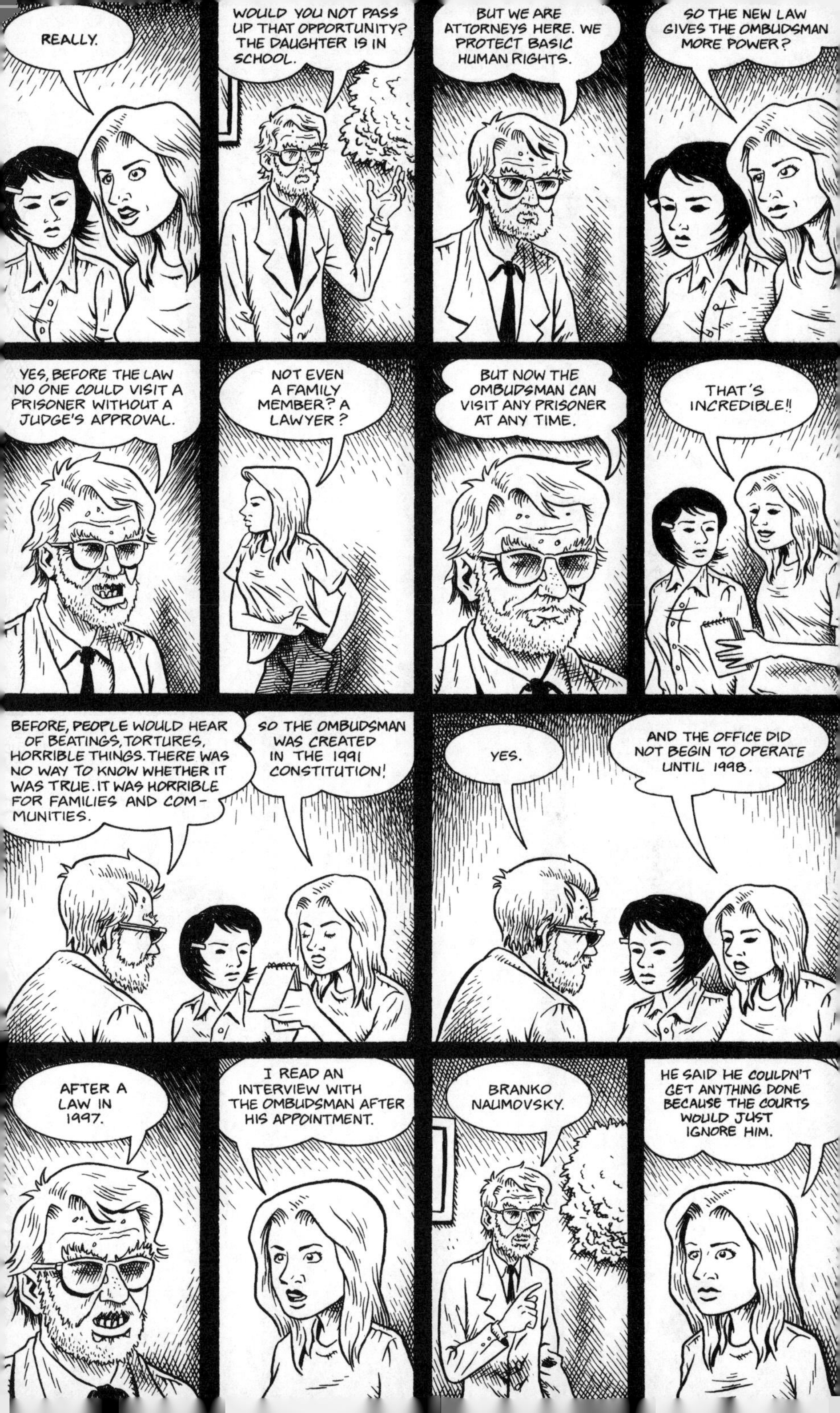
REALLY.
WOULD YOU NOT PASS UP THAT OPPORTUNITY? THE DAUGHTER IS IN SCHOOL.
BUT WE ARE ATTORNEYS HERE. WE PROTECT BASIC HUMAN RIGHTS.
SO THE NEW LAW GIVES THE OMBUDSMAN MORE POWER?
YES, BEFORE THE LAW NO ONE COULD VISIT A PRISONER WITHOUT A JUDGE'S APPROVAL.
NOT EVEN A FAMILY MEMBER? A LAWYER?
BUT NOW THE OMBUDSMAN CAN VISIT ANY PRISONER AT ANY TIME.
THAT'S INCREDIBLE!!
BEFORE, PEOPLE WOULD HEAR OF BEATINGS, TORTURES, HORRIBLE THINGS. THERE WAS NO WAY TO KNOW WHETHER IT WAS TRUE. IT WAS HORRIBLE FOR FAMILIES AND COMMUNITIES.
SO THE OMBUDSMAN WAS CREATED IN THE 1991 CONSTITUTION!
YES.
AND THE OFFICE DID NOT BEGIN TO OPERATE UNTIL 1998.
AFTER A LAW IN 1997.
I READ AN INTERVIEW WITH THE OMBUDSMAN AFTER HIS APPOINTMENT.
BRANKO NAUMOVSKY.
HE SAID HE COULDN'T GET ANYTHING DONE BECAUSE THE COURTS WOULD JUST IGNORE HIM.

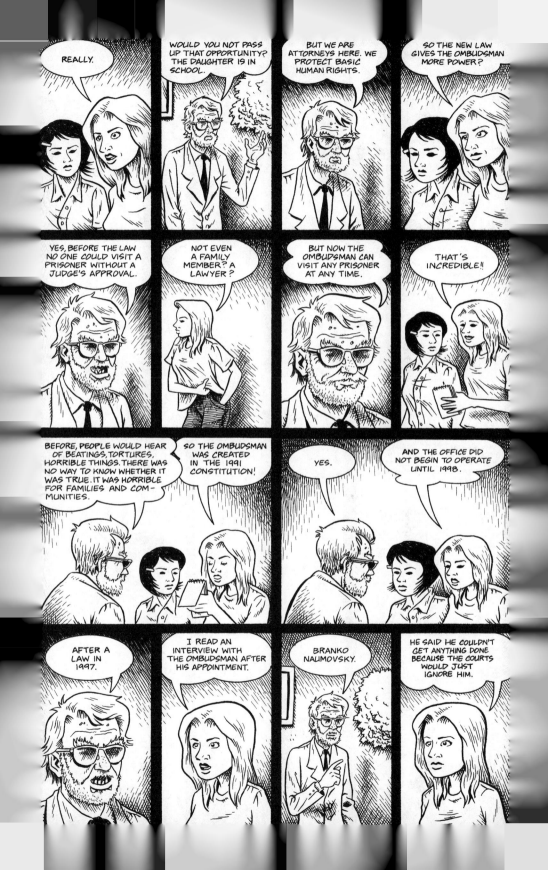

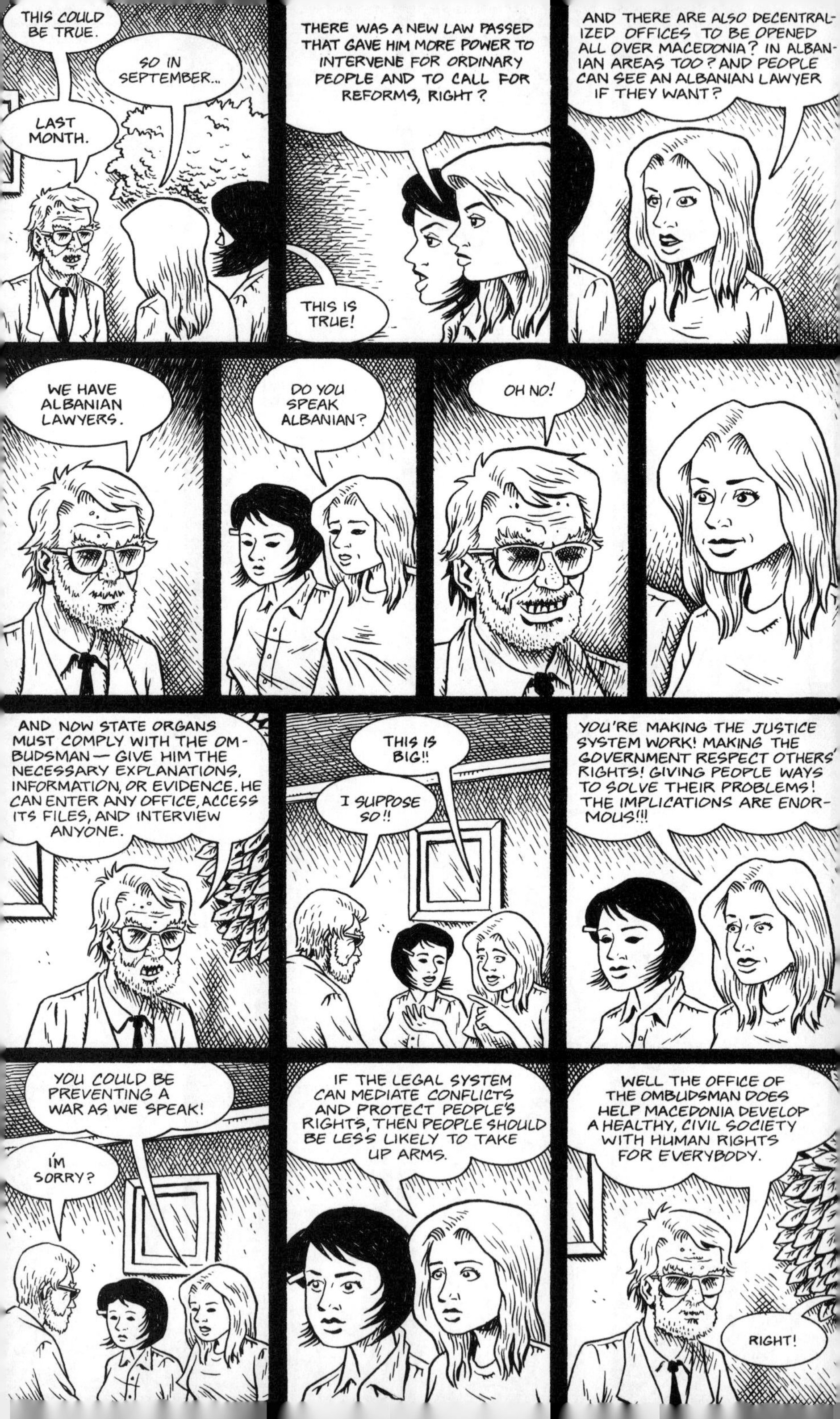
THIS COULD BE TRUE.
SO IN SEPTEMBER...
LAST MONTH.
THERE WAS A NEW LAW PASSED THAT GAVE HIM MORE POWER TO INTERVENE FOR ORDINARY PEOPLE AND TO CALL FOR REFORMS, RIGHT?
THIS IS TRUE!
AND THERE ARE ALSO DECENTRALIZED OFFICES TO BE OPENED ALL OVER MACEDONIA? IN ALBANIAN AREAS TOO? AND PEOPLE CAN SEE AN ALBANIAN LAWYER IF THEY WANT?
WE HAVE ALBANIAN LAWYERS.
DO YOU SPEAK ALBANIAN?
OH NO!
AND NOW STATE ORGANS MUST COMPLY WITH THE OMBUDSMAN — GIVE HIM THE NECESSARY EXPLANATIONS, INFORMATION, OR EVIDENCE. HE CAN ENTER ANY OFFICE, ACCESS ITS FILES, AND INTERVIEW ANYONE.
THIS IS BIG!!
I SUPPOSE SO!!
YOU'RE MAKING THE JUSTICE SYSTEM WORK! MAKING THE GOVERNMENT RESPECT OTHERS' RIGHTS! GIVING PEOPLE WAYS TO SOLVE THEIR PROBLEMS! THE IMPLICATIONS ARE ENORMOUS!!!
YOU COULD BE PREVENTING A WAR AS WE SPEAK!
I'M SORRY?
IF THE LEGAL SYSTEM CAN MEDIATE CONFLICTS AND PROTECT PEOPLE'S RIGHTS, THEN PEOPLE SHOULD BE LESS LIKELY TO TAKE UP ARMS.
WELL THE OFFICE OF THE OMBUDSMAN DOES HELP MACEDONIA DEVELOP A HEALTHY, CIVIL SOCIETY WITH HUMAN RIGHTS FOR EVERYBODY.
RIGHT!

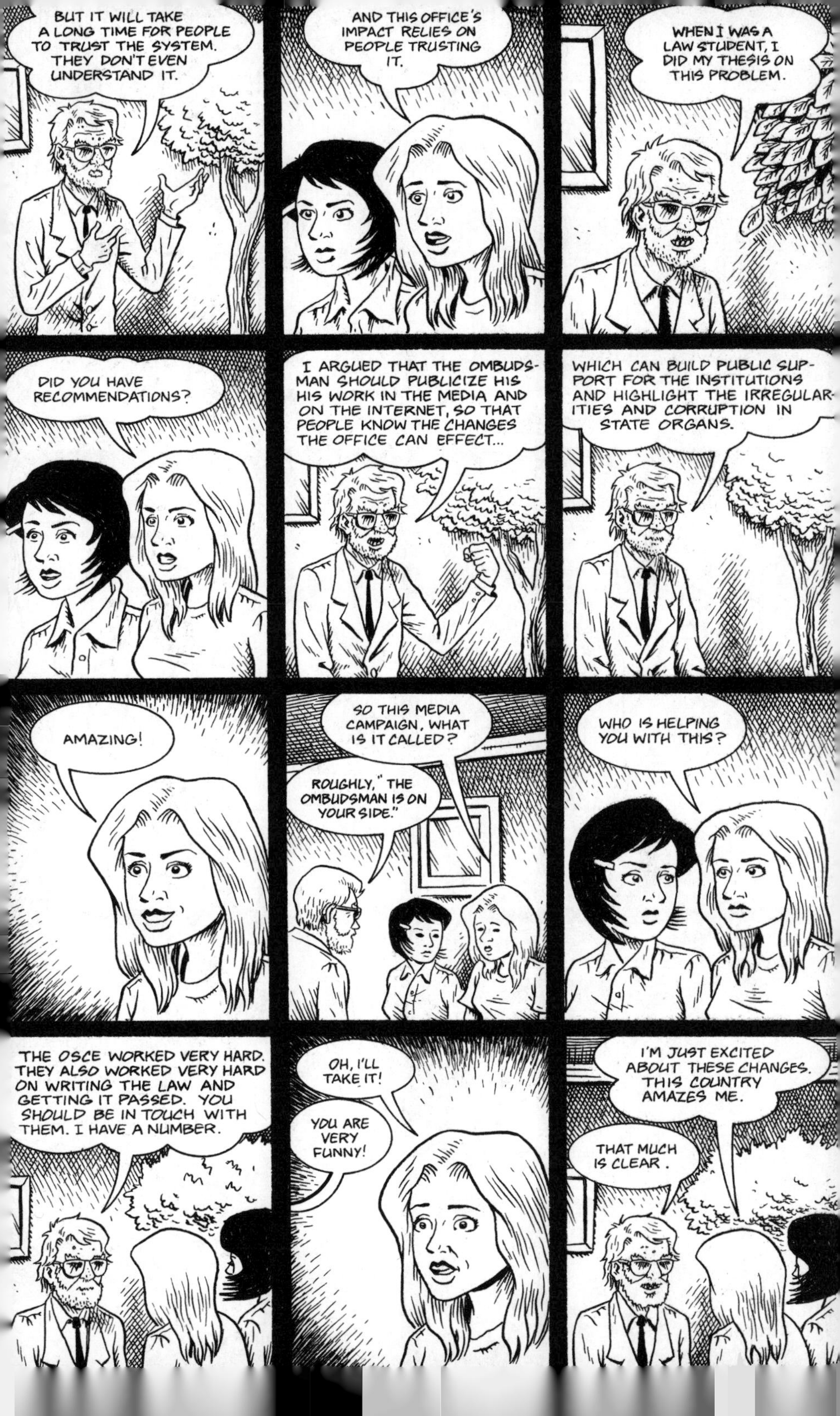
BUT IT WILL TAKE A LONG TIME FOR PEOPLE TO TRUST THE SYSTEM. THEY DON'T EVEN UNDERSTAND IT.
AND THIS OFFICE'S IMPACT RELIES ON PEOPLE TRUSTING IT.
WHEN I WAS A LAW STUDENT, I DID MY THESIS ON THIS PROBLEM.
DID YOU HAVE RECOMMENDATIONS?
I ARGUED THAT THE OMBUDSMAN SHOULD PUBLICIZE HIS HIS WORK IN THE MEDIA AND ON THE INTERNET, SO THAT PEOPLE KNOW THE CHANGES THE OFFICE CAN EFFECT...
WHICH CAN BUILD PUBLIC SUPPORT FOR THE INSTITUTIONS AND HIGHLIGHT THE IRREGULARITIES AND CORRUPTION IN STATE ORGANS.
AMAZING!
SO THIS MEDIA CAMPAIGN, WHAT IS IT CALLED?
ROUGHLY, "THE OMBUDSMAN IS ON YOUR SIDE."
WHO IS HELPING YOU WITH THIS?
THE OSCE WORKED VERY HARD. THEY ALSO WORKED VERY HARD ON WRITING THE LAW AND GETTING IT PASSED. YOU SHOULD BE IN TOUCH WITH THEM. I HAVE A NUMBER.
OH, I'LL TAKE IT!
YOU ARE VERY FUNNY!
I'M JUST EXCITED ABOUT THESE CHANGES. THIS COUNTRY AMAZES ME.
THAT MUCH IS CLEAR.

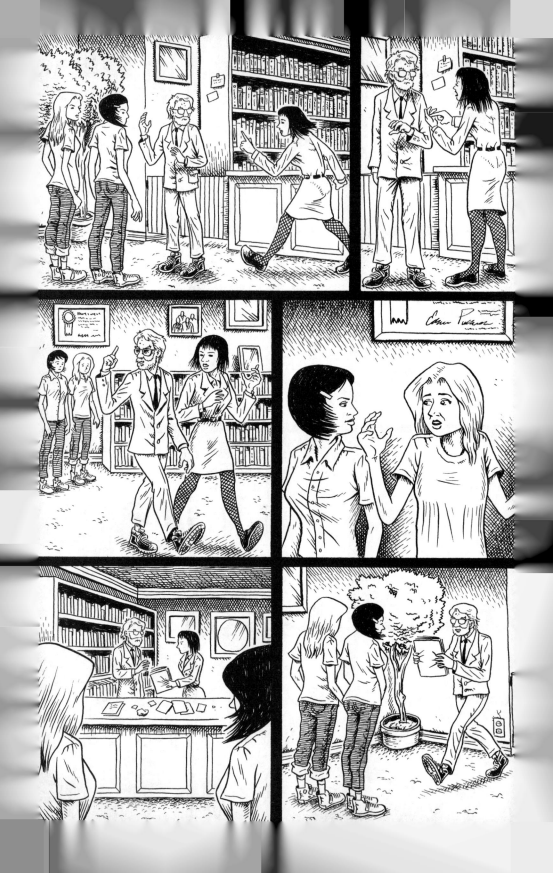

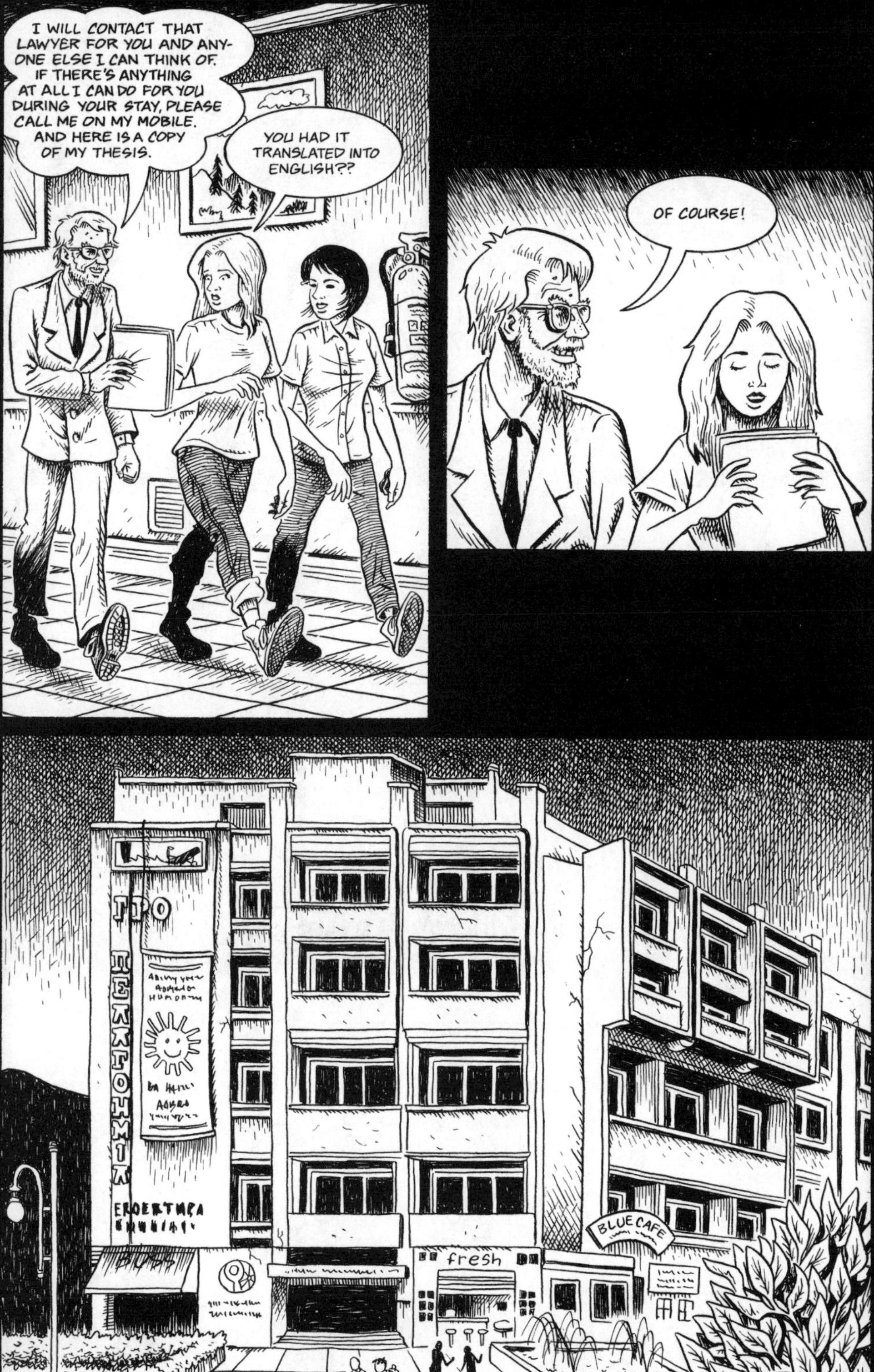
I WILL CONTACT THAT LAWYER FOR YOU AND ANYONE ELSE I CAN THINK OF. IF THERE'S ANYTHING AT ALL I CAN DO FOR YOU DURING YOUR STAY, PLEASE CALL ME ON MY MOBILE. AND HERE IS A COPY OF MY THESIS.
YOU HAD IT TRANSLATED INTO ENGLISH??
OF COURSE!
BLUE CAFE
fresh

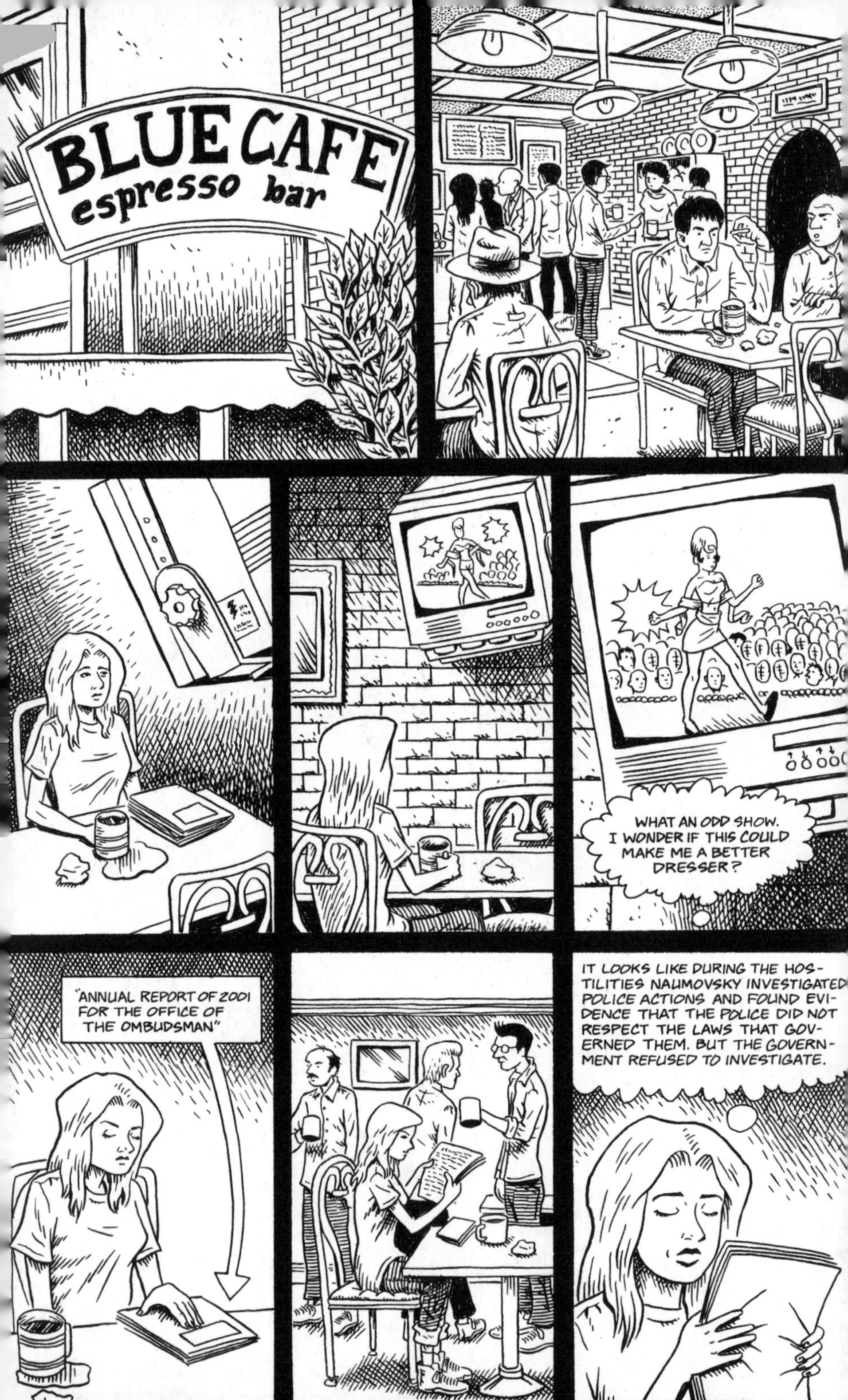
BLUE CAFE
espresso bar
WHAT AN ODD SHOW. I WONDER IF THIS COULD MAKE ME A BETTER DRESSER?
"ANNUAL REPORT OF 2001 FOR THE OFFICE OF THE OMBUDSMAN"
IT LOOKS LIKE DURING THE HOSTILITIES NAUMOVSKY INVESTIGATED POLICE ACTIONS AND FOUND EVIDENCE THAT THE POLICE DID NOT RESPECT THE LAWS THAT GOVERNED THEM. BUT THE GOVERNMENT REFUSED TO INVESTIGATE.

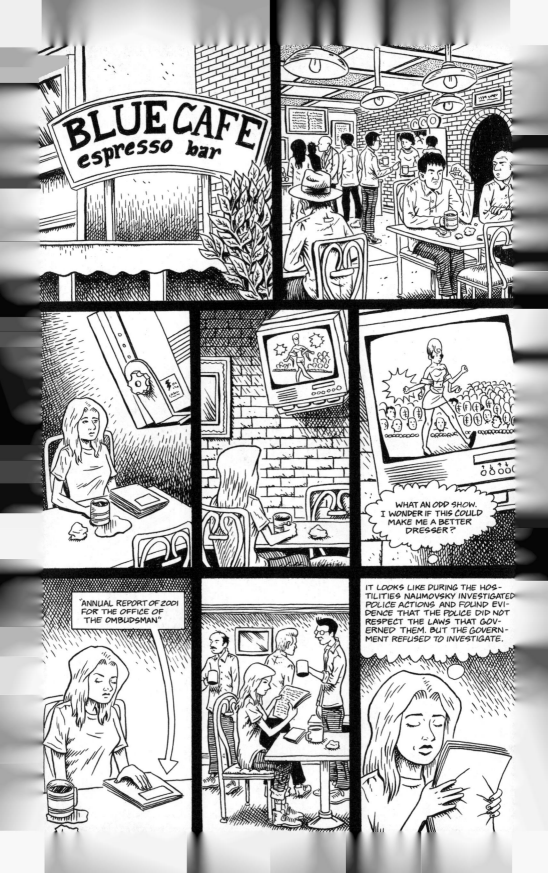

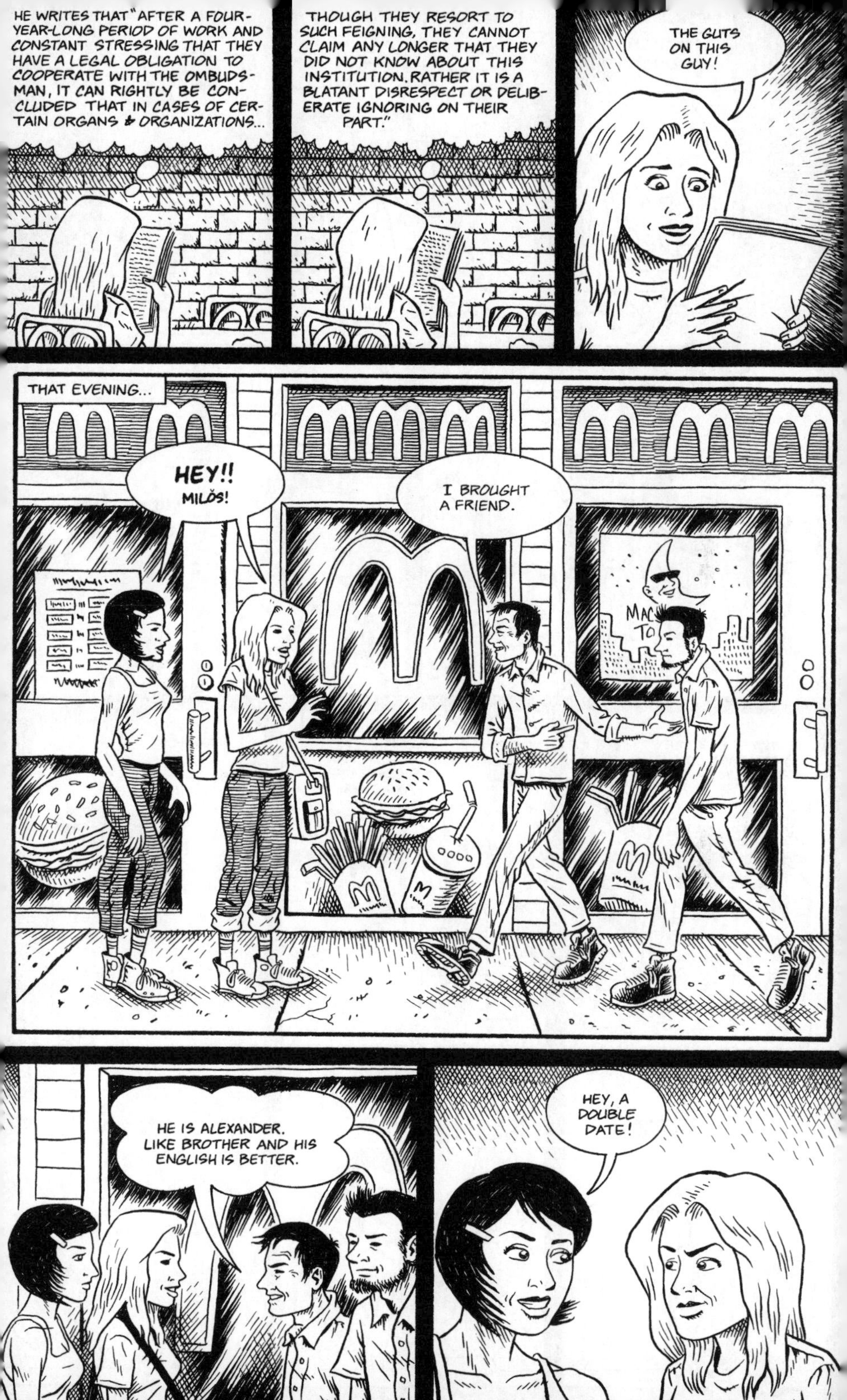
HE WRITES THAT "AFTER A FOUR-YEAR-LONG PERIOD OF WORK AND CONSTANT STRESSING THAT THEY HAVE A LEGAL OBLIGATION TO COOPERATE WITH THE OMBUDSMAN, IT CAN RIGHTLY BE CONCLUDED THAT IN CASES OF CERTAIN ORGANS & ORGANIZATIONS...
THOUGH THEY RESORT TO SUCH FEIGNING, THEY CANNOT CLAIM ANY LONGER THAT THEY DID NOT KNOW ABOUT THIS INSTITUTION. RATHER IT IS A BLATANT DISRESPECT OR DELIBERATE IGNORING ON THEIR PART."
THE GUTS ON THIS GUY!
THAT EVENING...
HEY!! MILÖS!
I BROUGHT A FRIEND.
HE IS ALEXANDER. LIKE BROTHER AND HIS ENGLISH IS BETTER.
HEY, A DOUBLE DATE!

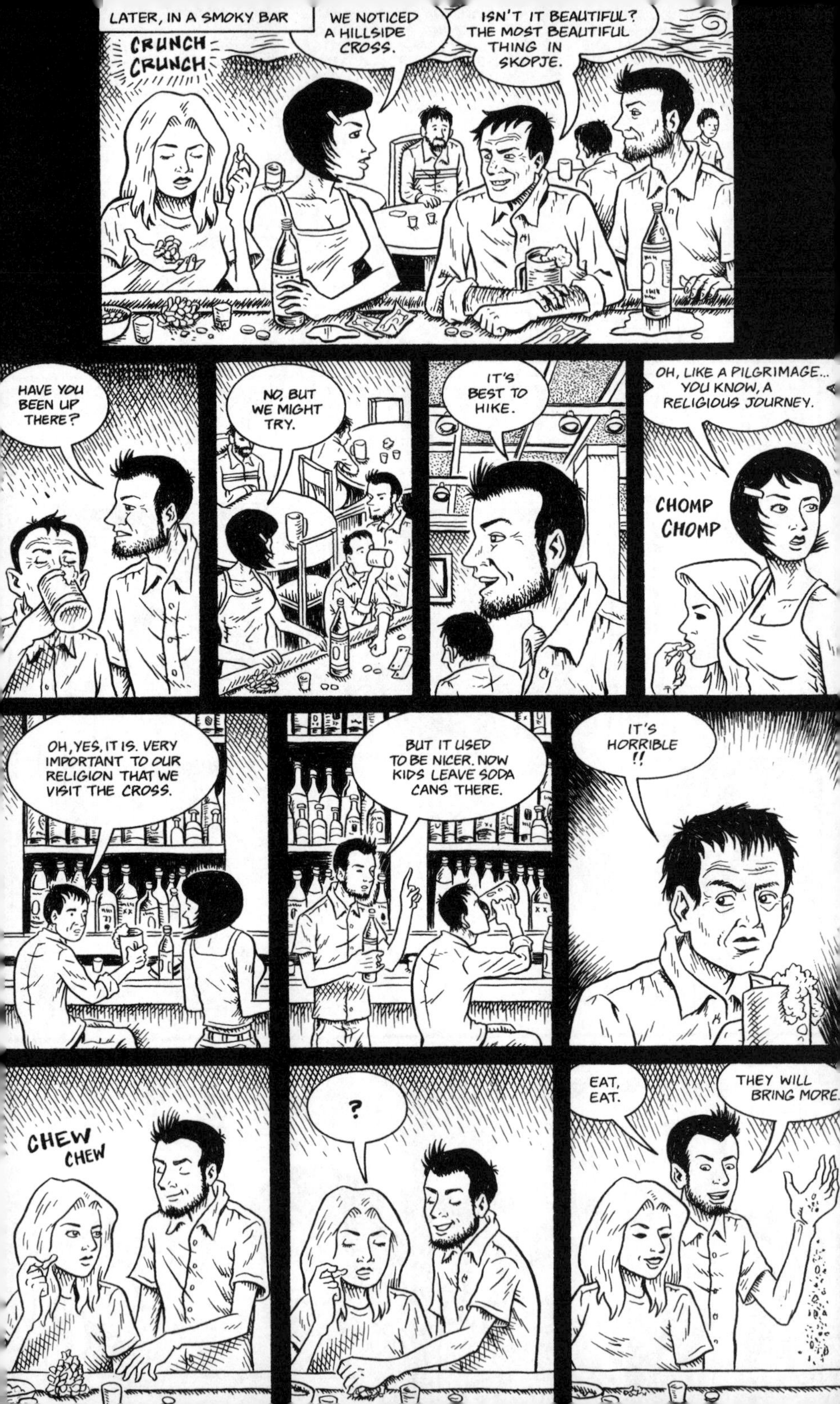

LATER, IN A SMOKY BAR
CRUNCH CRUNCH
WE NOTICED A HILLSIDE CROSS.
ISN'T IT BEAUTIFUL? THE MOST BEAUTIFUL THING IN SKOPJE.
HAVE YOU BEEN UP THERE?
NO, BUT WE MIGHT TRY.
IT'S BEST TO HIKE.
OH, LIKE A PILGRIMAGE... YOU KNOW, A RELIGIOUS JOURNEY.
CHOMP CHOMP
OH, YES, IT IS. VERY IMPORTANT TO OUR RELIGION THAT WE VISIT THE CROSS.
BUT IT USED TO BE NICER. NOW KIDS LEAVE SODA CANS THERE.
IT'S HORRIBLE !!
CHEW CHEW
?
EAT, EAT.
THEY WILL BRING MORE.

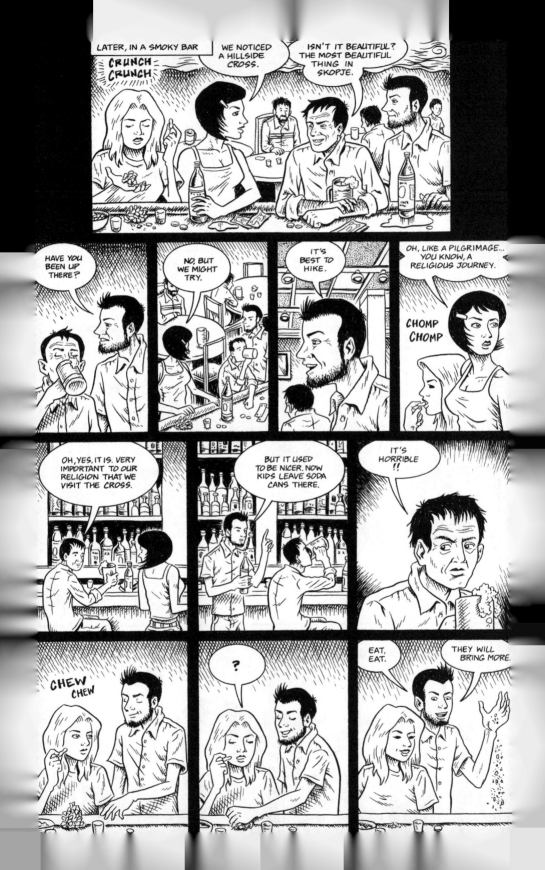

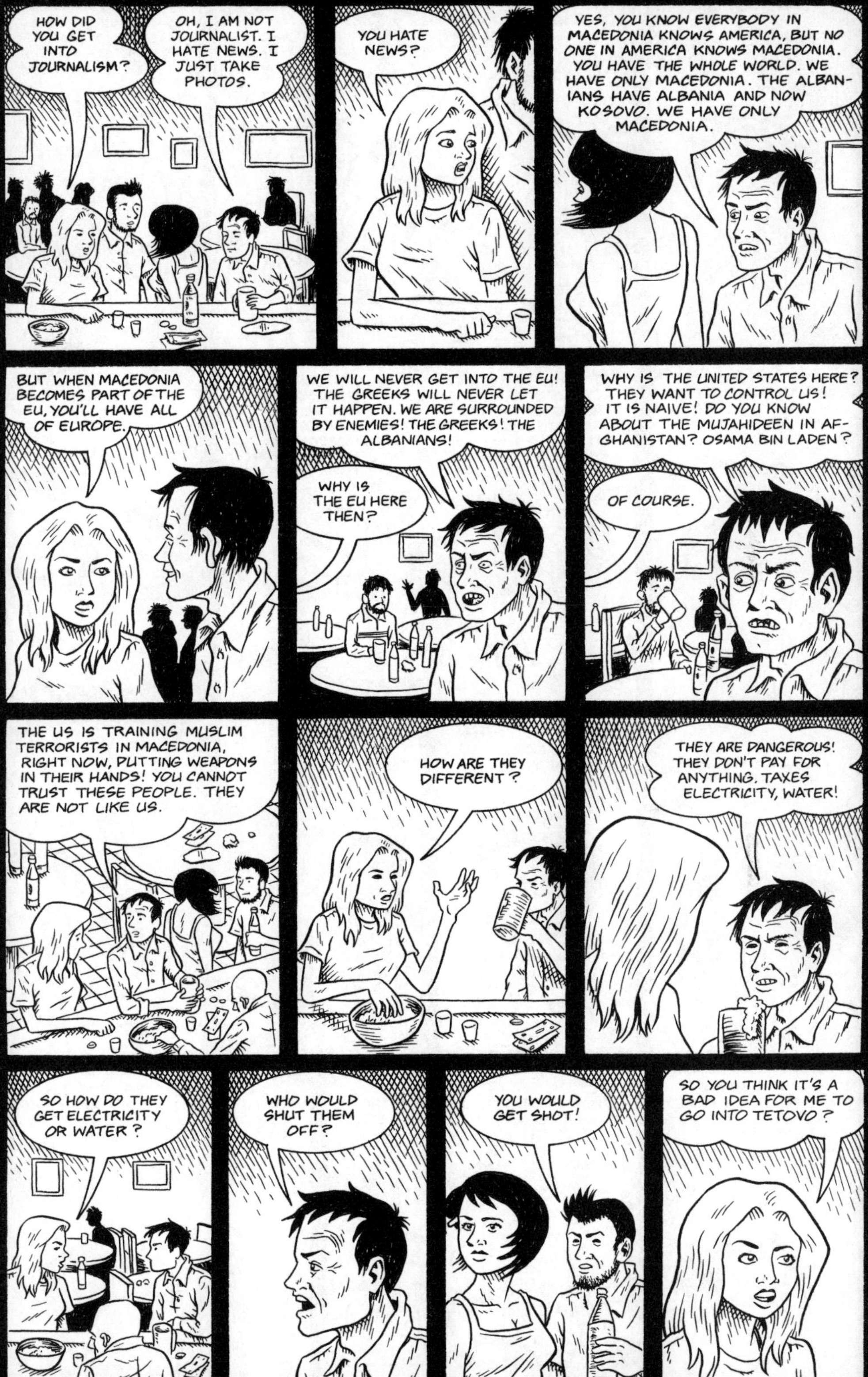
HOW DID YOU GET INTO JOURNALISM?
OH, I AM NOT JOURNALIST. I HATE NEWS. I JUST TAKE PHOTOS.
YOU HATE NEWS?
YES, YOU KNOW EVERYBODY IN MACEDONIA KNOWS AMERICA, BUT NO ONE IN AMERICA KNOWS MACEDONIA. YOU HAVE THE WHOLE WORLD. WE HAVE ONLY MACEDONIA. THE ALBANIANS HAVE ALBANIA AND NOW KOSOVO. WE HAVE ONLY MACEDONIA.
BUT WHEN MACEDONIA BECOMES PART OF THE EU, YOU'LL HAVE ALL OF EUROPE.
WE WILL NEVER GET INTO THE EU! THE GREEKS WILL NEVER LET IT HAPPEN. WE ARE SURROUNDED BY ENEMIES! THE GREEKS! THE ALBANIANS!
WHY IS THE EU HERE THEN?
WHY IS THE UNITED STATES HERE? THEY WANT TO CONTROL US! IT IS NAIVE! DO YOU KNOW ABOUT THE MUJAHIDEEN IN AFGHANISTAN? OSAMA BIN LADEN?
OF COURSE.
THE US IS TRAINING MUSLIM TERRORISTS IN MACEDONIA, RIGHT NOW, PUTTING WEAPONS IN THEIR HANDS! YOU CANNOT TRUST THESE PEOPLE. THEY ARE NOT LIKE US.
HOW ARE THEY DIFFERENT?
THEY ARE DANGEROUS! THEY DON'T PAY FOR ANYTHING. TAXES ELECTRICITY, WATER!
SO HOW DO THEY GET ELECTRICITY OR WATER?
WHO WOULD SHUT THEM OFF?
YOU WOULD GET SHOT!
SO YOU THINK IT'S A BAD IDEA FOR ME TO GO INTO TETOVO?

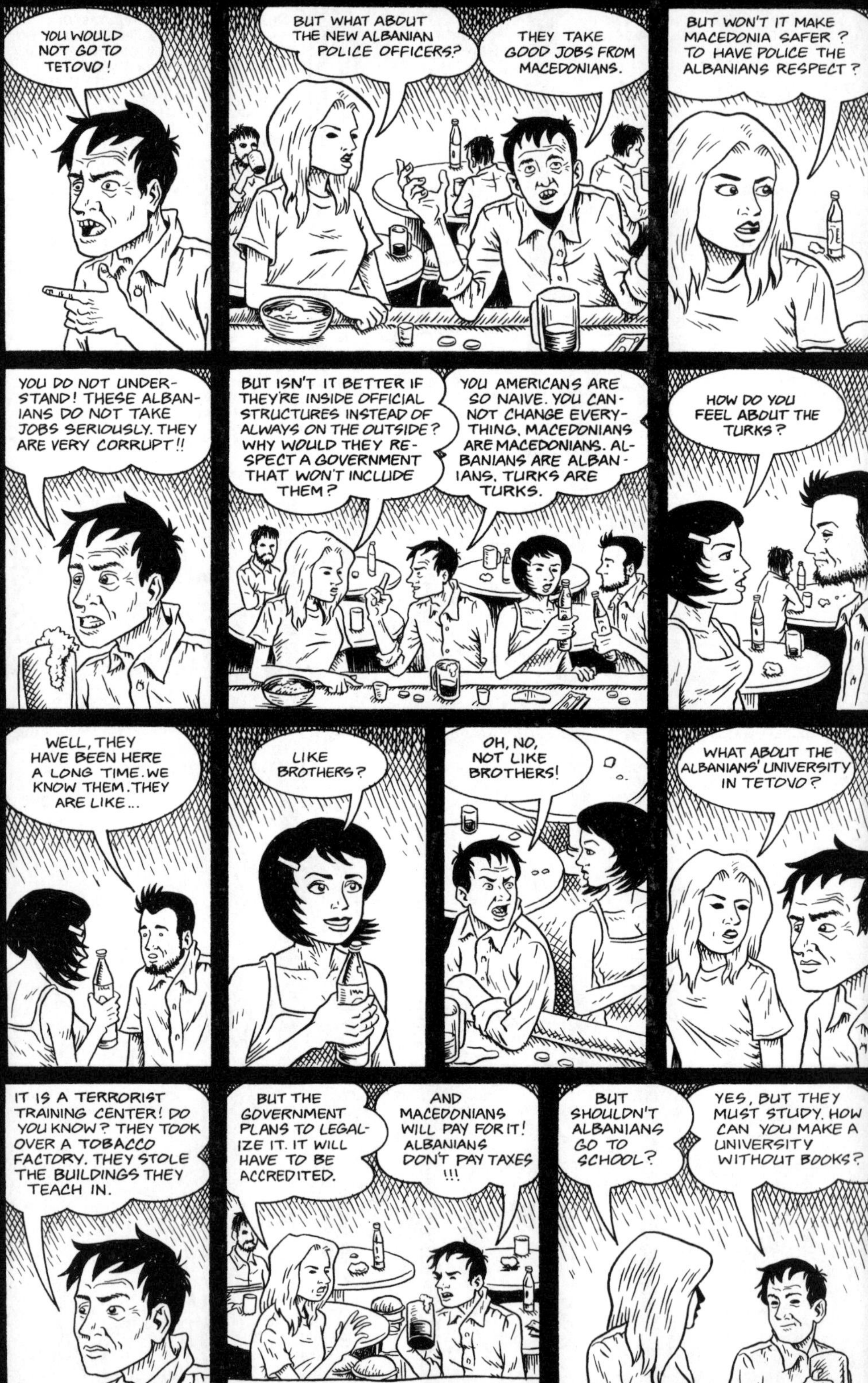
YOU WOULD NOT GO TO TETOVO!
BUT WHAT ABOUT THE NEW ALBANIAN POLICE OFFICERS?
THEY TAKE GOOD JOBS FROM MACEDONIANS.
BUT WON'T IT MAKE MACEDONIA SAFER? TO HAVE POLICE THE ALBANIANS RESPECT?
YOU DO NOT UNDERSTAND! THESE ALBANIANS DO NOT TAKE JOBS SERIOUSLY. THEY ARE VERY CORRUPT!!
BUT ISN'T IT BETTER IF THEY'RE INSIDE OFFICIAL STRUCTURES INSTEAD OF ALWAYS ON THE OUTSIDE? WHY WOULD THEY RESPECT A GOVERNMENT THAT WON'T INCLUDE THEM?
YOU AMERICANS ARE SO NAIVE. YOU CANNOT CHANGE EVERYTHING. MACEDONIANS ARE MACEDONIANS. ALBANIANS ARE ALBANIANS. TURKS ARE TURKS.
HOW DO YOU FEEL ABOUT THE TURKS?
WELL, THEY HAVE BEEN HERE A LONG TIME. WE KNOW THEM. THEY ARE LIKE...
LIKE BROTHERS?
OH, NO, NOT LIKE BROTHERS!
WHAT ABOUT THE ALBANIANS' UNIVERSITY IN TETOVO?
IT IS A TERRORIST TRAINING CENTER! DO YOU KNOW? THEY TOOK OVER A TOBACCO FACTORY. THEY STOLE THE BUILDINGS THEY TEACH IN.
BUT THE GOVERNMENT PLANS TO LEGALIZE IT. IT WILL HAVE TO BE ACCREDITED.
AND MACEDONIANS WILL PAY FOR IT! ALBANIANS DON'T PAY TAXES !!!
BUT SHOULDN'T ALBANIANS GO TO SCHOOL?
YES, BUT THEY MUST STUDY. HOW CAN YOU MAKE A UNIVERSITY WITHOUT BOOKS?

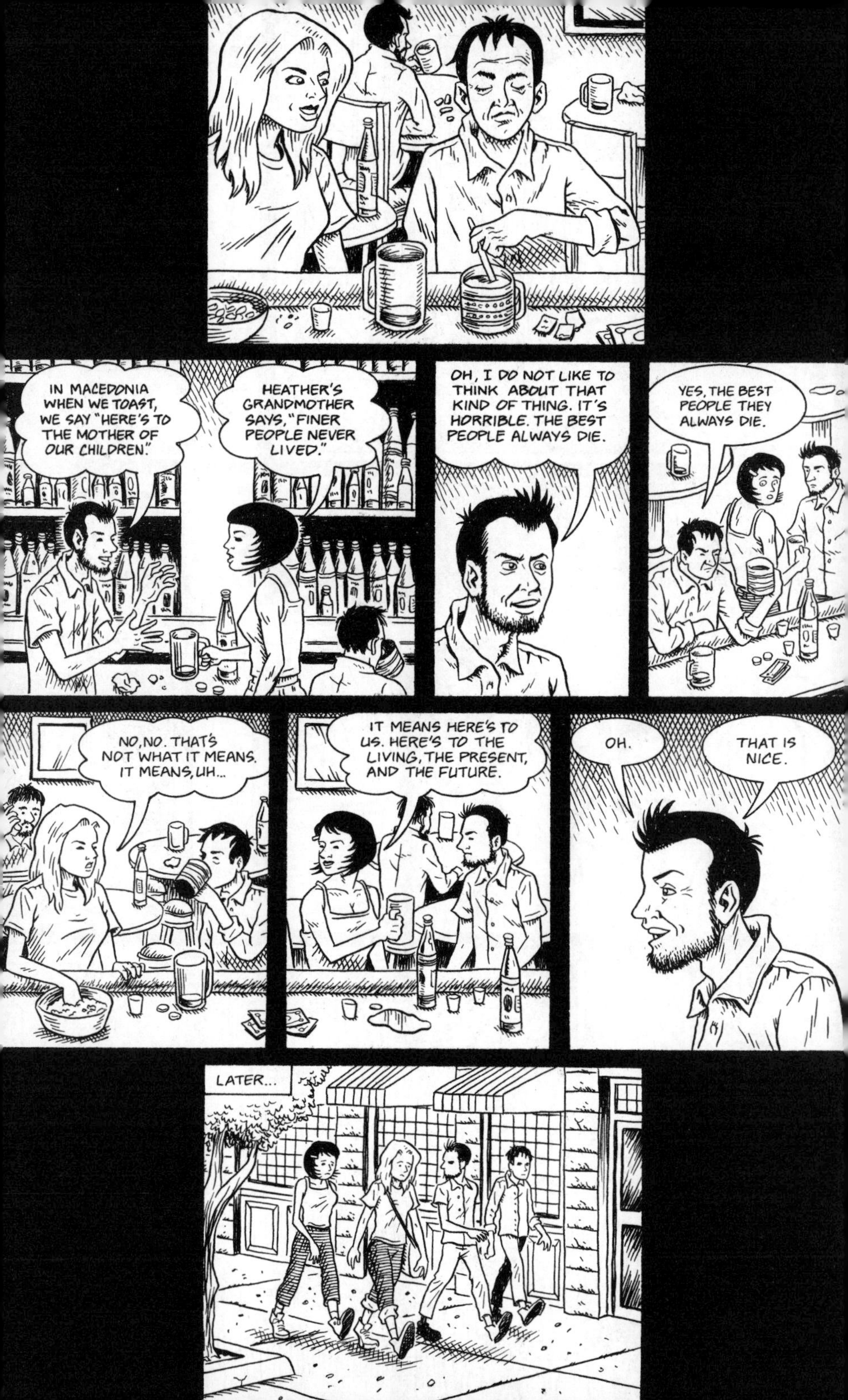
IN MACEDONIA WHEN WE TOAST, WE SAY "HERE'S TO THE MOTHER OF OUR CHILDREN."
HEATHER'S GRANDMOTHER SAYS, "FINER PEOPLE NEVER LIVED."
OH, I DO NOT LIKE TO THINK ABOUT THAT KIND OF THING. IT'S HORRIBLE. THE BEST PEOPLE ALWAYS DIE.
YES, THE BEST PEOPLE THEY ALWAYS DIE.
NO, NO. THAT'S NOT WHAT IT MEANS. IT MEANS, UH...
IT MEANS HERE'S TO US. HERE'S TO THE LIVING, THE PRESENT, AND THE FUTURE.
OH.
THAT IS NICE.
LATER...

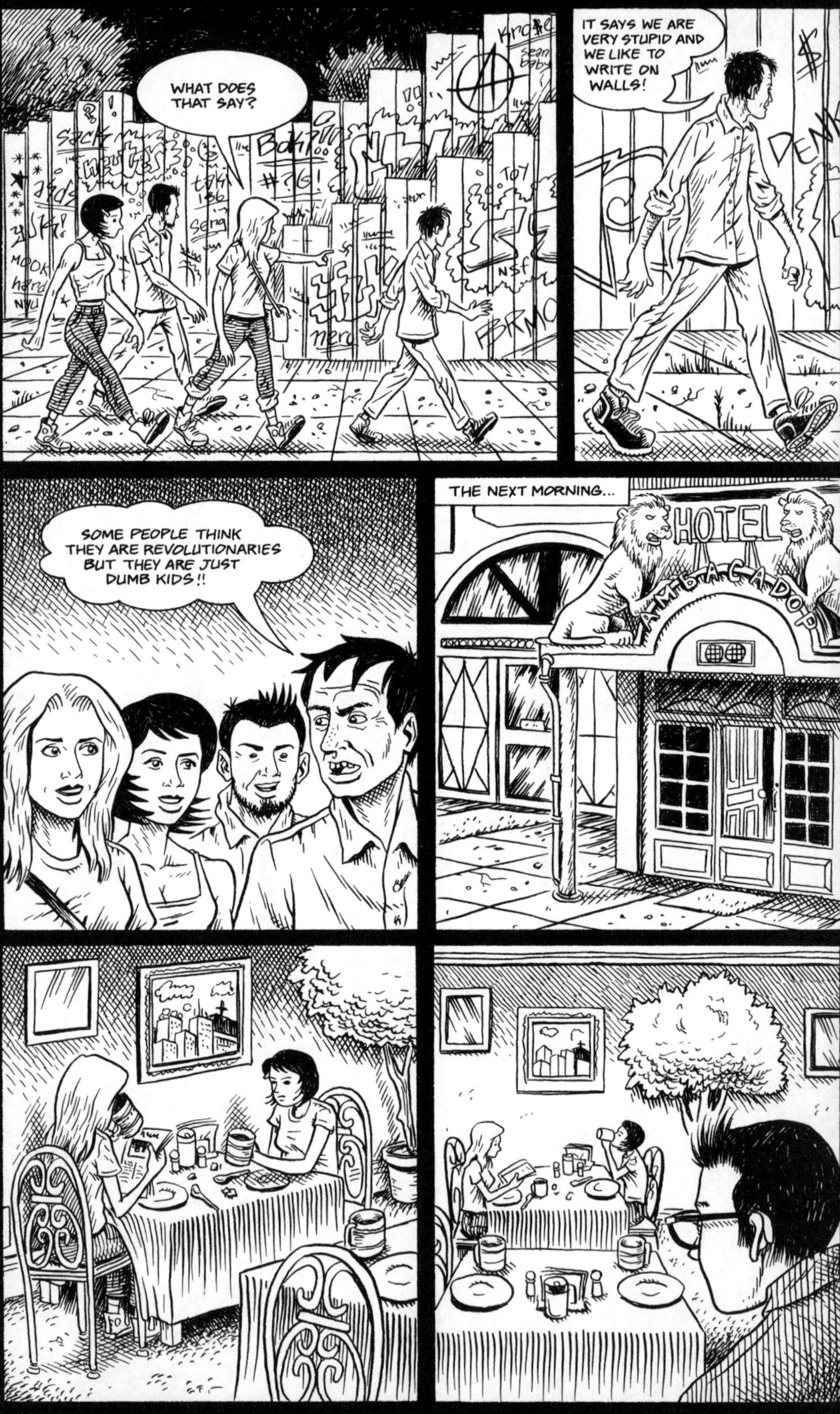
WHAT DOES THAT SAY?
IT SAYS WE ARE VERY STUPID AND WE LIKE TO WRITE ON WALLS!
SOME PEOPLE THINK THEY ARE REVOLUTIONARIES BUT THEY ARE JUST DUMB KIDS!!
THE NEXT MORNING...
HOTEL

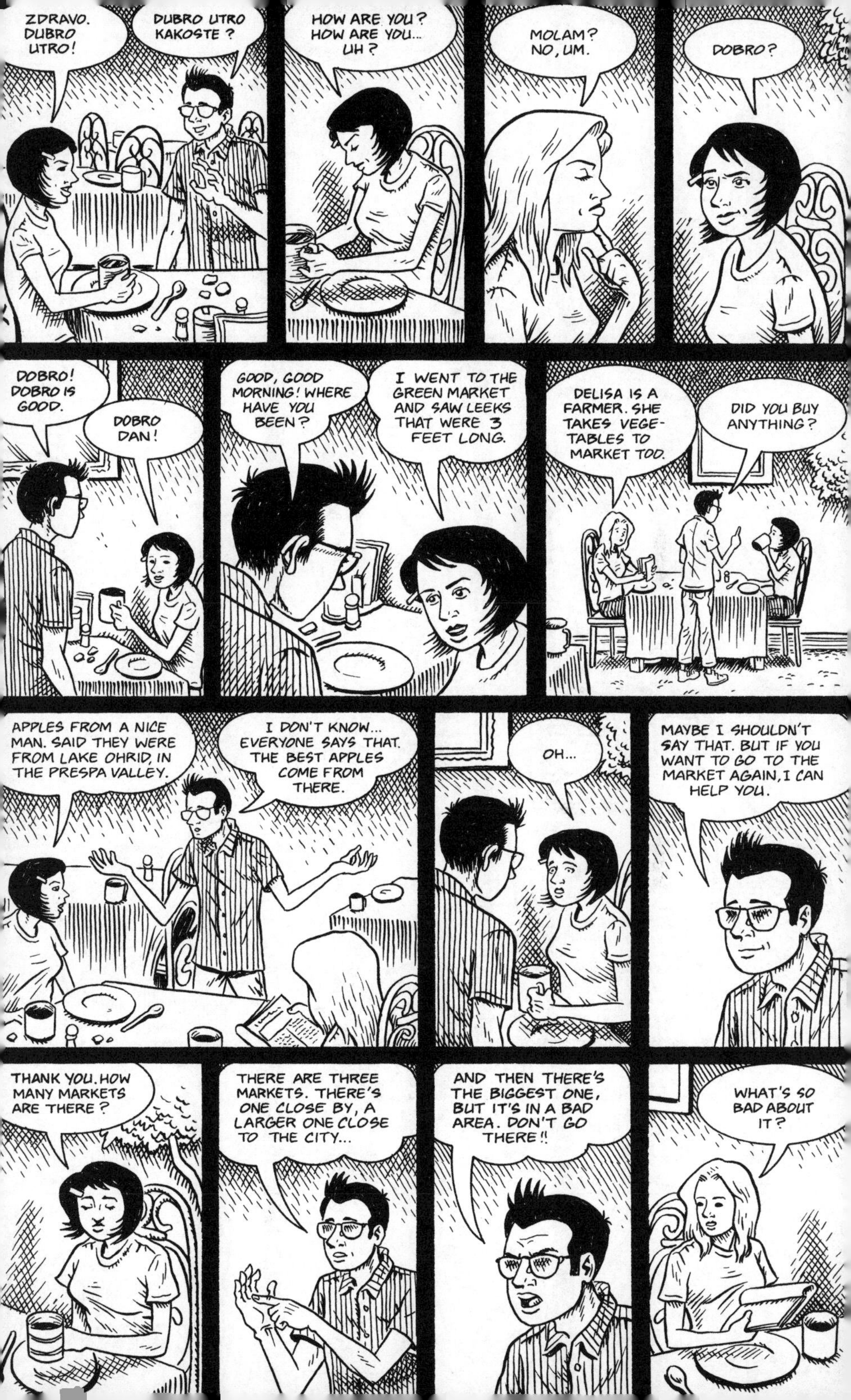
ZDRAVO. DUBRO UTRO!
DUBRO UTRO KAKOSTE?
HOW ARE YOU? HOW ARE YOU... UH?
MOLAM? NO, UM.
DOBRO?
DOBRO! DOBRO IS GOOD.
DOBRO DAN!
GOOD, GOOD MORNING! WHERE HAVE YOU BEEN?
I WENT TO THE GREEN MARKET AND SAW LEEKS THAT WERE 3 FEET LONG.
DELISA IS A FARMER. SHE TAKES VEGE-TABLES TO MARKET TOO.
DID YOU BUY ANYTHING?
APPLES FROM A NICE MAN. SAID THEY WERE FROM LAKE OHRID, IN THE PRESPA VALLEY.
I DON'T KNOW... EVERYONE SAYS THAT. THE BEST APPLES COME FROM THERE.
OH...
MAYBE I SHOULDN'T SAY THAT. BUT IF YOU WANT TO GO TO THE MARKET AGAIN, I CAN HELP YOU.
THANK YOU. HOW MANY MARKETS ARE THERE?
THERE ARE THREE MARKETS. THERE'S ONE CLOSE BY, A LARGER ONE CLOSE TO THE CITY...
AND THEN THERE'S THE BIGGEST ONE, BUT IT'S IN A BAD AREA. DON'T GO THERE!!
WHAT'S SO BAD ABOUT IT?

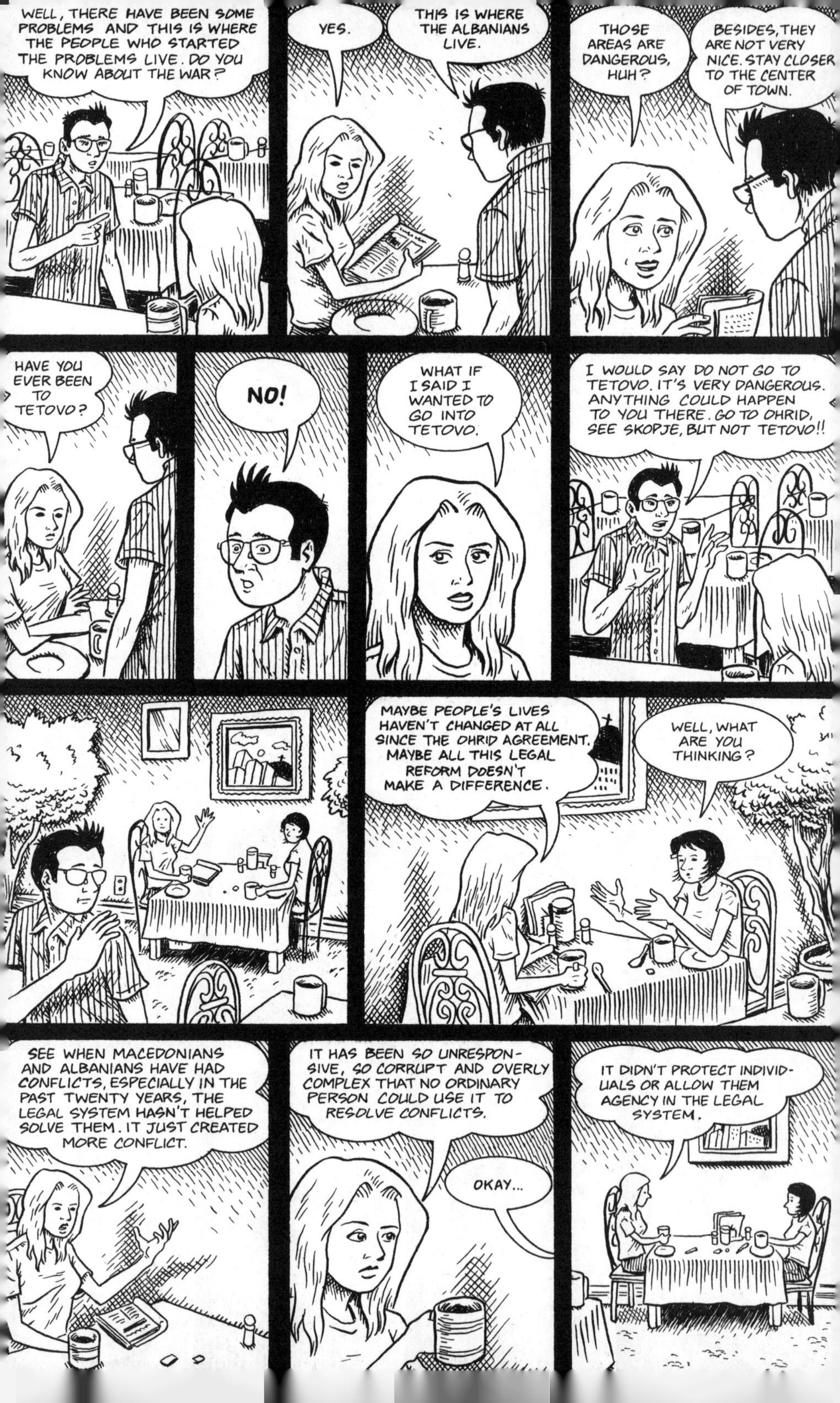
WELL, THERE HAVE BEEN SOME PROBLEMS AND THIS IS WHERE THE PEOPLE WHO STARTED THE PROBLEMS LIVE. DO YOU KNOW ABOUT THE WAR?
YES.
THIS IS WHERE THE ALBANIANS LIVE.
THOSE AREAS ARE DANGEROUS, HUH?
BESIDES, THEY ARE NOT VERY NICE. STAY CLOSER TO THE CENTER OF TOWN.
HAVE YOU EVER BEEN TO TETOVO?
NO!
WHAT IF I SAID I WANTED TO GO INTO TETOVO.
I WOULD SAY DO NOT GO TO TETOVO. IT'S VERY DANGEROUS. ANYTHING COULD HAPPEN TO YOU THERE. GO TO OHRID, SEE SKOPJE, BUT NOT TETOVO!!
MAYBE PEOPLE'S LIVES HAVEN'T CHANGED AT ALL SINCE THE OHRID AGREEMENT. MAYBE ALL THIS LEGAL REFORM DOESN'T MAKE A DIFFERENCE.
WELL, WHAT ARE YOU THINKING?
SEE WHEN MACEDONIANS AND ALBANIANS HAVE HAD CONFLICTS, ESPECIALLY IN THE PAST TWENTY YEARS, THE LEGAL SYSTEM HASN'T HELPED SOLVE THEM. IT JUST CREATED MORE CONFLICT.
IT HAS BEEN SO UNRESPONSIVE, SO CORRUPT AND OVERLY COMPLEX THAT NO ORDINARY PERSON COULD USE IT TO RESOLVE CONFLICTS.
OKAY...
IT DIDN'T PROTECT INDIVIDUALS OR ALLOW THEM AGENCY IN THE LEGAL SYSTEM.

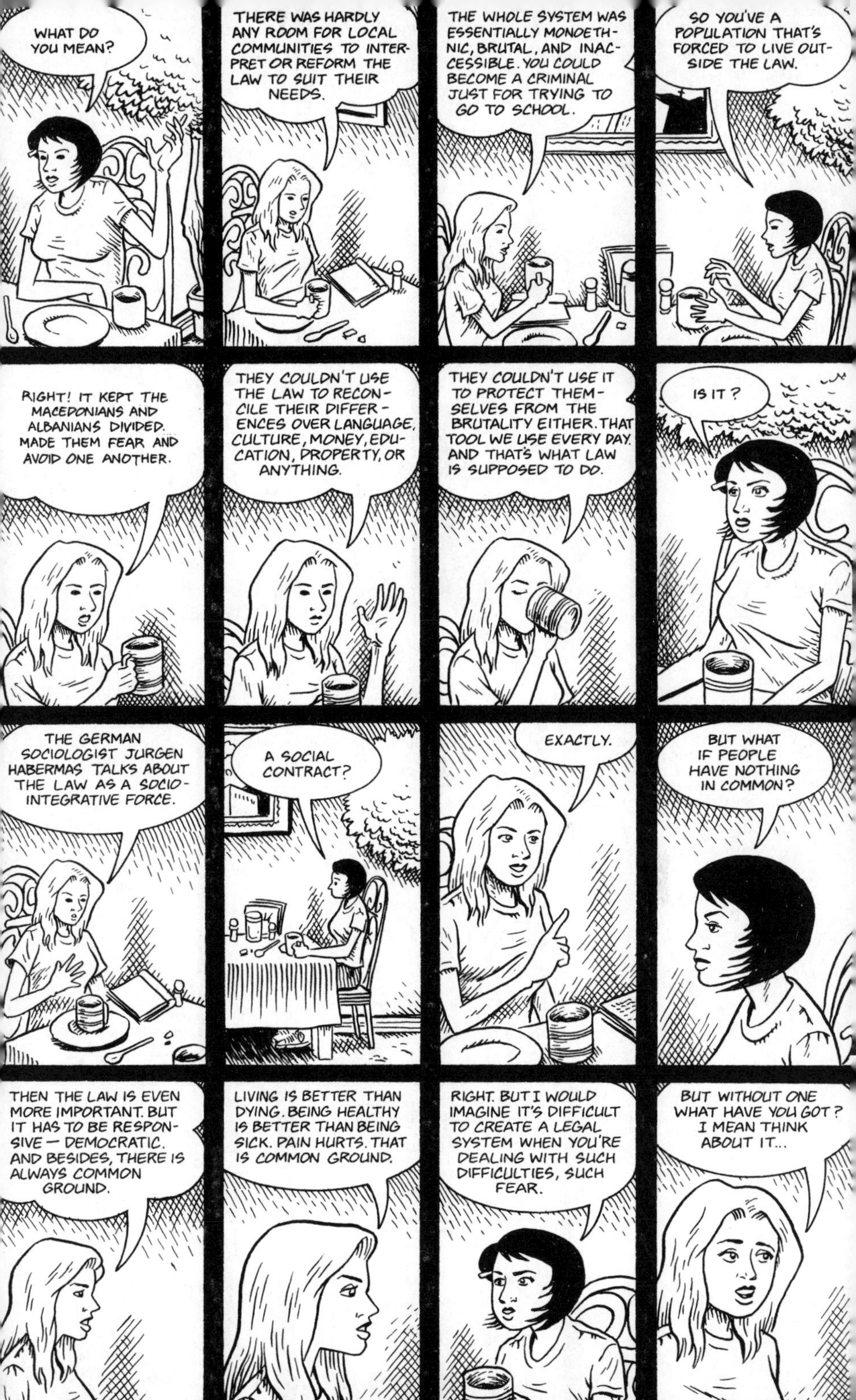
WHAT DO YOU MEAN?
THERE WAS HARDLY ANY ROOM FOR LOCAL COMMUNITIES TO INTERPRET OR REFORM THE LAW TO SUIT THEIR NEEDS.
THE WHOLE SYSTEM WAS ESSENTIALLY MONOETHNIC, BRUTAL, AND INACCESSIBLE. YOU COULD BECOME A CRIMINAL JUST FOR TRYING TO GO TO SCHOOL.
SO YOU'VE A POPULATION THAT'S FORCED TO LIVE OUTSIDE THE LAW.
RIGHT! IT KEPT THE MACEDONIANS AND ALBANIANS DIVIDED. MADE THEM FEAR AND AVOID ONE ANOTHER.
THEY COULDN'T USE THE LAW TO RECONCILE THEIR DIFFERENCES OVER LANGUAGE, CULTURE, MONEY, EDUCATION, PROPERTY, OR ANYTHING.
THEY COULDN'T USE IT TO PROTECT THEMSELVES FROM THE BRUTALITY EITHER. THAT TOOL WE USE EVERY DAY. AND THAT'S WHAT LAW IS SUPPOSED TO DO.
IS IT?
THE GERMAN SOCIOLOGIST JURGEN HABERMAS TALKS ABOUT THE LAW AS A SOCIO-INTEGRATIVE FORCE.
A SOCIAL CONTRACT?
EXACTLY.
BUT WHAT IF PEOPLE HAVE NOTHING IN COMMON?
THEN THE LAW IS EVEN MORE IMPORTANT. BUT IT HAS TO BE RESPONSIVE — DEMOCRATIC. AND BESIDES, THERE IS ALWAYS COMMON GROUND.
LIVING IS BETTER THAN DYING. BEING HEALTHY IS BETTER THAN BEING SICK. PAIN HURTS. THAT IS COMMON GROUND.
RIGHT. BUT I WOULD IMAGINE IT'S DIFFICULT TO CREATE A LEGAL SYSTEM WHEN YOU'RE DEALING WITH SUCH DIFFICULTIES, SUCH FEAR.
BUT WITHOUT ONE WHAT HAVE YOU GOT? I MEAN THINK ABOUT IT...

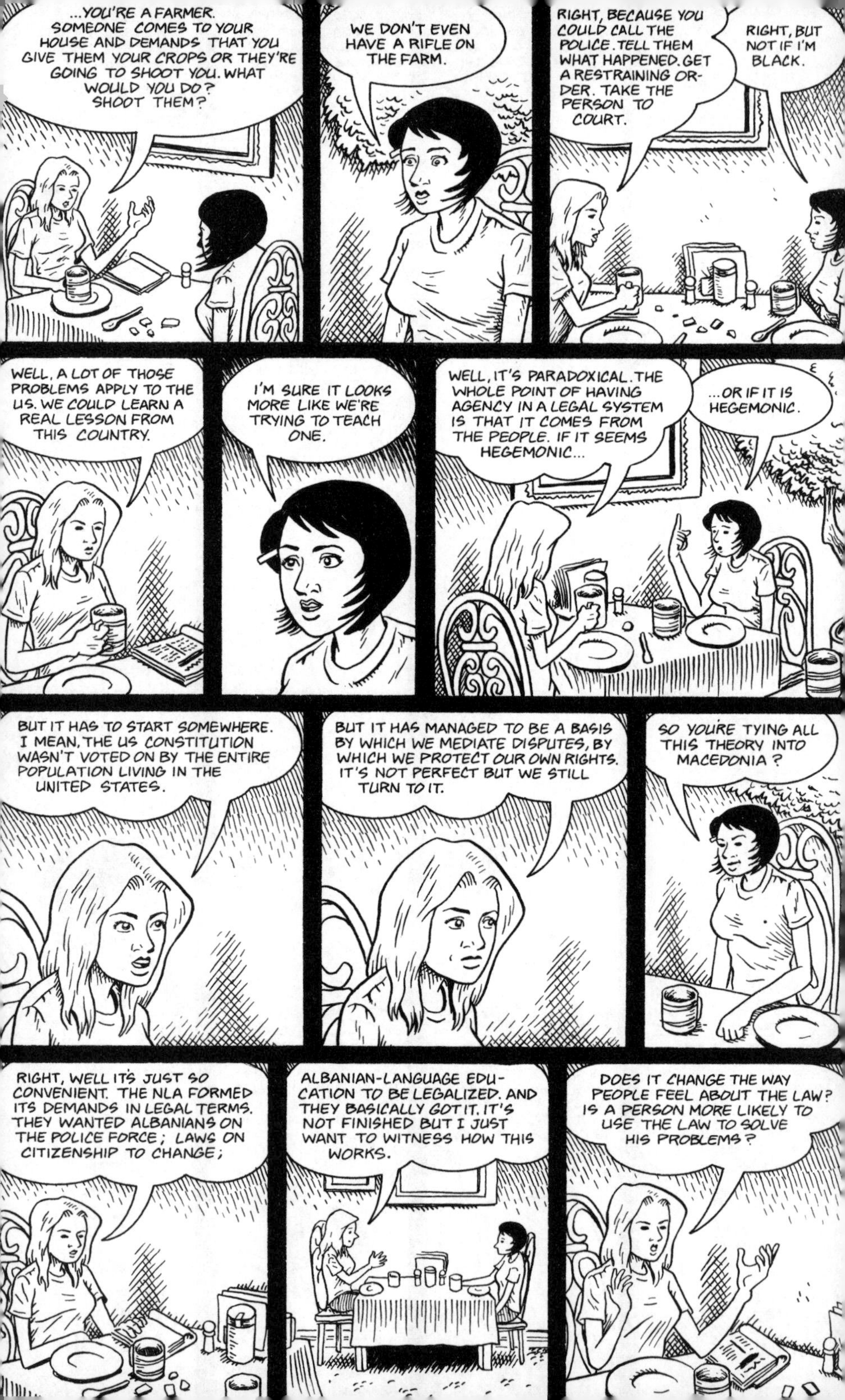
...YOU'RE A FARMER. SOMEONE COMES TO YOUR HOUSE AND DEMANDS THAT YOU GIVE THEM YOUR CROPS OR THEY'RE GOING TO SHOOT YOU. WHAT WOULD YOU DO? SHOOT THEM?
WE DON'T EVEN HAVE A RIFLE ON THE FARM.
RIGHT, BECAUSE YOU COULD CALL THE POLICE. TELL THEM WHAT HAPPENED. GET A RESTRAINING ORDER. TAKE THE PERSON TO COURT.
RIGHT, BUT NOT IF I'M BLACK.
WELL, A LOT OF THOSE PROBLEMS APPLY TO THE US. WE COULD LEARN A REAL LESSON FROM THIS COUNTRY.
I'M SURE IT LOOKS MORE LIKE WE'RE TRYING TO TEACH ONE.
WELL, IT'S PARADOXICAL. THE WHOLE POINT OF HAVING AGENCY IN A LEGAL SYSTEM IS THAT IT COMES FROM THE PEOPLE. IF IT SEEMS HEGEMONIC...
...OR IF IT IS HEGEMONIC.
BUT IT HAS TO START SOMEWHERE. I MEAN, THE US CONSTITUTION WASN'T VOTED ON BY THE ENTIRE POPULATION LIVING IN THE UNITED STATES.
BUT IT HAS MANAGED TO BE A BASIS BY WHICH WE MEDIATE DISPUTES, BY WHICH WE PROTECT OUR OWN RIGHTS. IT'S NOT PERFECT BUT WE STILL TURN TO IT.
SO YOU'RE TYING ALL THIS THEORY INTO MACEDONIA?
RIGHT, WELL IT'S JUST SO CONVENIENT. THE NLA FORMED ITS DEMANDS IN LEGAL TERMS. THEY WANTED ALBANIANS ON THE POLICE FORCE; LAWS ON CITIZENSHIP TO CHANGE;
ALBANIAN-LANGUAGE EDUCATION TO BE LEGALIZED. AND THEY BASICALLY GOT IT. IT'S NOT FINISHED BUT I JUST WANT TO WITNESS HOW THIS WORKS.
DOES IT CHANGE THE WAY PEOPLE FEEL ABOUT THE LAW? IS A PERSON MORE LIKELY TO USE THE LAW TO SOLVE HIS PROBLEMS?

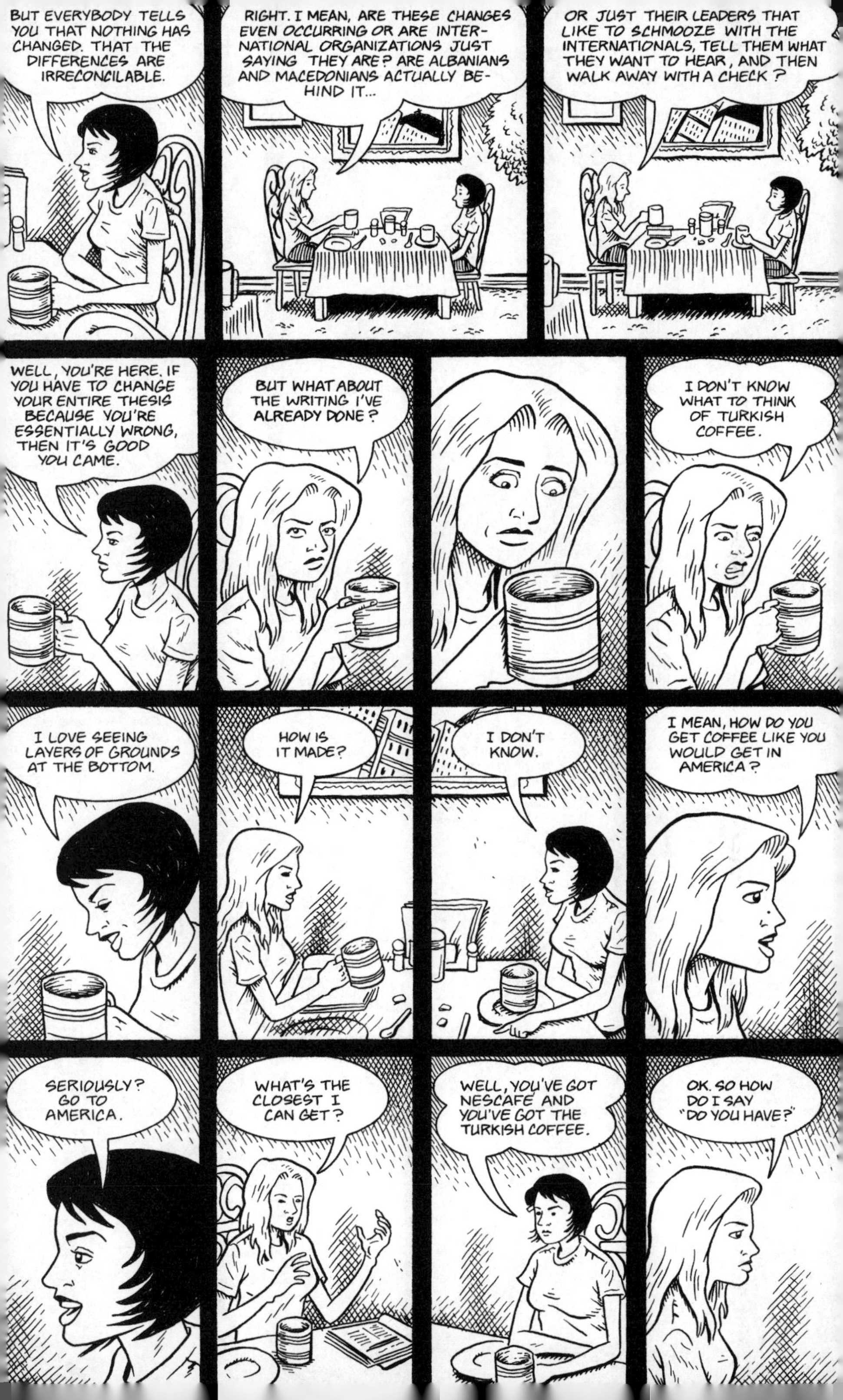
BUT EVERYBODY TELLS YOU THAT NOTHING HAS CHANGED. THAT THE DIFFERENCES ARE IRRECONCILABLE.
RIGHT. I MEAN, ARE THESE CHANGES EVEN OCCURRING OR ARE INTERNATIONAL ORGANIZATIONS JUST SAYING THEY ARE? ARE ALBANIANS AND MACEDONIANS ACTUALLY BEHIND IT...
OR JUST THEIR LEADERS THAT LIKE TO SCHMOOZE WITH THE INTERNATIONALS, TELL THEM WHAT THEY WANT TO HEAR, AND THEN WALK AWAY WITH A CHECK?
WELL, YOU'RE HERE. IF YOU HAVE TO CHANGE YOUR ENTIRE THESIS BECAUSE YOU'RE ESSENTIALLY WRONG, THEN IT'S GOOD YOU CAME.
BUT WHAT ABOUT THE WRITING I'VE ALREADY DONE?
I DON'T KNOW WHAT TO THINK OF TURKISH COFFEE.
I LOVE SEEING LAYERS OF GROUNDS AT THE BOTTOM.
HOW IS IT MADE?
I DON'T KNOW.
I MEAN, HOW DO YOU GET COFFEE LIKE YOU WOULD GET IN AMERICA?
SERIOUSLY? GO TO AMERICA.
WHAT'S THE CLOSEST I CAN GET?
WELL, YOU'VE GOT NESCAFE AND YOU'VE GOT THE TURKISH COFFEE.
O.K. SO HOW DO I SAY "DO YOU HAVE?"

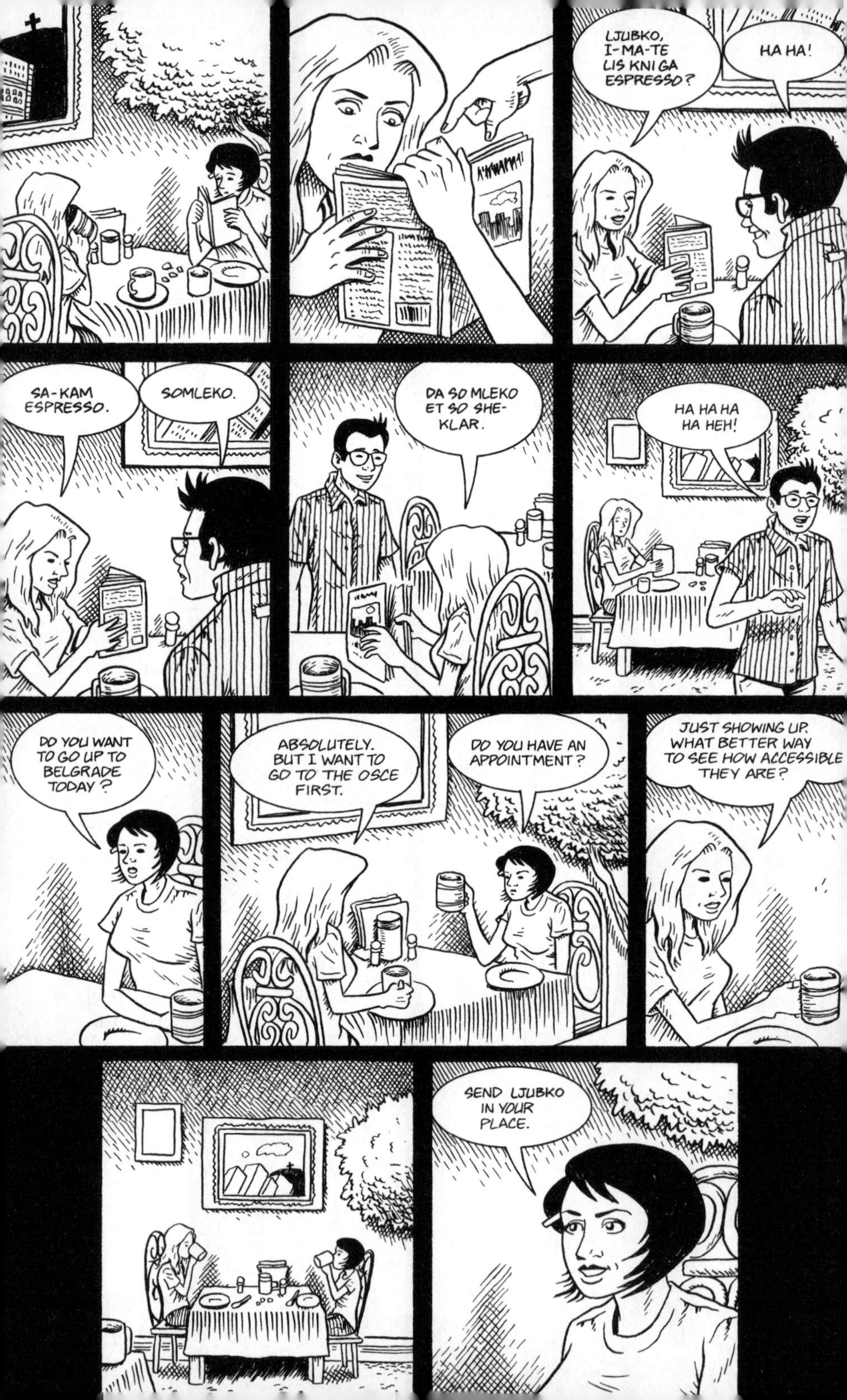

LJUBKO, I-MA-TE LIS KNI GA ESPRESSO?
HA HA!
SA-KAM ESPRESSO.
SOMLEKO.
DA SO MLEKO ET SO SHE-KLAR.
HA HA HA HA HEH!
DO YOU WANT TO GO UP TO BELGRADE TODAY?
ABSOLUTELY. BUT I WANT TO GO TO THE OSCE FIRST.
DO YOU HAVE AN APPOINTMENT?
JUST SHOWING UP. WHAT BETTER WAY TO SEE HOW ACCESSIBLE THEY ARE?
SEND LJUBKO IN YOUR PLACE.

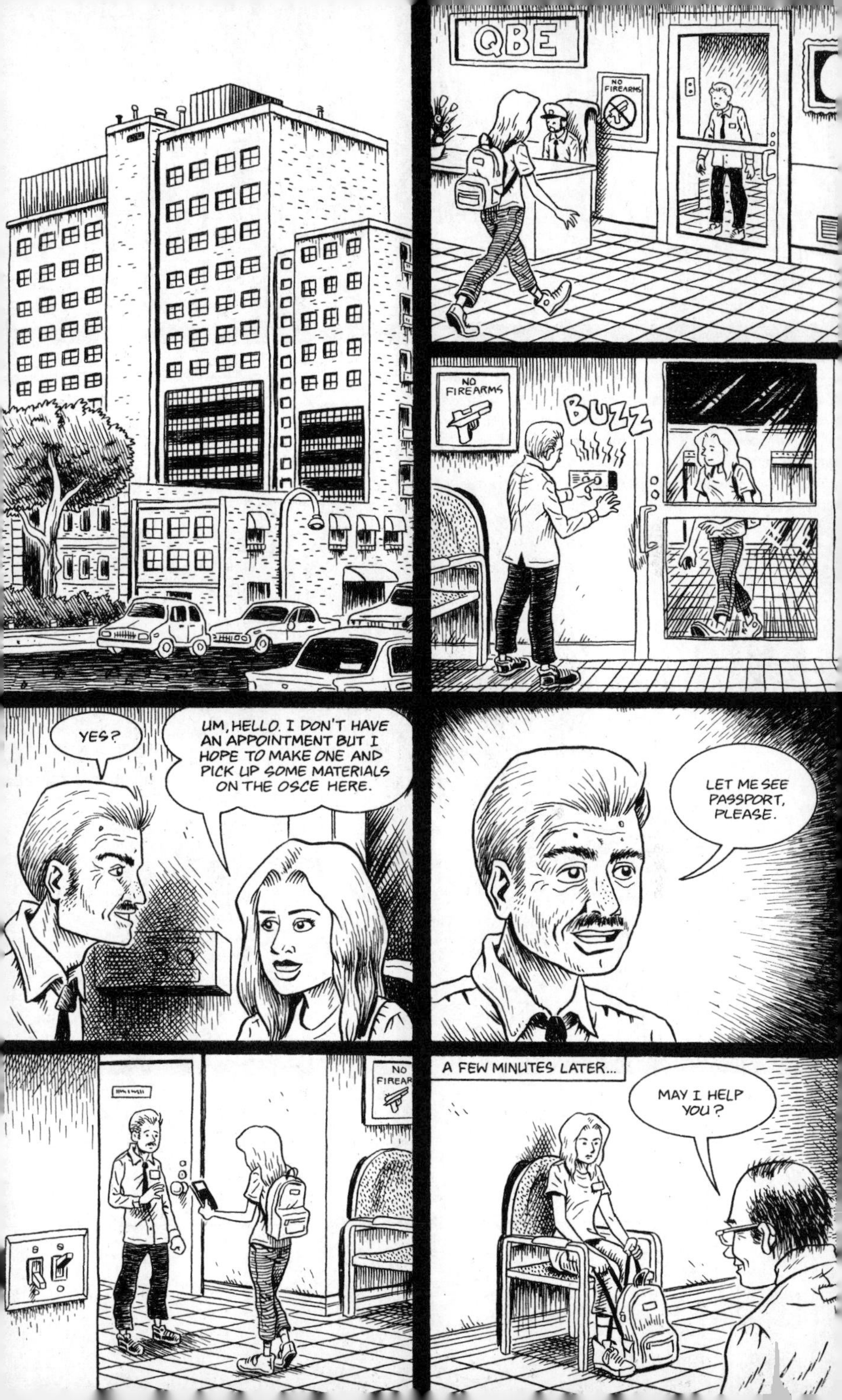
QBE
NO FIREARMS
NO FIREARMS
BUZZ
YES?
UM, HELLO. I DON'T HAVE AN APPOINTMENT BUT I HOPE TO MAKE ONE AND PICK UP SOME MATERIALS ON THE OSCE HERE.
LET ME SEE PASSPORT, PLEASE.
A FEW MINUTES LATER...
MAY I HELP YOU?

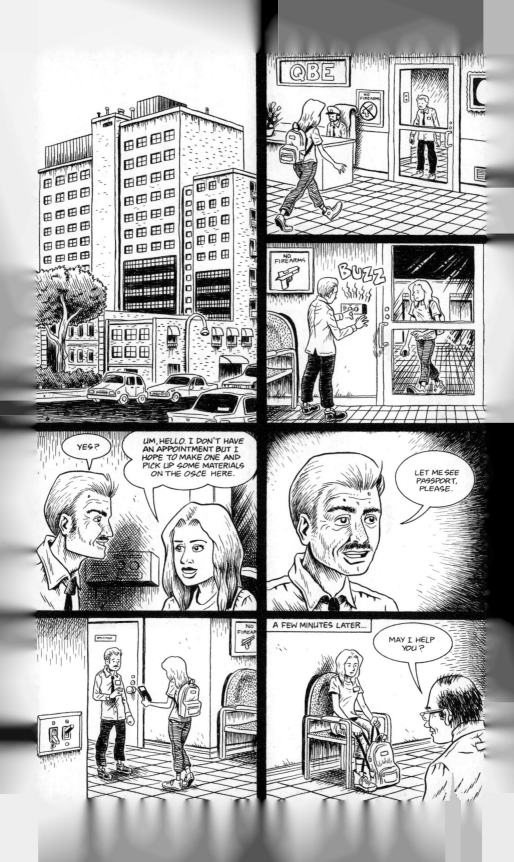

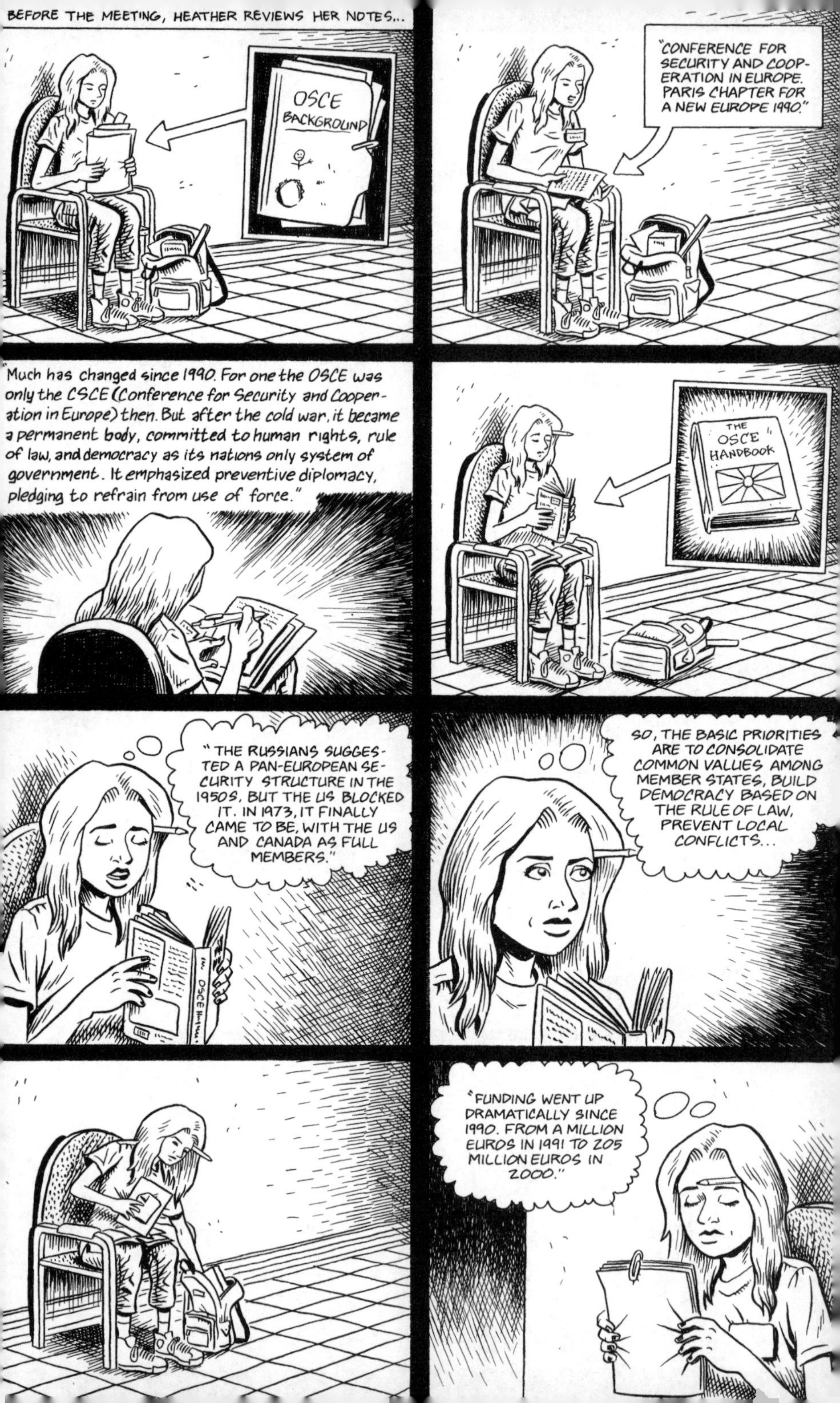
BEFORE THE MEETING, HEATHER REVIEWS HER NOTES...
OSCE BACKGROUND
"CONFERENCE FOR SECURITY AND COOPERATION IN EUROPE. PARIS CHAPTER FOR A NEW EUROPE 1990."
"Much has changed since 1990. For one the OSCE was only the CSCE (Conference for Security and Cooperation in Europe) then. But after the cold war, it became a permanent body, committed to human rights, rule of law, and democracy as its nations only system of government. It emphasized preventive diplomacy, pledging to refrain from use of force."
THE OSCE HANDBOOK
"THE RUSSIANS SUGGESTED A PAN-EUROPEAN SECURITY STRUCTURE IN THE 1950S, BUT THE US BLOCKED IT. IN 1973, IT FINALLY CAME TO BE, WITH THE US AND CANADA AS FULL MEMBERS."
SO, THE BASIC PRIORITIES ARE TO CONSOLIDATE COMMON VALUES AMONG MEMBER STATES, BUILD DEMOCRACY BASED ON THE RULE OF LAW, PREVENT LOCAL CONFLICTS...
"FUNDING WENT UP DRAMATICALLY SINCE 1990. FROM A MILLION EUROS IN 1991 TO 205 MILLION EUROS IN 2000."

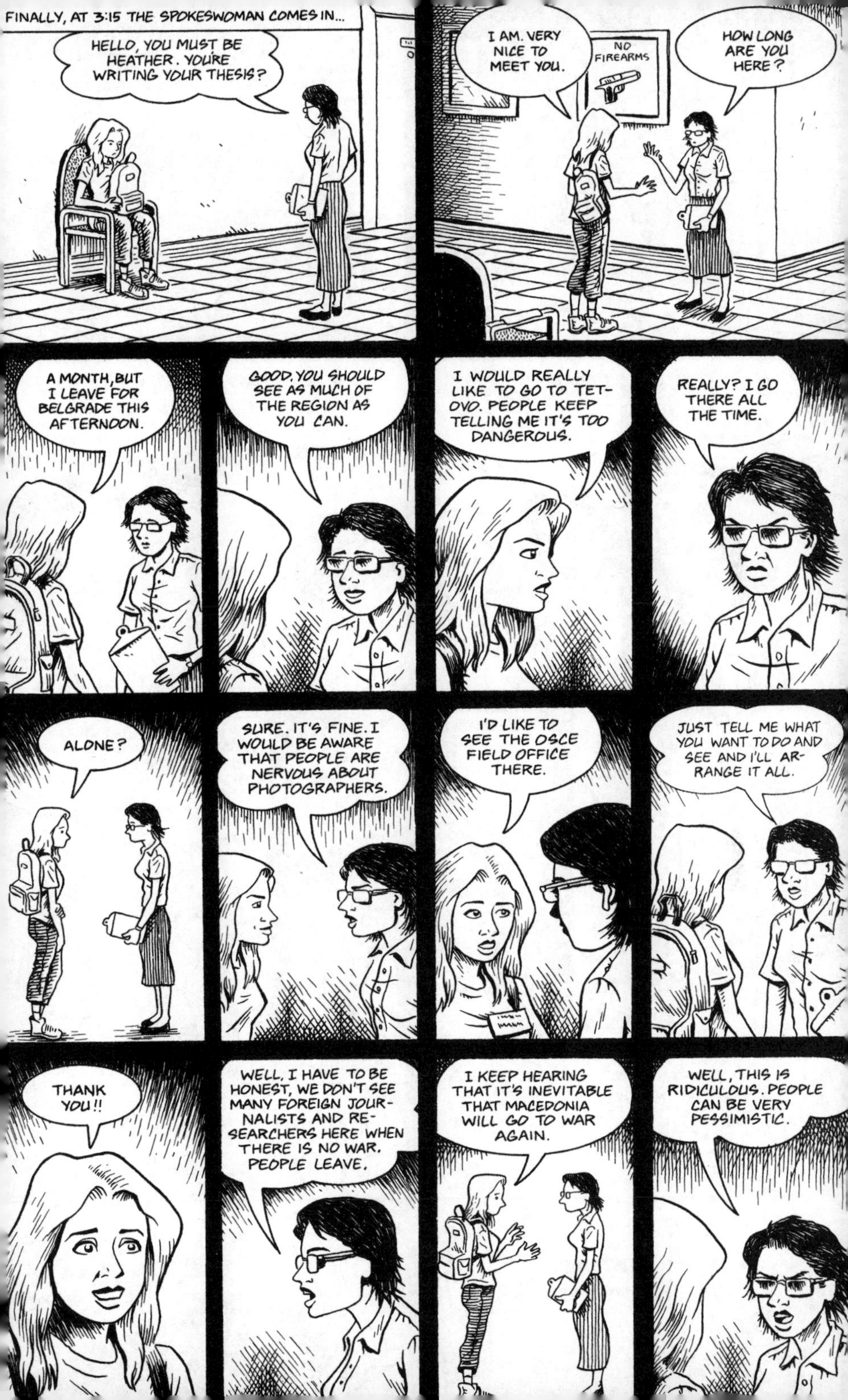
FINALLY, AT 3:15 THE SPOKESWOMAN COMES IN...
HELLO, YOU MUST BE HEATHER. YOU'RE WRITING YOUR THESIS?
I AM. VERY NICE TO MEET YOU.
NO FIREARMS
HOW LONG ARE YOU HERE?
A MONTH, BUT I LEAVE FOR BELGRADE THIS AFTERNOON.
GOOD, YOU SHOULD SEE AS MUCH OF THE REGION AS YOU CAN.
I WOULD REALLY LIKE TO GO TO TETOVO. PEOPLE KEEP TELLING ME IT'S TOO DANGEROUS.
REALLY? I GO THERE ALL THE TIME.
ALONE?
SURE. IT'S FINE. I WOULD BE AWARE THAT PEOPLE ARE NERVOUS ABOUT PHOTOGRAPHERS.
I'D LIKE TO SEE THE OSCE FIELD OFFICE THERE.
JUST TELL ME WHAT YOU WANT TO DO AND SEE AND I'LL ARRANGE IT ALL.
THANK YOU!!
WELL, I HAVE TO BE HONEST, WE DON'T SEE MANY FOREIGN JOURNALISTS AND RESEARCHERS HERE WHEN THERE IS NO WAR. PEOPLE LEAVE.
I KEEP HEARING THAT IT'S INEVITABLE THAT MACEDONIA WILL GO TO WAR AGAIN.
WELL, THIS IS RIDICULOUS. PEOPLE CAN BE VERY PESSIMISTIC.

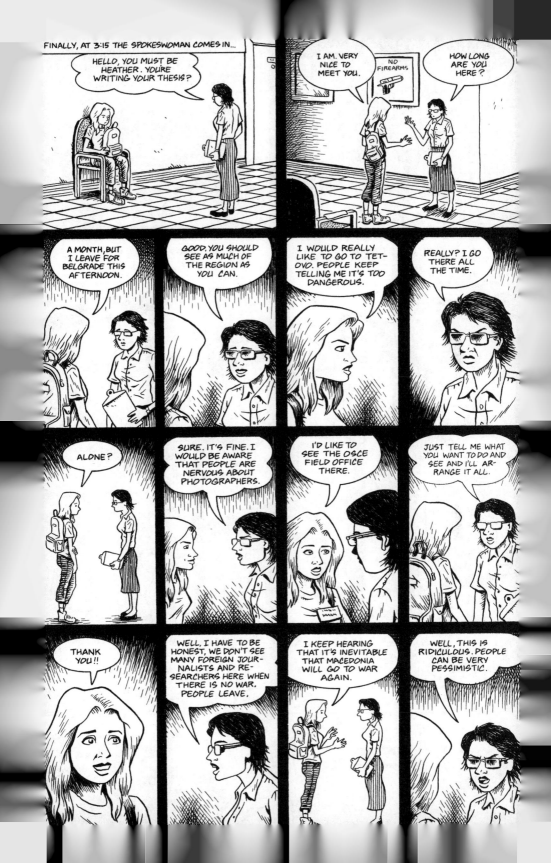

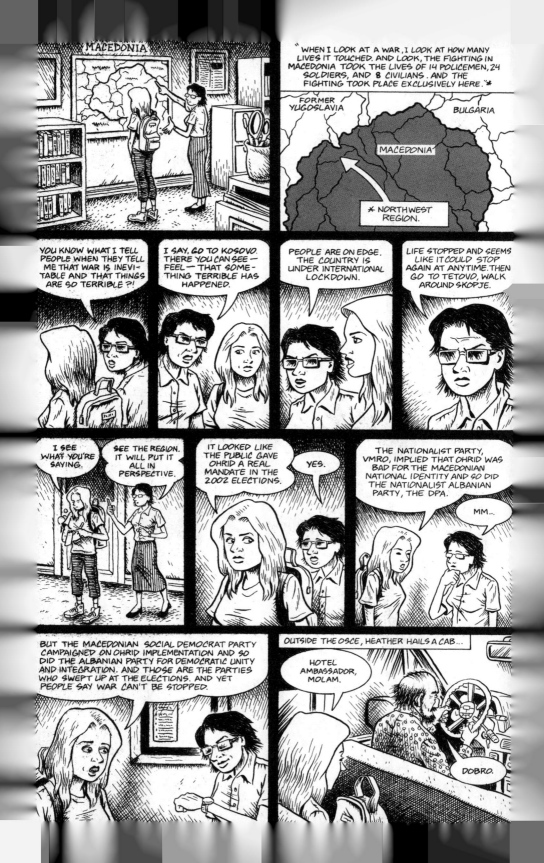

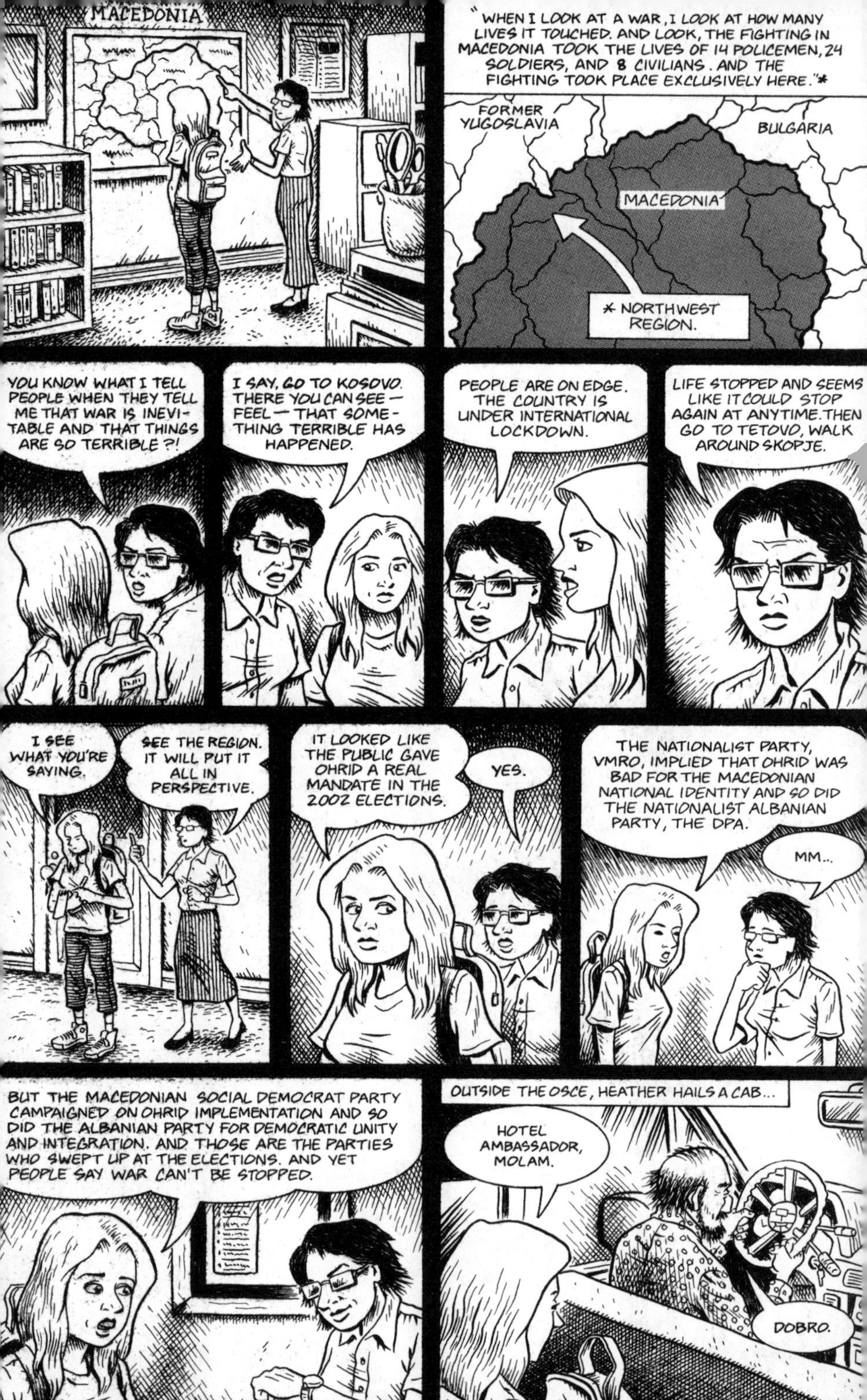
MACEDONIA
"WHEN I LOOK AT A WAR, I LOOK AT HOW MANY LIVES IT TOUCHED. AND LOOK, THE FIGHTING IN MACEDONIA TOOK THE LIVES OF 14 POLICEMEN, 24 SOLDIERS, AND 8 CIVILIANS. AND THE FIGHTING TOOK PLACE EXCLUSIVELY HERE."*
FORMER YUGOSLAVIA
BULGARIA
MACEDONIA
* NORTHWEST REGION.
YOU KNOW WHAT I TELL PEOPLE WHEN THEY TELL ME THAT WAR IS INEVITABLE AND THAT THINGS ARE SO TERRIBLE?!
I SAY, GO TO KOSOVO. THERE YOU CAN SEE— FEEL— THAT SOMETHING TERRIBLE HAS HAPPENED.
PEOPLE ARE ON EDGE. THE COUNTRY IS UNDER INTERNATIONAL LOCKDOWN.
LIFE STOPPED AND SEEMS LIKE IT COULD STOP AGAIN AT ANYTIME. THEN GO TO TETOVO, WALK AROUND SKOPJE.
I SEE WHAT YOU'RE SAYING.
SEE THE REGION. IT WILL PUT IT ALL IN PERSPECTIVE.
IT LOOKED LIKE THE PUBLIC GAVE OHRID A REAL MANDATE IN THE 2002 ELECTIONS.
YES.
THE NATIONALIST PARTY, VMRO, IMPLIED THAT OHRID WAS BAD FOR THE MACEDONIAN NATIONAL IDENTITY AND SO DID THE NATIONALIST ALBANIAN PARTY, THE DPA.
MM...
BUT THE MACEDONIAN SOCIAL DEMOCRAT PARTY CAMPAIGNED ON OHRID IMPLEMENTATION AND SO DID THE ALBANIAN PARTY FOR DEMOCRATIC UNITY AND INTEGRATION. AND THOSE ARE THE PARTIES WHO SWEPT UP AT THE ELECTIONS. AND YET PEOPLE SAY WAR CAN'T BE STOPPED.
OUTSIDE THE OSCE, HEATHER HAILS A CAB...
HOTEL AMBASSADOR, MOLAM.
DOBRO.

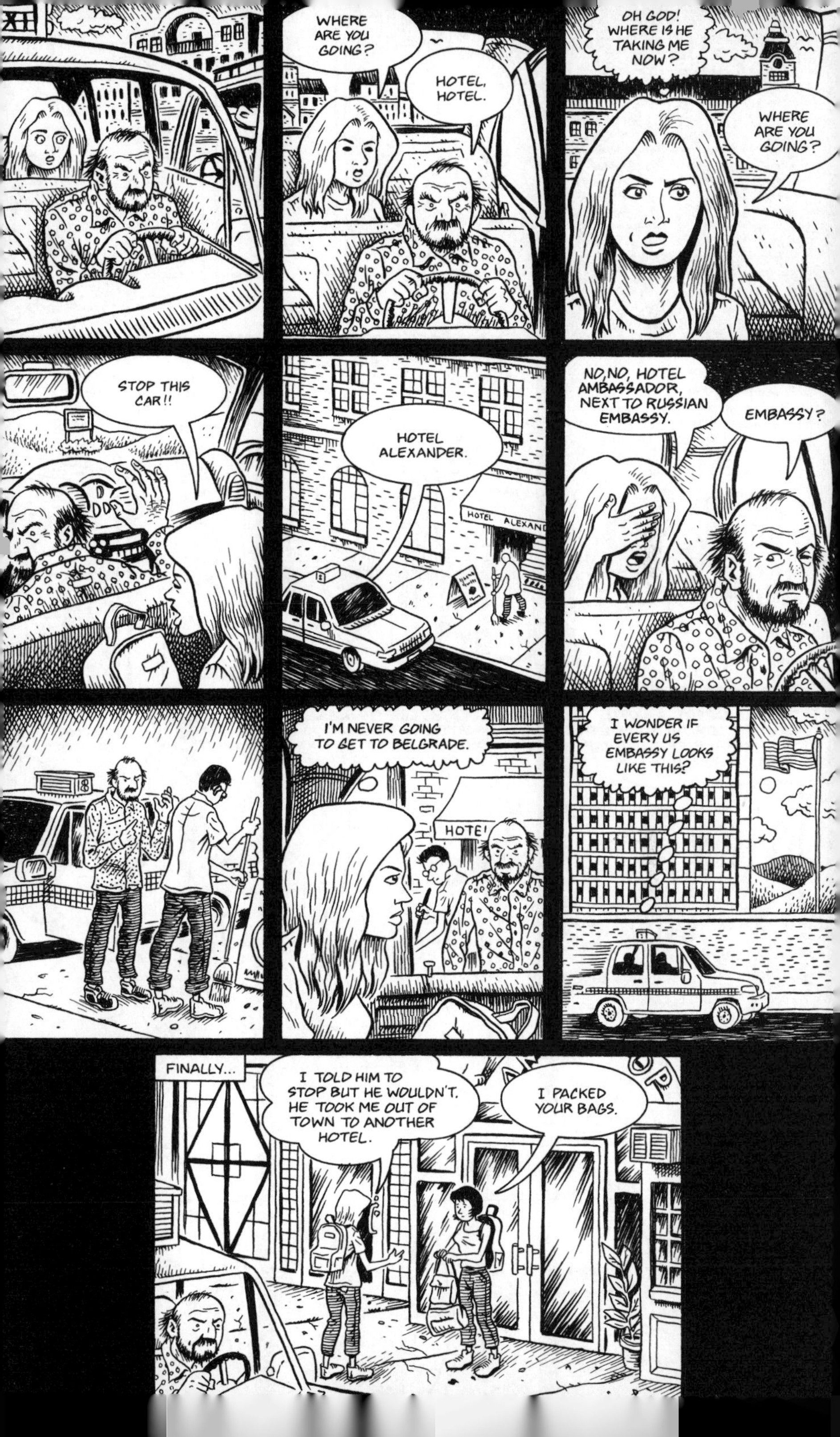
WHERE ARE YOU GOING?
HOTEL, HOTEL.
OH GOD! WHERE IS HE TAKING ME NOW?
WHERE ARE YOU GOING?
STOP THIS CAR!!
HOTEL ALEXANDER.
HOTEL ALEXAND
NO, NO, HOTEL AMBASSADOR, NEXT TO RUSSIAN EMBASSY.
EMBASSY?
I'M NEVER GOING TO GET TO BELGRADE.
HOTE
I WONDER IF EVERY US EMBASSY LOOKS LIKE THIS?
FINALLY...
I TOLD HIM TO STOP BUT HE WOULDN'T. HE TOOK ME OUT OF TOWN TO ANOTHER HOTEL.
I PACKED YOUR BAGS.

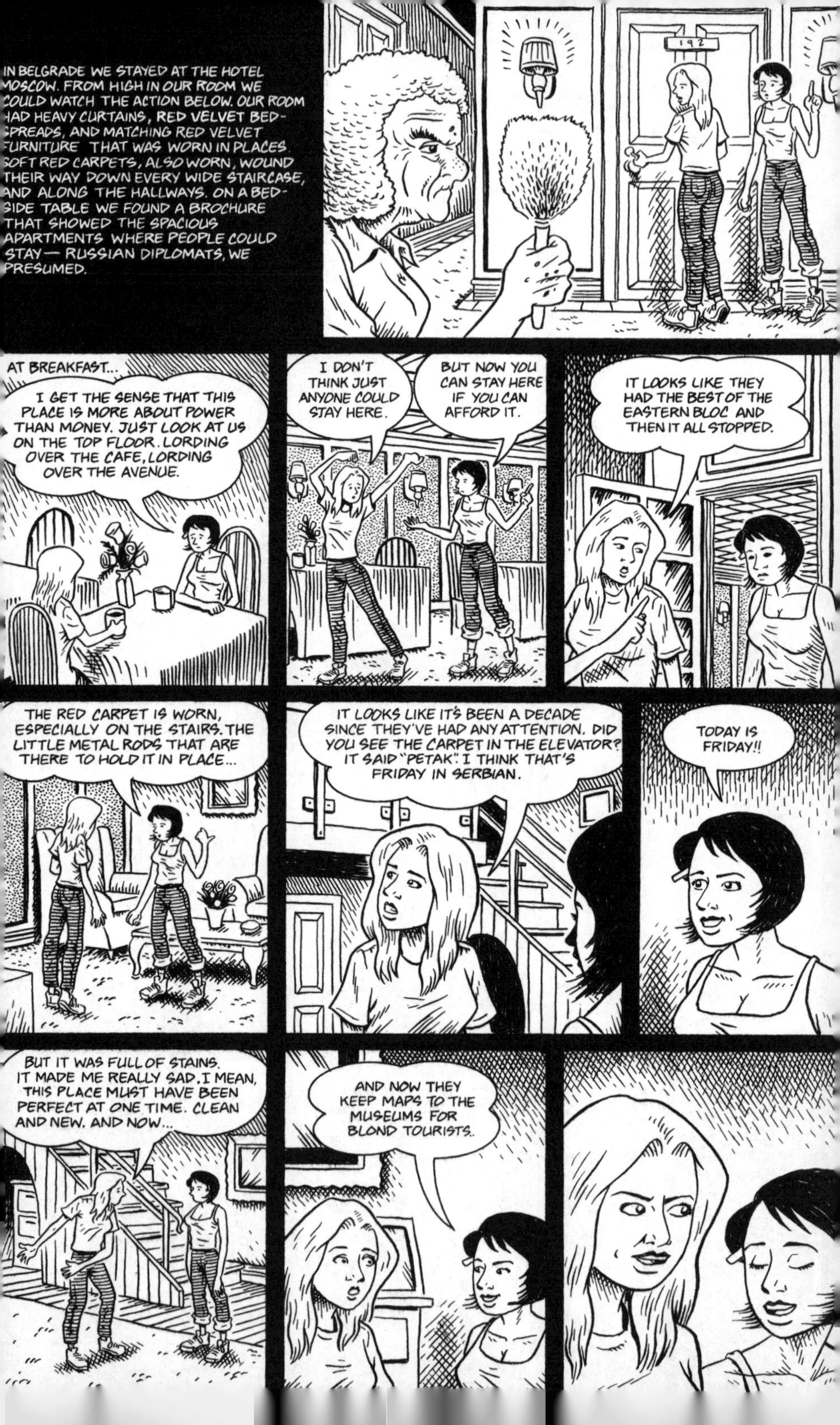

IN BELGRADE WE STAYED AT THE HOTEL MOSCOW. FROM HIGH IN OUR ROOM WE COULD WATCH THE ACTION BELOW. OUR ROOM HAD HEAVY CURTAINS, RED VELVET BEDSPREADS, AND MATCHING RED VELVET FURNITURE THAT WAS WORN IN PLACES. SOFT RED CARPETS, ALSO WORN, WOUND THEIR WAY DOWN EVERY WIDE STAIRCASE, AND ALONG THE HALLWAYS. ON A BEDSIDE TABLE WE FOUND A BROCHURE THAT SHOWED THE SPACIOUS APARTMENTS WHERE PEOPLE COULD STAY— RUSSIAN DIPLOMATS, WE PRESUMED.
192
AT BREAKFAST...
I GET THE SENSE THAT THIS PLACE IS MORE ABOUT POWER THAN MONEY. JUST LOOK AT US ON THE TOP FLOOR. LORDING OVER THE CAFE, LORDING OVER THE AVENUE.
I DON'T THINK JUST ANYONE COULD STAY HERE.
BUT NOW YOU CAN STAY HERE IF YOU CAN AFFORD IT.
IT LOOKS LIKE THEY HAD THE BEST OF THE EASTERN BLOC AND THEN IT ALL STOPPED.
THE RED CARPET IS WORN, ESPECIALLY ON THE STAIRS. THE LITTLE METAL RODS THAT ARE THERE TO HOLD IT IN PLACE...
IT LOOKS LIKE IT'S BEEN A DECADE SINCE THEY'VE HAD ANY ATTENTION. DID YOU SEE THE CARPET IN THE ELEVATOR? IT SAID "PETAK". I THINK THAT'S FRIDAY IN SERBIAN.
TODAY IS FRIDAY!!
BUT IT WAS FULL OF STAINS. IT MADE ME REALLY SAD. I MEAN, THIS PLACE MUST HAVE BEEN PERFECT AT ONE TIME. CLEAN AND NEW. AND NOW...
AND NOW THEY KEEP MAPS TO THE MUSEUMS FOR BLOND TOURISTS.

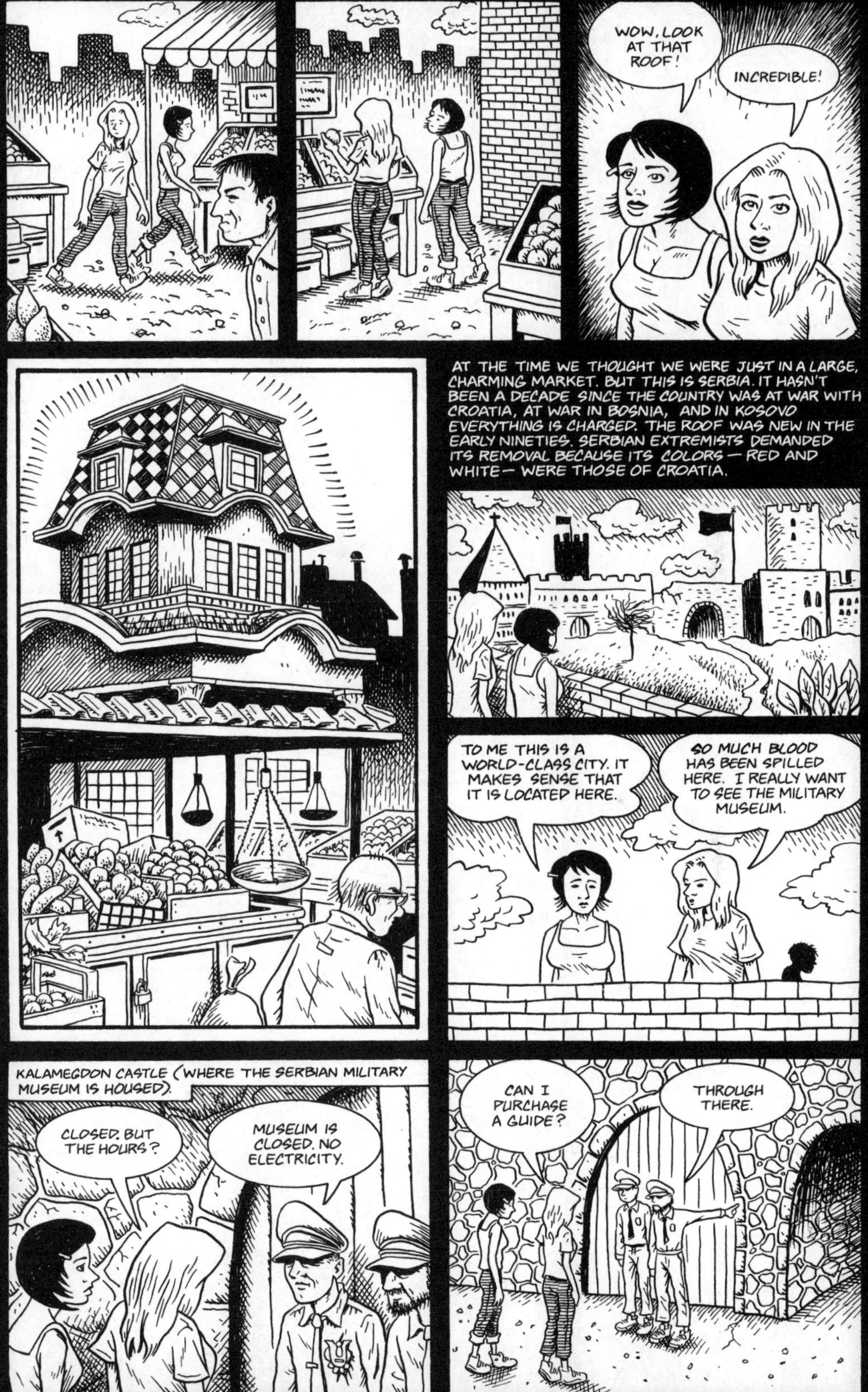
WOW, LOOK AT THAT ROOF!
INCREDIBLE!
AT THE TIME WE THOUGHT WE WERE JUST IN A LARGE, CHARMING MARKET. BUT THIS IS SERBIA. IT HASN'T BEEN A DECADE SINCE THE COUNTRY WAS AT WAR WITH CROATIA, AT WAR IN BOSNIA, AND IN KOSOVO EVERYTHING IS CHARGED. THE ROOF WAS NEW IN THE EARLY NINETIES. SERBIAN EXTREMISTS DEMANDED ITS REMOVAL BECAUSE ITS COLORS — RED AND WHITE — WERE THOSE OF CROATIA.
TO ME THIS IS A WORLD-CLASS CITY. IT MAKES SENSE THAT IT IS LOCATED HERE.
SO MUCH BLOOD HAS BEEN SPILLED HERE. I REALLY WANT TO SEE THE MILITARY MUSEUM.
KALAMEGDON CASTLE (WHERE THE SERBIAN MILITARY MUSEUM IS HOUSED).
MUSEUM IS CLOSED. NO ELECTRICITY.
CLOSED. BUT THE HOURS?
CAN I PURCHASE A GUIDE?
THROUGH THERE.

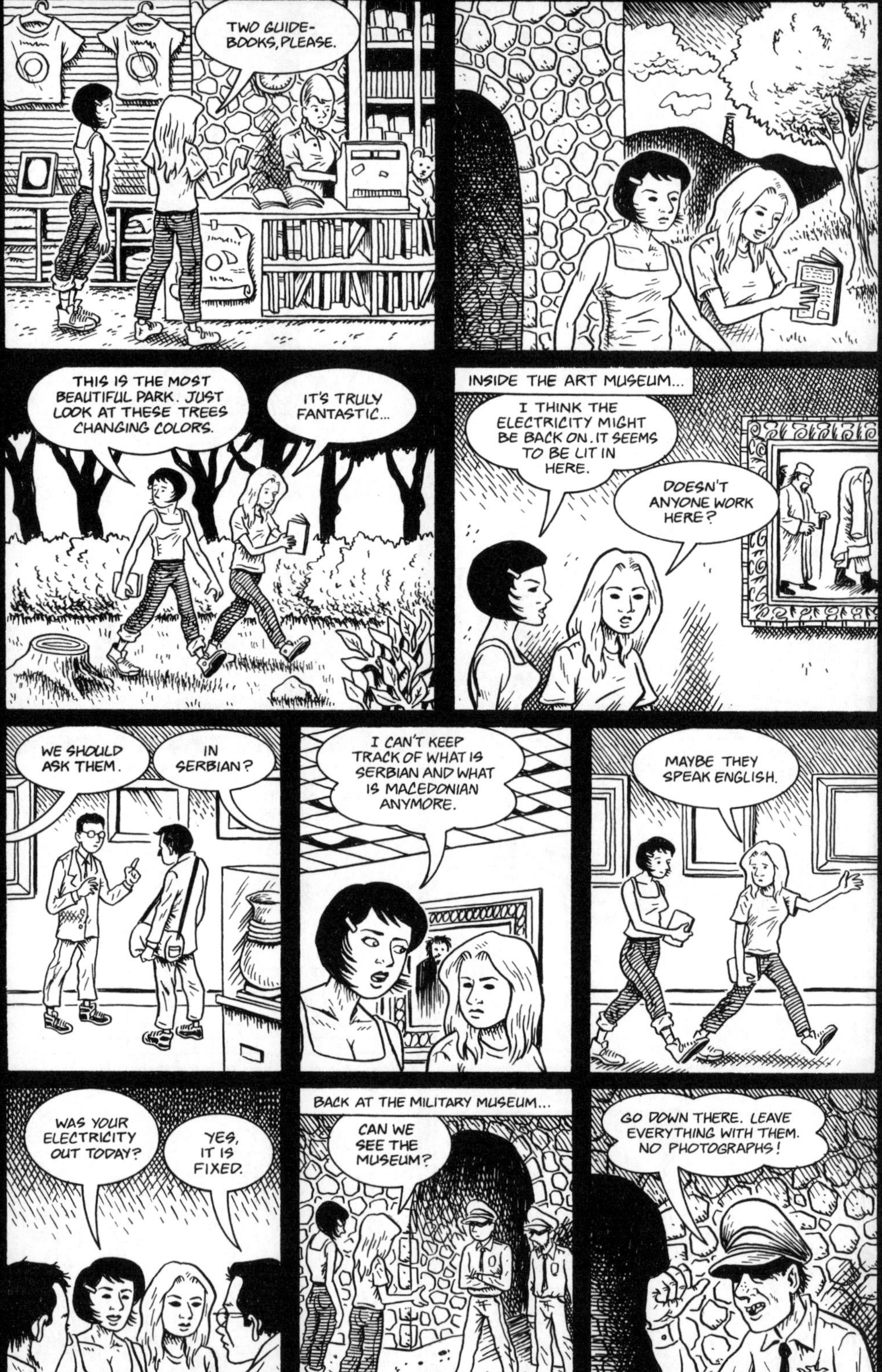
TWO GUIDE-BOOKS, PLEASE.
THIS IS THE MOST BEAUTIFUL PARK. JUST LOOK AT THESE TREES CHANGING COLORS.
IT'S TRULY FANTASTIC...
INSIDE THE ART MUSEUM...
I THINK THE ELECTRICITY MIGHT BE BACK ON. IT SEEMS TO BE LIT IN HERE.
DOESN'T ANYONE WORK HERE?
WE SHOULD ASK THEM.
IN SERBIAN?
I CAN'T KEEP TRACK OF WHAT IS SERBIAN AND WHAT IS MACEDONIAN ANYMORE.
MAYBE THEY SPEAK ENGLISH.
WAS YOUR ELECTRICITY OUT TODAY?
YES, IT IS FIXED.
BACK AT THE MILITARY MUSEUM...
CAN WE SEE THE MUSEUM?
GO DOWN THERE. LEAVE EVERYTHING WITH THEM. NO PHOTOGRAPHS!

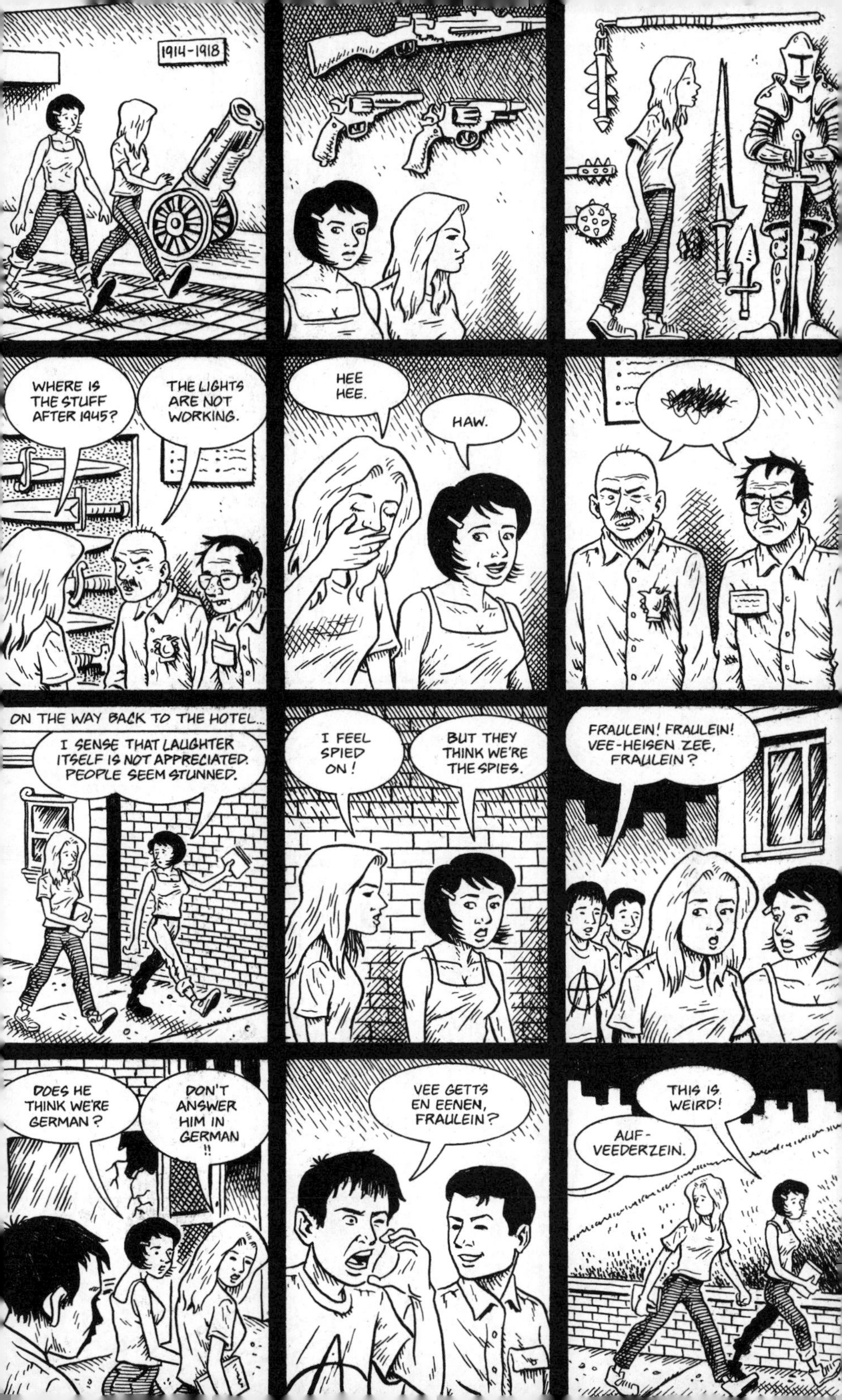
1914-1918
WHERE IS THE STUFF AFTER 1945?
THE LIGHTS ARE NOT WORKING.
HEE HEE.
HAW.
ON THE WAY BACK TO THE HOTEL...
I SENSE THAT LAUGHTER ITSELF IS NOT APPRECIATED. PEOPLE SEEM STUNNED.
I FEEL SPIED ON!
BUT THEY THINK WE'RE THE SPIES.
FRAULEIN! FRAULEIN! VEE-HEISEN ZEE, FRAULEIN?
DOES HE THINK WE'RE GERMAN?
DON'T ANSWER HIM IN GERMAN!!
VEE GETTS EN EENEN, FRAULEIN?
THIS IS WEIRD!
AUF-VEEDERZEIN.

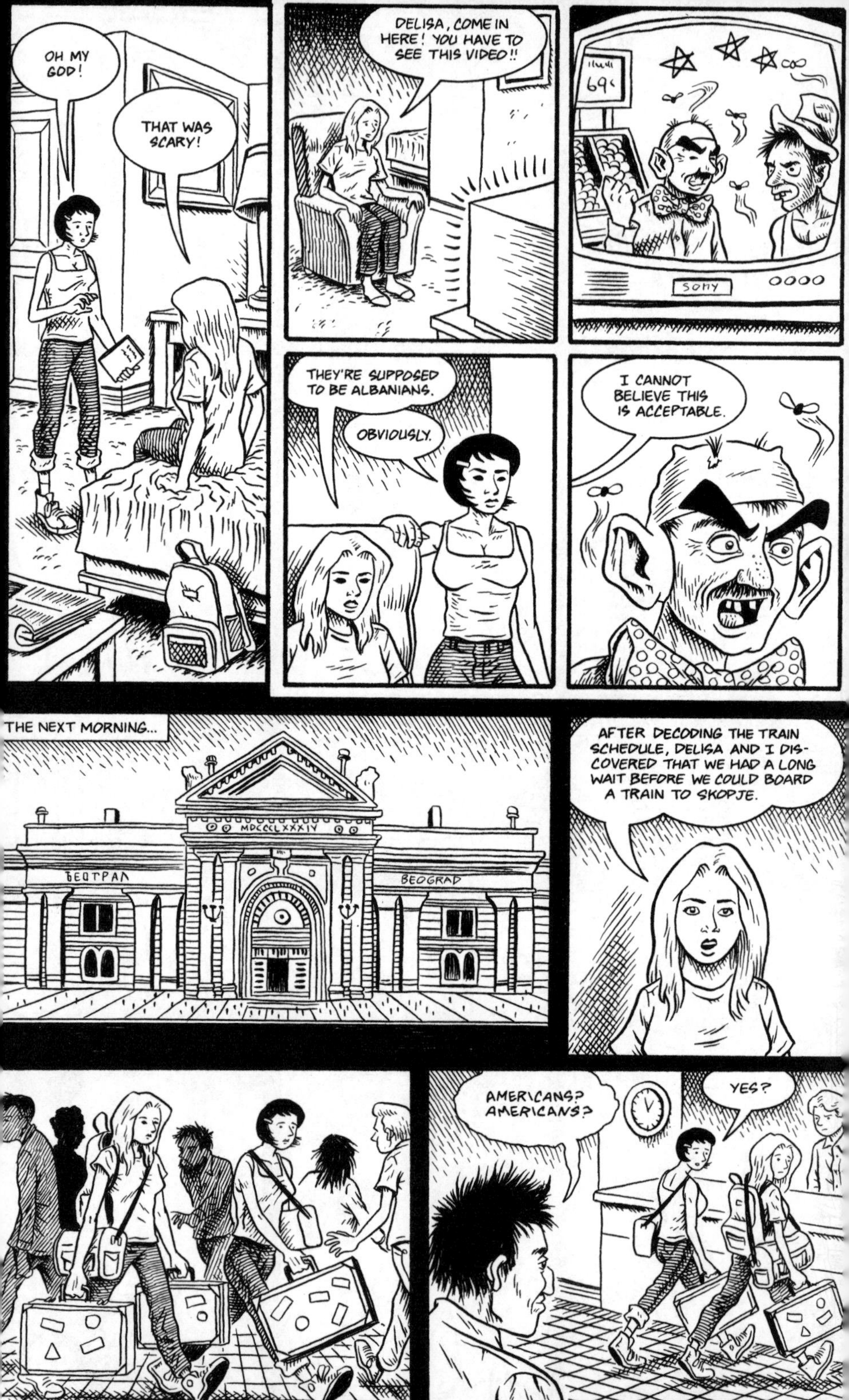
OH MY GOD!
THAT WAS SCARY!
DELISA, COME IN HERE! YOU HAVE TO SEE THIS VIDEO!!
69¢
SONY
THEY'RE SUPPOSED TO BE ALBANIANS.
OBVIOUSLY.
I CANNOT BELIEVE THIS IS ACCEPTABLE.
THE NEXT MORNING...
MDCCCLXXXIV
БЕОГРАД
BEOGRAD
AFTER DECODING THE TRAIN SCHEDULE, DELISA AND I DISCOVERED THAT WE HAD A LONG WAIT BEFORE WE COULD BOARD A TRAIN TO SKOPJE.
AMERICANS? AMERICANS?
YES?

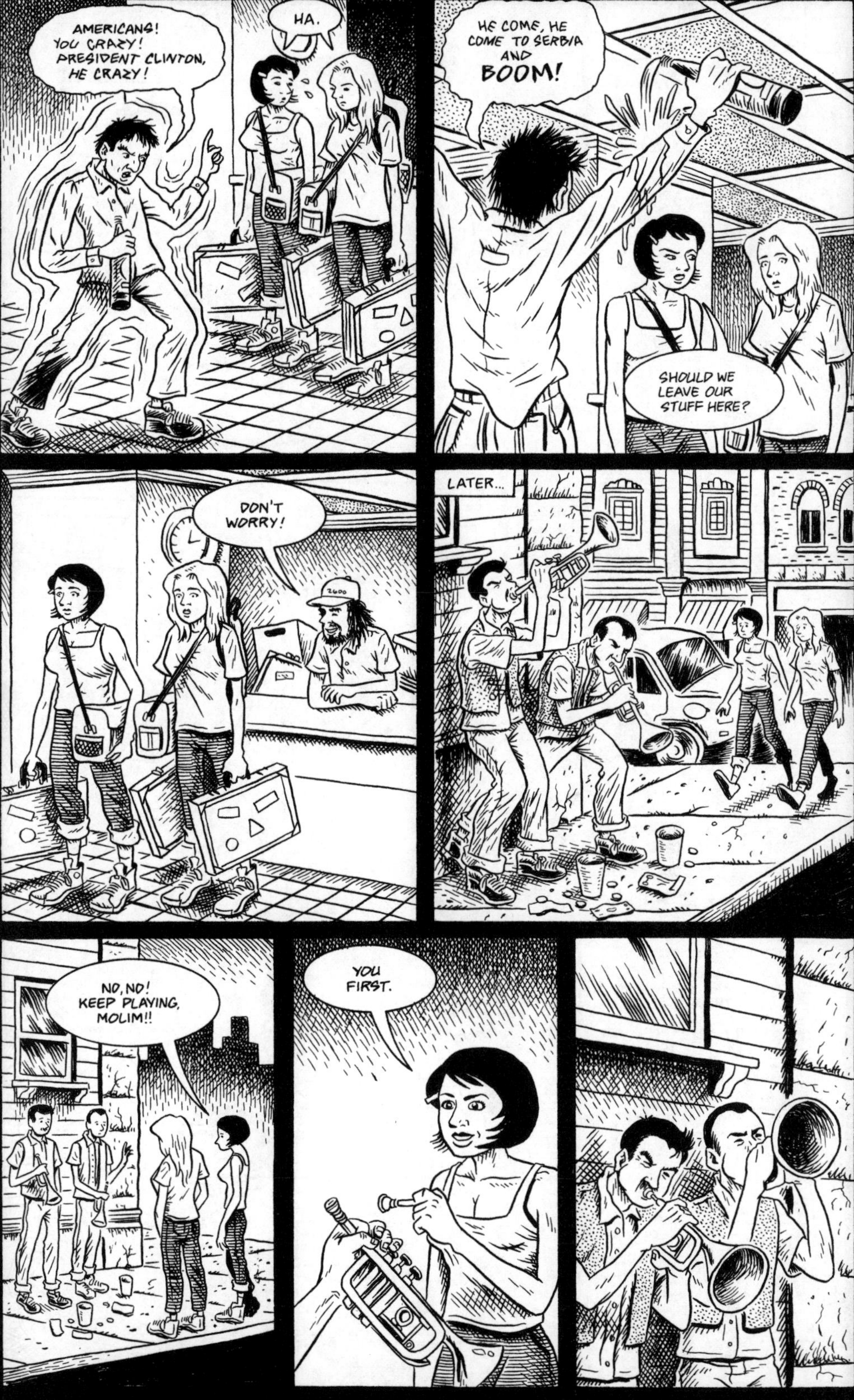
AMERICANS! YOU CRAZY! PRESIDENT CLINTON, HE CRAZY!
HA.
HE COME, HE COME TO SERBIA AND BOOM!
SHOULD WE LEAVE OUR STUFF HERE?
DON'T WORRY!
2600
LATER...
NO, NO! KEEP PLAYING, MOLIM!!
YOU FIRST.

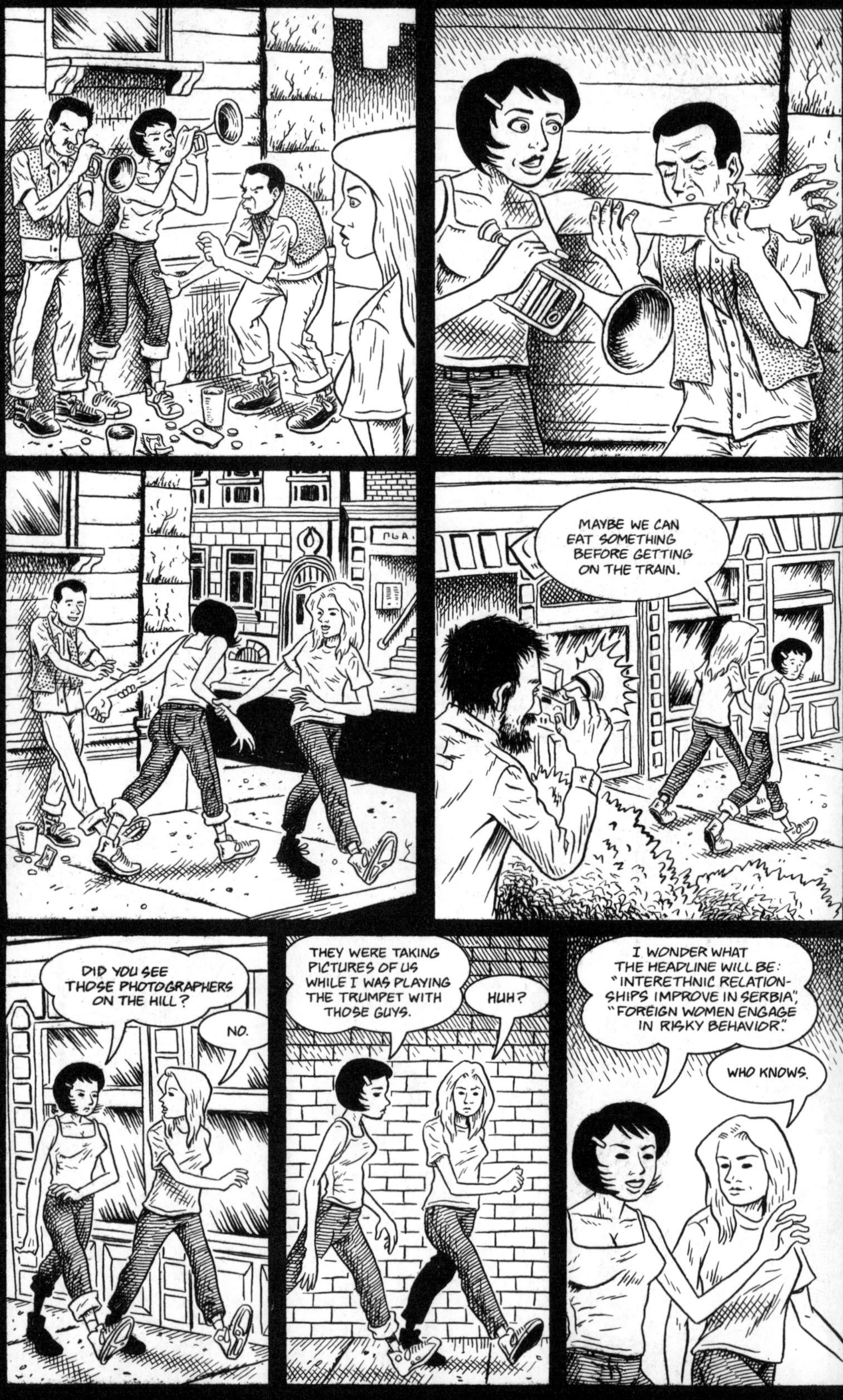

MAYBE WE CAN EAT SOMETHING BEFORE GETTING ON THE TRAIN.
DID YOU SEE THOSE PHOTOGRAPHERS ON THE HILL?
NO.
THEY WERE TAKING PICTURES OF US WHILE I WAS PLAYING THE TRUMPET WITH THOSE GUYS.
HUH?
I WONDER WHAT THE HEADLINE WILL BE: "INTERETHNIC RELATIONSHIPS IMPROVE IN SERBIA", "FOREIGN WOMEN ENGAGE IN RISKY BEHAVIOR".
WHO KNOWS.

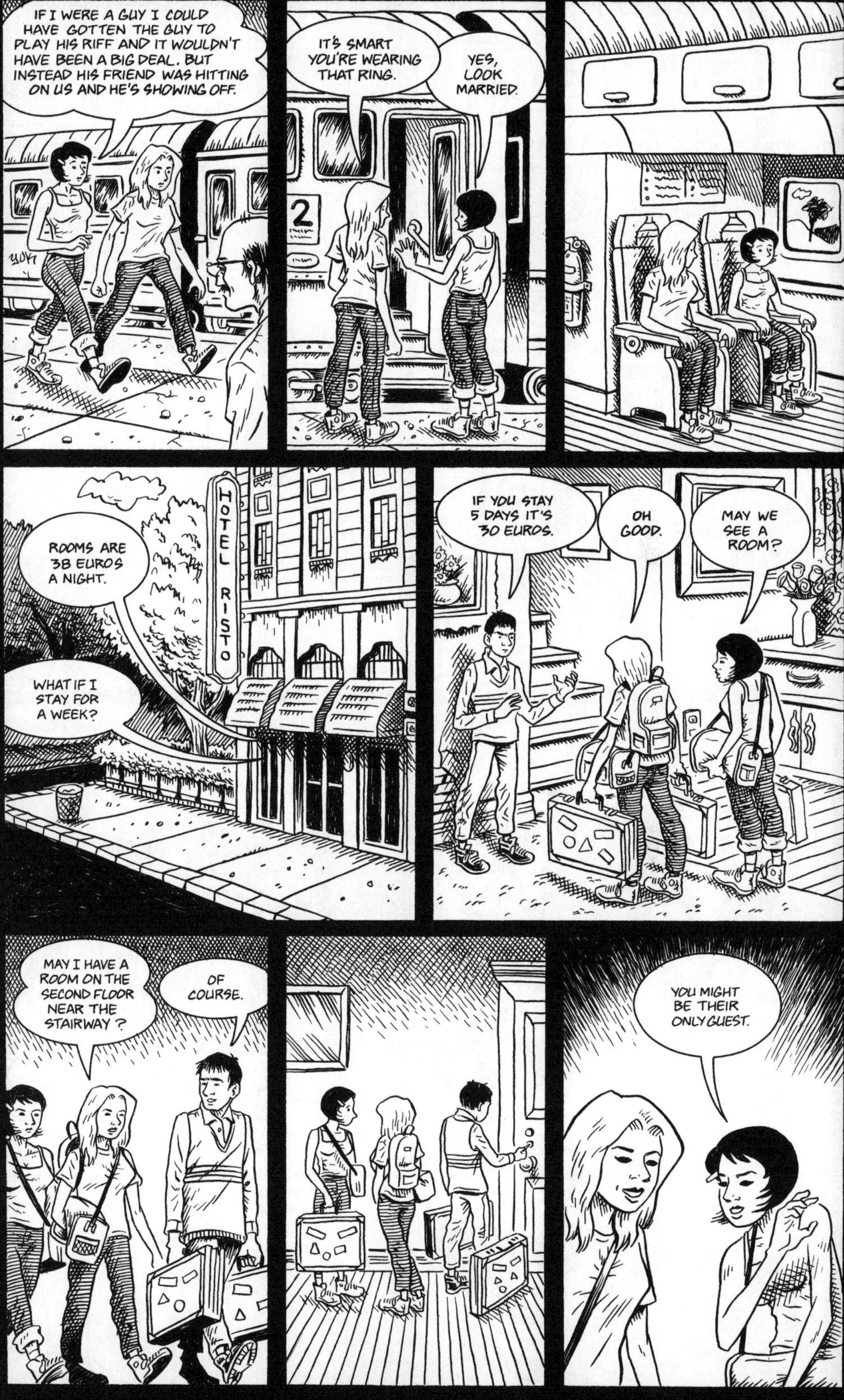
IF I WERE A GUY I COULD HAVE GOTTEN THE GUY TO PLAY HIS RIFF AND IT WOULDN'T HAVE BEEN A BIG DEAL. BUT INSTEAD HIS FRIEND WAS HITTING ON US AND HE'S SHOWING OFF.
IT'S SMART YOU'RE WEARING THAT RING.
YES, LOOK MARRIED.
2
HOTEL RISTO
ROOMS ARE 38 EUROS A NIGHT.
WHAT IF I STAY FOR A WEEK?
IF YOU STAY 5 DAYS IT'S 30 EUROS.
OH GOOD.
MAY WE SEE A ROOM?
MAY I HAVE A ROOM ON THE SECOND FLOOR NEAR THE STAIRWAY ?
OF COURSE.
YOU MIGHT BE THEIR ONLY GUEST.

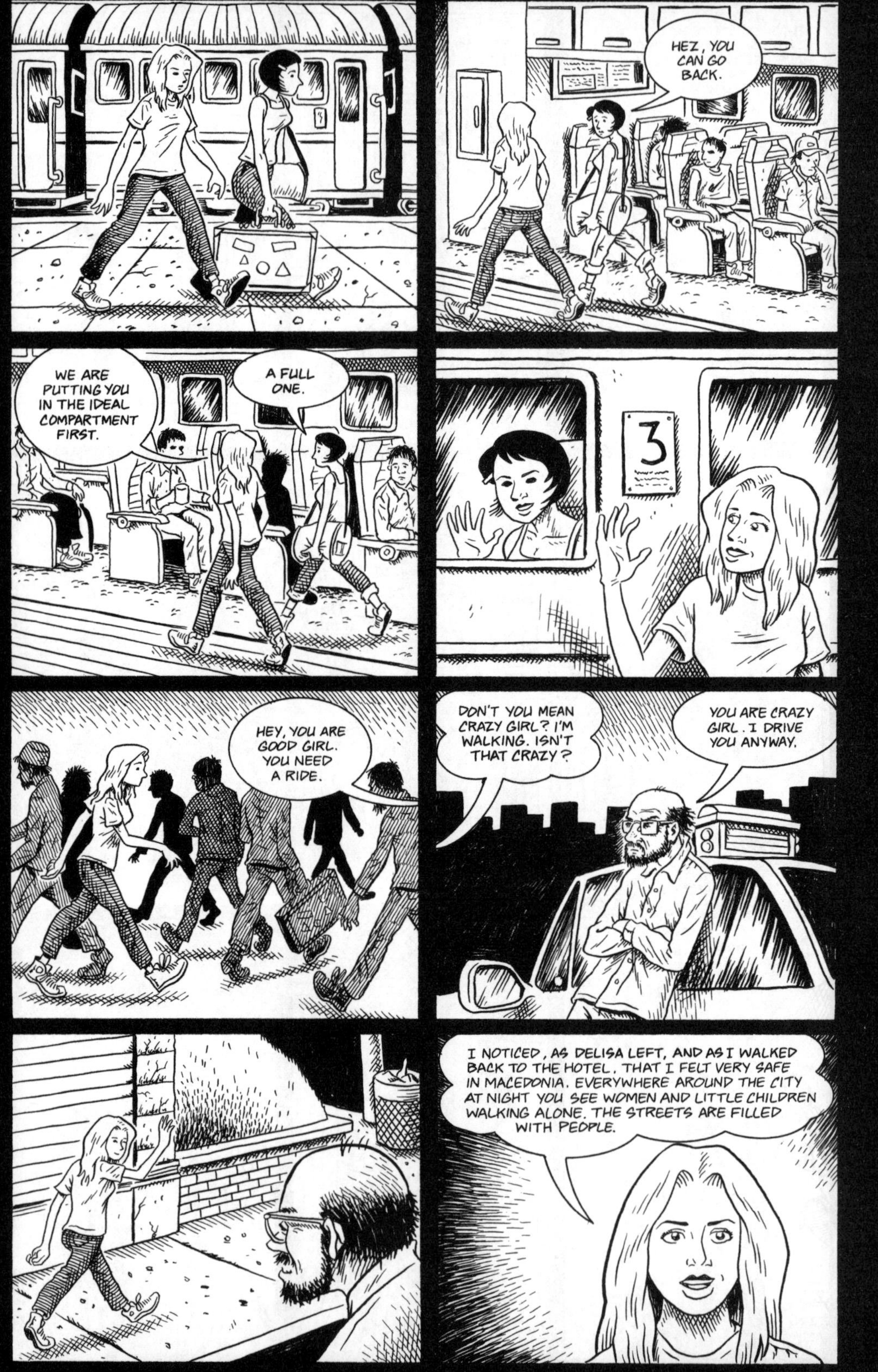
HEZ, YOU CAN GO BACK.
WE ARE PUTTING YOU IN THE IDEAL COMPARTMENT FIRST.
A FULL ONE.
3
HEY, YOU ARE GOOD GIRL. YOU NEED A RIDE.
DON'T YOU MEAN CRAZY GIRL? I'M WALKING. ISN'T THAT CRAZY?
YOU ARE CRAZY GIRL. I DRIVE YOU ANYWAY.
I NOTICED, AS DELISA LEFT, AND AS I WALKED BACK TO THE HOTEL, THAT I FELT VERY SAFE IN MACEDONIA. EVERYWHERE AROUND THE CITY AT NIGHT YOU SEE WOMEN AND LITTLE CHILDREN WALKING ALONE. THE STREETS ARE FILLED WITH PEOPLE.

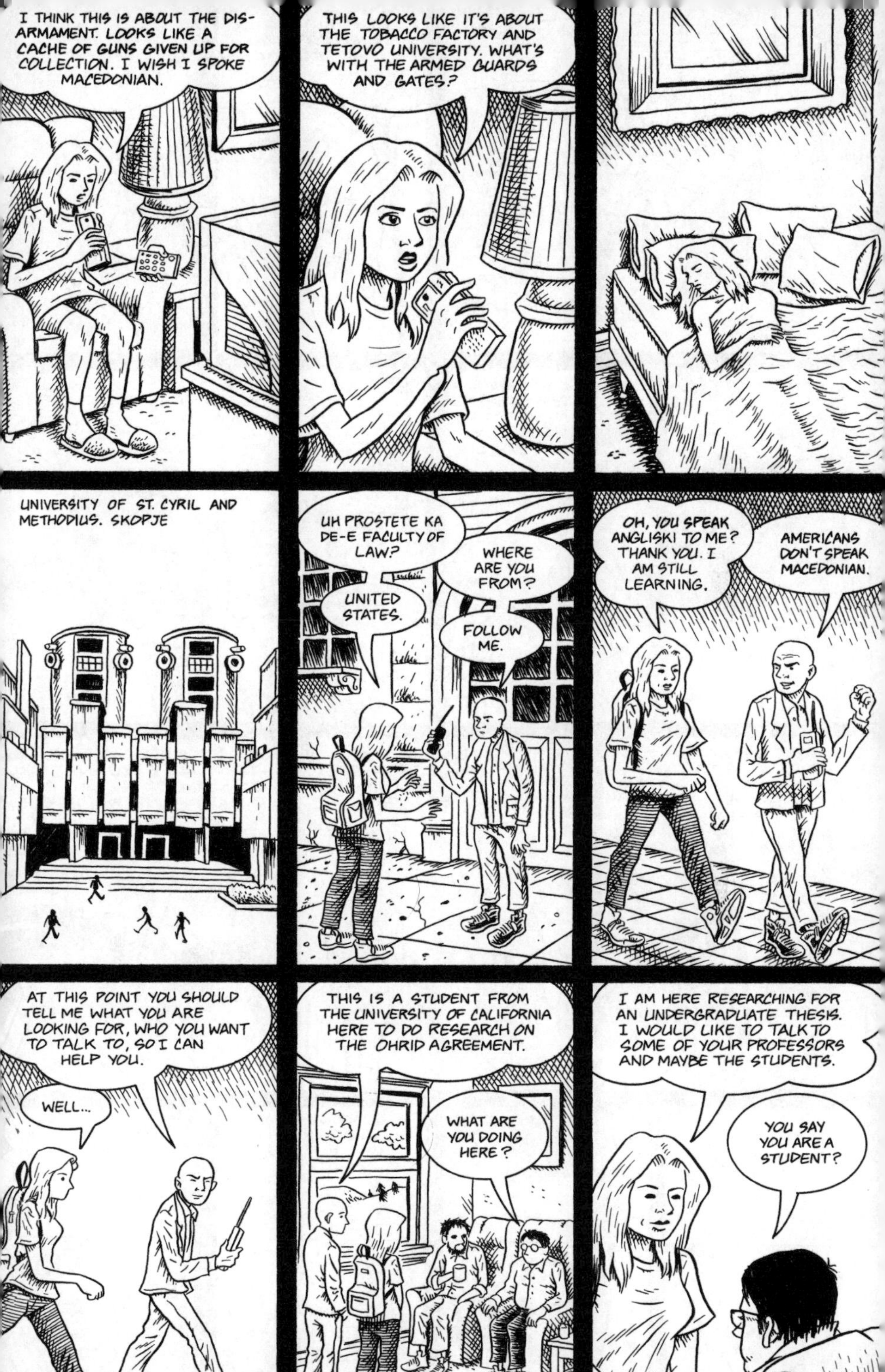

I THINK THIS IS ABOUT THE DIS-ARMAMENT. LOOKS LIKE A CACHE OF GUNS GIVEN UP FOR COLLECTION. I WISH I SPOKE MACEDONIAN.
THIS LOOKS LIKE IT'S ABOUT THE TOBACCO FACTORY AND TETOVO UNIVERSITY. WHAT'S WITH THE ARMED GUARDS AND GATES?
UNIVERSITY OF ST. CYRIL AND METHODIUS. SKOPJE
UH PROSTETE KA DE-E FACULTY OF LAW?
WHERE ARE YOU FROM?
UNITED STATES.
FOLLOW ME.
OH, YOU SPEAK ANGLISKI TO ME? THANK YOU. I AM STILL LEARNING.
AMERICANS DON'T SPEAK MACEDONIAN.
AT THIS POINT YOU SHOULD TELL ME WHAT YOU ARE LOOKING FOR, WHO YOU WANT TO TALK TO, SO I CAN HELP YOU.
WELL...
THIS IS A STUDENT FROM THE UNIVERSITY OF CALIFORNIA HERE TO DO RESEARCH ON THE OHRID AGREEMENT.
WHAT ARE YOU DOING HERE?
I AM HERE RESEARCHING FOR AN UNDERGRADUATE THESIS. I WOULD LIKE TO TALK TO SOME OF YOUR PROFESSORS AND MAYBE THE STUDENTS.
YOU SAY YOU ARE A STUDENT?

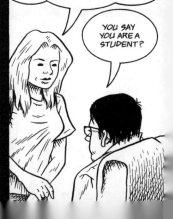

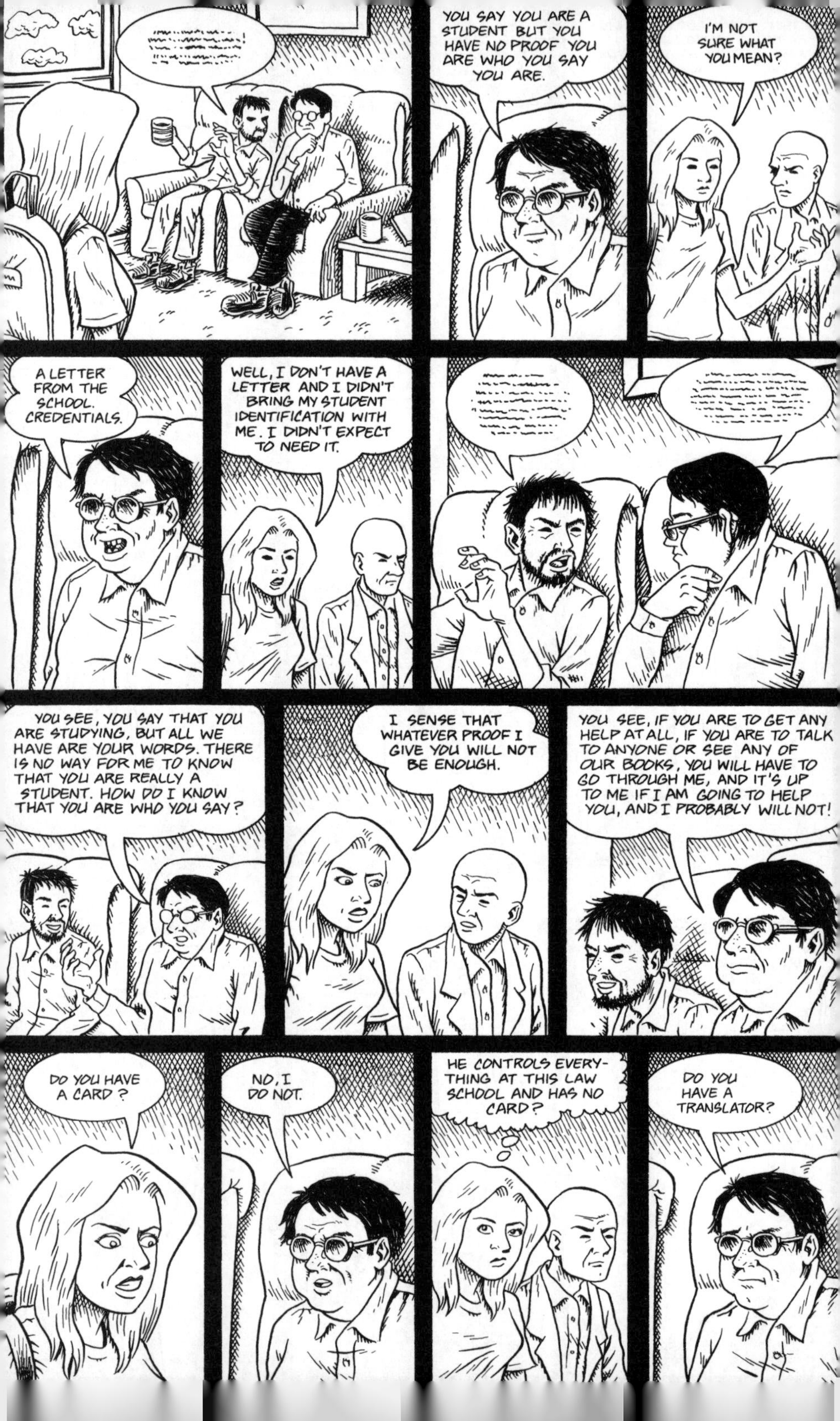
YOU SAY YOU ARE A STUDENT BUT YOU HAVE NO PROOF YOU ARE WHO YOU SAY YOU ARE.
I'M NOT SURE WHAT YOU MEAN?
A LETTER FROM THE SCHOOL. CREDENTIALS.
WELL, I DON'T HAVE A LETTER AND I DIDN'T BRING MY STUDENT IDENTIFICATION WITH ME. I DIDN'T EXPECT TO NEED IT.
YOU SEE, YOU SAY THAT YOU ARE STUDYING, BUT ALL WE HAVE ARE YOUR WORDS. THERE IS NO WAY FOR ME TO KNOW THAT YOU ARE REALLY A STUDENT. HOW DO I KNOW THAT YOU ARE WHO YOU SAY?
I SENSE THAT WHATEVER PROOF I GIVE YOU WILL NOT BE ENOUGH.
YOU SEE, IF YOU ARE TO GET ANY HELP AT ALL, IF YOU ARE TO TALK TO ANYONE OR SEE ANY OF OUR BOOKS, YOU WILL HAVE TO GO THROUGH ME, AND IT'S UP TO ME IF I AM GOING TO HELP YOU, AND I PROBABLY WILL NOT!
DO YOU HAVE A CARD?
NO, I DO NOT.
HE CONTROLS EVERYTHING AT THIS LAW SCHOOL AND HAS NO CARD?
DO YOU HAVE A TRANSLATOR?

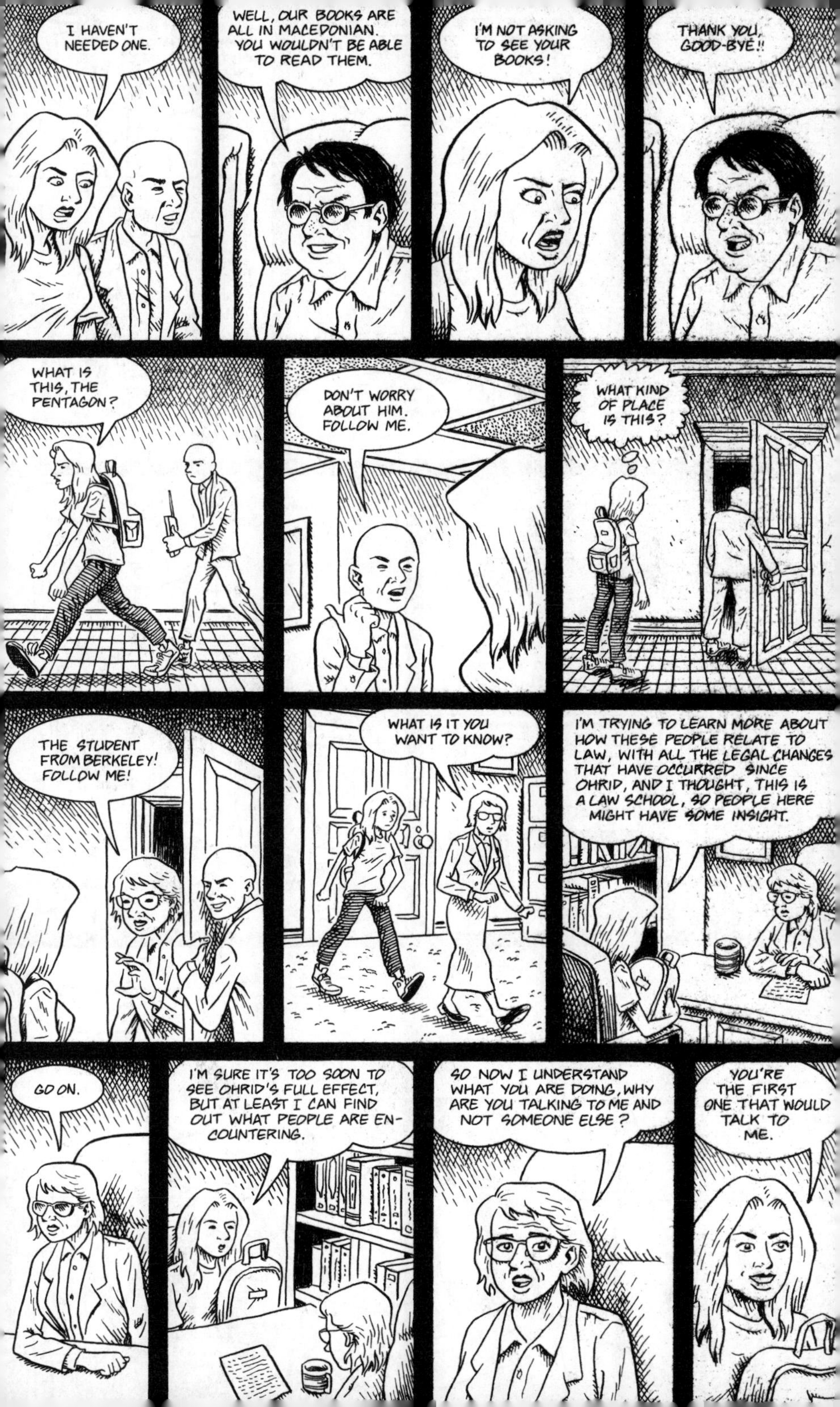
I HAVEN'T NEEDED ONE.
WELL, OUR BOOKS ARE ALL IN MACEDONIAN. YOU WOULDN'T BE ABLE TO READ THEM.
I'M NOT ASKING TO SEE YOUR BOOKS!
THANK YOU, GOOD-BYE!!
WHAT IS THIS, THE PENTAGON?
DON'T WORRY ABOUT HIM. FOLLOW ME.
WHAT KIND OF PLACE IS THIS?
THE STUDENT FROM BERKELEY! FOLLOW ME!
WHAT IS IT YOU WANT TO KNOW?
I'M TRYING TO LEARN MORE ABOUT HOW THESE PEOPLE RELATE TO LAW, WITH ALL THE LEGAL CHANGES THAT HAVE OCCURRED SINCE OHRID, AND I THOUGHT, THIS IS A LAW SCHOOL, SO PEOPLE HERE MIGHT HAVE SOME INSIGHT.
GO ON.
I'M SURE IT'S TOO SOON TO SEE OHRID'S FULL EFFECT, BUT AT LEAST I CAN FIND OUT WHAT PEOPLE ARE EN-COUNTERING.
SO NOW I UNDERSTAND WHAT YOU ARE DOING, WHY ARE YOU TALKING TO ME AND NOT SOMEONE ELSE?
YOU'RE THE FIRST ONE THAT WOULD TALK TO ME.

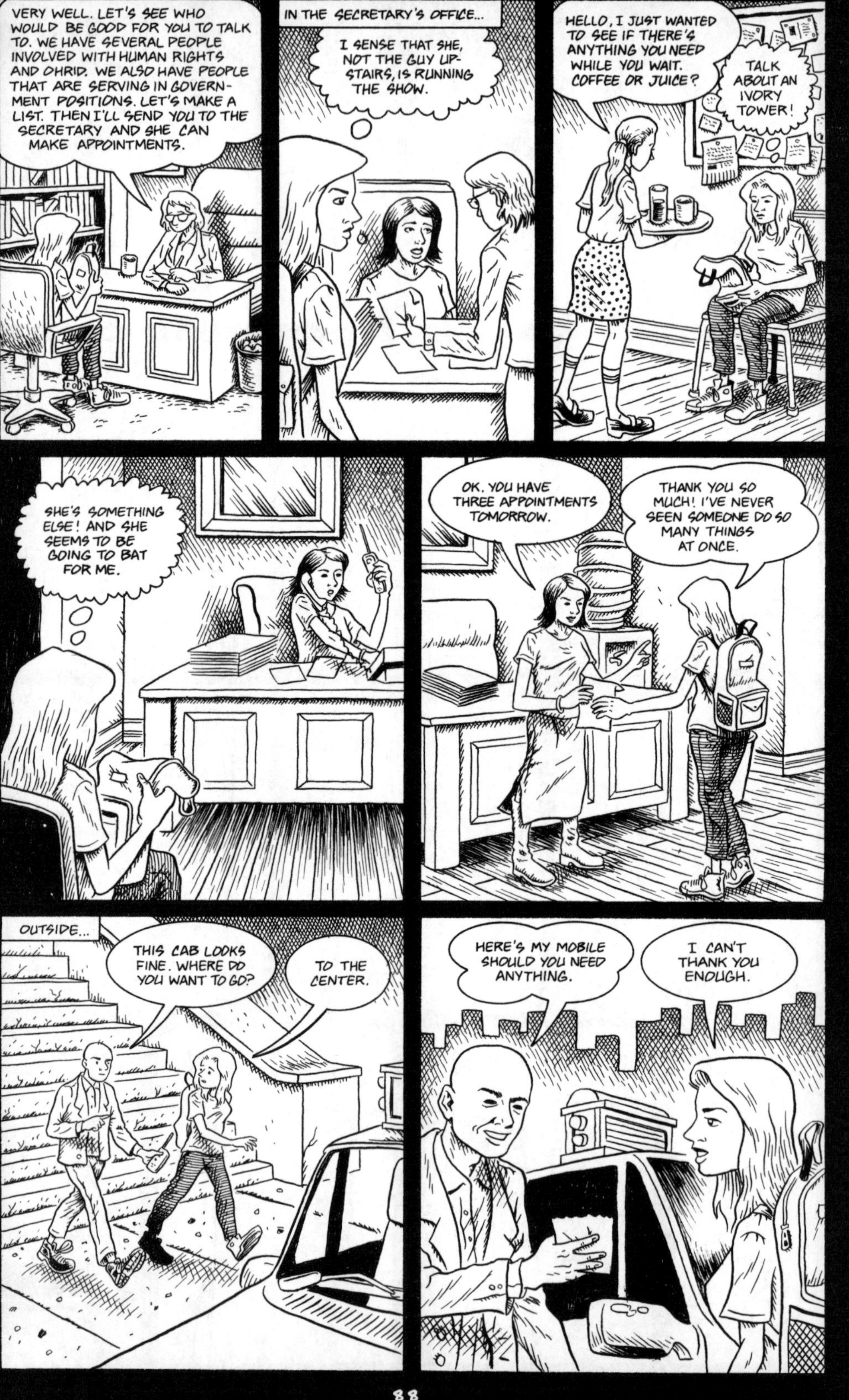

VERY WELL. LET'S SEE WHO WOULD BE GOOD FOR YOU TO TALK TO. WE HAVE SEVERAL PEOPLE INVOLVED WITH HUMAN RIGHTS AND OHRID. WE ALSO HAVE PEOPLE THAT ARE SERVING IN GOVERNMENT POSITIONS. LET'S MAKE A LIST. THEN I'LL SEND YOU TO THE SECRETARY AND SHE CAN MAKE APPOINTMENTS.
IN THE SECRETARY'S OFFICE...
I SENSE THAT SHE, NOT THE GUY UPSTAIRS, IS RUNNING THE SHOW.
HELLO, I JUST WANTED TO SEE IF THERE'S ANYTHING YOU NEED WHILE YOU WAIT. COFFEE OR JUICE?
TALK ABOUT AN IVORY TOWER!
SHE'S SOMETHING ELSE! AND SHE SEEMS TO BE GOING TO BAT FOR ME.
OK. YOU HAVE THREE APPOINTMENTS TOMORROW.
THANK YOU SO MUCH! I'VE NEVER SEEN SOMEONE DO SO MANY THINGS AT ONCE.
OUTSIDE...
THIS CAB LOOKS FINE. WHERE DO YOU WANT TO GO?
TO THE CENTER.
HERE'S MY MOBILE SHOULD YOU NEED ANYTHING.
I CAN'T THANK YOU ENOUGH.

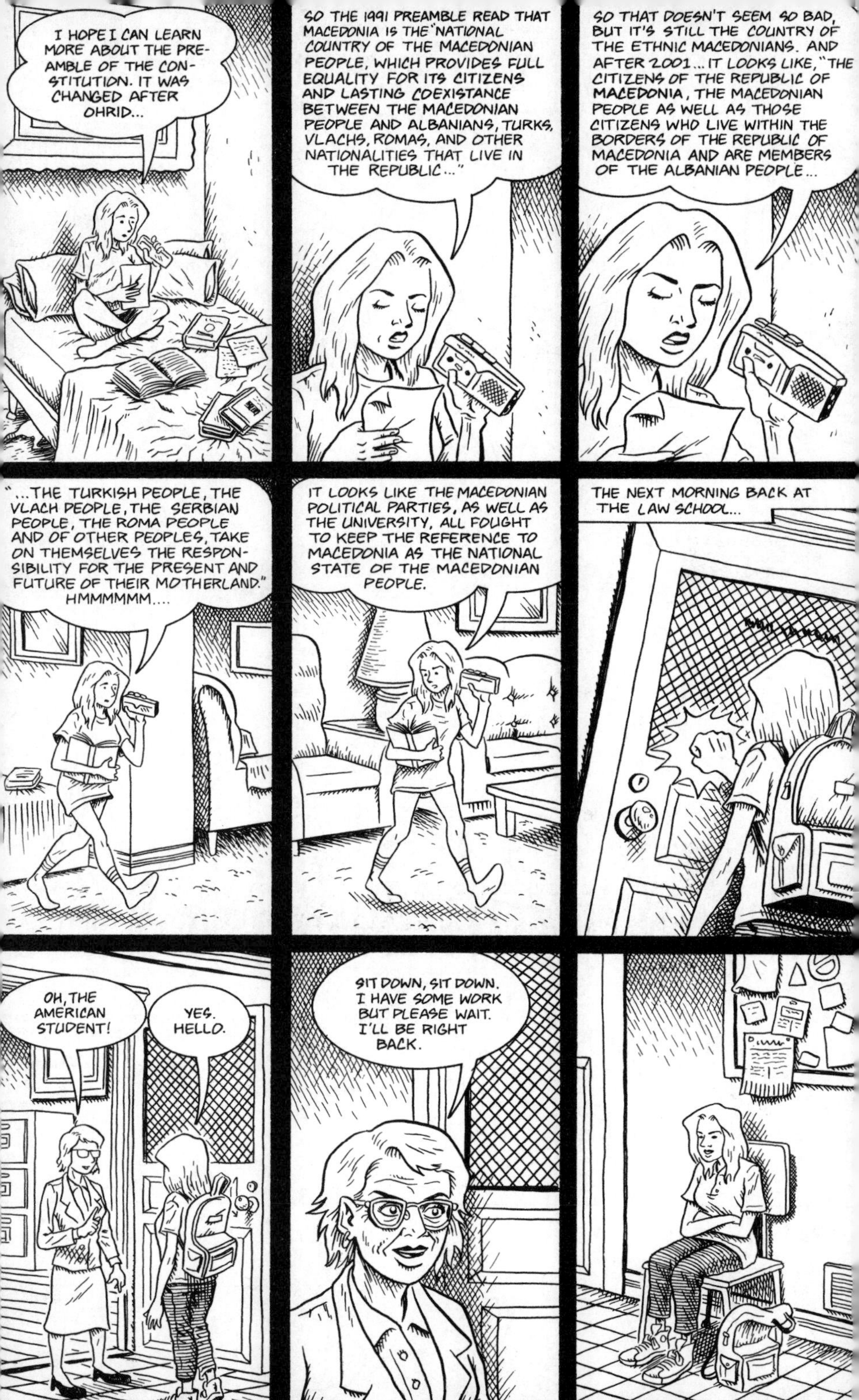
I HOPE I CAN LEARN MORE ABOUT THE PREAMBLE OF THE CONSTITUTION. IT WAS CHANGED AFTER OHRID...
SO THE 1991 PREAMBLE READ THAT MACEDONIA IS THE "NATIONAL COUNTRY OF THE MACEDONIAN PEOPLE, WHICH PROVIDES FULL EQUALITY FOR ITS CITIZENS AND LASTING COEXISTANCE BETWEEN THE MACEDONIAN PEOPLE AND ALBANIANS, TURKS, VLACHS, ROMAS, AND OTHER NATIONALITIES THAT LIVE IN THE REPUBLIC..."
SO THAT DOESN'T SEEM SO BAD, BUT IT'S STILL THE COUNTRY OF THE ETHNIC MACEDONIANS. AND AFTER 2001... IT LOOKS LIKE, "THE CITIZENS OF THE REPUBLIC OF MACEDONIA, THE MACEDONIAN PEOPLE AS WELL AS THOSE CITIZENS WHO LIVE WITHIN THE BORDERS OF THE REPUBLIC OF MACEDONIA AND ARE MEMBERS OF THE ALBANIAN PEOPLE...
"...THE TURKISH PEOPLE, THE VLACH PEOPLE, THE SERBIAN PEOPLE, THE ROMA PEOPLE AND OF OTHER PEOPLES, TAKE ON THEMSELVES THE RESPONSIBILITY FOR THE PRESENT AND FUTURE OF THEIR MOTHERLAND." HMMMMMM....
IT LOOKS LIKE THE MACEDONIAN POLITICAL PARTIES, AS WELL AS THE UNIVERSITY, ALL FOUGHT TO KEEP THE REFERENCE TO MACEDONIA AS THE NATIONAL STATE OF THE MACEDONIAN PEOPLE.
THE NEXT MORNING BACK AT THE LAW SCHOOL...
OH, THE AMERICAN STUDENT!
YES. HELLO.
SIT DOWN, SIT DOWN. I HAVE SOME WORK BUT PLEASE WAIT. I'LL BE RIGHT BACK.

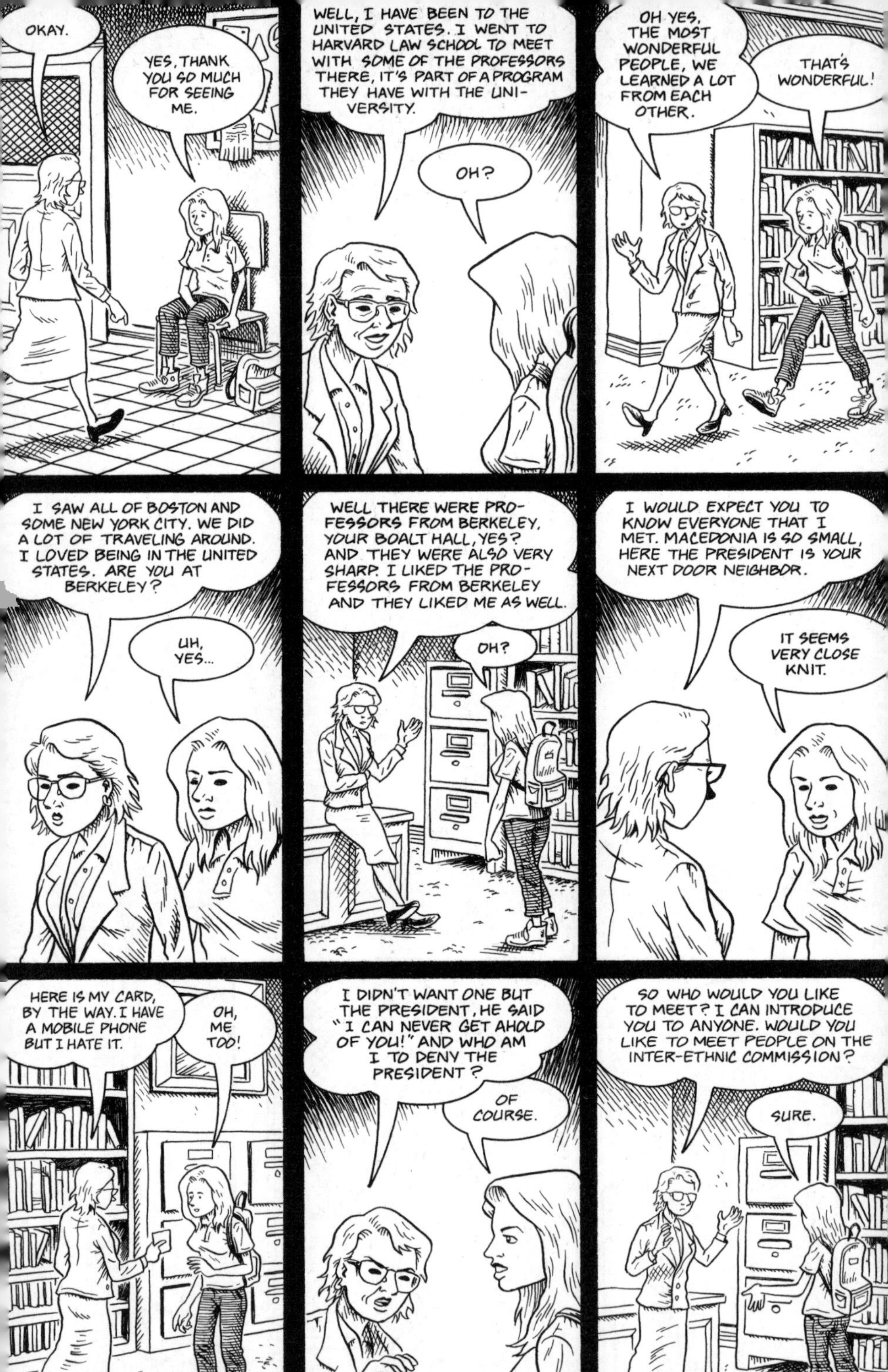
OKAY.
YES, THANK YOU SO MUCH FOR SEEING ME.
WELL, I HAVE BEEN TO THE UNITED STATES. I WENT TO HARVARD LAW SCHOOL TO MEET WITH SOME OF THE PROFESSORS THERE, IT'S PART OF A PROGRAM THEY HAVE WITH THE UNIVERSITY.
OH?
OH YES. THE MOST WONDERFUL PEOPLE, WE LEARNED A LOT FROM EACH OTHER.
THAT'S WONDERFUL!
I SAW ALL OF BOSTON AND SOME NEW YORK CITY. WE DID A LOT OF TRAVELING AROUND. I LOVED BEING IN THE UNITED STATES. ARE YOU AT BERKELEY?
UH, YES...
WELL THERE WERE PROFESSORS FROM BERKELEY, YOUR BOALT HALL, YES? AND THEY WERE ALSO VERY SHARP. I LIKED THE PROFESSORS FROM BERKELEY AND THEY LIKED ME AS WELL.
OH?
I WOULD EXPECT YOU TO KNOW EVERYONE THAT I MET. MACEDONIA IS SO SMALL, HERE THE PRESIDENT IS YOUR NEXT DOOR NEIGHBOR.
IT SEEMS VERY CLOSE KNIT.
HERE IS MY CARD, BY THE WAY. I HAVE A MOBILE PHONE BUT I HATE IT.
OH, ME TOO!
I DIDN'T WANT ONE BUT THE PRESIDENT, HE SAID "I CAN NEVER GET AHOLD OF YOU!" AND WHO AM I TO DENY THE PRESIDENT?
OF COURSE.
SO WHO WOULD YOU LIKE TO MEET? I CAN INTRODUCE YOU TO ANYONE. WOULD YOU LIKE TO MEET PEOPLE ON THE INTER-ETHNIC COMMISSION?
SURE.

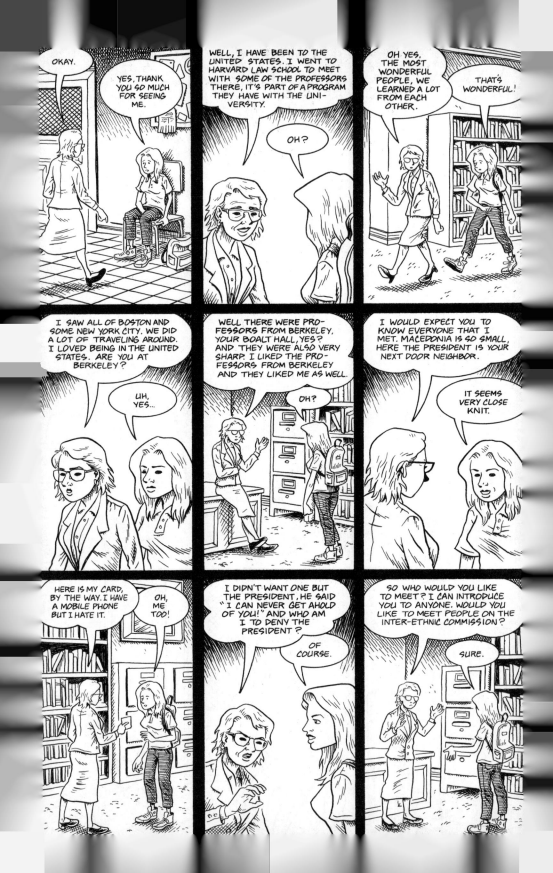

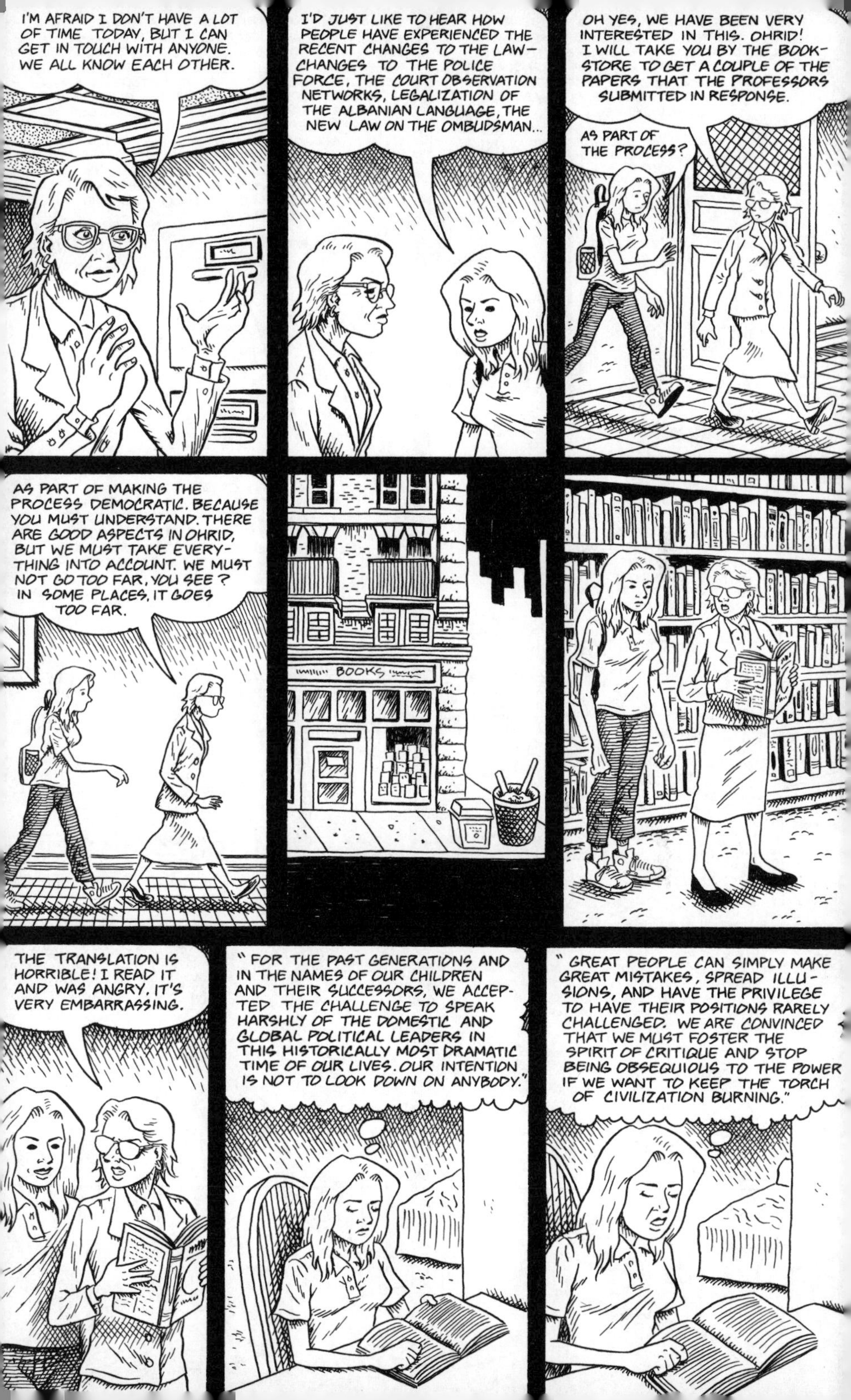
I'M AFRAID I DON'T HAVE A LOT OF TIME TODAY, BUT I CAN GET IN TOUCH WITH ANYONE. WE ALL KNOW EACH OTHER.
I'D JUST LIKE TO HEAR HOW PEOPLE HAVE EXPERIENCED THE RECENT CHANGES TO THE LAW—CHANGES TO THE POLICE FORCE, THE COURT OBSERVATION NETWORKS, LEGALIZATION OF THE ALBANIAN LANGUAGE, THE NEW LAW ON THE OMBUDSMAN...
OH YES, WE HAVE BEEN VERY INTERESTED IN THIS. OHRID! I WILL TAKE YOU BY THE BOOKSTORE TO GET A COUPLE OF THE PAPERS THAT THE PROFESSORS SUBMITTED IN RESPONSE.
AS PART OF THE PROCESS?
AS PART OF MAKING THE PROCESS DEMOCRATIC. BECAUSE YOU MUST UNDERSTAND. THERE ARE GOOD ASPECTS IN OHRID, BUT WE MUST TAKE EVERYTHING INTO ACCOUNT. WE MUST NOT GO TOO FAR, YOU SEE? IN SOME PLACES, IT GOES TOO FAR.
BOOKS
THE TRANSLATION IS HORRIBLE! I READ IT AND WAS ANGRY. IT'S VERY EMBARRASSING.
"FOR THE PAST GENERATIONS AND IN THE NAMES OF OUR CHILDREN AND THEIR SUCCESSORS, WE ACCEPTED THE CHALLENGE TO SPEAK HARSHLY OF THE DOMESTIC AND GLOBAL POLITICAL LEADERS IN THIS HISTORICALLY MOST DRAMATIC TIME OF OUR LIVES. OUR INTENTION IS NOT TO LOOK DOWN ON ANYBODY."
"GREAT PEOPLE CAN SIMPLY MAKE GREAT MISTAKES, SPREAD ILLUSIONS, AND HAVE THE PRIVILEGE TO HAVE THEIR POSITIONS RARELY CHALLENGED. WE ARE CONVINCED THAT WE MUST FOSTER THE SPIRIT OF CRITIQUE AND STOP BEING OBSEQUIOUS TO THE POWER IF WE WANT TO KEEP THE TORCH OF CIVILIZATION BURNING."

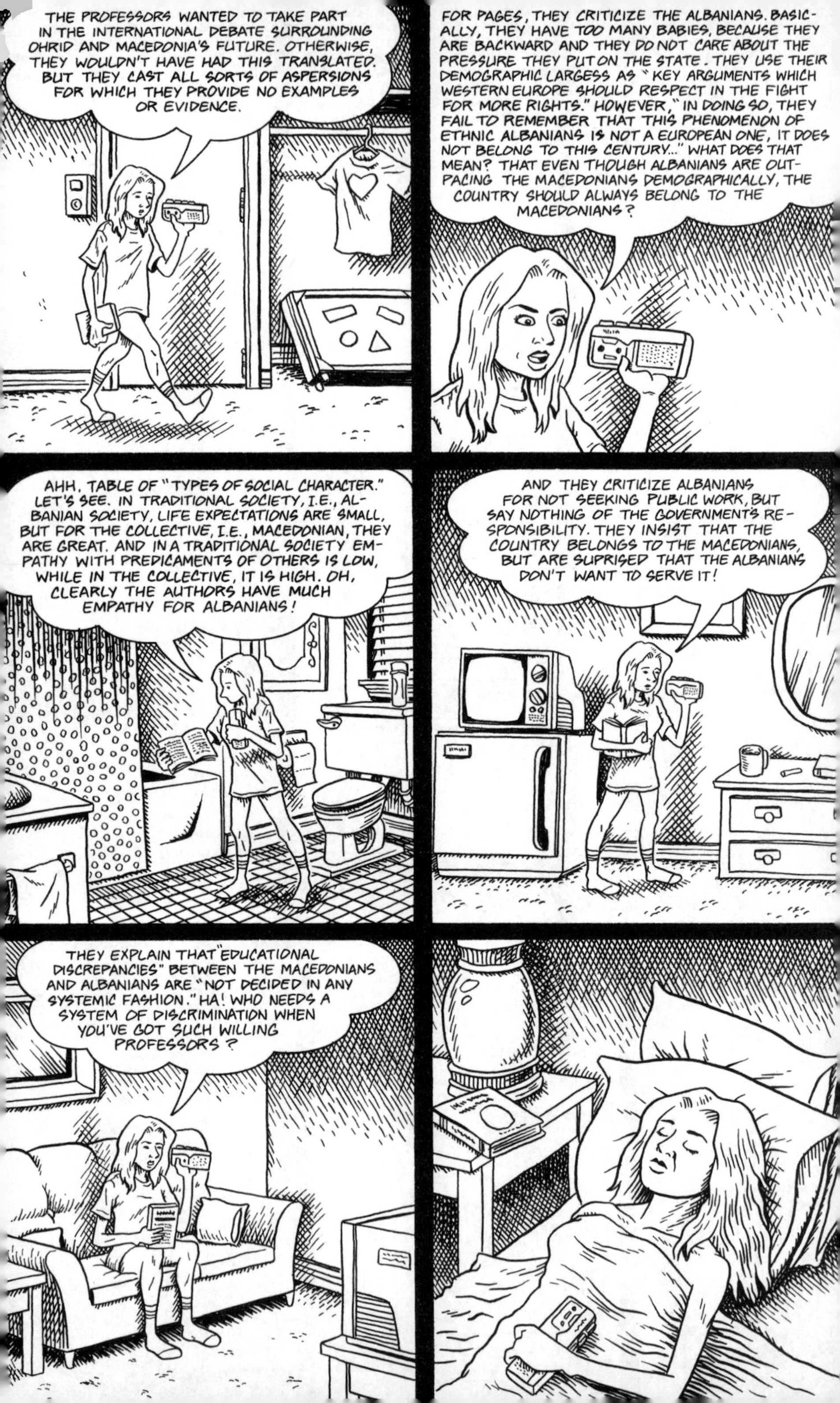
THE PROFESSORS WANTED TO TAKE PART IN THE INTERNATIONAL DEBATE SURROUNDING OHRID AND MACEDONIA'S FUTURE. OTHERWISE, THEY WOULDN'T HAVE HAD THIS TRANSLATED. BUT THEY CAST ALL SORTS OF ASPERSIONS FOR WHICH THEY PROVIDE NO EXAMPLES OR EVIDENCE.
FOR PAGES, THEY CRITICIZE THE ALBANIANS. BASICALLY, THEY HAVE TOO MANY BABIES, BECAUSE THEY ARE BACKWARD AND THEY DO NOT CARE ABOUT THE PRESSURE THEY PUT ON THE STATE. THEY USE THEIR DEMOGRAPHIC LARGESS AS "KEY ARGUMENTS WHICH WESTERN EUROPE SHOULD RESPECT IN THE FIGHT FOR MORE RIGHTS." HOWEVER, "IN DOING SO, THEY FAIL TO REMEMBER THAT THIS PHENOMENON OF ETHNIC ALBANIANS IS NOT A EUROPEAN ONE, IT DOES NOT BELONG TO THIS CENTURY..." WHAT DOES THAT MEAN? THAT EVEN THOUGH ALBANIANS ARE OUTPACING THE MACEDONIANS DEMOGRAPHICALLY, THE COUNTRY SHOULD ALWAYS BELONG TO THE MACEDONIANS?
AHH. TABLE OF "TYPES OF SOCIAL CHARACTER." LET'S SEE. IN TRADITIONAL SOCIETY, I.E., ALBANIAN SOCIETY, LIFE EXPECTATIONS ARE SMALL, BUT FOR THE COLLECTIVE, I.E., MACEDONIAN, THEY ARE GREAT. AND IN A TRADITIONAL SOCIETY EMPATHY WITH PREDICAMENTS OF OTHERS IS LOW, WHILE IN THE COLLECTIVE, IT IS HIGH. OH, CLEARLY THE AUTHORS HAVE MUCH EMPATHY FOR ALBANIANS!
AND THEY CRITICIZE ALBANIANS FOR NOT SEEKING PUBLIC WORK, BUT SAY NOTHING OF THE GOVERNMENT'S RESPONSIBILITY. THEY INSIST THAT THE COUNTRY BELONGS TO THE MACEDONIANS, BUT ARE SUPRISED THAT THE ALBANIANS DON'T WANT TO SERVE IT!
THEY EXPLAIN THAT "EDUCATIONAL DISCREPANCIES" BETWEEN THE MACEDONIANS AND ALBANIANS ARE "NOT DECIDED IN ANY SYSTEMIC FASHION." HA! WHO NEEDS A SYSTEM OF DISCRIMINATION WHEN YOU'VE GOT SUCH WILLING PROFESSORS?

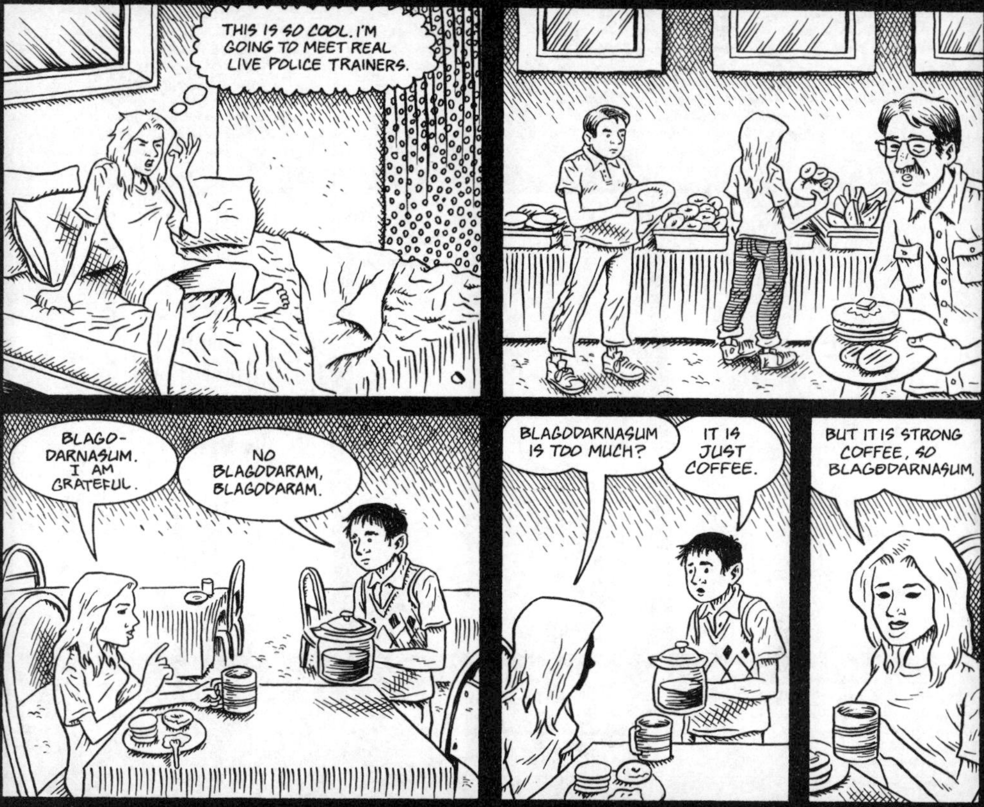
THIS IS SO COOL. I'M GOING TO MEET REAL LIVE POLICE TRAINERS.
BLAGO- DARNASUM. I AM GRATEFUL.
NO BLAGODARAM, BLAGODARAM.
BLAGODARNASUM IS TOO MUCH?
IT IS JUST COFFEE.
BUT IT IS STRONG COFFEE, SO BLAGODARNASUM.

WHEN MILOŠEVIĆ WITHDREW THE YNA IN 1991, THE MACEDONIAN GOVERNMENT FILLED THE SECURITY VACUUM BY QUICKLY ENLARGING ITS POLICE FORCE WITHOUT GIVING MUCH TRAINING OR PAY. THERE WERE HARDLY ANY ALBANIANS ON THE FORCE. THE NINETIES SAW RAMPANT POLICE BRUTALITY, ARBITRARY ARRESTS, HUMILIATION, AND TORTURE OF DETAINEES IN MACEDONIA. DETAINEES WERE ROUTINELY DENIED ACCESS TO LAWYERS AND TO MEDICAL CARE. POLICE COULD HOLD A DETAINEE UNTIL HIS WOUNDS WERE HEALED, OR UNTIL HE CONFESSED TO A CRIME SUFFICIENTLY ATROCIOUS TO EXCUSE, IN THE EYES OF THE COURT, THE ACTS OF INTERROGATORS. WHEN ILL TREATMENT OR TORTURE WAS UNDENIABLE, IT WAS THE POLICE'S WORD AGAINST THE DETAINEE'S. AND IT WASN'T JUST LIMITED TO ALBANIANS. IN 1994, A MACEDONIAN MAN REPORTED THAT POLICE SHOT HIM WHILE HE WAS AT THE POLICE STATION. POLICE ADMITTED THAT HE WAS WOUNDED IN CUSTODY, BUT SAID HE SHOT HIMSELF.

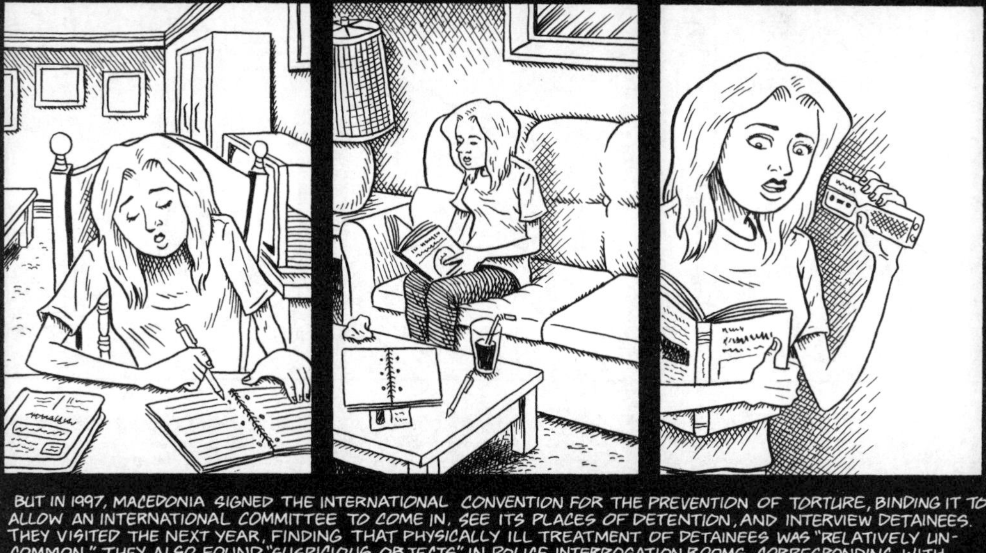

BUT IN 1997, MACEDONIA SIGNED THE INTERNATIONAL CONVENTION FOR THE PREVENTION OF TORTURE, BINDING IT TO ALLOW AN INTERNATIONAL COMMITTEE TO COME IN, SEE ITS PLACES OF DETENTION, AND INTERVIEW DETAINEES. THEY VISITED THE NEXT YEAR, FINDING THAT PHYSICALLY ILL TREATMENT OF DETAINEES WAS "RELATIVELY UNCOMMON." THEY ALSO FOUND "SUSPICIOUS OBJECTS" IN POLICE INTERROGATION ROOMS, CORRESPONDING WITH ACCOUNTS OF BEATINGS — A BASEBALL BAT, A METAL ROD. SOME POLICE STATIONS HAD A DOCTOR OR NURSE FOR POLICE AND CLAIMED THAT THESE WOULD ASSIST DETAINEES IF NECESSARY, BUT THE CPT FOUND FEW RECORDS OF ANY MEDICAL CARE AT ALL.

THE GOVERNMENT RESPONDED THAT MACEDONIAN LAW DID NOT GRANT THE RIGHT TO A DOCTOR FOR ARRESTED PERSONS, BUT THAT THE GOVERNMENT PROVIDED MEDICAL CARE ANYWAY. BUT IT SEEMED ASTOUNDED THAT THE COMMITTEE RECOMMENDED DETAINEES TO RECEIVE MEDICAL CARE "OUT OF THE TIME INTENDED FOR THE INTERROGATION AND OUT OF SIGHT OF THE POLICE OFFICERS," AND THAT RESULTS SHOULD BE FORMALLY RECORDED BUT IT PROMISED TO CODIFY THE REFORMS. AN ELABORATE BUREAUCRACY ATTENDED ANY COMPLAINT. THE GOVERNMENT EXPLAINED ITS PROCEDURES IN 2001: "AFTER RECEIVING A COMPLAINT, A SPECIAL DEPARTMENT WITHIN THE CABINET OF THE MINISTER CONSIDERS AND DIRECTS THE COMPLAINT TO THE DIVISION OF THE MINISTRY IT RELATES TO... THEN A PROPER COMMISSION TO REVIEW THE COMPLAINT IS ESTABLISHED. THIS COMMISSION CONSIDERS THE ACCOUNTS IN THE COMPLAINT, ESTABLISHES THE TYPE OF ABUSE OF POLICE POWER AND THEN FORMS A CHECK TEAM."

"THIS TEAM PREPARES A PLAN RELATIVE TO THE SPECIFIC TASKS AND METHODS TO BE APPLIED IN THE CHECK (FOR EXAMPLE, FOR COMPETENT DEPARTMENTS WITHIN THE MINISTRY TO VERIFY THE AUTHENTICITY OF THE PHOTO DOCUMENTATION). FULL CHECK OF THE ENTIRE CASE IS CONDUCTED, STARTING WITH THE CHECK OF THE DAILY REGISTRATION BOOK AT THE POLICE STATION... AFTER THIS, TALKS ARE MADE WITH THE IMMEDIATE SUPERIOR AND OTHER POLICE OFFICERS THAT WERE PRESENT OR TOOK PART IN THE CASE. AFTERWARDS, A FULL ANALYSIS OF THE POLICE DOCUMENTATION IS CONDUCTED... DEPENDING ON WHAT WAS ESTABLISHED, THE TEAM MAKES PROPOSALS ON MEASURES TO BE UNDERTAKEN.

AFTER THE GOSTIVAR PROTEST BEATINGS, THE SOBRANIE DID CREATE A COMMISSION TO INVESTIGATE POLICE MISCONDUCT. BUT THE REPORT WAS 2 PAGES! AFTER IT WAS REPORTED THAT POLICE HANDCUFFED DEMONSTRATORS, BEAT THEM WITH TRUNCHEONS! A 2-PAGE REPORT! IT DIDN'T EVEN IDENTIFY THE ABUSERS! THE ARMED HOSTILITIES JUST MADE IT WORSE. POLICE BECAME COMBATANTS. THE FEW ETHNIC ALBANIAN OFFICERS WHO WERE ON THE FORCE NOW LEFT, CITING FEARS FOR THEIR SAFETY AND PRESSURE FROM THEIR COMMUNITIES.

THEY CREATED A RAPID-REACTION UNIT, ALLOWING THE MINISTER OF INTERIOR, LJUBE BOSKOVSKI, TO COMPOSE IT. NOW, BOSKOVSKI IS A STAUNCH NATIONALIST, WHO OPPOSED PEACE WITH THE NLA. HE RECRUITED FROM THE RADICAL RANKS OF THE VMRO. BUT THE MINISTRY OF INTERIOR WAS CONSIDERED HIS MINISTRY JUST LIKE A MINISTRY IN MACEDONIA WAS CONSIDERED A PERSONAL EXTENSION OF AN INDIVIDUAL MINISTER. THIS WAS A TOP-DOWN SYSTEM. IF ANYONE QUESTIONED THE POLICE, IT WAS TAKEN AS A PERSONAL ATTACK ON BOSKOVSKI. SO ALL OF A SUDDEN, YOU HAVE AROUND 7,000 POLICE RESERVISTS WITH LITTLE TO NO TRAINING IN CRISIS RDLES. AND FROM THIS, HE FORMED A SECRET, RADICAL, ANTI-ALBANIAN UNIT CALLED "THE LIONS."

AT OHRID, NEGOTIATIONS ON THE POLICE WERE THE MOST DIFFICULT. ALBANIAN DELEGATES WANTED LOCAL CONTROL OF POLICE UNITS WHILE MACEDONIANS ARGUED THAT ONLY A CENTRALIZED FORCE COULD HOLD THE COUNT-

BOSKOVSKI DID HIS BEST TO DERAIL THE PEACE PROCESS. IN AUGUST, A LAND MINE KILLED 8 GOVERNMENT SOLDIERS AND BOSKOVSKI ORDERED HIS FORCES TO SEAL OFF A NEARBY ETHNIC ALBANIAN VILLAGE, LJUBOTEN. THEY SHELLED IT FOR 2 DAYS, AFTER WHICH THEY CONDUCTED A HOUSE-TO-HOUSE ATTACK. THEY KILLED 8 CIVILIANS, INCLUDING A 6-YEAR-OLD BOY AND A 60-YEAR-OLD MAN, AND BURNED AT LEAST 22 HOUSES, SHEDS, AND STORES. AS CIVILIANS FLED, POLICE BEAT AND SHOT THEM. BOSKOVSKI CLAIMED THAT THE PEOPLE KILLED WERE TERRORISTS, BUT THERE WAS NO EVIDENCE OF ANY NLA PRESENCE IN THE TOWN.

BOSKOVSKI RECRUITED FOR THE LIONS AND REWARDED THEIR VIOLENCE, EVEN DURING THE DISARMAMENT. IN 2002, THEY WERE CONSECRATED IN AN ORTHODOX CEREMONY, GIVEN MEDALLIONS THAT READ: "GOD PROTECT ME FROM EVIL AND GIVE ME THE STRENGTH TO DEFEND MY HOME, MY PEOPLE, MY MACEDONIA."

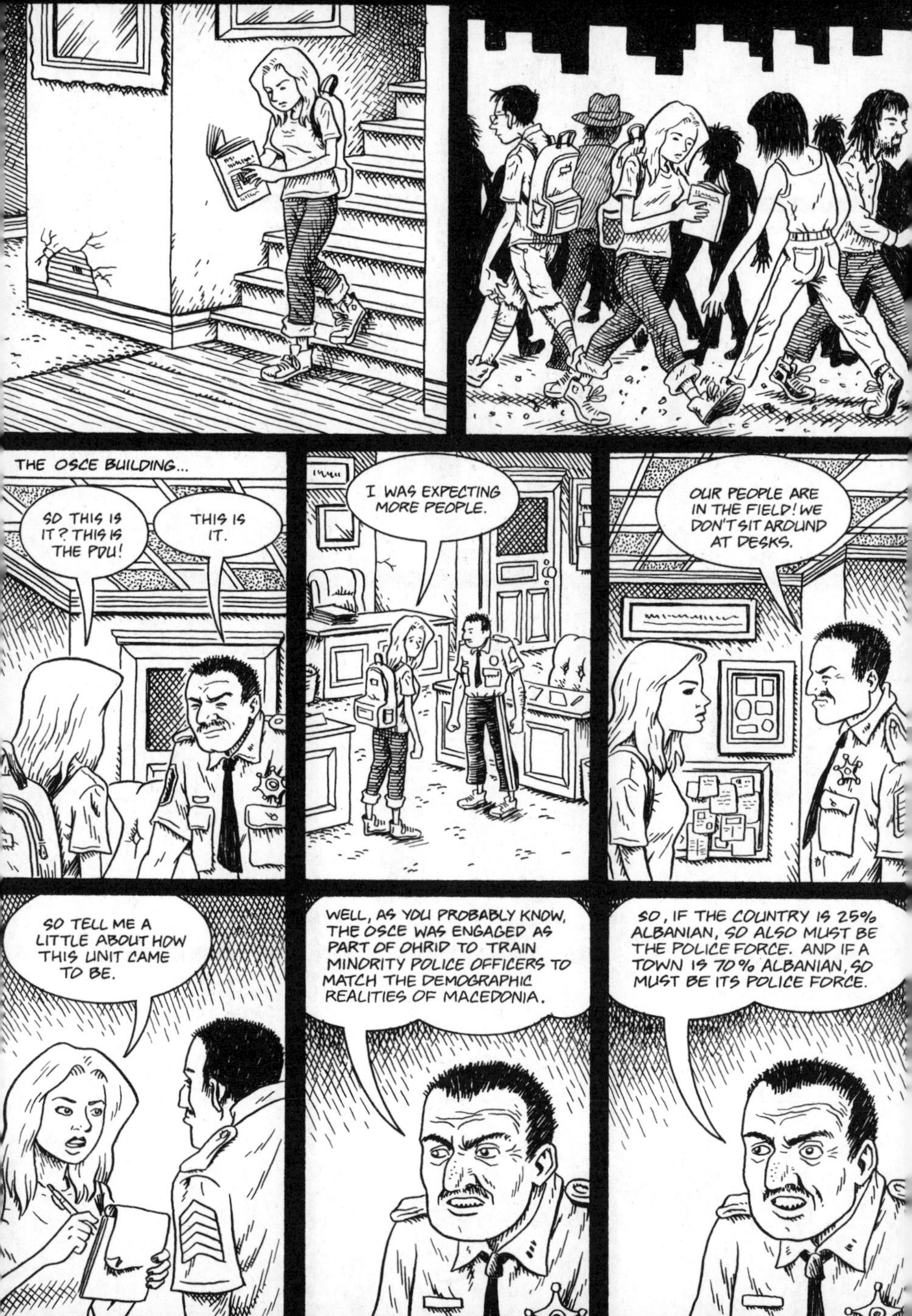
THE OSCE BUILDING...
SO THIS IS IT? THIS IS THE PDU!
THIS IS IT.
I WAS EXPECTING MORE PEOPLE.
OUR PEOPLE ARE IN THE FIELD! WE DON'T SIT AROUND AT DESKS.
SO TELL ME A LITTLE ABOUT HOW THIS UNIT CAME TO BE.
WELL, AS YOU PROBABLY KNOW, THE OSCE WAS ENGAGED AS PART OF OHRID TO TRAIN MINORITY POLICE OFFICERS TO MATCH THE DEMOGRAPHIC REALITIES OF MACEDONIA.
SO, IF THE COUNTRY IS 25% ALBANIAN, SO ALSO MUST BE THE POLICE FORCE. AND IF A TOWN IS 70% ALBANIAN, SO MUST BE ITS POLICE FORCE.

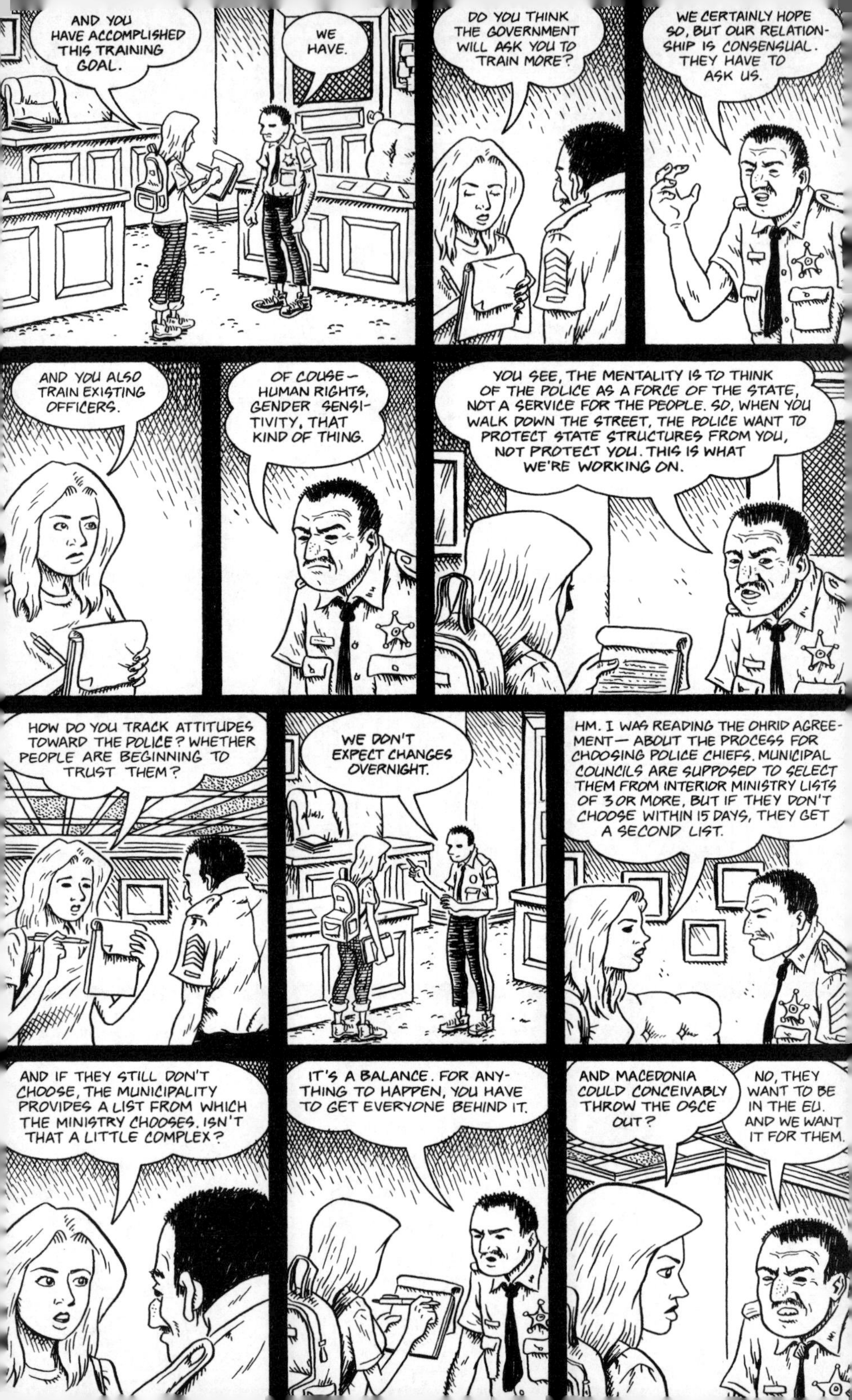
AND YOU HAVE ACCOMPLISHED THIS TRAINING GOAL.
WE HAVE.
DO YOU THINK THE GOVERNMENT WILL ASK YOU TO TRAIN MORE?
WE CERTAINLY HOPE SO, BUT OUR RELATIONSHIP IS CONSENSUAL. THEY HAVE TO ASK US.
AND YOU ALSO TRAIN EXISTING OFFICERS.
OF COUSE— HUMAN RIGHTS, GENDER SENSITIVITY, THAT KIND OF THING.
YOU SEE, THE MENTALITY IS TO THINK OF THE POLICE AS A FORCE OF THE STATE, NOT A SERVICE FOR THE PEOPLE. SO, WHEN YOU WALK DOWN THE STREET, THE POLICE WANT TO PROTECT STATE STRUCTURES FROM YOU, NOT PROTECT YOU. THIS IS WHAT WE'RE WORKING ON.
HOW DO YOU TRACK ATTITUDES TOWARD THE POLICE? WHETHER PEOPLE ARE BEGINNING TO TRUST THEM?
WE DON'T EXPECT CHANGES OVERNIGHT.
HM. I WAS READING THE OHRID AGREEMENT— ABOUT THE PROCESS FOR CHOOSING POLICE CHIEFS. MUNICIPAL COUNCILS ARE SUPPOSED TO SELECT THEM FROM INTERIOR MINISTRY LISTS OF 3 OR MORE, BUT IF THEY DON'T CHOOSE WITHIN 15 DAYS, THEY GET A SECOND LIST.
AND IF THEY STILL DON'T CHOOSE, THE MUNICIPALITY PROVIDES A LIST FROM WHICH THE MINISTRY CHOOSES. ISN'T THAT A LITTLE COMPLEX?
IT'S A BALANCE. FOR ANYTHING TO HAPPEN, YOU HAVE TO GET EVERYONE BEHIND IT.
AND MACEDONIA COULD CONCEIVABLY THROW THE OSCE OUT?
NO, THEY WANT TO BE IN THE EU. AND WE WANT IT FOR THEM.

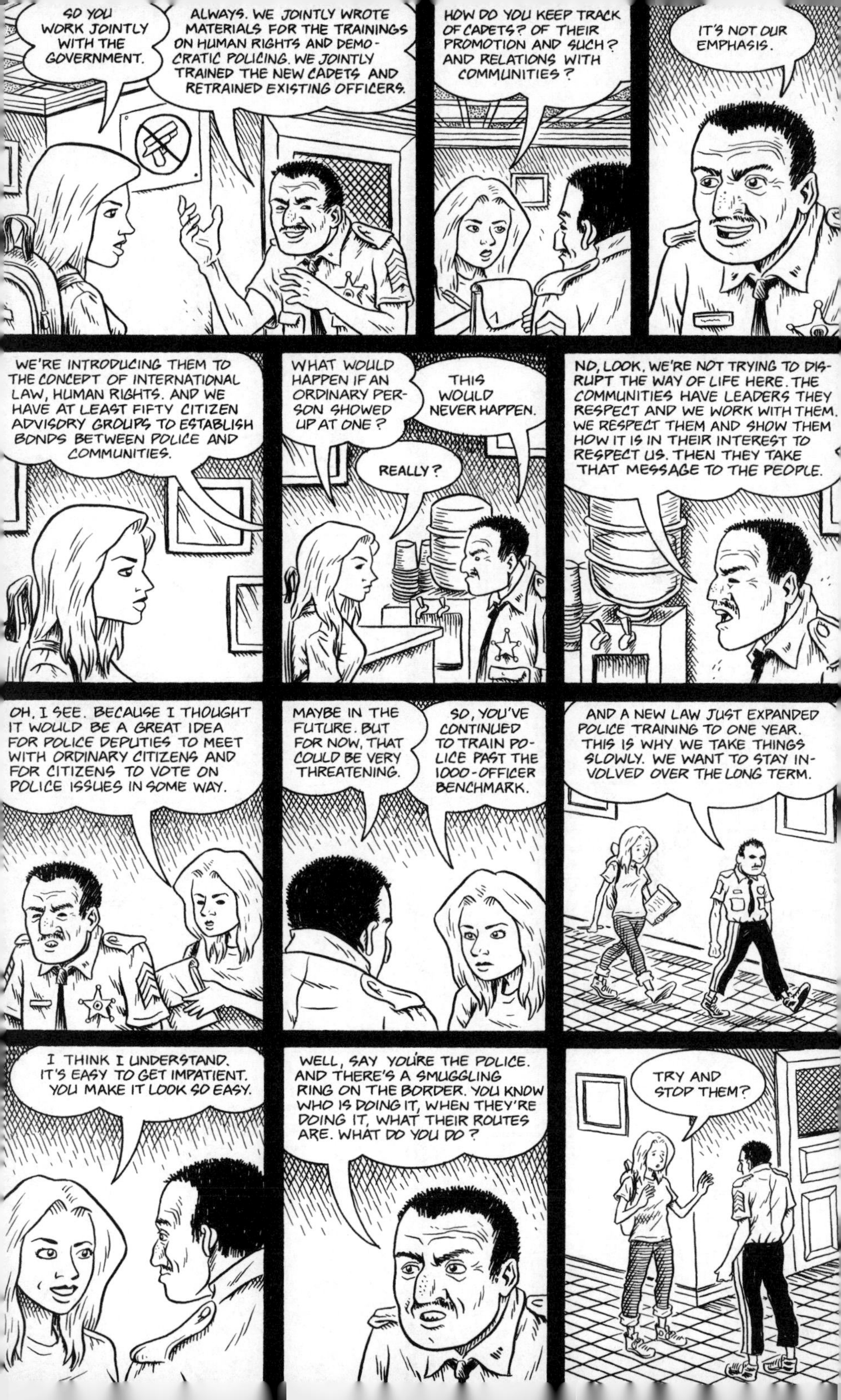
SO YOU WORK JOINTLY WITH THE GOVERNMENT.
ALWAYS. WE JOINTLY WROTE MATERIALS FOR THE TRAININGS ON HUMAN RIGHTS AND DEMO-CRATIC POLICING. WE JOINTLY TRAINED THE NEW CADETS AND RETRAINED EXISTING OFFICERS.
HOW DO YOU KEEP TRACK OF CADETS? OF THEIR PROMOTION AND SUCH? AND RELATIONS WITH COMMUNITIES?
IT'S NOT OUR EMPHASIS.
WE'RE INTRODUCING THEM TO THE CONCEPT OF INTERNATIONAL LAW, HUMAN RIGHTS. AND WE HAVE AT LEAST FIFTY CITIZEN ADVISORY GROUPS TO ESTABLISH BONDS BETWEEN POLICE AND COMMUNITIES.
WHAT WOULD HAPPEN IF AN ORDINARY PER-SON SHOWED UP AT ONE?
THIS WOULD NEVER HAPPEN.
REALLY?
NO, LOOK. WE'RE NOT TRYING TO DIS-RUPT THE WAY OF LIFE HERE. THE COMMUNITIES HAVE LEADERS THEY RESPECT AND WE WORK WITH THEM. WE RESPECT THEM AND SHOW THEM HOW IT IS IN THEIR INTEREST TO RESPECT US. THEN THEY TAKE THAT MESSAGE TO THE PEOPLE.
OH, I SEE. BECAUSE I THOUGHT IT WOULD BE A GREAT IDEA FOR POLICE DEPUTIES TO MEET WITH ORDINARY CITIZENS AND FOR CITIZENS TO VOTE ON POLICE ISSUES IN SOME WAY.
MAYBE IN THE FUTURE. BUT FOR NOW, THAT COULD BE VERY THREATENING.
SO, YOU'VE CONTINUED TO TRAIN PO-LICE PAST THE 1000-OFFICER BENCHMARK.
AND A NEW LAW JUST EXPANDED POLICE TRAINING TO ONE YEAR. THIS IS WHY WE TAKE THINGS SLOWLY. WE WANT TO STAY IN-VOLVED OVER THE LONG TERM.
I THINK I UNDERSTAND. IT'S EASY TO GET IMPATIENT. YOU MAKE IT LOOK SO EASY.
WELL, SAY YOU'RE THE POLICE. AND THERE'S A SMUGGLING RING ON THE BORDER. YOU KNOW WHO IS DOING IT, WHEN THEY'RE DOING IT, WHAT THEIR ROUTES ARE. WHAT DO YOU DO?
TRY AND STOP THEM?

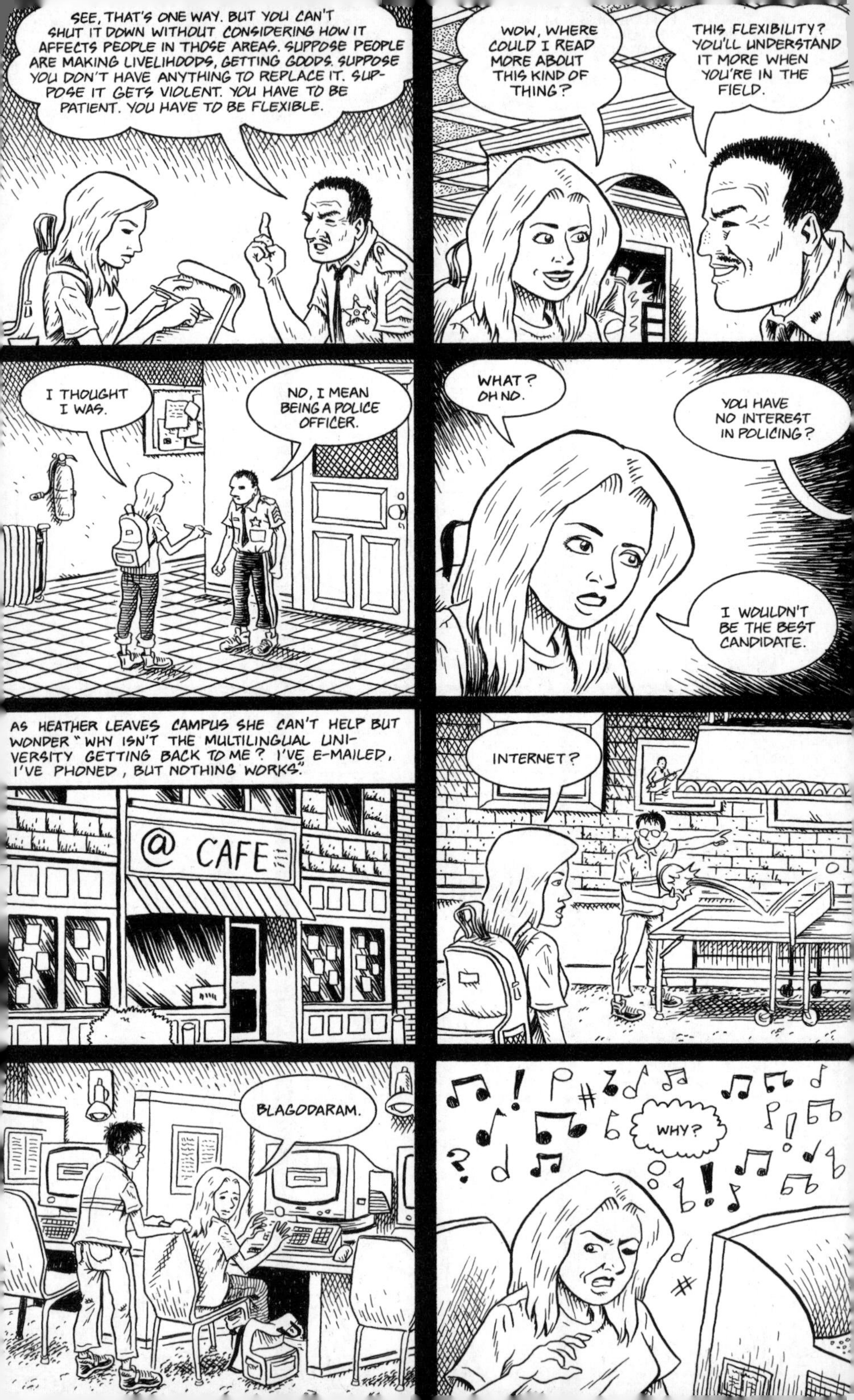
SEE, THAT'S ONE WAY. BUT YOU CAN'T SHUT IT DOWN WITHOUT CONSIDERING HOW IT AFFECTS PEOPLE IN THOSE AREAS. SUPPOSE PEOPLE ARE MAKING LIVELIHOODS, GETTING GOODS. SUPPOSE YOU DON'T HAVE ANYTHING TO REPLACE IT. SUPPOSE IT GETS VIOLENT. YOU HAVE TO BE PATIENT. YOU HAVE TO BE FLEXIBLE.
WOW, WHERE COULD I READ MORE ABOUT THIS KIND OF THING?
THIS FLEXIBILITY? YOU'LL UNDERSTAND IT MORE WHEN YOU'RE IN THE FIELD.
I THOUGHT I WAS.
NO, I MEAN BEING A POLICE OFFICER.
WHAT? OH NO.
YOU HAVE NO INTEREST IN POLICING?
I WOULDN'T BE THE BEST CANDIDATE.
AS HEATHER LEAVES CAMPUS SHE CAN'T HELP BUT WONDER "WHY ISN'T THE MULTILINGUAL UNIVERSITY GETTING BACK TO ME? I'VE E-MAILED, I'VE PHONED, BUT NOTHING WORKS."
@ CAFE
INTERNET?
BLAGODARAM.
WHY?

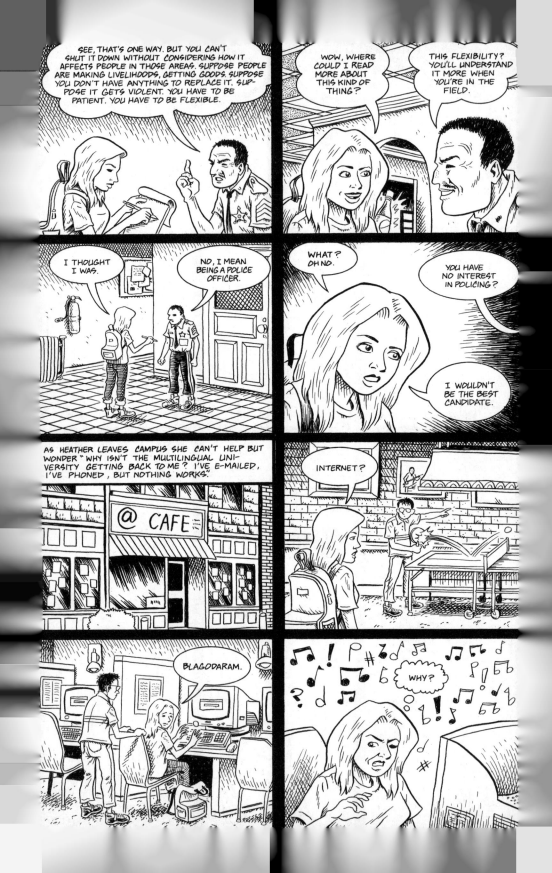

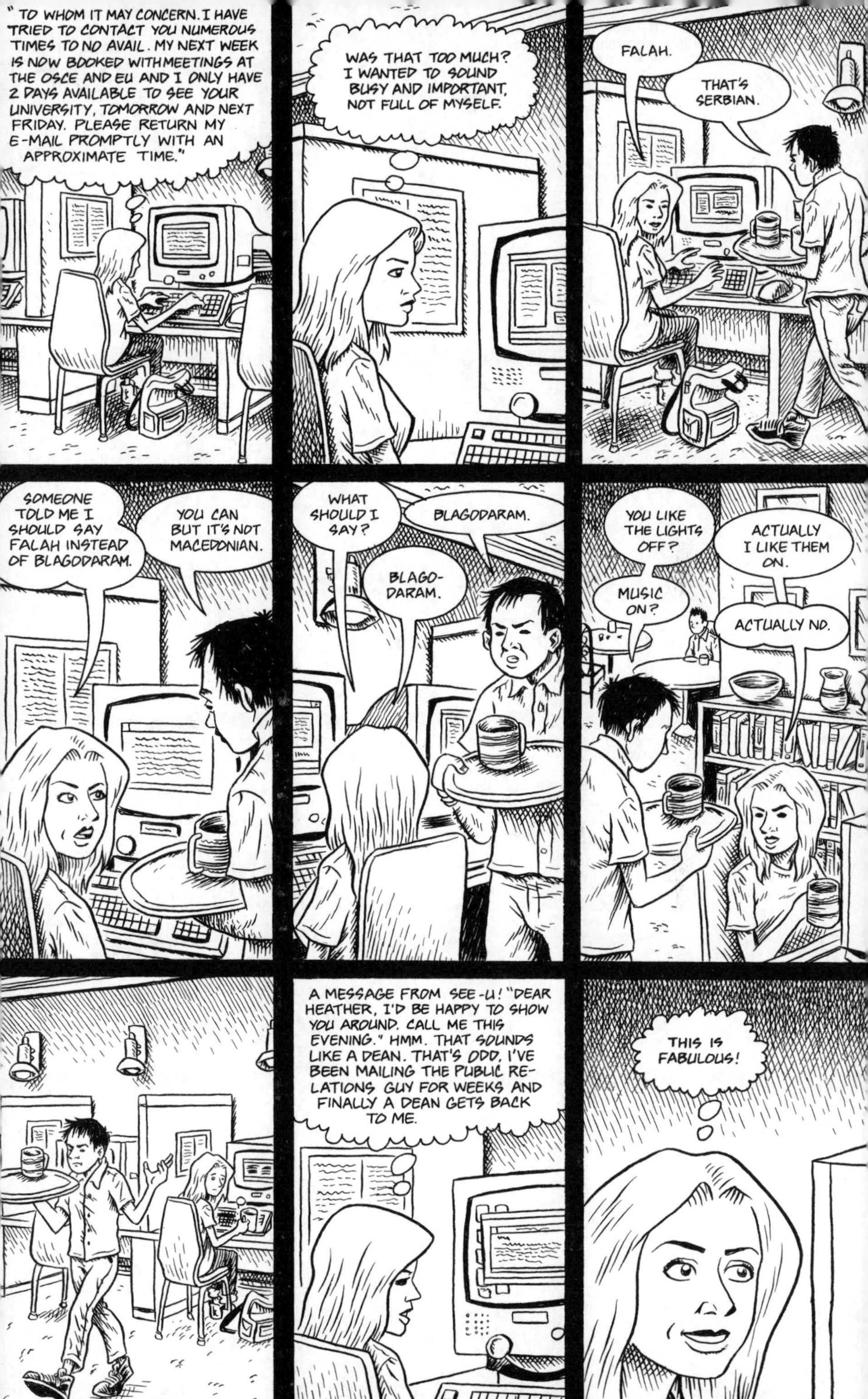
"TO WHOM IT MAY CONCERN. I HAVE TRIED TO CONTACT YOU NUMEROUS TIMES TO NO AVAIL. MY NEXT WEEK IS NOW BOOKED WITH MEETINGS AT THE OSCE AND EU AND I ONLY HAVE 2 DAYS AVAILABLE TO SEE YOUR UNIVERSITY, TOMORROW AND NEXT FRIDAY. PLEASE RETURN MY E-MAIL PROMPTLY WITH AN APPROXIMATE TIME."
WAS THAT TOO MUCH? I WANTED TO SOUND BUSY AND IMPORTANT, NOT FULL OF MYSELF.
FALAH.
THAT'S SERBIAN.
SOMEONE TOLD ME I SHOULD SAY FALAH INSTEAD OF BLAGODARAM.
YOU CAN BUT IT'S NOT MACEDONIAN.
WHAT SHOULD I SAY?
BLAGODARAM.
BLAGO-DARAM.
YOU LIKE THE LIGHTS OFF?
ACTUALLY I LIKE THEM ON.
MUSIC ON?
ACTUALLY NO.
A MESSAGE FROM SEE-U! "DEAR HEATHER, I'D BE HAPPY TO SHOW YOU AROUND. CALL ME THIS EVENING." HMM. THAT SOUNDS LIKE A DEAN. THAT'S ODD, I'VE BEEN MAILING THE PUBLIC RE-LATIONS GUY FOR WEEKS AND FINALLY A DEAN GETS BACK TO ME.
THIS IS FABULOUS!

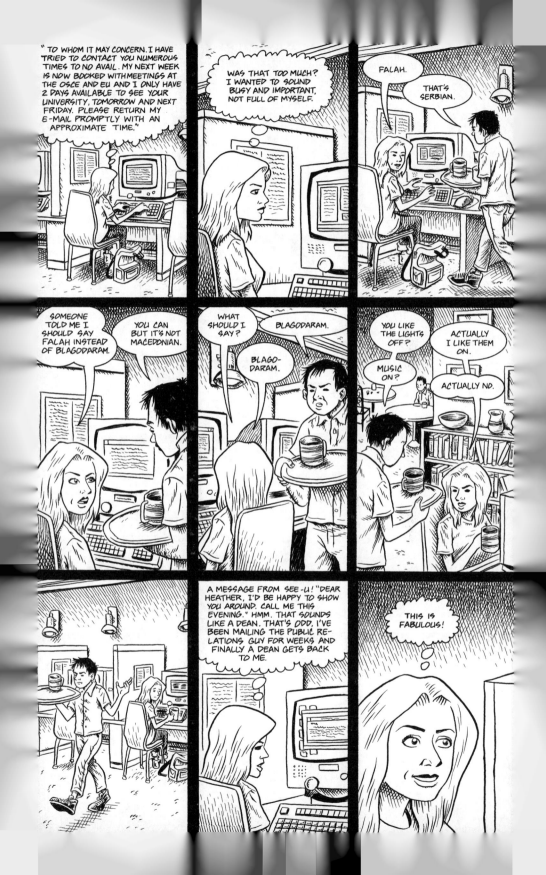

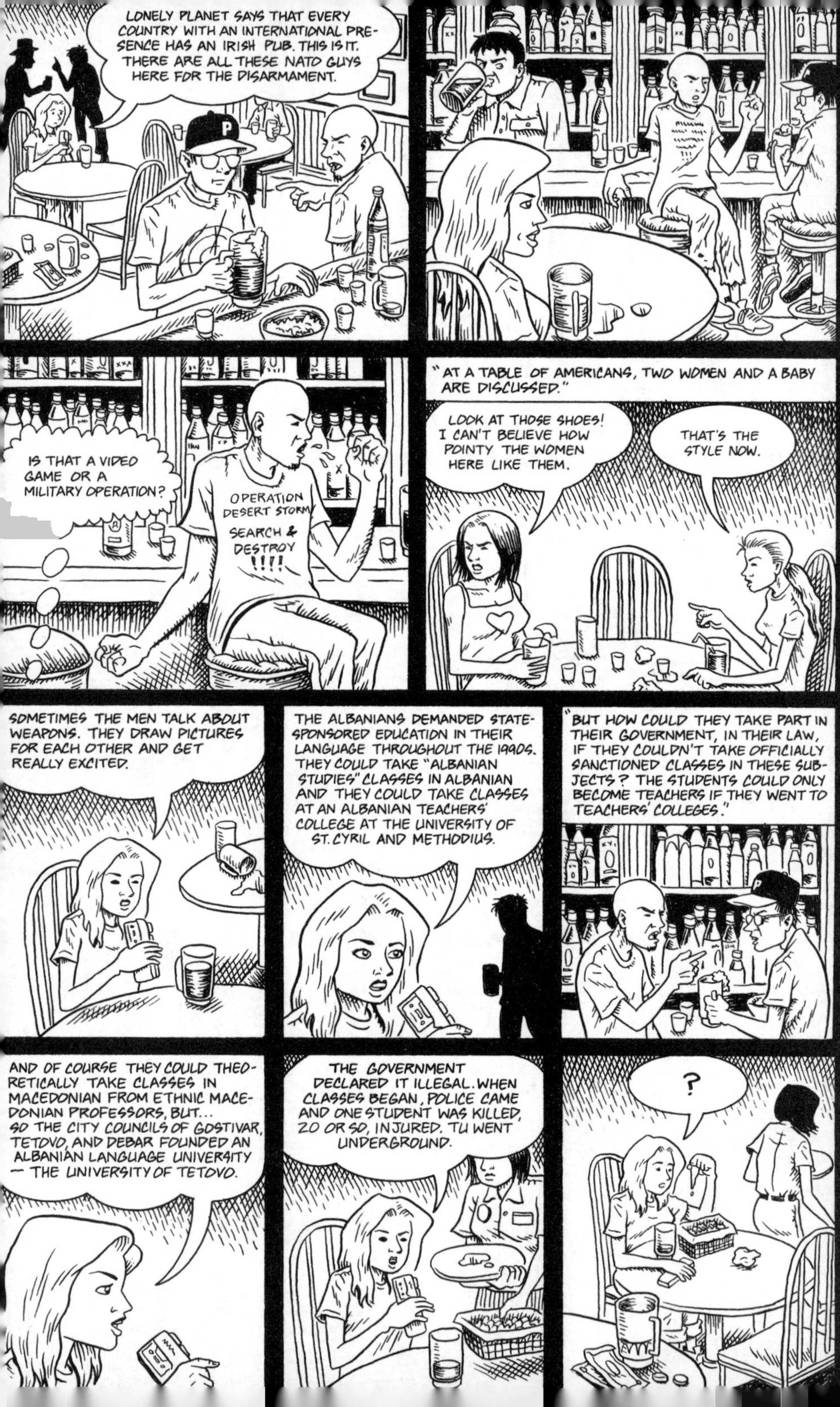
LONELY PLANET SAYS THAT EVERY COUNTRY WITH AN INTERNATIONAL PRESENCE HAS AN IRISH PUB. THIS IS IT. THERE ARE ALL THESE NATO GUYS HERE FOR THE DISARMAMENT.
IS THAT A VIDEO GAME OR A MILITARY OPERATION?
OPERATION DESERT STORM
SEARCH & DESTROY !!!!
"AT A TABLE OF AMERICANS, TWO WOMEN AND A BABY ARE DISCUSSED."
LOOK AT THOSE SHOES! I CAN'T BELIEVE HOW POINTY THE WOMEN HERE LIKE THEM.
THAT'S THE STYLE NOW.
SOMETIMES THE MEN TALK ABOUT WEAPONS. THEY DRAW PICTURES FOR EACH OTHER AND GET REALLY EXCITED.
THE ALBANIANS DEMANDED STATE-SPONSORED EDUCATION IN THEIR LANGUAGE THROUGHOUT THE 1990S. THEY COULD TAKE "ALBANIAN STUDIES" CLASSES IN ALBANIAN AND THEY COULD TAKE CLASSES AT AN ALBANIAN TEACHERS' COLLEGE AT THE UNIVERSITY OF ST. CYRIL AND METHODIUS.
"BUT HOW COULD THEY TAKE PART IN THEIR GOVERNMENT, IN THEIR LAW, IF THEY COULDN'T TAKE OFFICIALLY SANCTIONED CLASSES IN THESE SUBJECTS? THE STUDENTS COULD ONLY BECOME TEACHERS IF THEY WENT TO TEACHERS' COLLEGES."
AND OF COURSE THEY COULD THEORETICALLY TAKE CLASSES IN MACEDONIAN FROM ETHNIC MACEDONIAN PROFESSORS, BUT... SO THE CITY COUNCILS OF GOSTIVAR, TETOVO, AND DEBAR FOUNDED AN ALBANIAN LANGUAGE UNIVERSITY — THE UNIVERSITY OF TETOVO.
THE GOVERNMENT DECLARED IT ILLEGAL. WHEN CLASSES BEGAN, POLICE CAME AND ONE STUDENT WAS KILLED, 20 OR SO, INJURED. TU WENT UNDERGROUND.
?

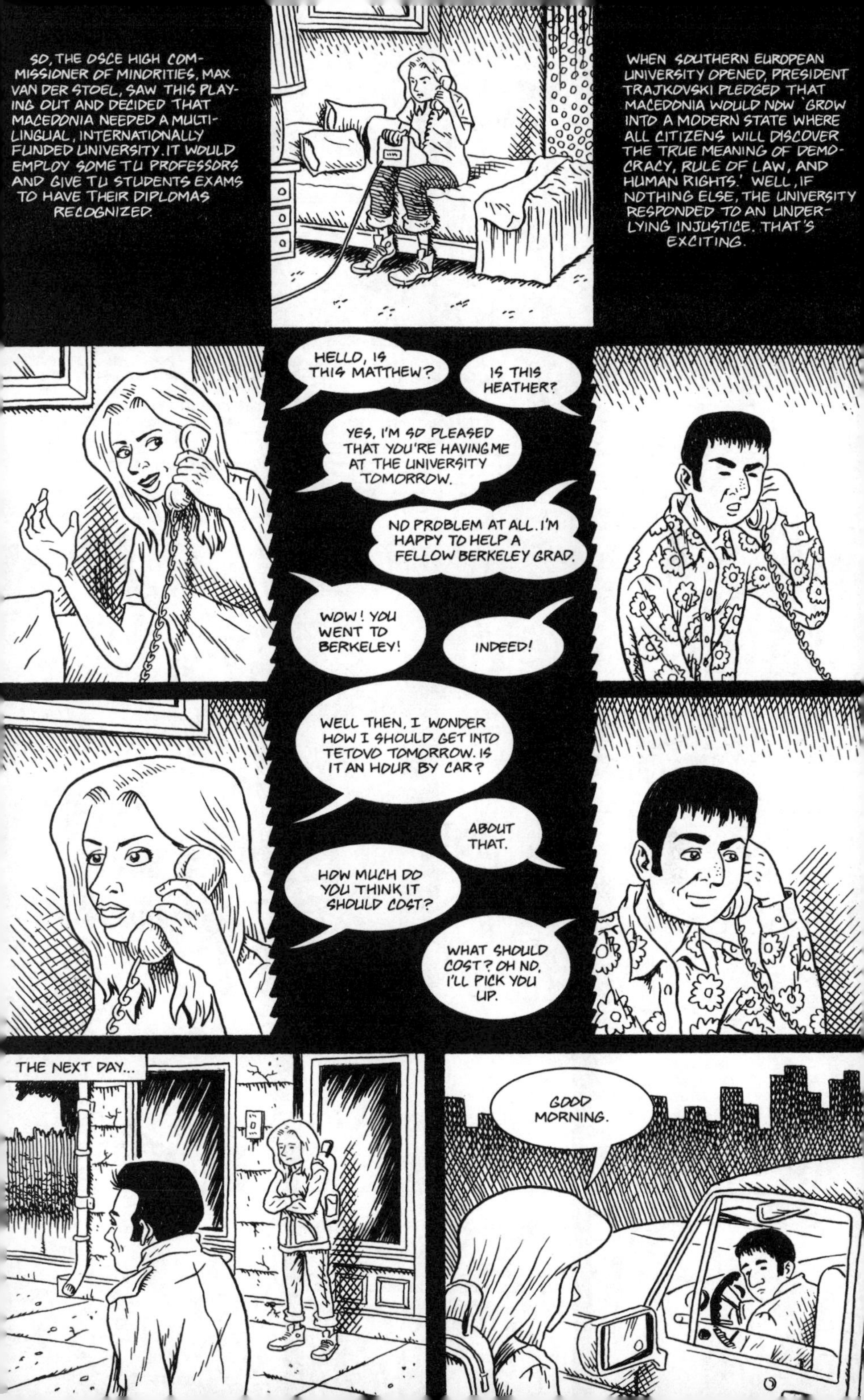
SO, THE OSCE HIGH COMMISSIONER OF MINORITIES, MAX VAN DER STOEL, SAW THIS PLAYING OUT AND DECIDED THAT MACEDONIA NEEDED A MULTILINGUAL, INTERNATIONALLY FUNDED UNIVERSITY. IT WOULD EMPLOY SOME TU PROFESSORS AND GIVE TU STUDENTS EXAMS TO HAVE THEIR DIPLOMAS RECOGNIZED.
WHEN SOUTHERN EUROPEAN UNIVERSITY OPENED, PRESIDENT TRAJKOVSKI PLEDGED THAT MACEDONIA WOULD NOW 'GROW INTO A MODERN STATE WHERE ALL CITIZENS WILL DISCOVER THE TRUE MEANING OF DEMOCRACY, RULE OF LAW, AND HUMAN RIGHTS.' WELL, IF NOTHING ELSE, THE UNIVERSITY RESPONDED TO AN UNDERLYING INJUSTICE. THAT'S EXCITING.
HELLO, IS THIS MATTHEW?
IS THIS HEATHER?
YES, I'M SO PLEASED THAT YOU'RE HAVING ME AT THE UNIVERSITY TOMORROW.
NO PROBLEM AT ALL. I'M HAPPY TO HELP A FELLOW BERKELEY GRAD.
WOW! YOU WENT TO BERKELEY!
INDEED!
WELL THEN, I WONDER HOW I SHOULD GET INTO TETOVO TOMORROW. IS IT AN HOUR BY CAR?
ABOUT THAT.
HOW MUCH DO YOU THINK IT SHOULD COST?
WHAT SHOULD COST? OH NO, I'LL PICK YOU UP.
THE NEXT DAY...
GOOD MORNING.

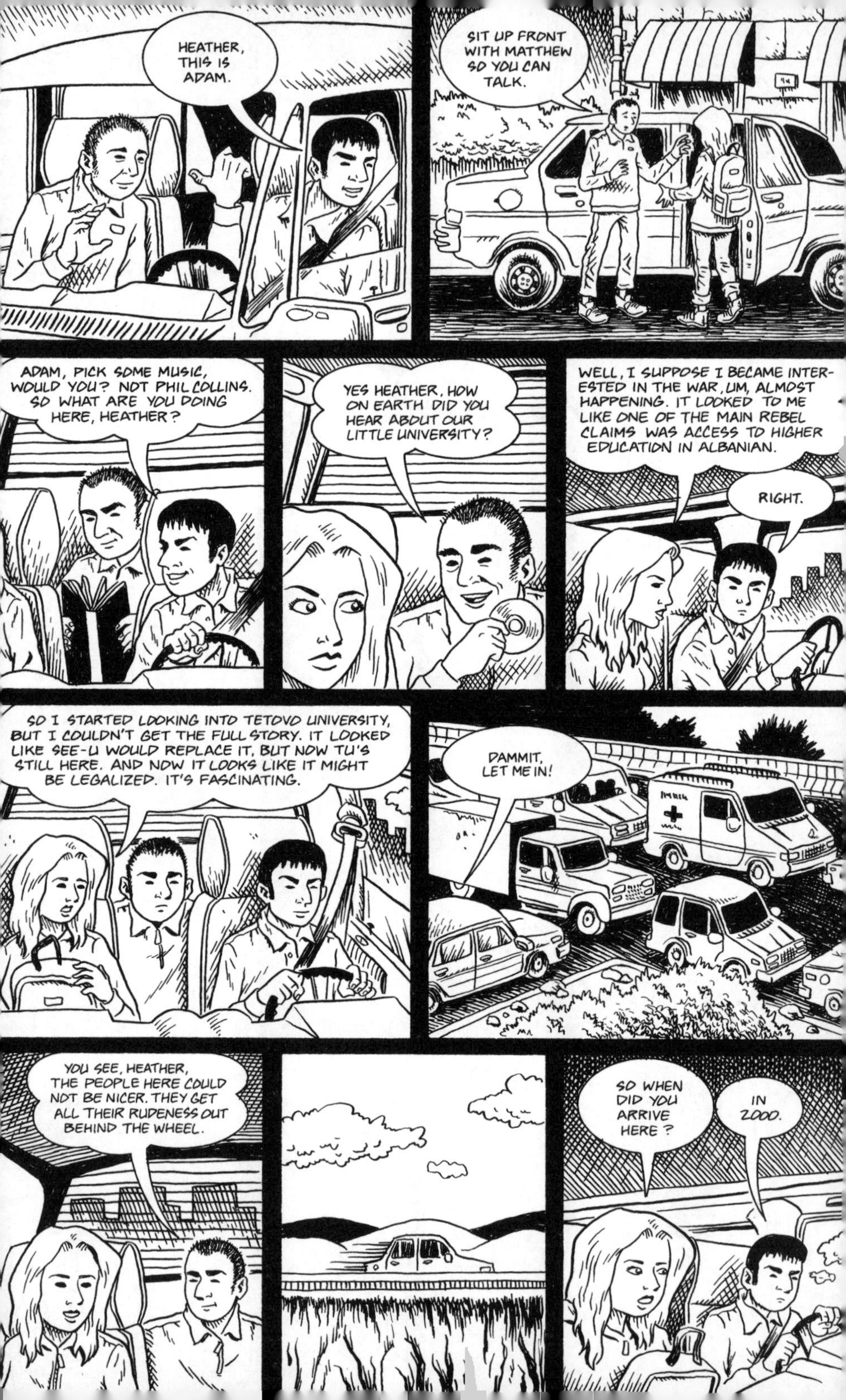
HEATHER, THIS IS ADAM.
SIT UP FRONT WITH MATTHEW SO YOU CAN TALK.
ADAM, PICK SOME MUSIC, WOULD YOU? NOT PHIL COLLINS. SO WHAT ARE YOU DOING HERE, HEATHER?
YES HEATHER, HOW ON EARTH DID YOU HEAR ABOUT OUR LITTLE UNIVERSITY?
WELL, I SUPPOSE I BECAME INTERESTED IN THE WAR, UM, ALMOST HAPPENING. IT LOOKED TO ME LIKE ONE OF THE MAIN REBEL CLAIMS WAS ACCESS TO HIGHER EDUCATION IN ALBANIAN.
RIGHT.
SO I STARTED LOOKING INTO TETOVO UNIVERSITY, BUT I COULDN'T GET THE FULL STORY. IT LOOKED LIKE SEE-U WOULD REPLACE IT, BUT NOW TU'S STILL HERE. AND NOW IT LOOKS LIKE IT MIGHT BE LEGALIZED. IT'S FASCINATING.
DAMMIT, LET ME IN!
YOU SEE, HEATHER, THE PEOPLE HERE COULD NOT BE NICER. THEY GET ALL THEIR RUDENESS OUT BEHIND THE WHEEL.
SO WHEN DID YOU ARRIVE HERE?
IN 2000.

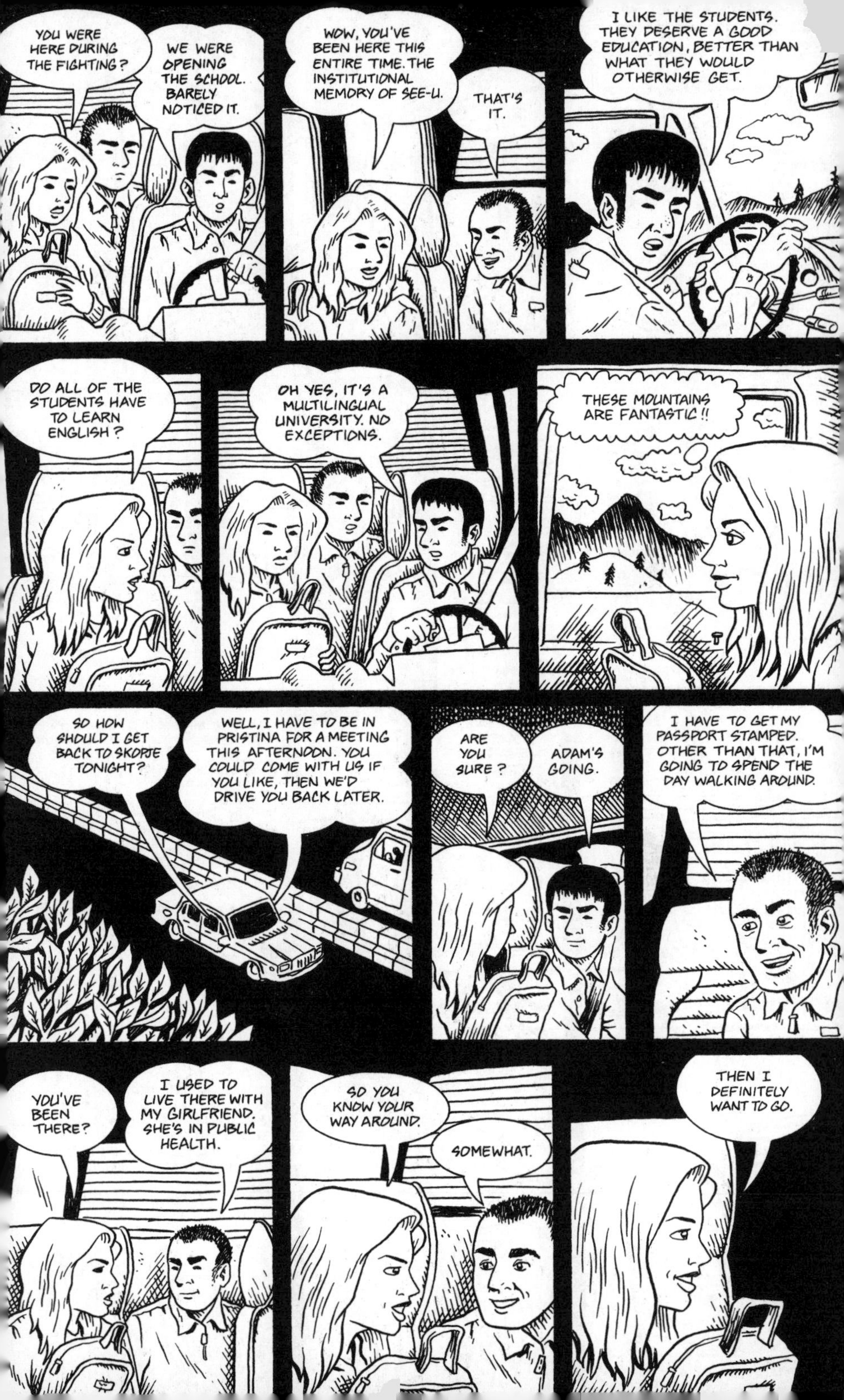
YOU WERE HERE DURING THE FIGHTING?
WE WERE OPENING THE SCHOOL. BARELY NOTICED IT.
WOW, YOU'VE BEEN HERE THIS ENTIRE TIME. THE INSTITUTIONAL MEMORY OF SEE-U.
THAT'S IT.
I LIKE THE STUDENTS. THEY DESERVE A GOOD EDUCATION, BETTER THAN WHAT THEY WOULD OTHERWISE GET.
DO ALL OF THE STUDENTS HAVE TO LEARN ENGLISH?
OH YES, IT'S A MULTILINGUAL UNIVERSITY. NO EXCEPTIONS.
THESE MOUNTAINS ARE FANTASTIC!!
SO HOW SHOULD I GET BACK TO SKOPJE TONIGHT?
WELL, I HAVE TO BE IN PRISTINA FOR A MEETING THIS AFTERNOON. YOU COULD COME WITH US IF YOU LIKE, THEN WE'D DRIVE YOU BACK LATER.
ARE YOU SURE?
ADAM'S GOING.
I HAVE TO GET MY PASSPORT STAMPED. OTHER THAN THAT, I'M GOING TO SPEND THE DAY WALKING AROUND.
YOU'VE BEEN THERE?
I USED TO LIVE THERE WITH MY GIRLFRIEND. SHE'S IN PUBLIC HEALTH.
SO YOU KNOW YOUR WAY AROUND.
SOMEWHAT.
THEN I DEFINITELY WANT TO GO.

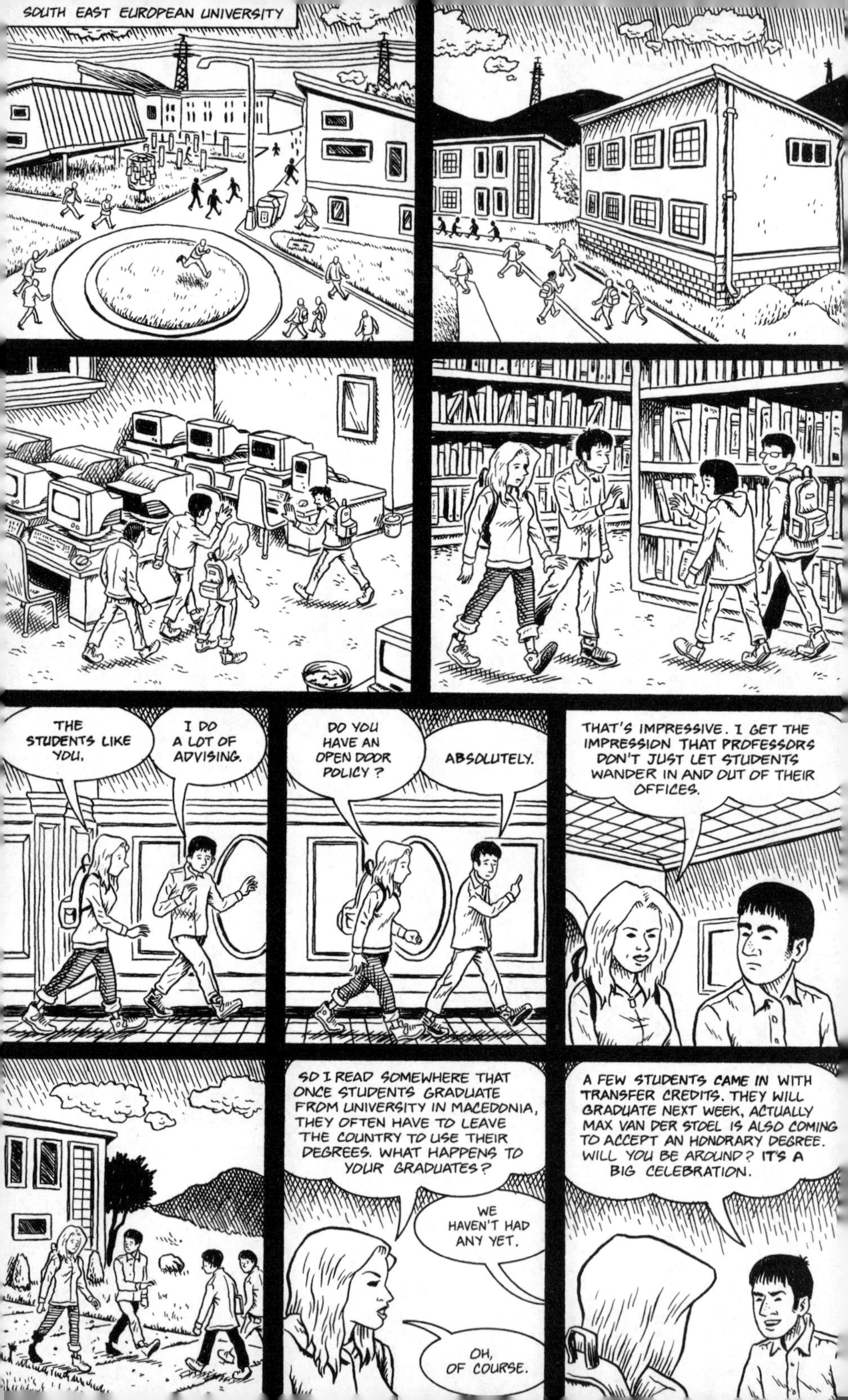
SOUTH EAST EUROPEAN UNIVERSITY
THE STUDENTS LIKE YOU.
I DO A LOT OF ADVISING.
DO YOU HAVE AN OPEN DOOR POLICY?
ABSOLUTELY.
THAT'S IMPRESSIVE. I GET THE IMPRESSION THAT PROFESSORS DON'T JUST LET STUDENTS WANDER IN AND OUT OF THEIR OFFICES.
SO I READ SOMEWHERE THAT ONCE STUDENTS GRADUATE FROM UNIVERSITY IN MACEDONIA, THEY OFTEN HAVE TO LEAVE THE COUNTRY TO USE THEIR DEGREES. WHAT HAPPENS TO YOUR GRADUATES?
WE HAVEN'T HAD ANY YET.
OH, OF COURSE.
A FEW STUDENTS CAME IN WITH TRANSFER CREDITS. THEY WILL GRADUATE NEXT WEEK, ACTUALLY MAX VAN DER STOEL IS ALSO COMING TO ACCEPT AN HONORARY DEGREE. WILL YOU BE AROUND? IT'S A BIG CELEBRATION.

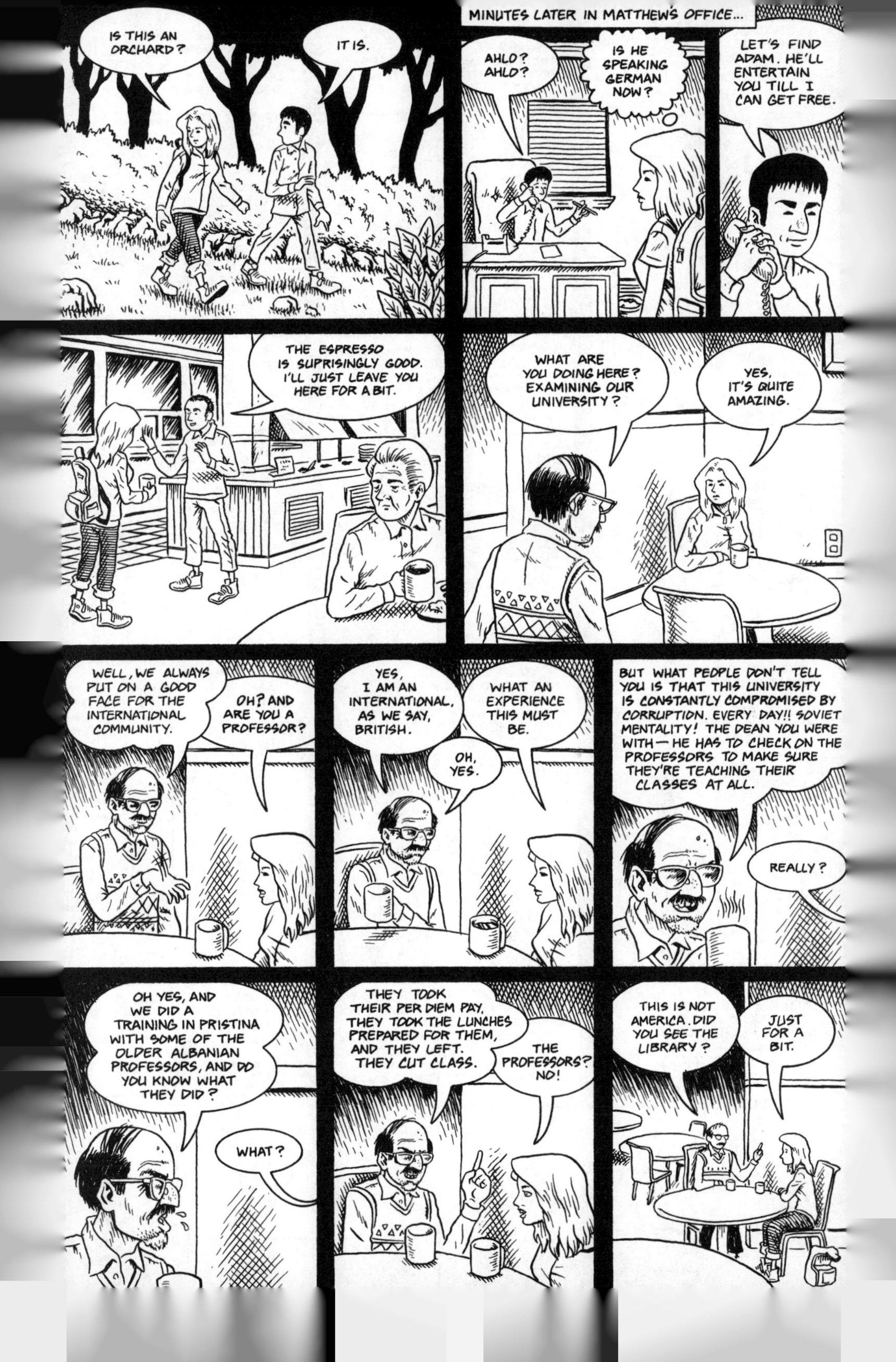
IS THIS AN ORCHARD?
IT IS.
MINUTES LATER IN MATTHEW'S OFFICE...
AHLO? AHLO?
IS HE SPEAKING GERMAN NOW?
LET'S FIND ADAM. HE'LL ENTERTAIN YOU TILL I CAN GET FREE.
THE ESPRESSO IS SUPRISINGLY GOOD. I'LL JUST LEAVE YOU HERE FOR A BIT.
WHAT ARE YOU DOING HERE? EXAMINING OUR UNIVERSITY?
YES, IT'S QUITE AMAZING.
WELL, WE ALWAYS PUT ON A GOOD FACE FOR THE INTERNATIONAL COMMUNITY.
OH? AND ARE YOU A PROFESSOR?
YES, I AM AN INTERNATIONAL, AS WE SAY, BRITISH.
WHAT AN EXPERIENCE THIS MUST BE.
OH, YES.
BUT WHAT PEOPLE DON'T TELL YOU IS THAT THIS UNIVERSITY IS CONSTANTLY COMPROMISED BY CORRUPTION. EVERY DAY!! SOVIET MENTALITY! THE DEAN YOU WERE WITH— HE HAS TO CHECK ON THE PROFESSORS TO MAKE SURE THEY'RE TEACHING THEIR CLASSES AT ALL.
REALLY?
OH YES, AND WE DID A TRAINING IN PRISTINA WITH SOME OF THE OLDER ALBANIAN PROFESSORS, AND DO YOU KNOW WHAT THEY DID?
WHAT?
THEY TOOK THEIR PER DIEM PAY, THEY TOOK THE LUNCHES PREPARED FOR THEM, AND THEY LEFT. THEY CUT CLASS.
THE PROFESSORS? NO!
THIS IS NOT AMERICA. DID YOU SEE THE LIBRARY?
JUST FOR A BIT.

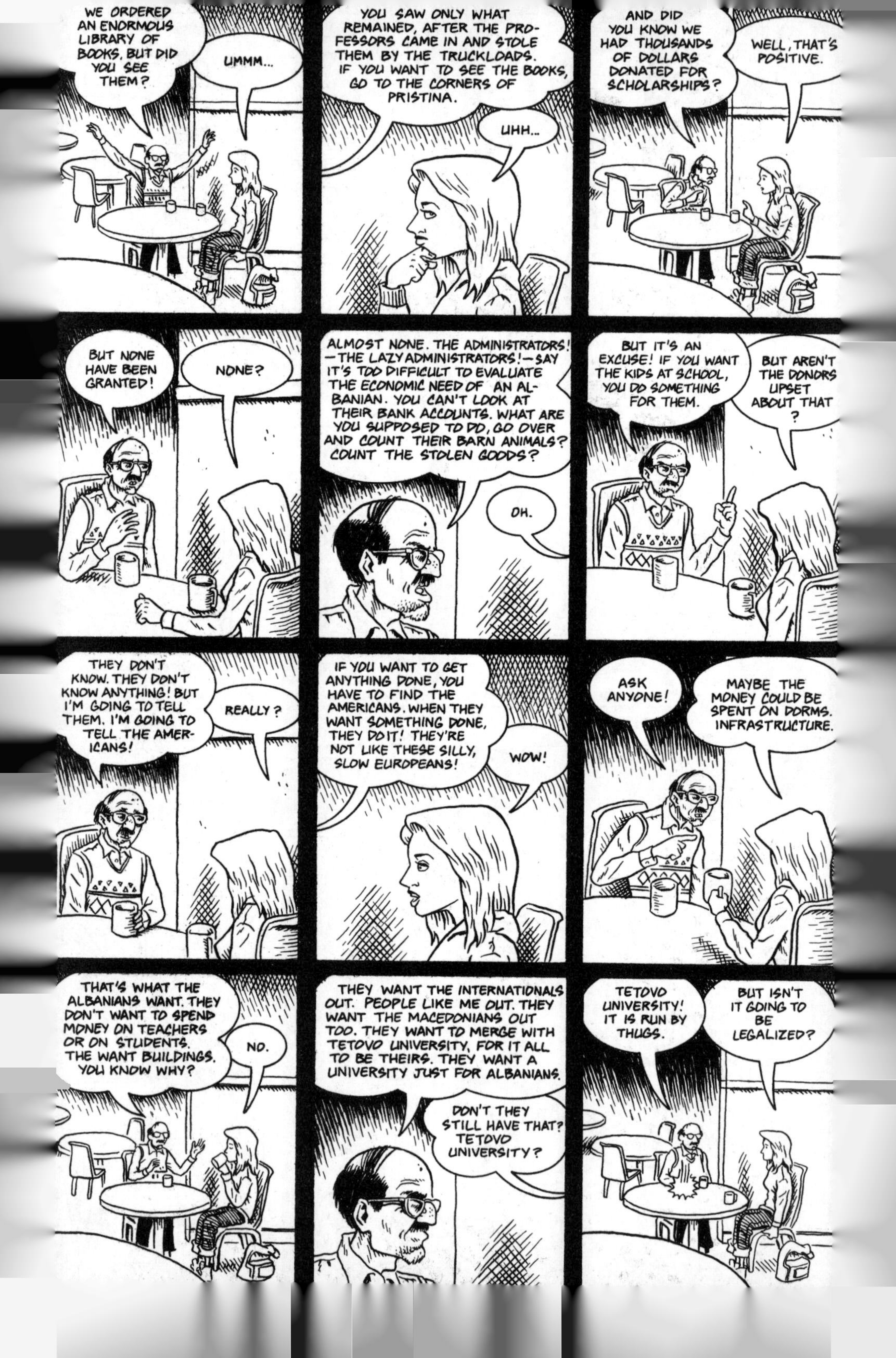
WE ORDERED AN ENORMOUS LIBRARY OF BOOKS, BUT DID YOU SEE THEM?
UMMM...
YOU SAW ONLY WHAT REMAINED, AFTER THE PROFESSORS CAME IN AND STOLE THEM BY THE TRUCKLOADS. IF YOU WANT TO SEE THE BOOKS, GO TO THE CORNERS OF PRISTINA.
UHH...
AND DID YOU KNOW WE HAD THOUSANDS OF DOLLARS DONATED FOR SCHOLARSHIPS?
WELL, THAT'S POSITIVE.
BUT NONE HAVE BEEN GRANTED!
NONE?
ALMOST NONE. THE ADMINISTRATORS! —THE LAZY ADMINISTRATORS!—SAY IT'S TOO DIFFICULT TO EVALUATE THE ECONOMIC NEED OF AN ALBANIAN. YOU CAN'T LOOK AT THEIR BANK ACCOUNTS. WHAT ARE YOU SUPPOSED TO DO, GO OVER AND COUNT THEIR BARN ANIMALS? COUNT THE STOLEN GOODS?
OH.
BUT IT'S AN EXCUSE! IF YOU WANT THE KIDS AT SCHOOL, YOU DO SOMETHING FOR THEM.
BUT AREN'T THE DONORS UPSET ABOUT THAT?
THEY DON'T KNOW. THEY DON'T KNOW ANYTHING! BUT I'M GOING TO TELL THEM. I'M GOING TO TELL THE AMERICANS!
REALLY?
IF YOU WANT TO GET ANYTHING DONE, YOU HAVE TO FIND THE AMERICANS. WHEN THEY WANT SOMETHING DONE, THEY DO IT! THEY'RE NOT LIKE THESE SILLY, SLOW EUROPEANS!
WOW!
ASK ANYONE!
MAYBE THE MONEY COULD BE SPENT ON DORMS. INFRASTRUCTURE.
THAT'S WHAT THE ALBANIANS WANT. THEY DON'T WANT TO SPEND MONEY ON TEACHERS OR ON STUDENTS. THE WANT BUILDINGS. YOU KNOW WHY?
NO.
THEY WANT THE INTERNATIONALS OUT. PEOPLE LIKE ME OUT. THEY WANT THE MACEDONIANS OUT TOO. THEY WANT TO MERGE WITH TETOVO UNIVERSITY, FOR IT ALL TO BE THEIRS. THEY WANT A UNIVERSITY JUST FOR ALBANIANS.
DON'T THEY STILL HAVE THAT? TETOVO UNIVERSITY?
TETOVO UNIVERSITY! IT IS RUN BY THUGS.
BUT ISN'T IT GOING TO BE LEGALIZED?

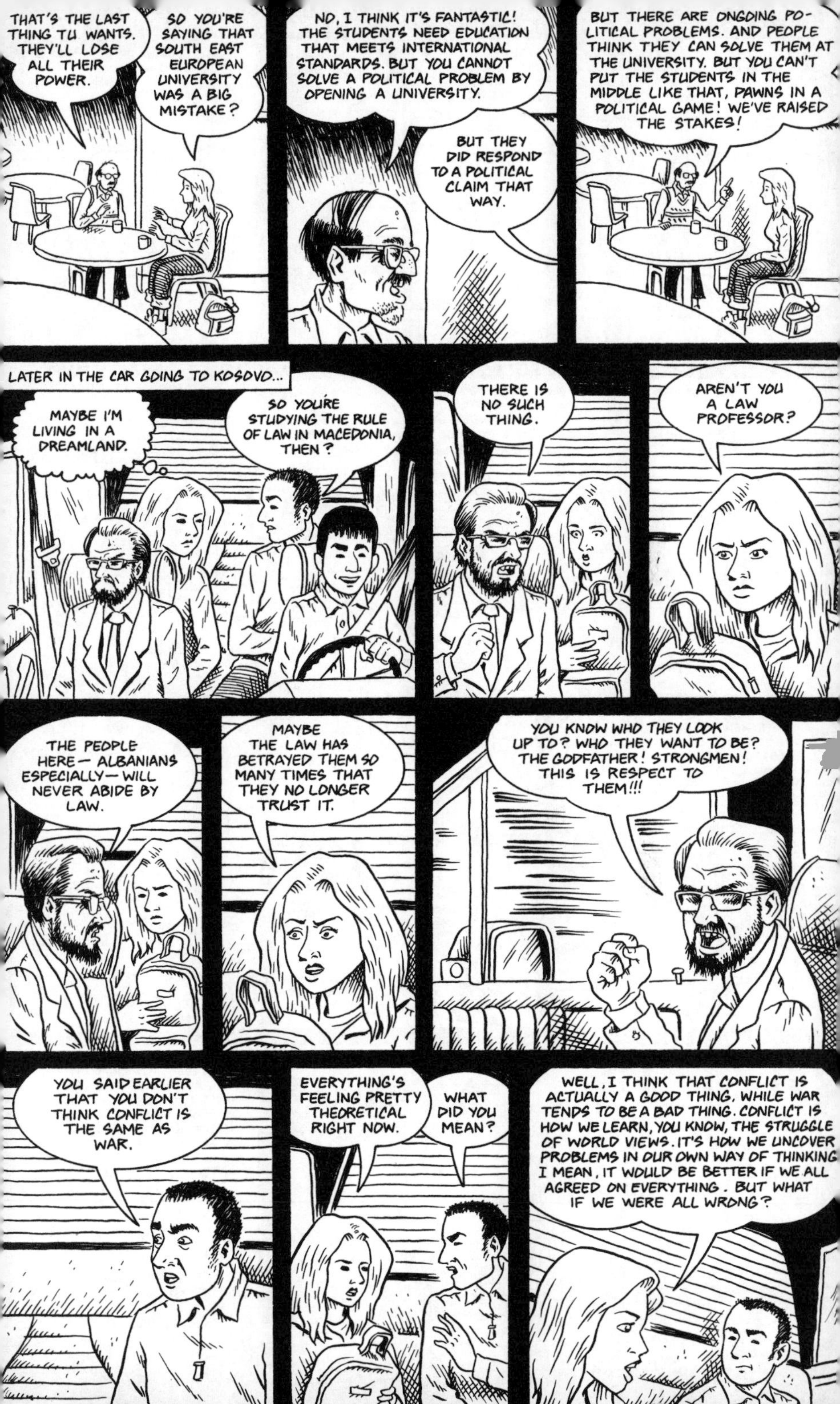
THAT'S THE LAST THING TU WANTS. THEY'LL LOSE ALL THEIR POWER.
SO YOU'RE SAYING THAT SOUTH EAST EUROPEAN UNIVERSITY WAS A BIG MISTAKE?
NO, I THINK IT'S FANTASTIC! THE STUDENTS NEED EDUCATION THAT MEETS INTERNATIONAL STANDARDS. BUT YOU CANNOT SOLVE A POLITICAL PROBLEM BY OPENING A UNIVERSITY.
BUT THEY DID RESPOND TO A POLITICAL CLAIM THAT WAY.
BUT THERE ARE ONGOING POLITICAL PROBLEMS. AND PEOPLE THINK THEY CAN SOLVE THEM AT THE UNIVERSITY. BUT YOU CAN'T PUT THE STUDENTS IN THE MIDDLE LIKE THAT, PAWNS IN A POLITICAL GAME! WE'VE RAISED THE STAKES!
LATER IN THE CAR GOING TO KOSOVO...
MAYBE I'M LIVING IN A DREAMLAND.
SO YOU'RE STUDYING THE RULE OF LAW IN MACEDONIA, THEN?
THERE IS NO SUCH THING.
AREN'T YOU A LAW PROFESSOR?
THE PEOPLE HERE— ALBANIANS ESPECIALLY— WILL NEVER ABIDE BY LAW.
MAYBE THE LAW HAS BETRAYED THEM SO MANY TIMES THAT THEY NO LONGER TRUST IT.
YOU KNOW WHO THEY LOOK UP TO? WHO THEY WANT TO BE? THE GODFATHER! STRONGMEN! THIS IS RESPECT TO THEM!!!
YOU SAID EARLIER THAT YOU DON'T THINK CONFLICT IS THE SAME AS WAR.
EVERYTHING'S FEELING PRETTY THEORETICAL RIGHT NOW.
WHAT DID YOU MEAN?
WELL, I THINK THAT CONFLICT IS ACTUALLY A GOOD THING, WHILE WAR TENDS TO BE A BAD THING. CONFLICT IS HOW WE LEARN, YOU KNOW, THE STRUGGLE OF WORLD VIEWS. IT'S HOW WE UNCOVER PROBLEMS IN OUR OWN WAY OF THINKING. I MEAN, IT WOULD BE BETTER IF WE ALL AGREED ON EVERYTHING. BUT WHAT IF WE WERE ALL WRONG?

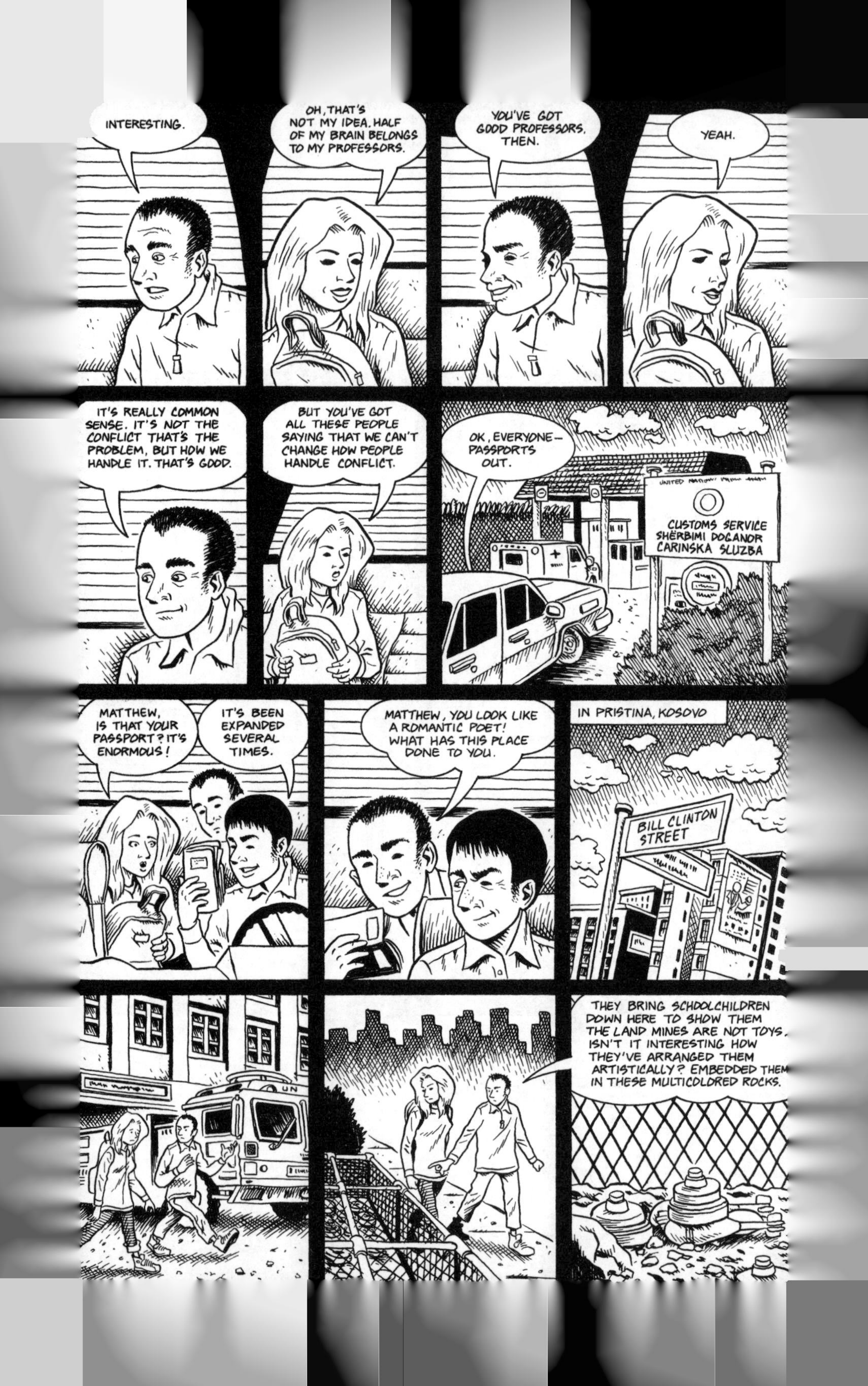
INTERESTING.
OH, THAT'S NOT MY IDEA. HALF OF MY BRAIN BELONGS TO MY PROFESSORS.
YOU'VE GOT GOOD PROFESSORS, THEN.
YEAH.
IT'S REALLY COMMON SENSE. IT'S NOT THE CONFLICT THAT'S THE PROBLEM, BUT HOW WE HANDLE IT. THAT'S GOOD.
BUT YOU'VE GOT ALL THESE PEOPLE SAYING THAT WE CAN'T CHANGE HOW PEOPLE HANDLE CONFLICT.
OK, EVERYONE— PASSPORTS OUT.
CUSTOMS SERVICE
SHËRBIMI DOGANOR
CARINSKA SLUZBA
MATTHEW, IS THAT YOUR PASSPORT? IT'S ENORMOUS!
IT'S BEEN EXPANDED SEVERAL TIMES.
MATTHEW, YOU LOOK LIKE A ROMANTIC POET! WHAT HAS THIS PLACE DONE TO YOU.
IN PRISTINA, KOSOVO
BILL CLINTON STREET
UN
THEY BRING SCHOOLCHILDREN DOWN HERE TO SHOW THEM THE LAND MINES ARE NOT TOYS. ISN'T IT INTERESTING HOW THEY'VE ARRANGED THEM ARTISTICALLY? EMBEDDED THEM IN THESE MULTICOLORED ROCKS.

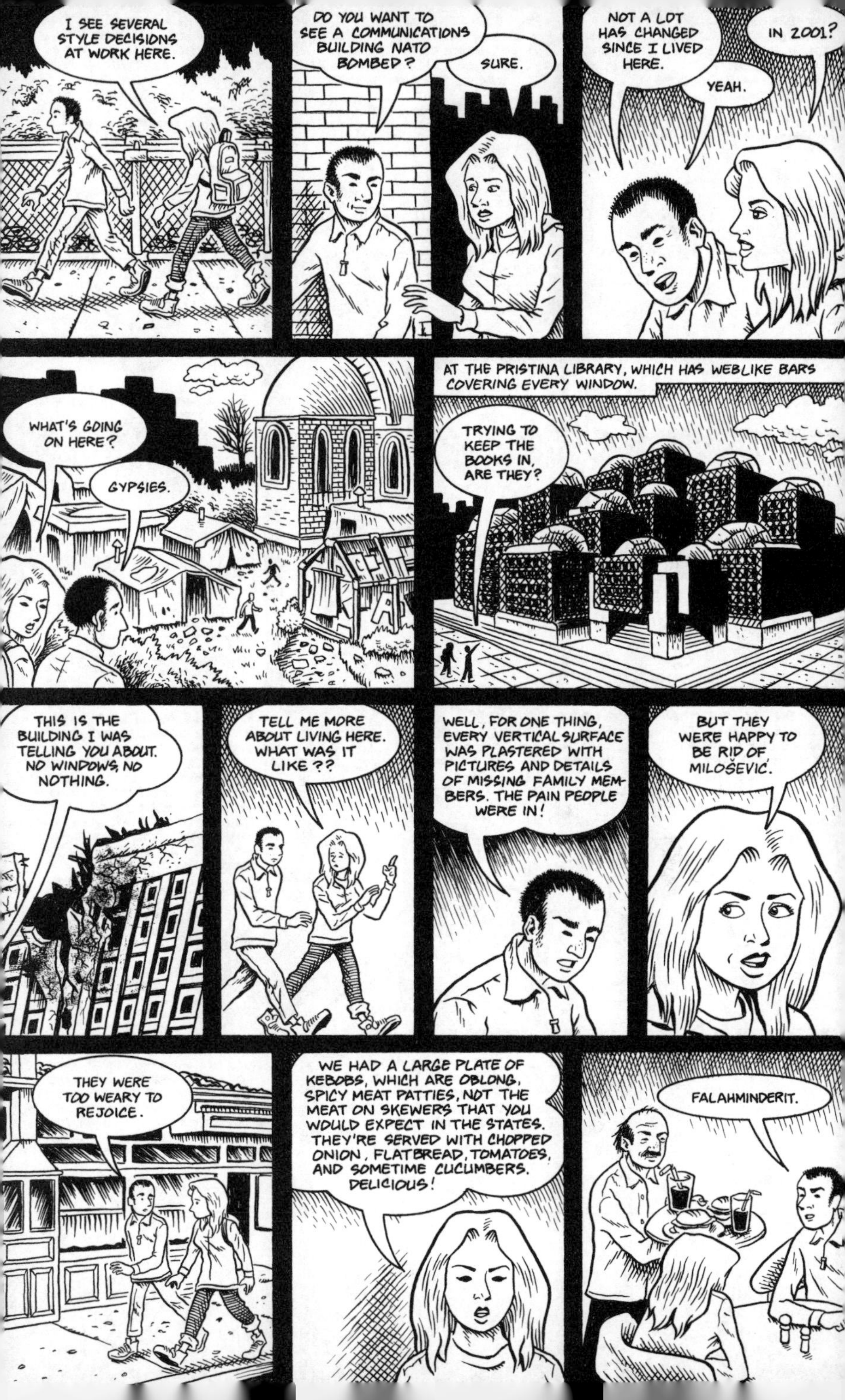
I SEE SEVERAL STYLE DECISIONS AT WORK HERE.
DO YOU WANT TO SEE A COMMUNICATIONS BUILDING NATO BOMBED?
SURE.
NOT A LOT HAS CHANGED SINCE I LIVED HERE.
YEAH.
IN 2001?
WHAT'S GOING ON HERE?
GYPSIES.
AT THE PRISTINA LIBRARY, WHICH HAS WEBLIKE BARS COVERING EVERY WINDOW.
TRYING TO KEEP THE BOOKS IN, ARE THEY?
THIS IS THE BUILDING I WAS TELLING YOU ABOUT. NO WINDOWS, NO NOTHING.
TELL ME MORE ABOUT LIVING HERE. WHAT WAS IT LIKE??
WELL, FOR ONE THING, EVERY VERTICAL SURFACE WAS PLASTERED WITH PICTURES AND DETAILS OF MISSING FAMILY MEMBERS. THE PAIN PEOPLE WERE IN!
BUT THEY WERE HAPPY TO BE RID OF MILOŠEVIĆ.
THEY WERE TOO WEARY TO REJOICE.
WE HAD A LARGE PLATE OF KEBOBS, WHICH ARE OBLONG, SPICY MEAT PATTIES, NOT THE MEAT ON SKEWERS THAT YOU WOULD EXPECT IN THE STATES. THEY'RE SERVED WITH CHOPPED ONION, FLATBREAD, TOMATOES, AND SOMETIME CUCUMBERS. DELICIOUS!
FALAHMINDERIT.

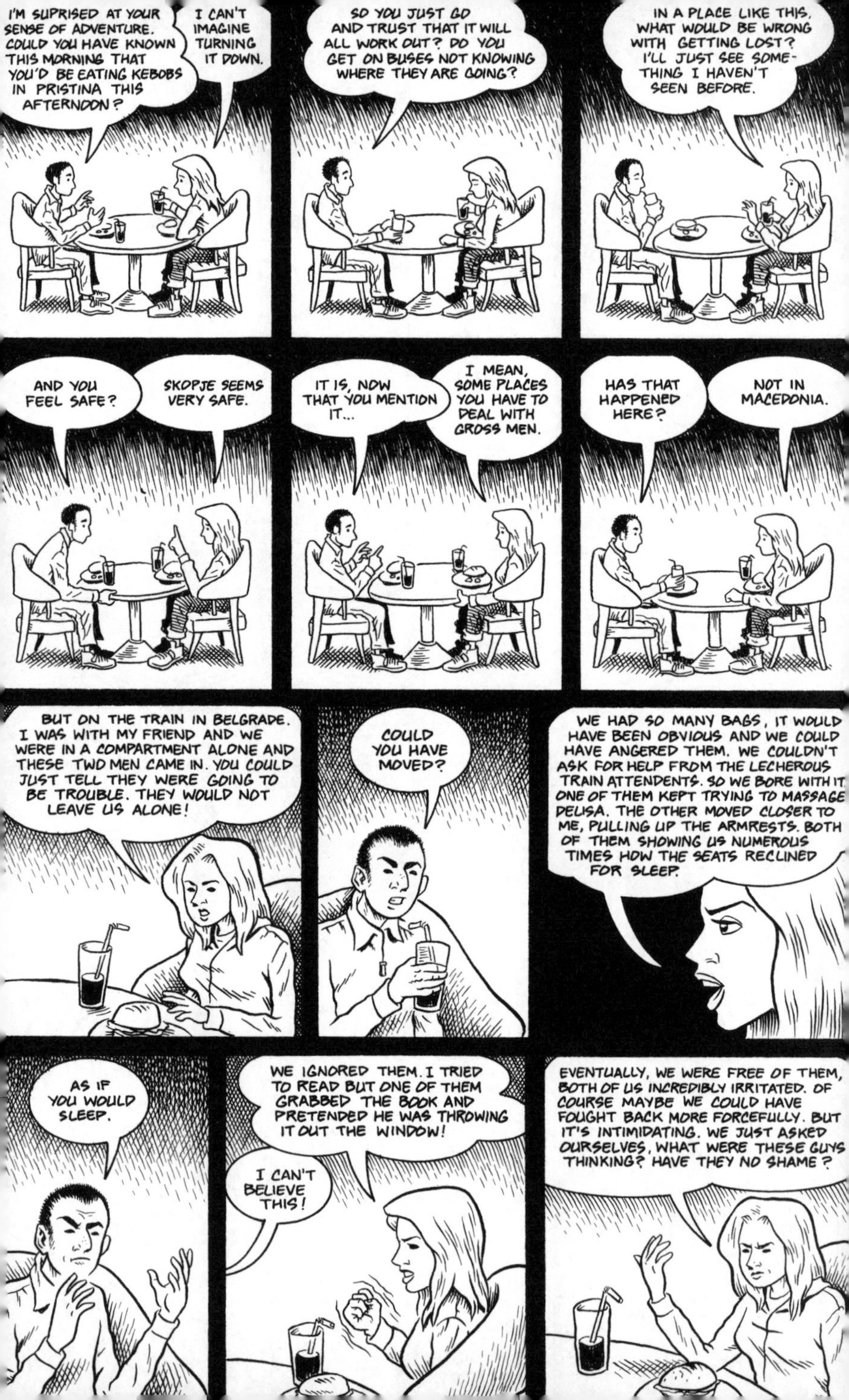
I'M SUPRISED AT YOUR SENSE OF ADVENTURE. COULD YOU HAVE KNOWN THIS MORNING THAT YOU'D BE EATING KEBOBS IN PRISTINA THIS AFTERNOON?
I CAN'T IMAGINE TURNING IT DOWN.
SO YOU JUST GO AND TRUST THAT IT WILL ALL WORK OUT? DO YOU GET ON BUSES NOT KNOWING WHERE THEY ARE GOING?
IN A PLACE LIKE THIS, WHAT WOULD BE WRONG WITH GETTING LOST? I'LL JUST SEE SOMETHING I HAVEN'T SEEN BEFORE.
AND YOU FEEL SAFE?
SKOPJE SEEMS VERY SAFE.
IT IS, NOW THAT YOU MENTION IT...
I MEAN, SOME PLACES YOU HAVE TO DEAL WITH GROSS MEN.
HAS THAT HAPPENED HERE?
NOT IN MACEDONIA.
BUT ON THE TRAIN IN BELGRADE. I WAS WITH MY FRIEND AND WE WERE IN A COMPARTMENT ALONE AND THESE TWO MEN CAME IN. YOU COULD JUST TELL THEY WERE GOING TO BE TROUBLE. THEY WOULD NOT LEAVE US ALONE!
COULD YOU HAVE MOVED?
WE HAD SO MANY BAGS, IT WOULD HAVE BEEN OBVIOUS AND WE COULD HAVE ANGERED THEM. WE COULDN'T ASK FOR HELP FROM THE LECHEROUS TRAIN ATTENDENTS. SO WE BORE WITH IT. ONE OF THEM KEPT TRYING TO MASSAGE DELISA. THE OTHER MOVED CLOSER TO ME, PULLING UP THE ARMRESTS. BOTH OF THEM SHOWING US NUMEROUS TIMES HOW THE SEATS RECLINED FOR SLEEP.
AS IF YOU WOULD SLEEP.
WE IGNORED THEM. I TRIED TO READ BUT ONE OF THEM GRABBED THE BOOK AND PRETENDED HE WAS THROWING IT OUT THE WINDOW!
I CAN'T BELIEVE THIS!
EVENTUALLY, WE WERE FREE OF THEM, BOTH OF US INCREDIBLY IRRITATED. OF COURSE MAYBE WE COULD HAVE FOUGHT BACK MORE FORCEFULLY. BUT IT'S INTIMIDATING. WE JUST ASKED OURSELVES, WHAT WERE THESE GUYS THINKING? HAVE THEY NO SHAME?

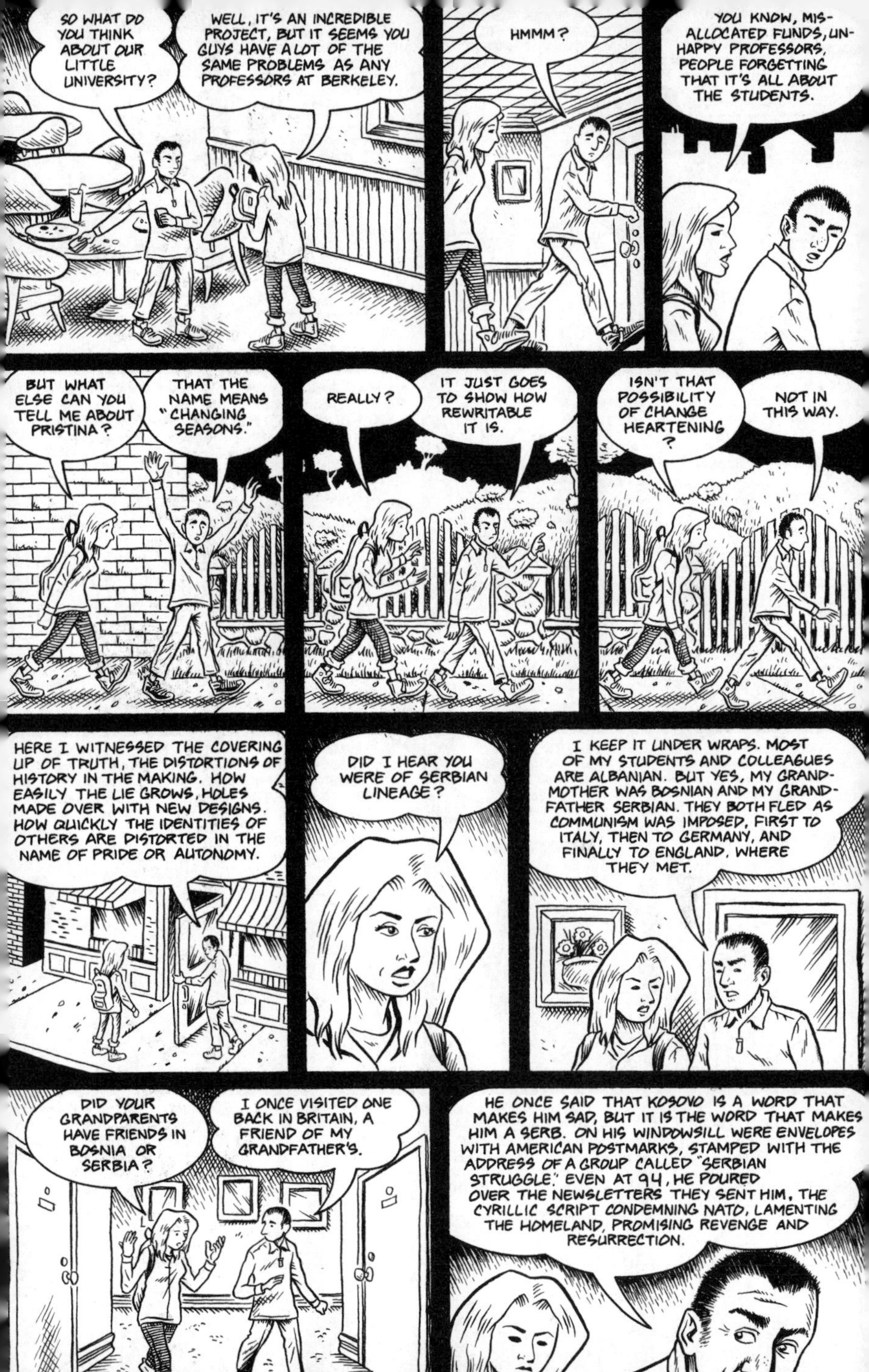
SO WHAT DO YOU THINK ABOUT OUR LITTLE UNIVERSITY?
WELL, IT'S AN INCREDIBLE PROJECT, BUT IT SEEMS YOU GUYS HAVE A LOT OF THE SAME PROBLEMS AS ANY PROFESSORS AT BERKELEY.
HMMM?
YOU KNOW, MIS-ALLOCATED FUNDS, UN-HAPPY PROFESSORS, PEOPLE FORGETTING THAT IT'S ALL ABOUT THE STUDENTS.
BUT WHAT ELSE CAN YOU TELL ME ABOUT PRISTINA?
THAT THE NAME MEANS "CHANGING SEASONS."
REALLY?
IT JUST GOES TO SHOW HOW REWRITABLE IT IS.
ISN'T THAT POSSIBILITY OF CHANGE HEARTENING?
NOT IN THIS WAY.
HERE I WITNESSED THE COVERING UP OF TRUTH, THE DISTORTIONS OF HISTORY IN THE MAKING. HOW EASILY THE LIE GROWS, HOLES MADE OVER WITH NEW DESIGNS. HOW QUICKLY THE IDENTITIES OF OTHERS ARE DISTORTED IN THE NAME OF PRIDE OR AUTONOMY.
DID I HEAR YOU WERE OF SERBIAN LINEAGE?
I KEEP IT UNDER WRAPS. MOST OF MY STUDENTS AND COLLEAGUES ARE ALBANIAN. BUT YES, MY GRAND-MOTHER WAS BOSNIAN AND MY GRAND-FATHER SERBIAN. THEY BOTH FLED AS COMMUNISM WAS IMPOSED, FIRST TO ITALY, THEN TO GERMANY, AND FINALLY TO ENGLAND, WHERE THEY MET.
DID YOUR GRANDPARENTS HAVE FRIENDS IN BOSNIA OR SERBIA?
I ONCE VISITED ONE BACK IN BRITAIN, A FRIEND OF MY GRANDFATHER'S.
HE ONCE SAID THAT KOSOVO IS A WORD THAT MAKES HIM SAD, BUT IT IS THE WORD THAT MAKES HIM A SERB. ON HIS WINDOWSILL WERE ENVELOPES WITH AMERICAN POSTMARKS, STAMPED WITH THE ADDRESS OF A GROUP CALLED "SERBIAN STRUGGLE." EVEN AT 94, HE POURED OVER THE NEWSLETTERS THEY SENT HIM, THE CYRILLIC SCRIPT CONDEMNING NATO, LAMENTING THE HOMELAND, PROMISING REVENGE AND RESURRECTION.

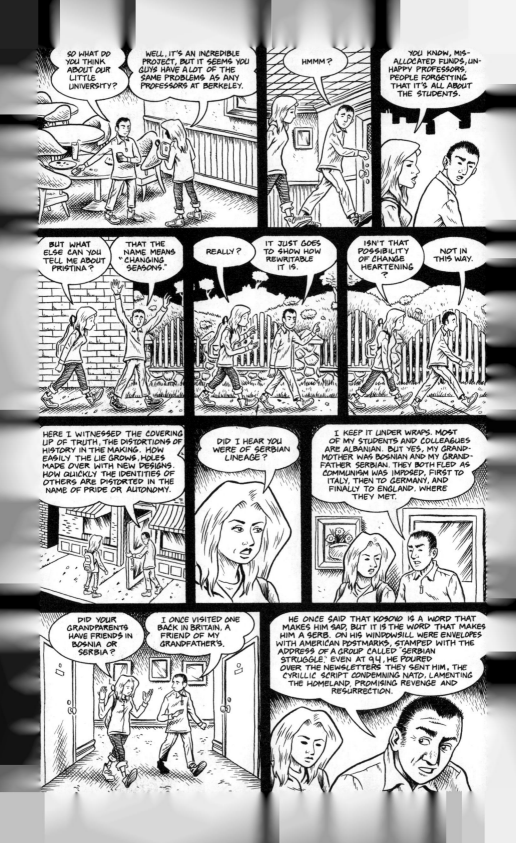

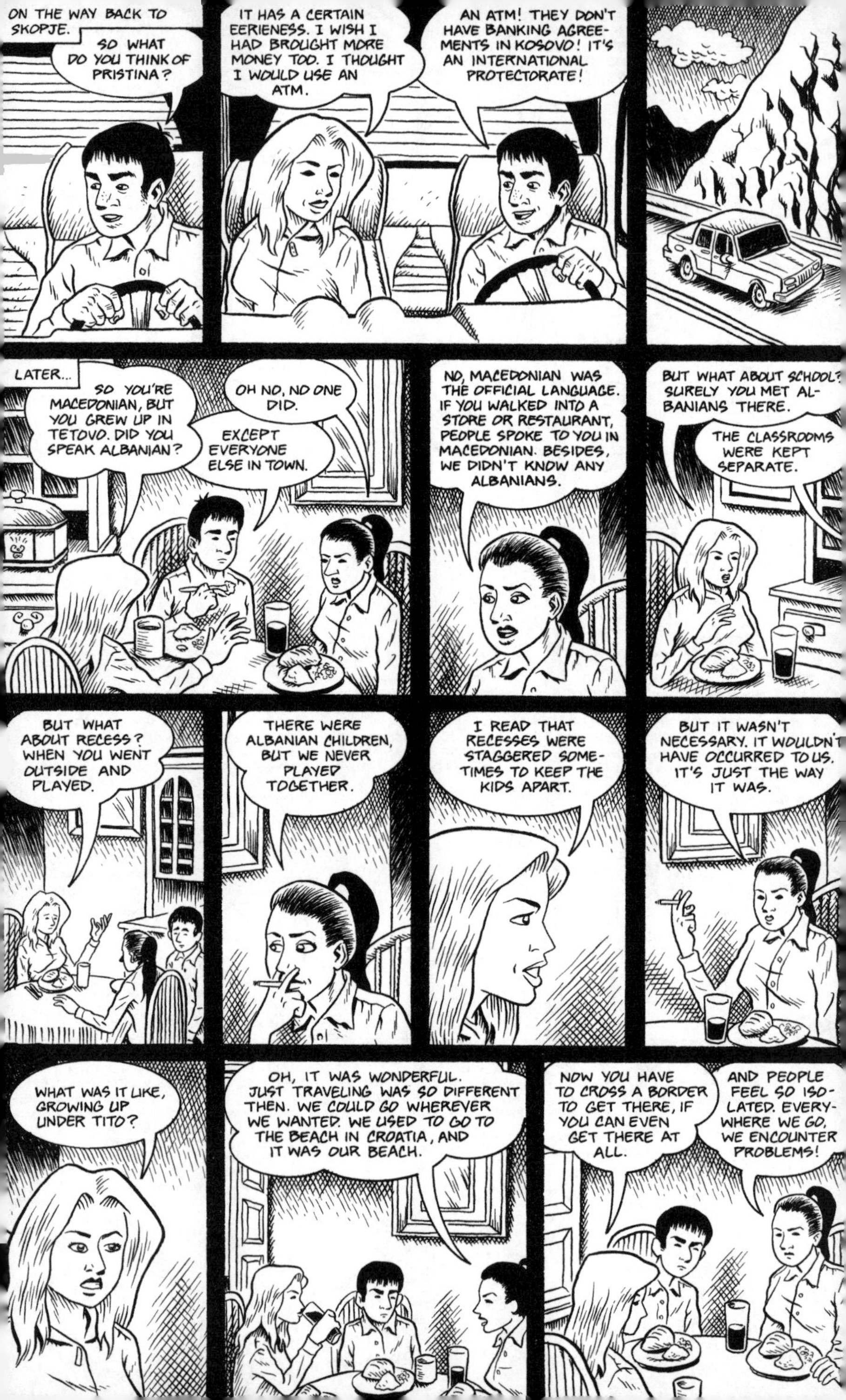
ON THE WAY BACK TO SKOPJE.
SO WHAT DO YOU THINK OF PRISTINA?
IT HAS A CERTAIN EERIENESS. I WISH I HAD BROUGHT MORE MONEY TOO. I THOUGHT I WOULD USE AN ATM.
AN ATM! THEY DON'T HAVE BANKING AGREEMENTS IN KOSOVO! IT'S AN INTERNATIONAL PROTECTORATE!
LATER...
SO YOU'RE MACEDONIAN, BUT YOU GREW UP IN TETOVO. DID YOU SPEAK ALBANIAN?
OH NO, NO ONE DID.
EXCEPT EVERYONE ELSE IN TOWN.
NO, MACEDONIAN WAS THE OFFICIAL LANGUAGE. IF YOU WALKED INTO A STORE OR RESTAURANT, PEOPLE SPOKE TO YOU IN MACEDONIAN. BESIDES, WE DIDN'T KNOW ANY ALBANIANS.
BUT WHAT ABOUT SCHOOL? SURELY YOU MET ALBANIANS THERE.
THE CLASSROOMS WERE KEPT SEPARATE.
BUT WHAT ABOUT RECESS? WHEN YOU WENT OUTSIDE AND PLAYED.
THERE WERE ALBANIAN CHILDREN, BUT WE NEVER PLAYED TOGETHER.
I READ THAT RECESSES WERE STAGGERED SOMETIMES TO KEEP THE KIDS APART.
BUT IT WASN'T NECESSARY. IT WOULDN'T HAVE OCCURRED TO US. IT'S JUST THE WAY IT WAS.
WHAT WAS IT LIKE, GROWING UP UNDER TITO?
OH, IT WAS WONDERFUL. JUST TRAVELING WAS SO DIFFERENT THEN. WE COULD GO WHEREVER WE WANTED. WE USED TO GO TO THE BEACH IN CROATIA, AND IT WAS OUR BEACH.
NOW YOU HAVE TO CROSS A BORDER TO GET THERE, IF YOU CAN EVEN GET THERE AT ALL.
AND PEOPLE FEEL SO ISOLATED. EVERYWHERE WE GO, WE ENCOUNTER PROBLEMS!

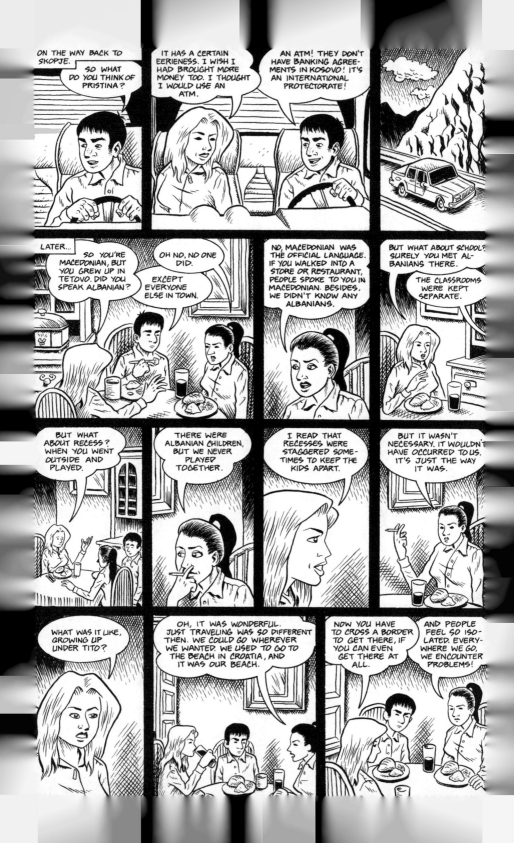

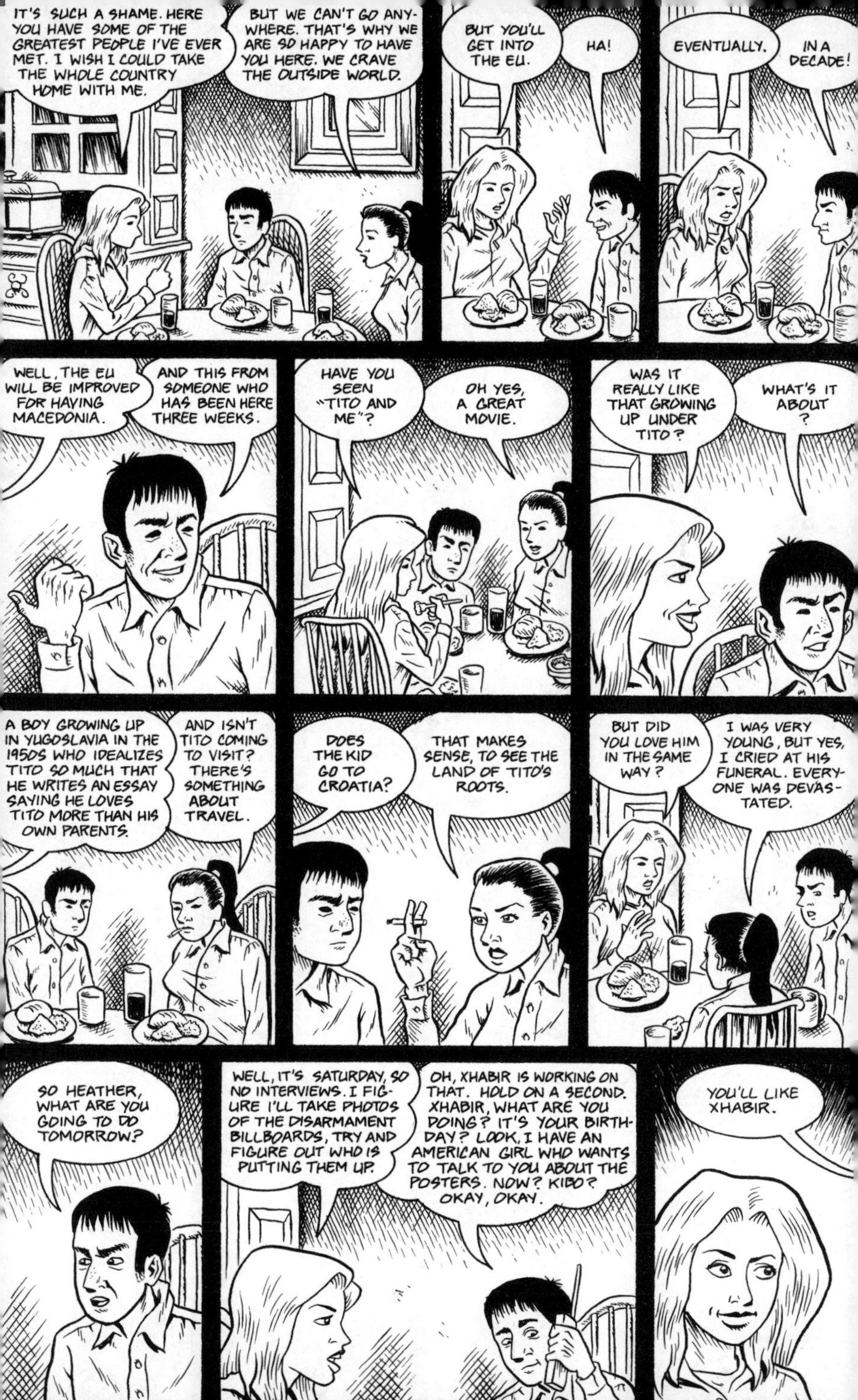
IT'S SUCH A SHAME. HERE YOU HAVE SOME OF THE GREATEST PEOPLE I'VE EVER MET. I WISH I COULD TAKE THE WHOLE COUNTRY HOME WITH ME.
BUT WE CAN'T GO ANYWHERE. THAT'S WHY WE ARE SO HAPPY TO HAVE YOU HERE. WE CRAVE THE OUTSIDE WORLD.
BUT YOU'LL GET INTO THE EU.
HA!
EVENTUALLY.
IN A DECADE!
WELL, THE EU WILL BE IMPROVED FOR HAVING MACEDONIA.
AND THIS FROM SOMEONE WHO HAS BEEN HERE THREE WEEKS.
HAVE YOU SEEN "TITO AND ME"?
OH YES, A GREAT MOVIE.
WAS IT REALLY LIKE THAT GROWING UP UNDER TITO?
WHAT'S IT ABOUT?
A BOY GROWING UP IN YUGOSLAVIA IN THE 1950S WHO IDEALIZES TITO SO MUCH THAT HE WRITES AN ESSAY SAYING HE LOVES TITO MORE THAN HIS OWN PARENTS.
AND ISN'T TITO COMING TO VISIT? THERE'S SOMETHING ABOUT TRAVEL.
DOES THE KID GO TO CROATIA?
THAT MAKES SENSE, TO SEE THE LAND OF TITO'S ROOTS.
BUT DID YOU LOVE HIM IN THE SAME WAY?
I WAS VERY YOUNG, BUT YES, I CRIED AT HIS FUNERAL. EVERYONE WAS DEVASTATED.
SO HEATHER, WHAT ARE YOU GOING TO DO TOMORROW?
WELL, IT'S SATURDAY, SO NO INTERVIEWS. I FIGURE I'LL TAKE PHOTOS OF THE DISARMAMENT BILLBOARDS, TRY AND FIGURE OUT WHO IS PUTTING THEM UP.
OH, XHABIR IS WORKING ON THAT. HOLD ON A SECOND. XHABIR, WHAT ARE YOU DOING? IT'S YOUR BIRTHDAY? LOOK, I HAVE AN AMERICAN GIRL WHO WANTS TO TALK TO YOU ABOUT THE POSTERS. NOW? KIBO? OKAY, OKAY.
YOU'LL LIKE XHABIR.

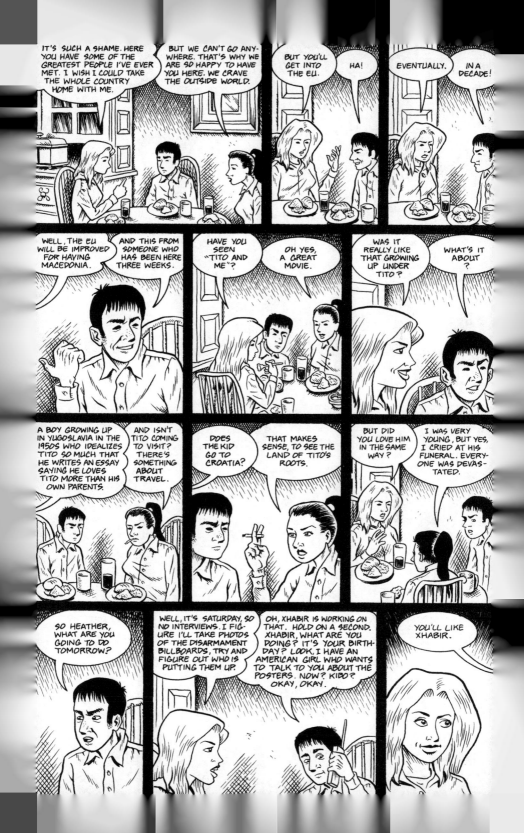

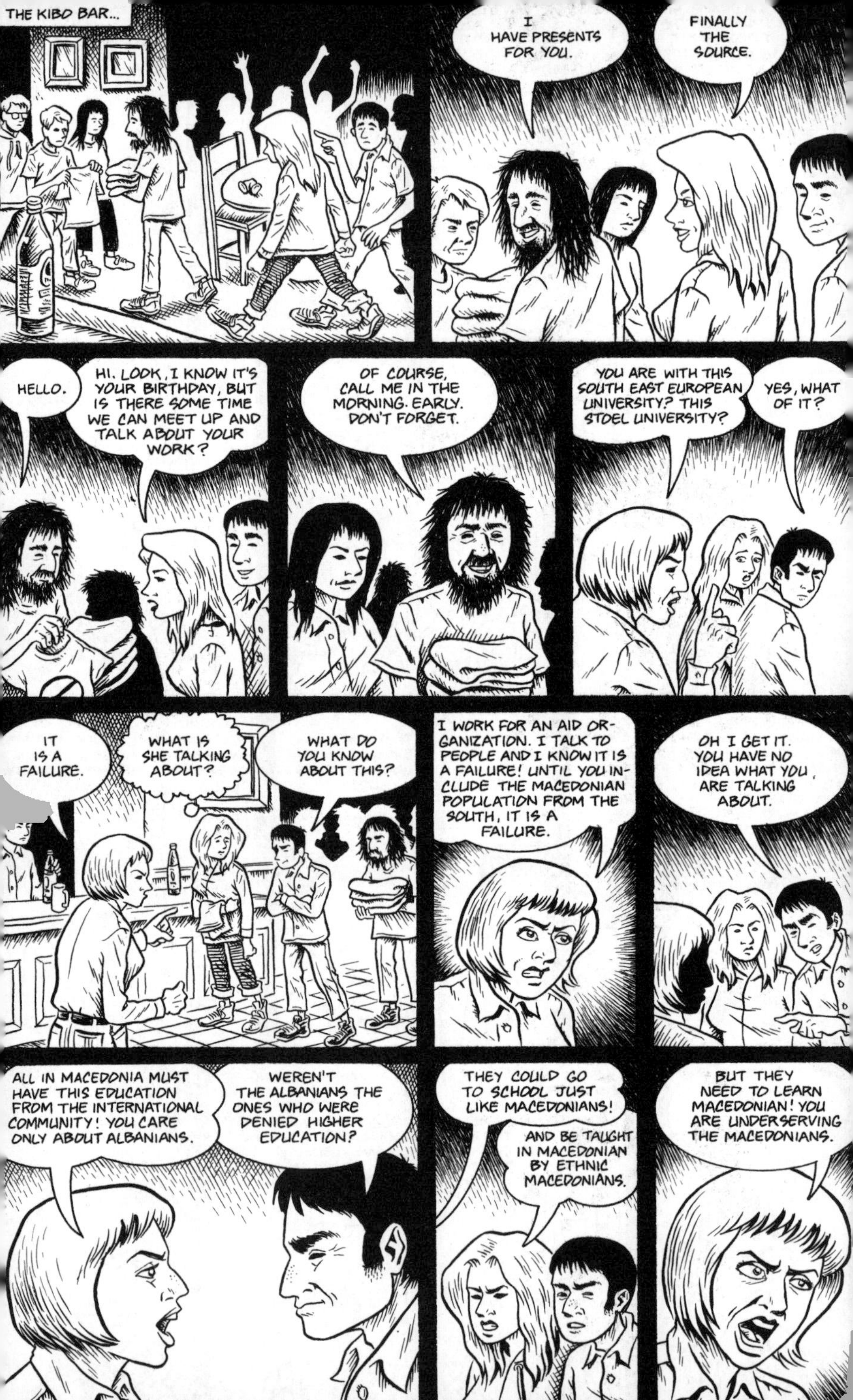
THE KIBO BAR...
I HAVE PRESENTS FOR YOU.
FINALLY THE SOURCE.
HELLO.
HI. LOOK, I KNOW IT'S YOUR BIRTHDAY, BUT IS THERE SOME TIME WE CAN MEET UP AND TALK ABOUT YOUR WORK?
OF COURSE, CALL ME IN THE MORNING. EARLY. DON'T FORGET.
YOU ARE WITH THIS SOUTH EAST EUROPEAN UNIVERSITY? THIS STOEL UNIVERSITY?
YES, WHAT OF IT?
IT IS A FAILURE.
WHAT IS SHE TALKING ABOUT?
WHAT DO YOU KNOW ABOUT THIS?
I WORK FOR AN AID ORGANIZATION. I TALK TO PEOPLE AND I KNOW IT IS A FAILURE! UNTIL YOU INCLUDE THE MACEDONIAN POPULATION FROM THE SOUTH, IT IS A FAILURE.
OH I GET IT. YOU HAVE NO IDEA WHAT YOU ARE TALKING ABOUT.
ALL IN MACEDONIA MUST HAVE THIS EDUCATION FROM THE INTERNATIONAL COMMUNITY! YOU CARE ONLY ABOUT ALBANIANS.
WEREN'T THE ALBANIANS THE ONES WHO WERE DENIED HIGHER EDUCATION?
THEY COULD GO TO SCHOOL JUST LIKE MACEDONIANS!
AND BE TAUGHT IN MACEDONIAN BY ETHNIC MACEDONIANS.
BUT THEY NEED TO LEARN MACEDONIAN! YOU ARE UNDERSERVING THE MACEDONIANS.

THAT NIGHT... TO THINK THAT AFTER JUST ONE DESPERATE E-MAIL, I COULD MEET ALL OF THESE PEOPLE. MATTHEW DIDN'T HAVE TO PICK ME UP THIS MORNING AND SHOW ME AROUND THE SCHOOL, LET ALONE TAKE ME INTO KOSOVO, OUT TO DINNER, AND TO THE PERSON I'VE BEEN LOOKING FOR SINCE MY FIRST DAY HERE.

I FEEL AN AFFINITY WITH THIS PLACE—THE PEOPLE FROM HERE, THE PEOPLE WHO CAME HERE. I FEEL MORE LIKE THEM THAN ANYONE I'VE EVER MET IN MY LIFE. I'M SURE THERE'S A SELECTION AT WORK AS FAR AS THE INTERNATIONALS ARE CONCERNED. MY FAMILY THOUGHT I WAS CRAZY TO COME HERE, AND THEIRS PROBABLY DID TOO, BUT EVERYONE'S HAVING THE TIME OF THEIR LIVES. I CAN'T IMAGINE HOW CLAUSTROPHOBIC IT MUST FEEL TO NOT BE ABLE TO LEAVE YOUR COUNTRY.

THE CONVERSATION WITH ADAM REALLY MADE ME THINK ABOUT HOW WE LOOK AT CONFLICT, MADE ME REMEMBER SOMETHING A PROFESSOR SAID ONE DAY. WE WERE PLOTTING A CONFLICT ALONG A CURVE, WHICH IN CONFLICT MODELING IS ALWAYS A CURVE UP TOWARD ARMED CONFLICT AND DOWN TOWARD A RECESSION OF HOSTILITIES AND FURTHER DOWN TOWARD PEACE-BUILDING. ANYHOW HE SUDDENLY ASKED "WHY IS IT THAT THE TAKING UP OF ARMS AND THE TAKING OF LIFE IS SIGNIFIED BY A RISE IN THE CURVE RATHER THAN SINKING? A RISE IMPLIES THINGS ARE GETTING BETTER." AND HE WAS SO RIGHT!

PUTTING IT ON A CURVE THAT RISES ALONG WITH THE DEATH TOLL JUST REINFORCES THE IDEA THAT VIOLENCE WILL BRING RESOLUTION, BECAUSE WE LOOK AT IT AS A FEVER RISING OF TENSIONS THAT WILL SOON BE LET OUT. A PRESSURE VALVE LET GO, AND PEOPLE EXHAUSTING THEMSELVES. WHAT GOES UP MUST COME DOWN, WE THINK. BUT REALLY IT'S ATROPHY AND DEGENERATION. YOU MIGHT SAY "THE MORE THIS BODY IS ABUSED AT TWENTY, THE BETTER SHAPE IT'LL BE IN AT FIFTY."

IT'S COMPLETELY ILLOGICAL, JUST AS IT'S ILLOGICAL TO THINK THAT PEOPLE WILL GET ALONG BETTER AFTER THEY EXPERIENCE DEVASTATING WAR.

THE NEXT MORNING...

YOU'LL LIKE FABIAN HE'S A PROFESSOR AT THE UNIVERSITY. HE'S FRENCH.

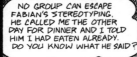

AH, THE AMERICAN STUDENT! ENCHANTÉ!

PLEASED TO MEET YOU.

AND JOLLY GOOD TO SEE YOU, OLD CHAP. YES, YES, JOLLY GOOD.

NO GROUP CAN ESCAPE FABIAN'S STEREOTYPING. HE CALLED ME THE OTHER DAY FOR DINNER AND I TOLD HIM I HAD EATEN ALREADY. DO YOU KNOW WHAT HE SAID?

WHAT?

"YOU FUCKING BRIT!"

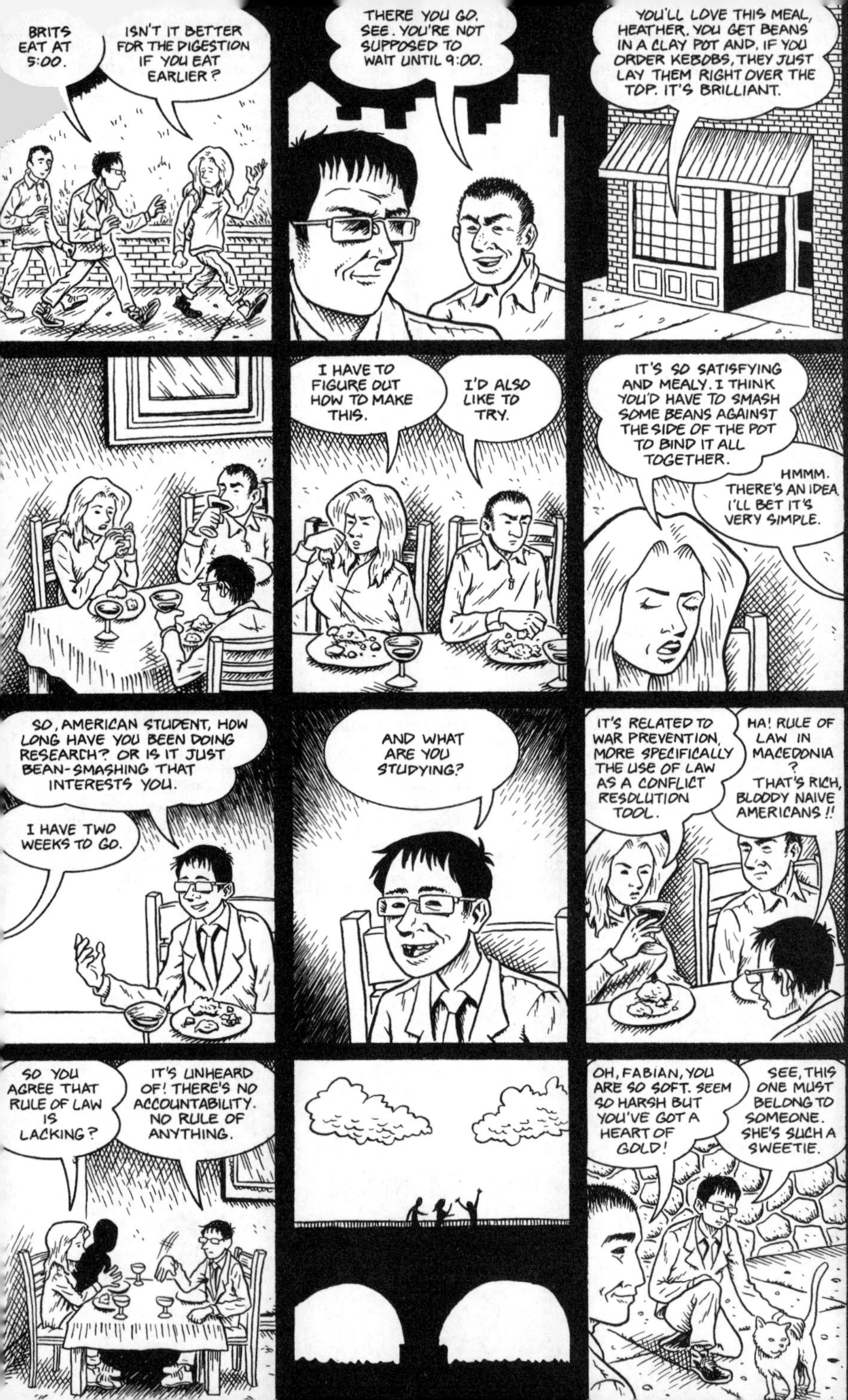
BRITS EAT AT 5:00.
ISN'T IT BETTER FOR THE DIGESTION IF YOU EAT EARLIER?
THERE YOU GO. SEE. YOU'RE NOT SUPPOSED TO WAIT UNTIL 9:00.
YOU'LL LOVE THIS MEAL, HEATHER. YOU GET BEANS IN A CLAY POT AND, IF YOU ORDER KEBOBS, THEY JUST LAY THEM RIGHT OVER THE TOP. IT'S BRILLIANT.
I HAVE TO FIGURE OUT HOW TO MAKE THIS.
I'D ALSO LIKE TO TRY.
IT'S SO SATISFYING AND MEALY. I THINK YOU'D HAVE TO SMASH SOME BEANS AGAINST THE SIDE OF THE POT TO BIND IT ALL TOGETHER.
HMMM. THERE'S AN IDEA. I'LL BET IT'S VERY SIMPLE.
SO, AMERICAN STUDENT, HOW LONG HAVE YOU BEEN DOING RESEARCH? OR IS IT JUST BEAN-SMASHING THAT INTERESTS YOU.
I HAVE TWO WEEKS TO GO.
AND WHAT ARE YOU STUDYING?
IT'S RELATED TO WAR PREVENTION, MORE SPECIFICALLY THE USE OF LAW AS A CONFLICT RESOLUTION TOOL.
HA! RULE OF LAW IN MACEDONIA? THAT'S RICH, BLOODY NAIVE AMERICANS!!
SO YOU AGREE THAT RULE OF LAW IS LACKING?
IT'S UNHEARD OF! THERE'S NO ACCOUNTABILITY. NO RULE OF ANYTHING.
OH, FABIAN, YOU ARE SO SOFT. SEEM SO HARSH BUT YOU'VE GOT A HEART OF GOLD!
SEE, THIS ONE MUST BELONG TO SOMEONE. SHE'S SUCH A SWEETIE.

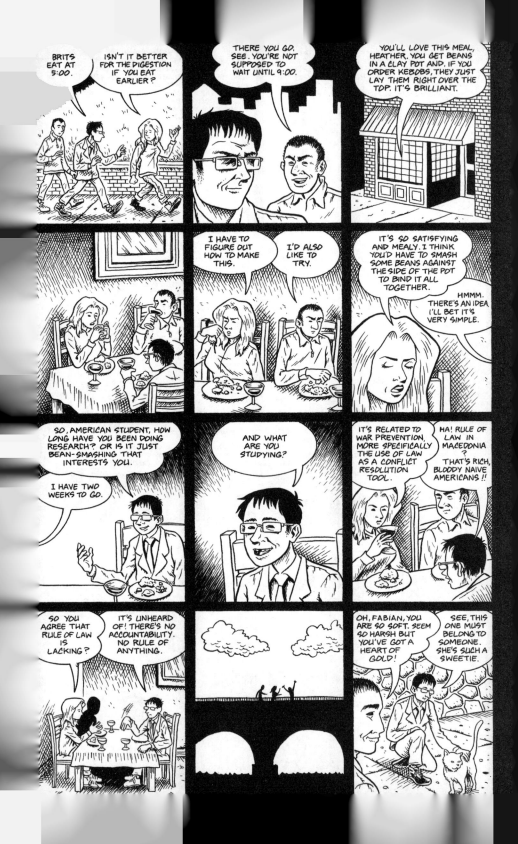

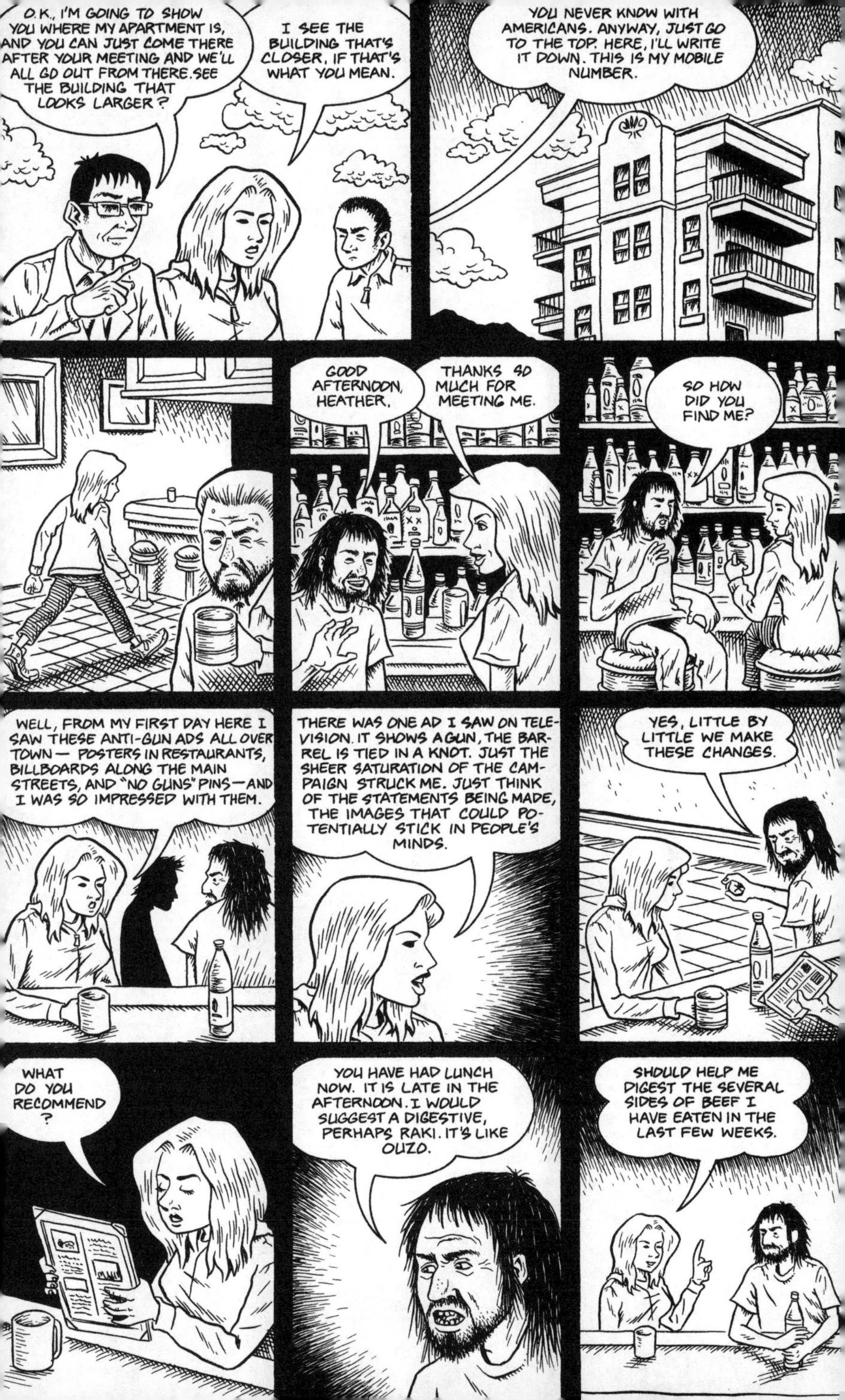
O.K., I'M GOING TO SHOW YOU WHERE MY APARTMENT IS, AND YOU CAN JUST COME THERE AFTER YOUR MEETING AND WE'LL ALL GO OUT FROM THERE. SEE THE BUILDING THAT LOOKS LARGER?
I SEE THE BUILDING THAT'S CLOSER, IF THAT'S WHAT YOU MEAN.
YOU NEVER KNOW WITH AMERICANS. ANYWAY, JUST GO TO THE TOP. HERE, I'LL WRITE IT DOWN. THIS IS MY MOBILE NUMBER.
GOOD AFTERNOON, HEATHER.
THANKS SO MUCH FOR MEETING ME.
SO HOW DID YOU FIND ME?
WELL, FROM MY FIRST DAY HERE I SAW THESE ANTI-GUN ADS ALL OVER TOWN— POSTERS IN RESTAURANTS, BILLBOARDS ALONG THE MAIN STREETS, AND "NO GUNS" PINS—AND I WAS SO IMPRESSED WITH THEM.
THERE WAS ONE AD I SAW ON TELEVISION. IT SHOWS A GUN, THE BARREL IS TIED IN A KNOT. JUST THE SHEER SATURATION OF THE CAMPAIGN STRUCK ME. JUST THINK OF THE STATEMENTS BEING MADE, THE IMAGES THAT COULD POTENTIALLY STICK IN PEOPLE'S MINDS.
YES, LITTLE BY LITTLE WE MAKE THESE CHANGES.
WHAT DO YOU RECOMMEND?
YOU HAVE HAD LUNCH NOW. IT IS LATE IN THE AFTERNOON. I WOULD SUGGEST A DIGESTIVE, PERHAPS RAKI. IT'S LIKE OUZO.
SHOULD HELP ME DIGEST THE SEVERAL SIDES OF BEEF I HAVE EATEN IN THE LAST FEW WEEKS.

SO DID YOU GROW UP SPEAKING ALBANIAN?

NO, I NEVER SPOKE ALBANIAN. ACTUALLY, I SPEAK MACEDONIAN AND TURKISH.

BUT I THOUGHT YOU WERE ALBANIAN.

WELL, PEOPLE LIKE ETHNIC LABELS, BUT IT'S MORE COMPLI- CATED THAN THAT.

WHAT HAVE YOU BEEN UP TO SINCE YOU ARRIVED?

OH, LOTS OF STUFF, MEETING WITH THE OSCE, SEEING LAW PROFESSORS.

SOMETIMES IT IS THE INTELLECTUALS THAT ARE VERY DANGEROUS.

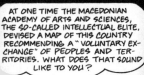

I'VE GOTTEN SOME MATERIALS FROM LAW PROFESSORS AND IT AMAZES ME HOW MUCH THEY SEE THE RHETORIC OF HUMAN RIGHTS TO JUSTIFY HARD- CORE NATIONALIST CLAIMS!

SO YOU SEE THIS.

THEY USE THE RIGHT CATCHPHRASES, BUT WHEN YOU READ CLOSELY...

AT ONE TIME THE MACEDONIAN ACADEMY OF ARTS AND SCIENCES, THE SO-CALLED INTELLECTUAL ELITE, DEVISED A MAP OF THIS COUNTRY RECOMMENDING A "VOLUNTARY EX- CHANGE" OF PEOPLES AND TER- RITORIES. WHAT DOES THAT SOUND LIKE TO YOU?

ETHNIC CLEANSING?

RIGHT, VOLUNTARY ETHNIC CLEANSING, VOLUN- TARY REMOVAL OF PEOPLE FROM THEIR NEIGHBORHOODS, TOWNS, FARMS. BUT YOU HAVE NOT ASKED A QUESTION.

HERE'S ONE. WHAT DO YOU THINK OF THAT HUGE HILLSIDE CROSS?

I'VE HEARD IT'S THE SECOND LARGEST OF ITS KIND.

THE FIRST NIGHT I ARRIVED, IT WAS THE FIRST THING I SAW. IT STRUCK ME AS BEAUTIFUL, BUT THEN I THOUGHT ABOUT WHAT IT MUST MEAN TO AL- BANIANS LIVING HERE. YOU CAN SEE IT FROM EVERYWHERE IN TOWN.

IT SAYS TO EVERYONE, "THIS IS AN ORTHO- DOX COUNTRY."

WHAT WAS IT LIKE GROWING UP AND SEEING IT?

AS A CHILD? IT WAS DEDICATED IN 2002.

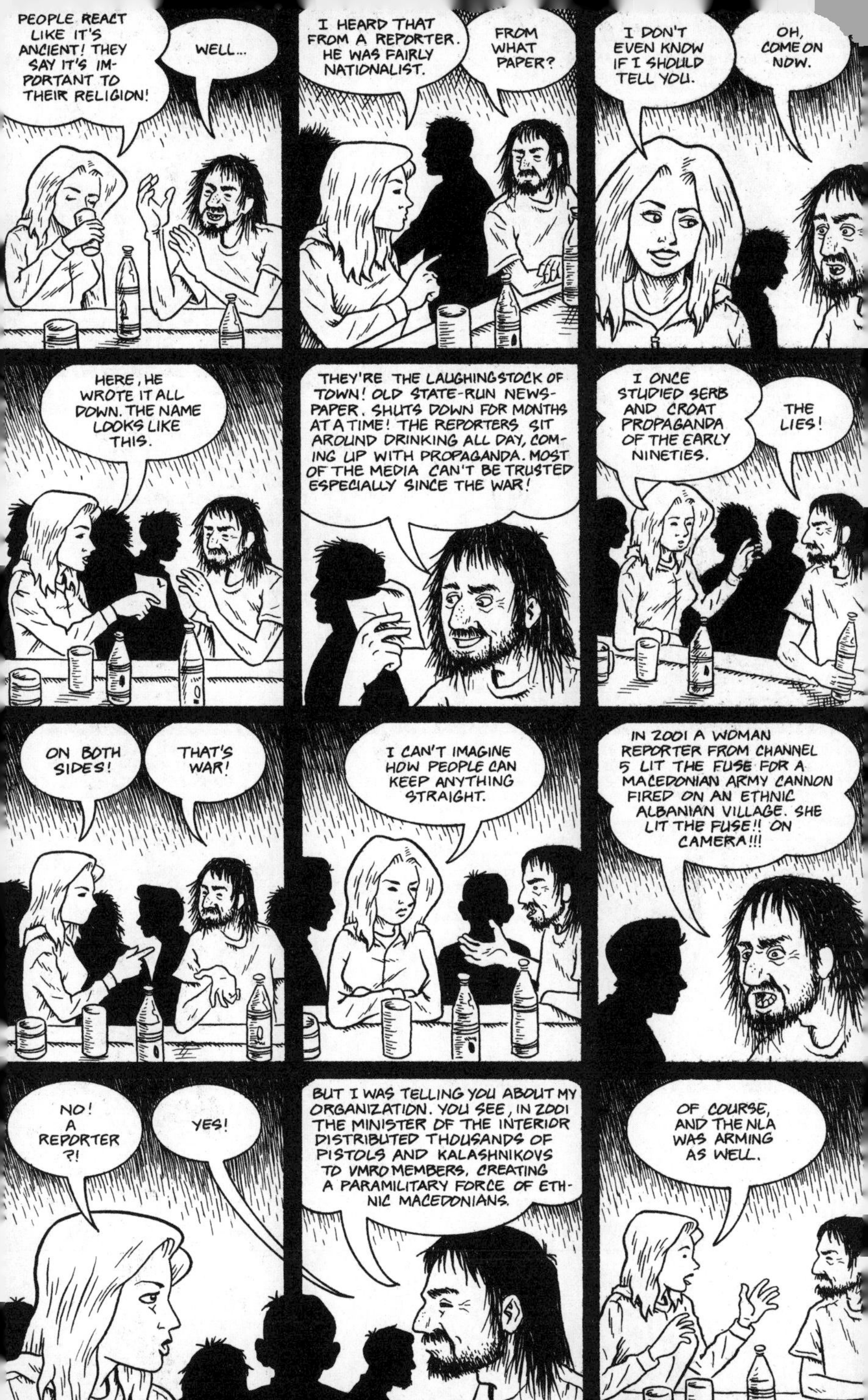
PEOPLE REACT LIKE IT'S ANCIENT! THEY SAY IT'S IMPORTANT TO THEIR RELIGION!
WELL...
I HEARD THAT FROM A REPORTER. HE WAS FAIRLY NATIONALIST.
FROM WHAT PAPER?
I DON'T EVEN KNOW IF I SHOULD TELL YOU.
OH, COME ON NOW.
HERE, HE WROTE IT ALL DOWN. THE NAME LOOKS LIKE THIS.
THEY'RE THE LAUGHINGSTOCK OF TOWN! OLD STATE-RUN NEWSPAPER. SHUTS DOWN FOR MONTHS AT A TIME! THE REPORTERS SIT AROUND DRINKING ALL DAY, COMING UP WITH PROPAGANDA. MOST OF THE MEDIA CAN'T BE TRUSTED ESPECIALLY SINCE THE WAR!
I ONCE STUDIED SERB AND CROAT PROPAGANDA OF THE EARLY NINETIES.
THE LIES!
ON BOTH SIDES!
THAT'S WAR!
I CAN'T IMAGINE HOW PEOPLE CAN KEEP ANYTHING STRAIGHT.
IN 2001 A WOMAN REPORTER FROM CHANNEL 5 LIT THE FUSE FOR A MACEDONIAN ARMY CANNON FIRED ON AN ETHNIC ALBANIAN VILLAGE. SHE LIT THE FUSE!! ON CAMERA!!!
NO! A REPORTER?!
YES!
BUT I WAS TELLING YOU ABOUT MY ORGANIZATION. YOU SEE, IN 2001 THE MINISTER OF THE INTERIOR DISTRIBUTED THOUSANDS OF PISTOLS AND KALASHNIKOVS TO VMRO MEMBERS, CREATING A PARAMILITARY FORCE OF ETHNIC MACEDONIANS.
OF COURSE, AND THE NLA WAS ARMING AS WELL.

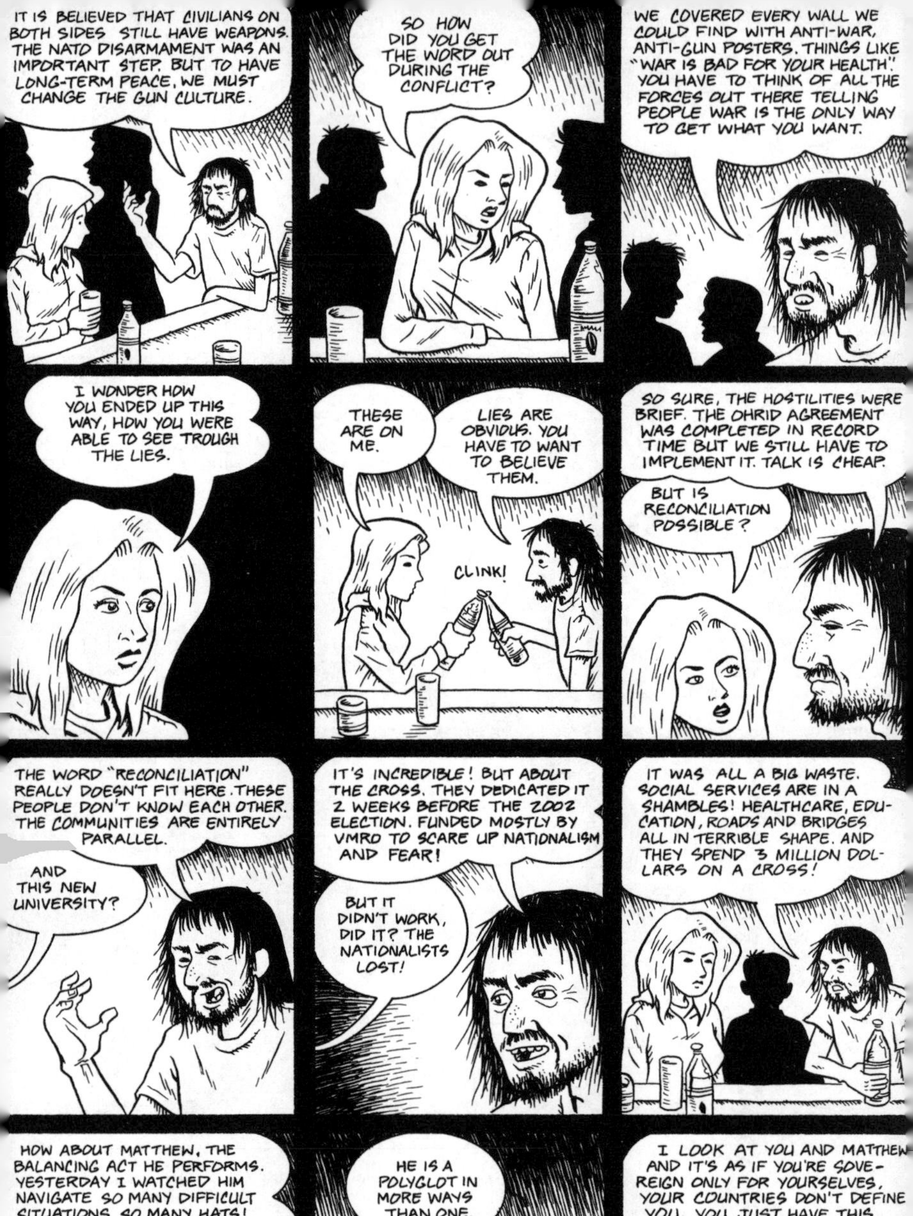
IT IS BELIEVED THAT CIVILIANS ON BOTH SIDES STILL HAVE WEAPONS. THE NATO DISARMAMENT WAS AN IMPORTANT STEP. BUT TO HAVE LONG-TERM PEACE, WE MUST CHANGE THE GUN CULTURE.
SO HOW DID YOU GET THE WORD OUT DURING THE CONFLICT?
WE COVERED EVERY WALL WE COULD FIND WITH ANTI-WAR, ANTI-GUN POSTERS. THINGS LIKE "WAR IS BAD FOR YOUR HEALTH". YOU HAVE TO THINK OF ALL THE FORCES OUT THERE TELLING PEOPLE WAR IS THE ONLY WAY TO GET WHAT YOU WANT.
I WONDER HOW YOU ENDED UP THIS WAY, HOW YOU WERE ABLE TO SEE TROUGH THE LIES.
THESE ARE ON ME.
LIES ARE OBVIOUS. YOU HAVE TO WANT TO BELIEVE THEM.
CLINK!
SO SURE, THE HOSTILITIES WERE BRIEF. THE OHRID AGREEMENT WAS COMPLETED IN RECORD TIME BUT WE STILL HAVE TO IMPLEMENT IT. TALK IS CHEAP.
BUT IS RECONCILIATION POSSIBLE?
THE WORD "RECONCILIATION" REALLY DOESN'T FIT HERE. THESE PEOPLE DON'T KNOW EACH OTHER. THE COMMUNITIES ARE ENTIRELY PARALLEL.
AND THIS NEW UNIVERSITY?
IT'S INCREDIBLE! BUT ABOUT THE CROSS. THEY DEDICATED IT 2 WEEKS BEFORE THE 2002 ELECTION. FUNDED MOSTLY BY VMRO TO SCARE UP NATIONALISM AND FEAR!
BUT IT DIDN'T WORK, DID IT? THE NATIONALISTS LOST!
IT WAS ALL A BIG WASTE. SOCIAL SERVICES ARE IN A SHAMBLES! HEALTHCARE, EDUCATION, ROADS AND BRIDGES ALL IN TERRIBLE SHAPE. AND THEY SPEND 3 MILLION DOLLARS ON A CROSS!
HOW ABOUT MATTHEW, THE BALANCING ACT HE PERFORMS. YESTERDAY I WATCHED HIM NAVIGATE SO MANY DIFFICULT SITUATIONS. SO MANY HATS! EDUCATOR, ADMINISTRATOR, DIPLOMAT, ADVOCATE, GOOD GUY, BAD GUY, JEEZ!
HE IS A POLYGLOT IN MORE WAYS THAN ONE.
I LOOK AT YOU AND MATTHEW AND IT'S AS IF YOU'RE SOVEREIGN ONLY FOR YOURSELVES. YOUR COUNTRIES DON'T DEFINE YOU. YOU JUST HAVE THIS SENSE OF RIGHT AND WRONG AND THAT'S WHAT YOU DO.

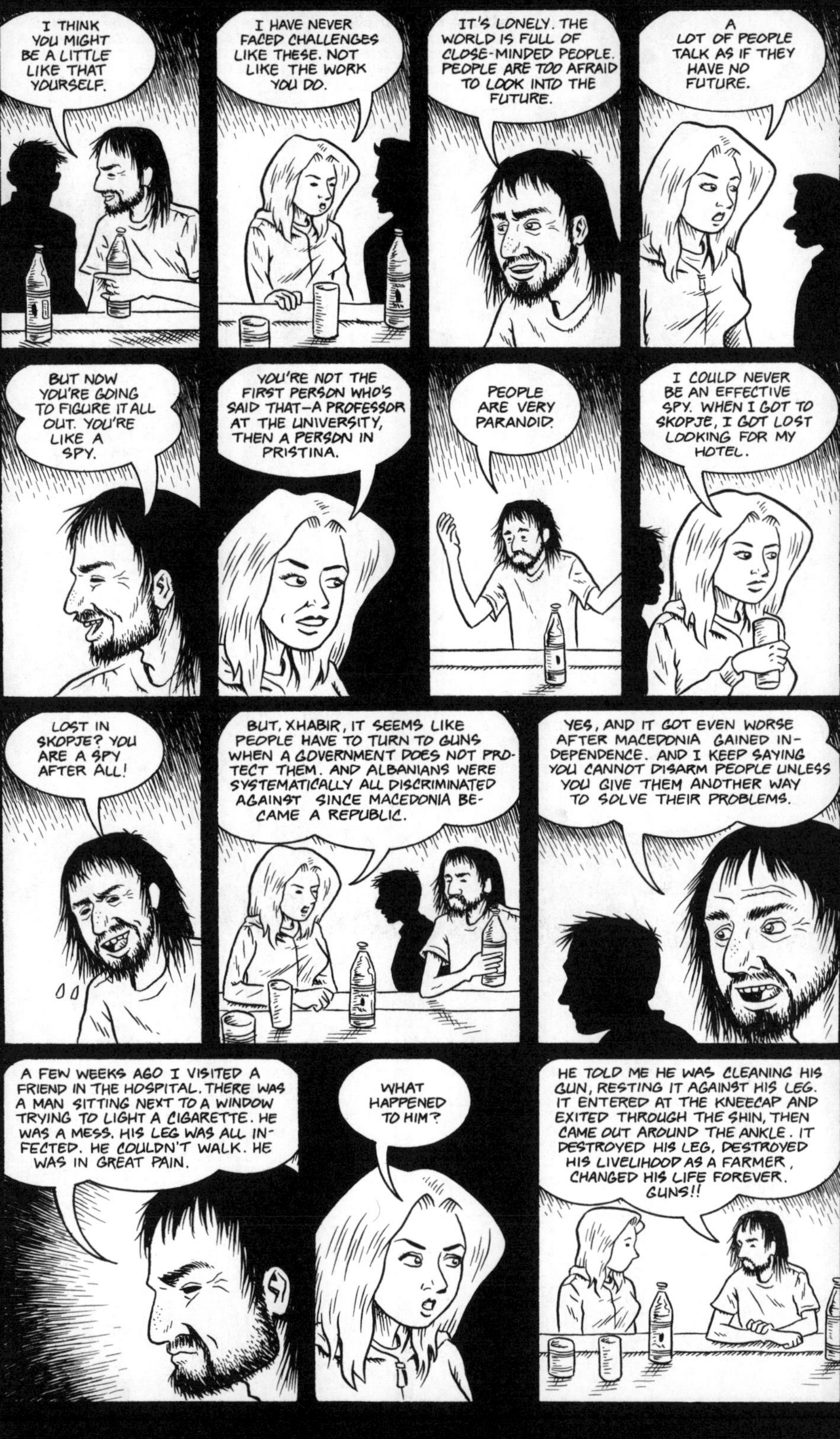
I THINK YOU MIGHT BE A LITTLE LIKE THAT YOURSELF.
I HAVE NEVER FACED CHALLENGES LIKE THESE. NOT LIKE THE WORK YOU DO.
IT'S LONELY. THE WORLD IS FULL OF CLOSE-MINDED PEOPLE. PEOPLE ARE TOO AFRAID TO LOOK INTO THE FUTURE.
A LOT OF PEOPLE TALK AS IF THEY HAVE NO FUTURE.
BUT NOW YOU'RE GOING TO FIGURE IT ALL OUT. YOU'RE LIKE A SPY.
YOU'RE NOT THE FIRST PERSON WHO'S SAID THAT—A PROFESSOR AT THE UNIVERSITY, THEN A PERSON IN PRISTINA.
PEOPLE ARE VERY PARANOID.
I COULD NEVER BE AN EFFECTIVE SPY. WHEN I GOT TO SKOPJE, I GOT LOST LOOKING FOR MY HOTEL.
LOST IN SKOPJE? YOU ARE A SPY AFTER ALL!
BUT, XHABIR, IT SEEMS LIKE PEOPLE HAVE TO TURN TO GUNS WHEN A GOVERNMENT DOES NOT PROTECT THEM. AND ALBANIANS WERE SYSTEMATICALLY ALL DISCRIMINATED AGAINST SINCE MACEDONIA BECAME A REPUBLIC.
YES, AND IT GOT EVEN WORSE AFTER MACEDONIA GAINED INDEPENDENCE. AND I KEEP SAYING YOU CANNOT DISARM PEOPLE UNLESS YOU GIVE THEM ANOTHER WAY TO SOLVE THEIR PROBLEMS.
A FEW WEEKS AGO I VISITED A FRIEND IN THE HOSPITAL. THERE WAS A MAN SITTING NEXT TO A WINDOW TRYING TO LIGHT A CIGARETTE. HE WAS A MESS. HIS LEG WAS ALL INFECTED. HE COULDN'T WALK. HE WAS IN GREAT PAIN.
WHAT HAPPENED TO HIM?
HE TOLD ME HE WAS CLEANING HIS GUN, RESTING IT AGAINST HIS LEG. IT ENTERED AT THE KNEECAP AND EXITED THROUGH THE SHIN, THEN CAME OUT AROUND THE ANKLE. IT DESTROYED HIS LEG, DESTROYED HIS LIVELIHOOD AS A FARMER, CHANGED HIS LIFE FOREVER. GUNS!!

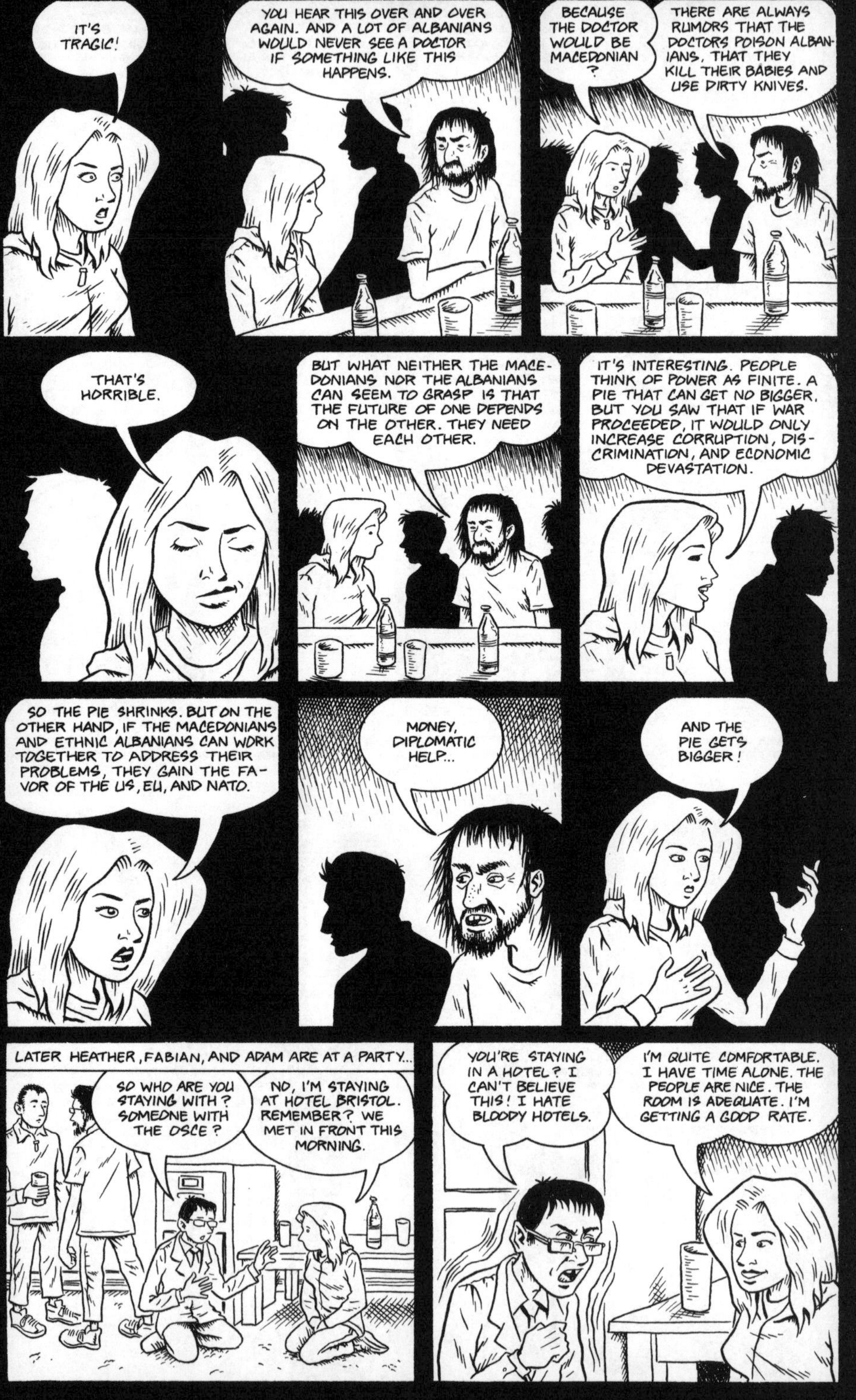
IT'S TRAGIC!
YOU HEAR THIS OVER AND OVER AGAIN. AND A LOT OF ALBANIANS WOULD NEVER SEE A DOCTOR IF SOMETHING LIKE THIS HAPPENS.
BECAUSE THE DOCTOR WOULD BE MACEDONIAN?
THERE ARE ALWAYS RUMORS THAT THE DOCTORS POISON ALBANIANS, THAT THEY KILL THEIR BABIES AND USE DIRTY KNIVES.
THAT'S HORRIBLE.
BUT WHAT NEITHER THE MACEDONIANS NOR THE ALBANIANS CAN SEEM TO GRASP IS THAT THE FUTURE OF ONE DEPENDS ON THE OTHER. THEY NEED EACH OTHER.
IT'S INTERESTING. PEOPLE THINK OF POWER AS FINITE. A PIE THAT CAN GET NO BIGGER. BUT YOU SAW THAT IF WAR PROCEEDED, IT WOULD ONLY INCREASE CORRUPTION, DISCRIMINATION, AND ECONOMIC DEVASTATION.
SO THE PIE SHRINKS. BUT ON THE OTHER HAND, IF THE MACEDONIANS AND ETHNIC ALBANIANS CAN WORK TOGETHER TO ADDRESS THEIR PROBLEMS, THEY GAIN THE FAVOR OF THE US, EU, AND NATO.
MONEY, DIPLOMATIC HELP...
AND THE PIE GETS BIGGER!
LATER HEATHER, FABIAN, AND ADAM ARE AT A PARTY...
SO WHO ARE YOU STAYING WITH? SOMEONE WITH THE OSCE?
NO, I'M STAYING AT HOTEL BRISTOL. REMEMBER? WE MET IN FRONT THIS MORNING.
YOU'RE STAYING IN A HOTEL? I CAN'T BELIEVE THIS! I HATE BLOODY HOTELS.
I'M QUITE COMFORTABLE. I HAVE TIME ALONE. THE PEOPLE ARE NICE. THE ROOM IS ADEQUATE. I'M GETTING A GOOD RATE.

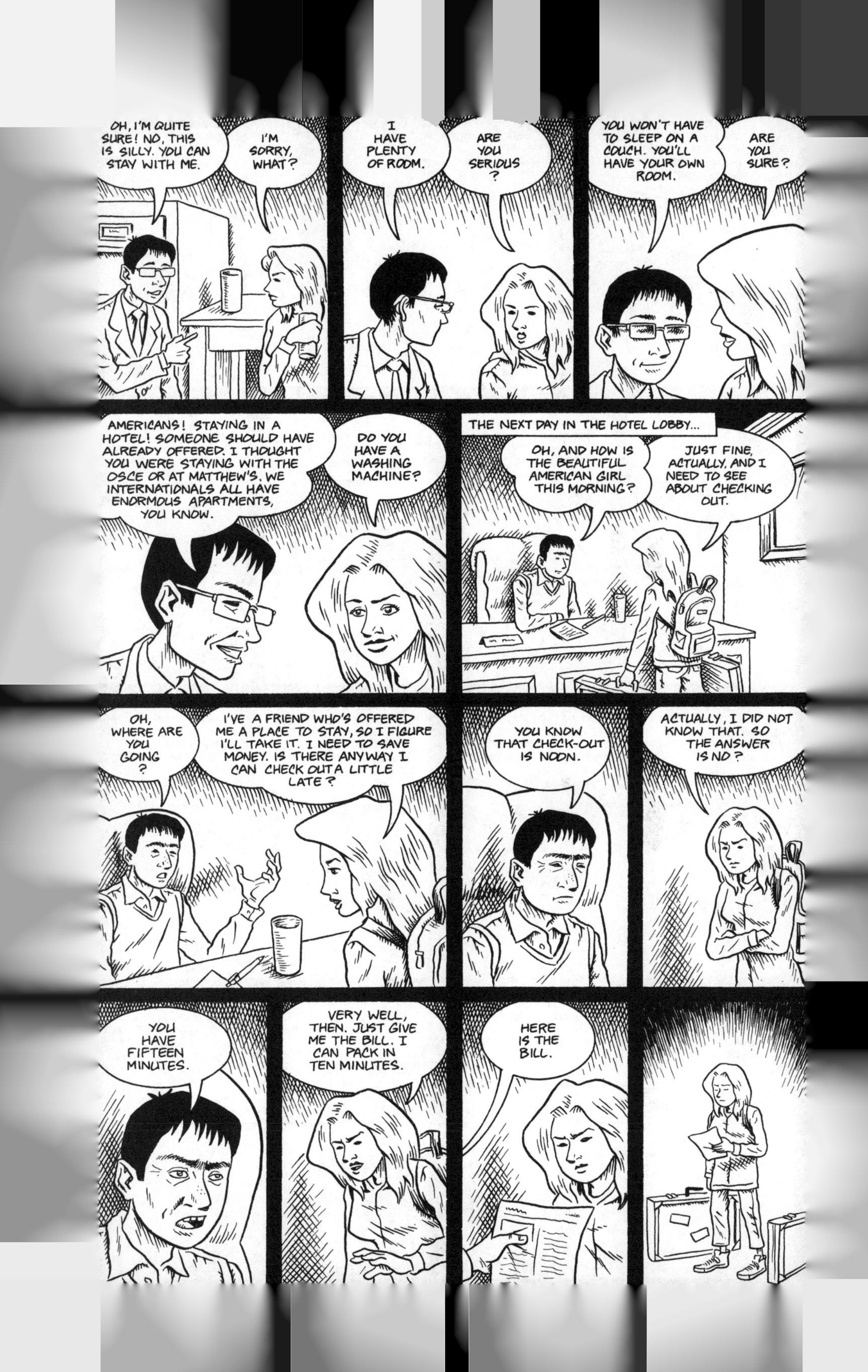
OH, I'M QUITE SURE! NO, THIS IS SILLY. YOU CAN STAY WITH ME.
I'M SORRY, WHAT?
I HAVE PLENTY OF ROOM.
ARE YOU SERIOUS?
YOU WON'T HAVE TO SLEEP ON A COUCH. YOU'LL HAVE YOUR OWN ROOM.
ARE YOU SURE?
AMERICANS! STAYING IN A HOTEL! SOMEONE SHOULD HAVE ALREADY OFFERED. I THOUGHT YOU WERE STAYING WITH THE OSCE OR AT MATTHEW'S. WE INTERNATIONALS ALL HAVE ENORMOUS APARTMENTS, YOU KNOW.
DO YOU HAVE A WASHING MACHINE?
THE NEXT DAY IN THE HOTEL LOBBY...
OH, AND HOW IS THE BEAUTIFUL AMERICAN GIRL THIS MORNING?
JUST FINE, ACTUALLY, AND I NEED TO SEE ABOUT CHECKING OUT.
OH, WHERE ARE YOU GOING?
I'VE A FRIEND WHO'S OFFERED ME A PLACE TO STAY, SO I FIGURE I'LL TAKE IT. I NEED TO SAVE MONEY. IS THERE ANYWAY I CAN CHECK OUT A LITTLE LATE?
YOU KNOW THAT CHECK-OUT IS NOON.
ACTUALLY, I DID NOT KNOW THAT. SO THE ANSWER IS NO?
YOU HAVE FIFTEEN MINUTES.
VERY WELL, THEN. JUST GIVE ME THE BILL. I CAN PACK IN TEN MINUTES.
HERE IS THE BILL.

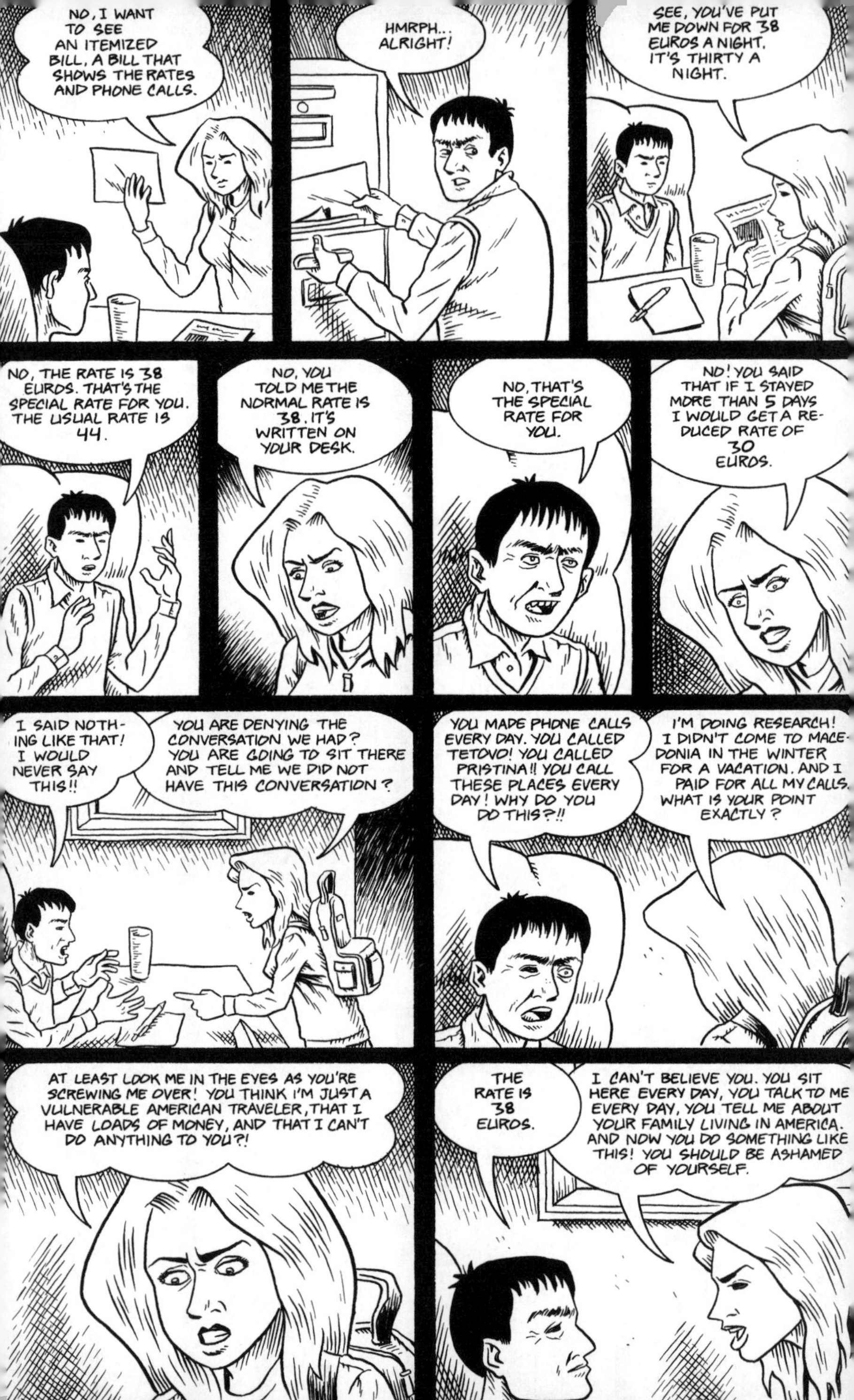

NO, I WANT TO SEE AN ITEMIZED BILL, A BILL THAT SHOWS THE RATES AND PHONE CALLS.
HMRPH... ALRIGHT!
SEE, YOU'VE PUT ME DOWN FOR 38 EUROS A NIGHT. IT'S THIRTY A NIGHT.
NO, THE RATE IS 38 EUROS. THAT'S THE SPECIAL RATE FOR YOU. THE USUAL RATE IS 44.
NO, YOU TOLD ME THE NORMAL RATE IS 38. IT'S WRITTEN ON YOUR DESK.
NO, THAT'S THE SPECIAL RATE FOR YOU.
NO! YOU SAID THAT IF I STAYED MORE THAN 5 DAYS I WOULD GET A REDUCED RATE OF 30 EUROS.
I SAID NOTHING LIKE THAT! I WOULD NEVER SAY THIS!!
YOU ARE DENYING THE CONVERSATION WE HAD? YOU ARE GOING TO SIT THERE AND TELL ME WE DID NOT HAVE THIS CONVERSATION?
YOU MADE PHONE CALLS EVERY DAY. YOU CALLED TETOVO! YOU CALLED PRISTINA!! YOU CALL THESE PLACES EVERY DAY! WHY DO YOU DO THIS?!!
I'M DOING RESEARCH! I DIDN'T COME TO MACEDONIA IN THE WINTER FOR A VACATION. AND I PAID FOR ALL MY CALLS. WHAT IS YOUR POINT EXACTLY?
AT LEAST LOOK ME IN THE EYES AS YOU'RE SCREWING ME OVER! YOU THINK I'M JUST A VULNERABLE AMERICAN TRAVELER, THAT I HAVE LOADS OF MONEY, AND THAT I CAN'T DO ANYTHING TO YOU?!
THE RATE IS 38 EUROS.
I CAN'T BELIEVE YOU. YOU SIT HERE EVERY DAY, YOU TALK TO ME EVERY DAY, YOU TELL ME ABOUT YOUR FAMILY LIVING IN AMERICA. AND NOW YOU DO SOMETHING LIKE THIS! YOU SHOULD BE ASHAMED OF YOURSELF.

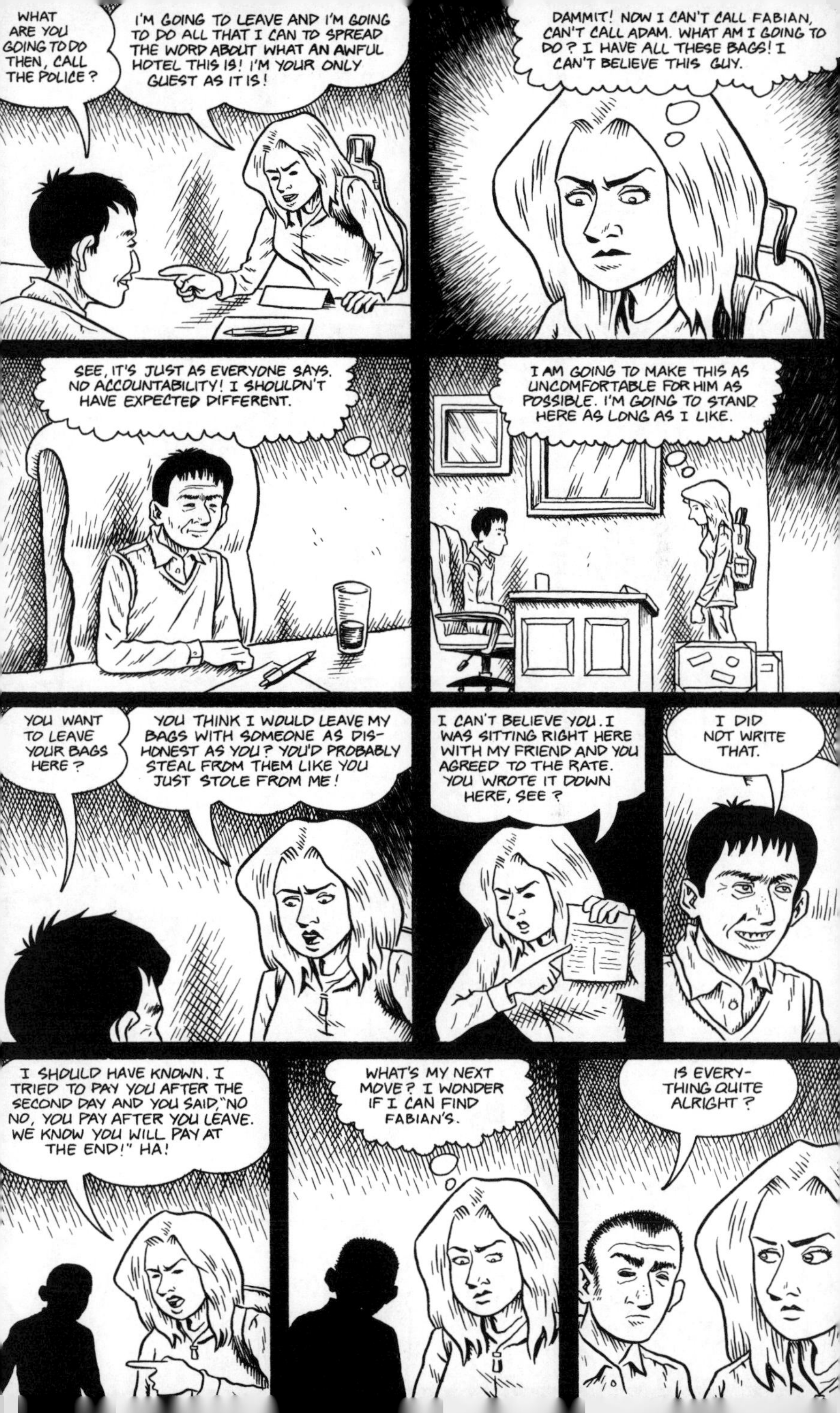
WHAT ARE YOU GOING TO DO THEN, CALL THE POLICE?
I'M GOING TO LEAVE AND I'M GOING TO DO ALL THAT I CAN TO SPREAD THE WORD ABOUT WHAT AN AWFUL HOTEL THIS IS! I'M YOUR ONLY GUEST AS IT IS!
DAMMIT! NOW I CAN'T CALL FABIAN, CAN'T CALL ADAM. WHAT AM I GOING TO DO? I HAVE ALL THESE BAGS! I CAN'T BELIEVE THIS GUY.
SEE, IT'S JUST AS EVERYONE SAYS. NO ACCOUNTABILITY! I SHOULDN'T HAVE EXPECTED DIFFERENT.
I AM GOING TO MAKE THIS AS UNCOMFORTABLE FOR HIM AS POSSIBLE. I'M GOING TO STAND HERE AS LONG AS I LIKE.
YOU WANT TO LEAVE YOUR BAGS HERE?
YOU THINK I WOULD LEAVE MY BAGS WITH SOMEONE AS DIS-HONEST AS YOU? YOU'D PROBABLY STEAL FROM THEM LIKE YOU JUST STOLE FROM ME!
I CAN'T BELIEVE YOU. I WAS SITTING RIGHT HERE WITH MY FRIEND AND YOU AGREED TO THE RATE. YOU WROTE IT DOWN HERE, SEE?
I DID NOT WRITE THAT.
I SHOULD HAVE KNOWN. I TRIED TO PAY YOU AFTER THE SECOND DAY AND YOU SAID, "NO NO, YOU PAY AFTER YOU LEAVE. WE KNOW YOU WILL PAY AT THE END!" HA!
WHAT'S MY NEXT MOVE? I WONDER IF I CAN FIND FABIAN'S.
IS EVERY-THING QUITE ALRIGHT?

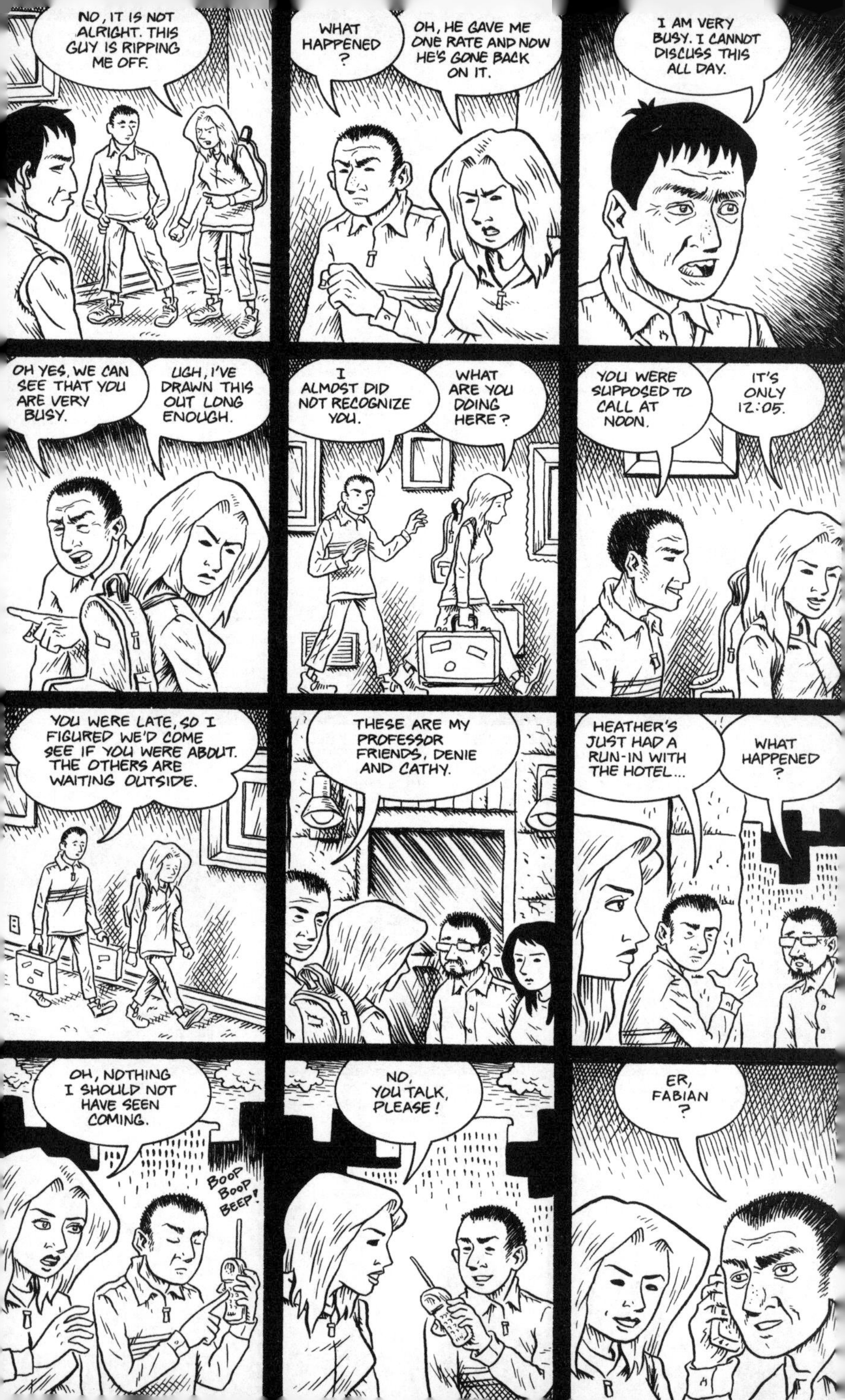
NO, IT IS NOT ALRIGHT. THIS GUY IS RIPPING ME OFF.
WHAT HAPPENED ?
OH, HE GAVE ME ONE RATE AND NOW HE'S GONE BACK ON IT.
I AM VERY BUSY. I CANNOT DISCUSS THIS ALL DAY.
OH YES, WE CAN SEE THAT YOU ARE VERY BUSY.
UGH, I'VE DRAWN THIS OUT LONG ENOUGH.
I ALMOST DID NOT RECOGNIZE YOU.
WHAT ARE YOU DOING HERE?
YOU WERE SUPPOSED TO CALL AT NOON.
IT'S ONLY 12:05.
YOU WERE LATE, SO I FIGURED WE'D COME SEE IF YOU WERE ABOUT. THE OTHERS ARE WAITING OUTSIDE.
THESE ARE MY PROFESSOR FRIENDS, DENIE AND CATHY.
HEATHER'S JUST HAD A RUN-IN WITH THE HOTEL...
WHAT HAPPENED ?
OH, NOTHING I SHOULD NOT HAVE SEEN COMING.
BOOP BOOP BEEP!
NO, YOU TALK, PLEASE!
ER, FABIAN ?

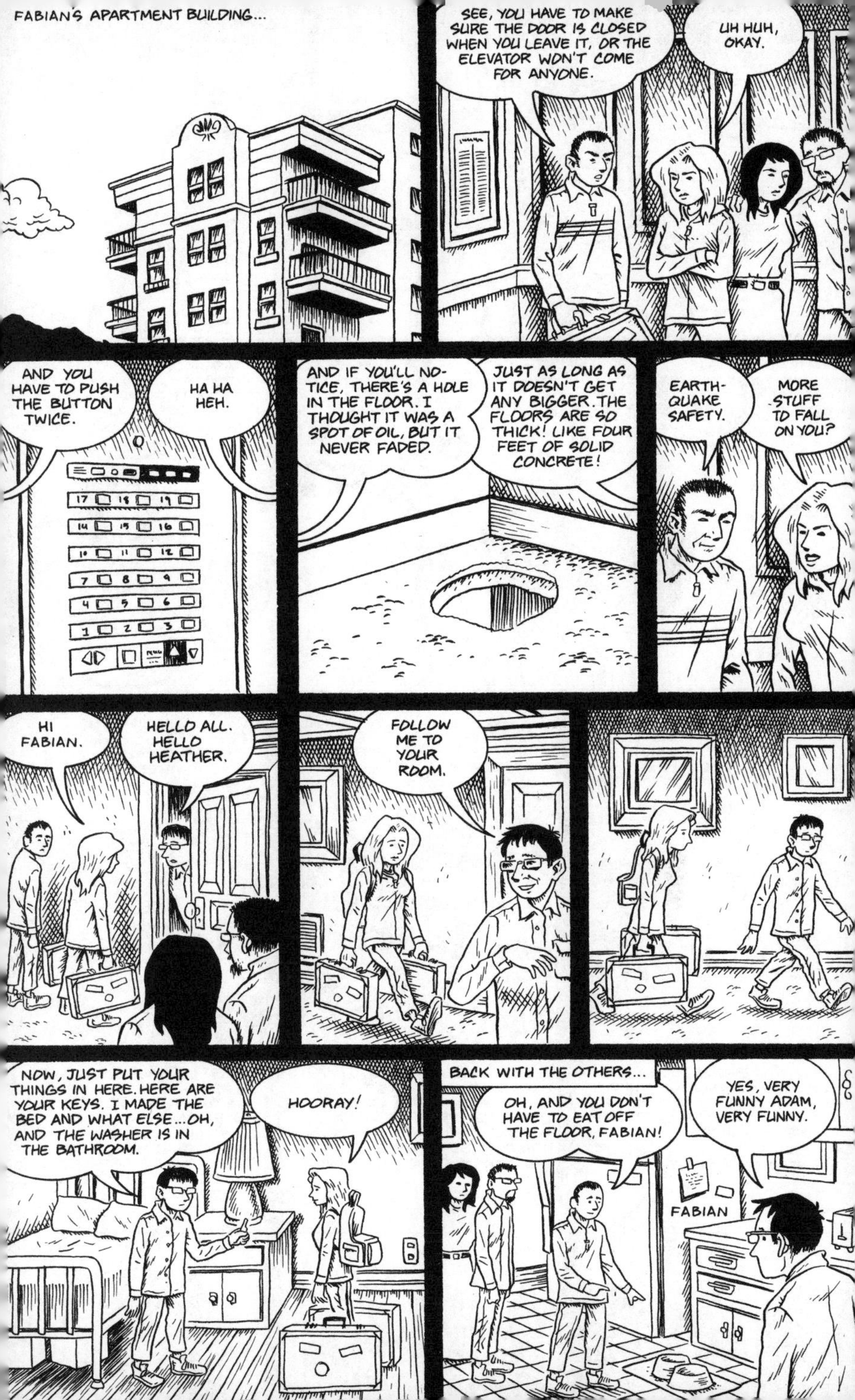
FABIAN'S APARTMENT BUILDING...
SEE, YOU HAVE TO MAKE SURE THE DOOR IS CLOSED WHEN YOU LEAVE IT, OR THE ELEVATOR WON'T COME FOR ANYONE.
UH HUH, OKAY.
AND YOU HAVE TO PUSH THE BUTTON TWICE.
HA HA HEH.
AND IF YOU'LL NOTICE, THERE'S A HOLE IN THE FLOOR. I THOUGHT IT WAS A SPOT OF OIL, BUT IT NEVER FADED.
JUST AS LONG AS IT DOESN'T GET ANY BIGGER. THE FLOORS ARE SO THICK! LIKE FOUR FEET OF SOLID CONCRETE!
EARTHQUAKE SAFETY.
MORE STUFF TO FALL ON YOU?
HI FABIAN.
HELLO ALL. HELLO HEATHER.
FOLLOW ME TO YOUR ROOM.
NOW, JUST PUT YOUR THINGS IN HERE. HERE ARE YOUR KEYS. I MADE THE BED AND WHAT ELSE...OH, AND THE WASHER IS IN THE BATHROOM.
HOORAY!
BACK WITH THE OTHERS...
OH, AND YOU DON'T HAVE TO EAT OFF THE FLOOR, FABIAN!
YES, VERY FUNNY ADAM, VERY FUNNY.
FABIAN

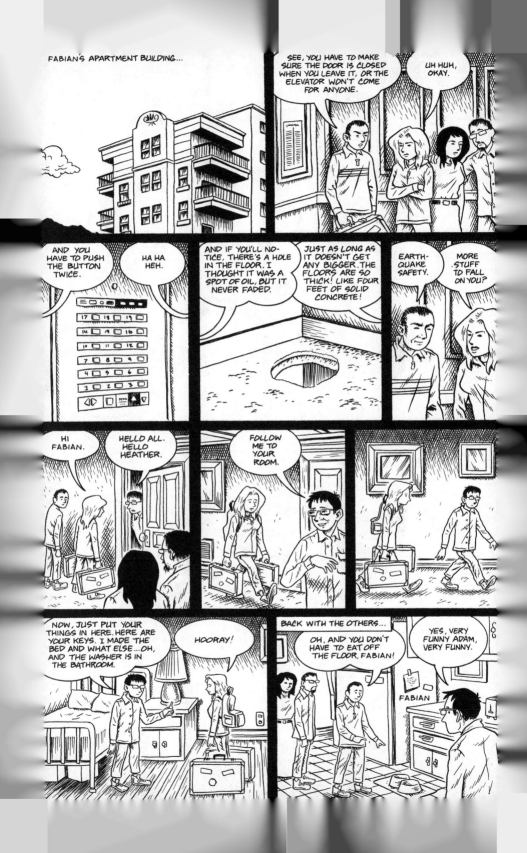

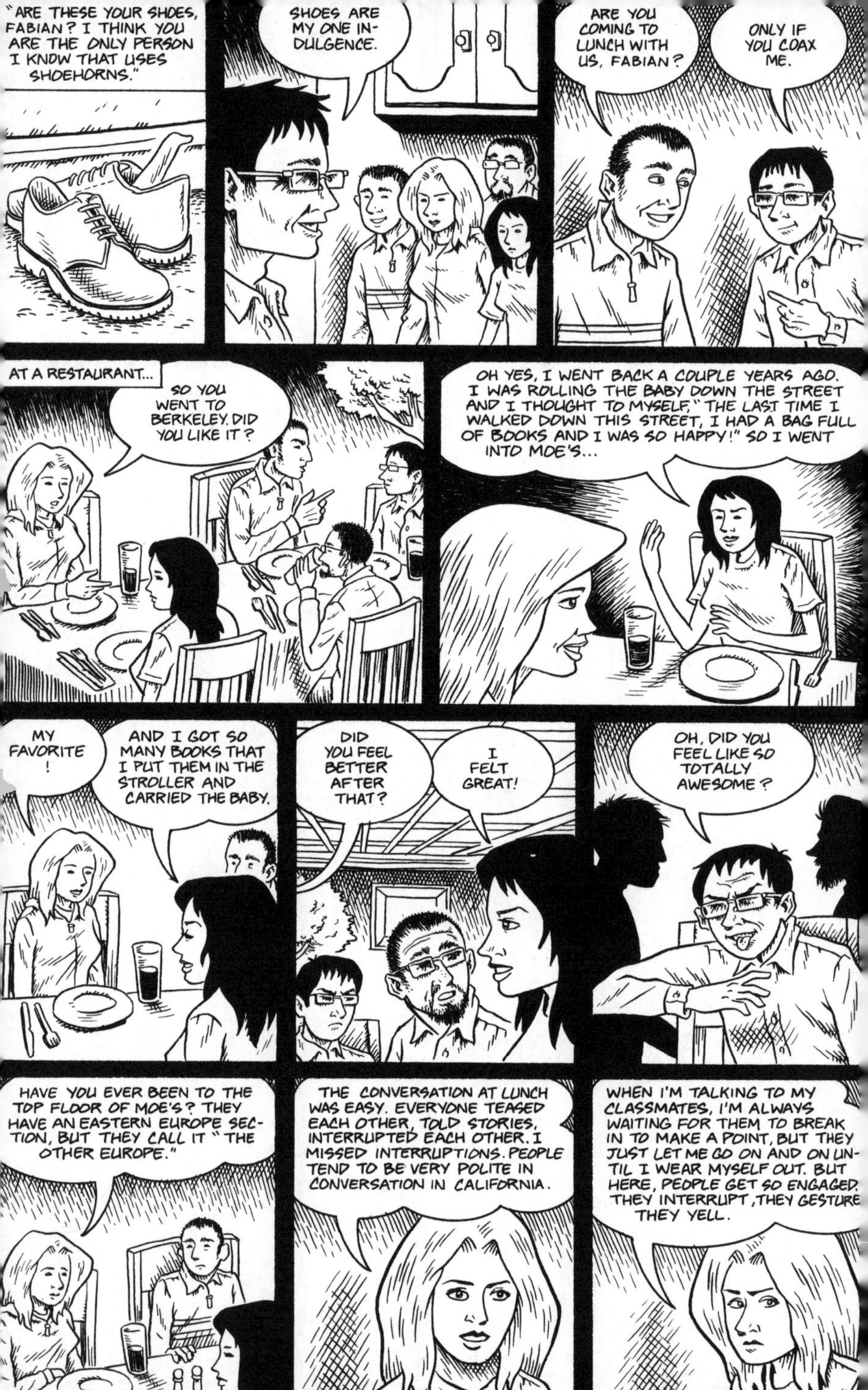
"ARE THESE YOUR SHOES, FABIAN? I THINK YOU ARE THE ONLY PERSON I KNOW THAT USES SHOEHORNS."
SHOES ARE MY ONE INDULGENCE.
ARE YOU COMING TO LUNCH WITH US, FABIAN?
ONLY IF YOU COAX ME.
AT A RESTAURANT...
SO YOU WENT TO BERKELEY. DID YOU LIKE IT?
OH YES, I WENT BACK A COUPLE YEARS AGO. I WAS ROLLING THE BABY DOWN THE STREET AND I THOUGHT TO MYSELF, "THE LAST TIME I WALKED DOWN THIS STREET, I HAD A BAG FULL OF BOOKS AND I WAS SO HAPPY!" SO I WENT INTO MOE'S...
MY FAVORITE!
AND I GOT SO MANY BOOKS THAT I PUT THEM IN THE STROLLER AND CARRIED THE BABY.
DID YOU FEEL BETTER AFTER THAT?
I FELT GREAT!
OH, DID YOU FEEL LIKE SO TOTALLY AWESOME?
HAVE YOU EVER BEEN TO THE TOP FLOOR OF MOE'S? THEY HAVE AN EASTERN EUROPE SECTION, BUT THEY CALL IT "THE OTHER EUROPE."
THE CONVERSATION AT LUNCH WAS EASY. EVERYONE TEASED EACH OTHER, TOLD STORIES, INTERRUPTED EACH OTHER. I MISSED INTERRUPTIONS. PEOPLE TEND TO BE VERY POLITE IN CONVERSATION IN CALIFORNIA.
WHEN I'M TALKING TO MY CLASSMATES, I'M ALWAYS WAITING FOR THEM TO BREAK IN TO MAKE A POINT, BUT THEY JUST LET ME GO ON AND ON UNTIL I WEAR MYSELF OUT. BUT HERE, PEOPLE GET SO ENGAGED. THEY INTERRUPT, THEY GESTURE THEY YELL.

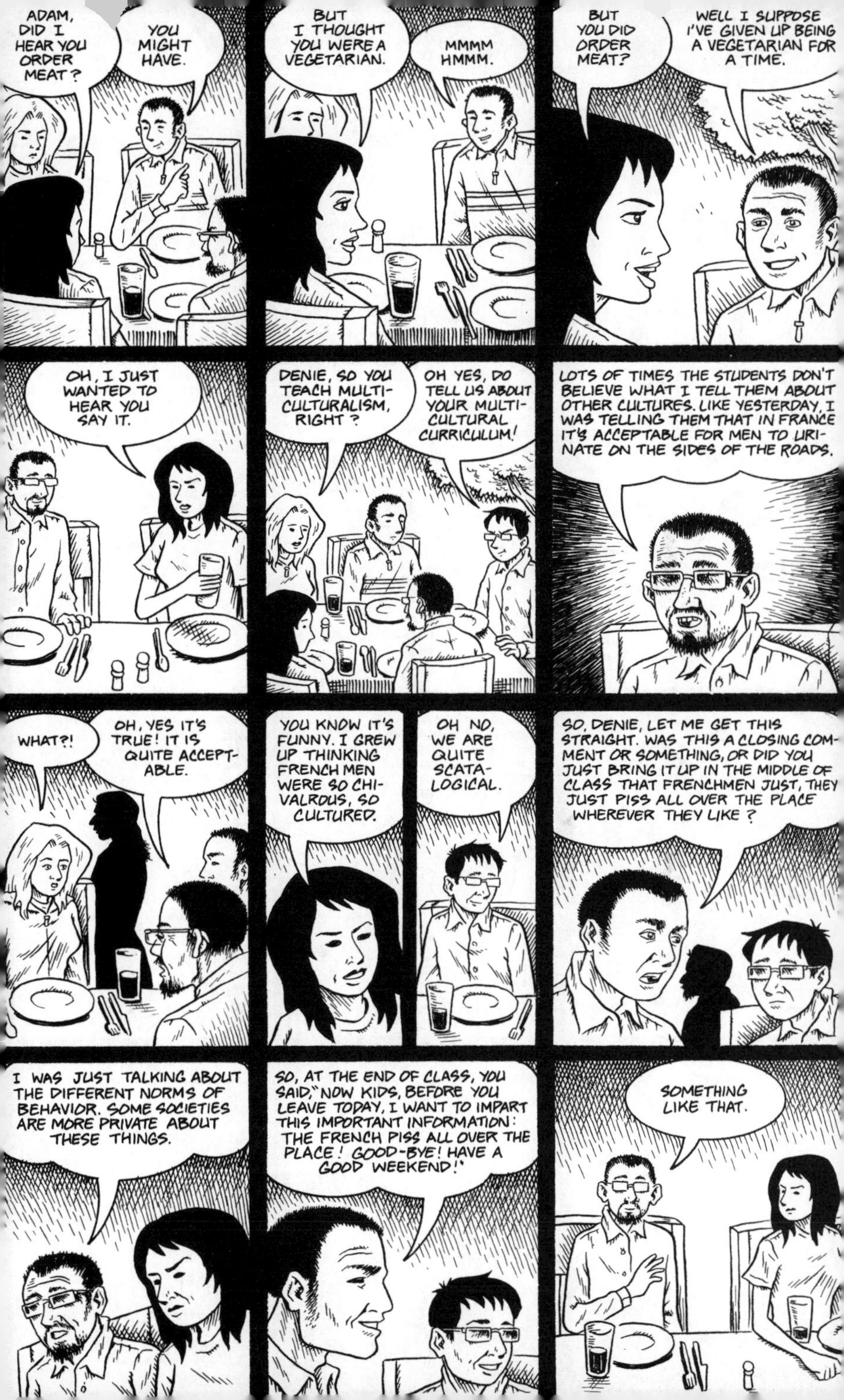
ADAM, DID I HEAR YOU ORDER MEAT?
YOU MIGHT HAVE.
BUT I THOUGHT YOU WERE A VEGETARIAN.
MMMM HMMM.
BUT YOU DID ORDER MEAT?
WELL I SUPPOSE I'VE GIVEN UP BEING A VEGETARIAN FOR A TIME.
OH, I JUST WANTED TO HEAR YOU SAY IT.
DENIE, SO YOU TEACH MULTI-CULTURALISM, RIGHT?
OH YES, DO TELL US ABOUT YOUR MULTI-CULTURAL CURRICULUM!
LOTS OF TIMES THE STUDENTS DON'T BELIEVE WHAT I TELL THEM ABOUT OTHER CULTURES. LIKE YESTERDAY, I WAS TELLING THEM THAT IN FRANCE IT'S ACCEPTABLE FOR MEN TO URINATE ON THE SIDES OF THE ROADS.
WHAT?!
OH, YES IT'S TRUE! IT IS QUITE ACCEPTABLE.
YOU KNOW IT'S FUNNY. I GREW UP THINKING FRENCH MEN WERE SO CHIVALROUS, SO CULTURED.
OH NO, WE ARE QUITE SCATALOGICAL.
SO, DENIE, LET ME GET THIS STRAIGHT. WAS THIS A CLOSING COMMENT OR SOMETHING, OR DID YOU JUST BRING IT UP IN THE MIDDLE OF CLASS THAT FRENCHMEN JUST, THEY JUST PISS ALL OVER THE PLACE WHEREVER THEY LIKE?
I WAS JUST TALKING ABOUT THE DIFFERENT NORMS OF BEHAVIOR. SOME SOCIETIES ARE MORE PRIVATE ABOUT THESE THINGS.
SO, AT THE END OF CLASS, YOU SAID, "NOW KIDS, BEFORE YOU LEAVE TODAY, I WANT TO IMPART THIS IMPORTANT INFORMATION: THE FRENCH PISS ALL OVER THE PLACE! GOOD-BYE! HAVE A GOOD WEEKEND!"
SOMETHING LIKE THAT.

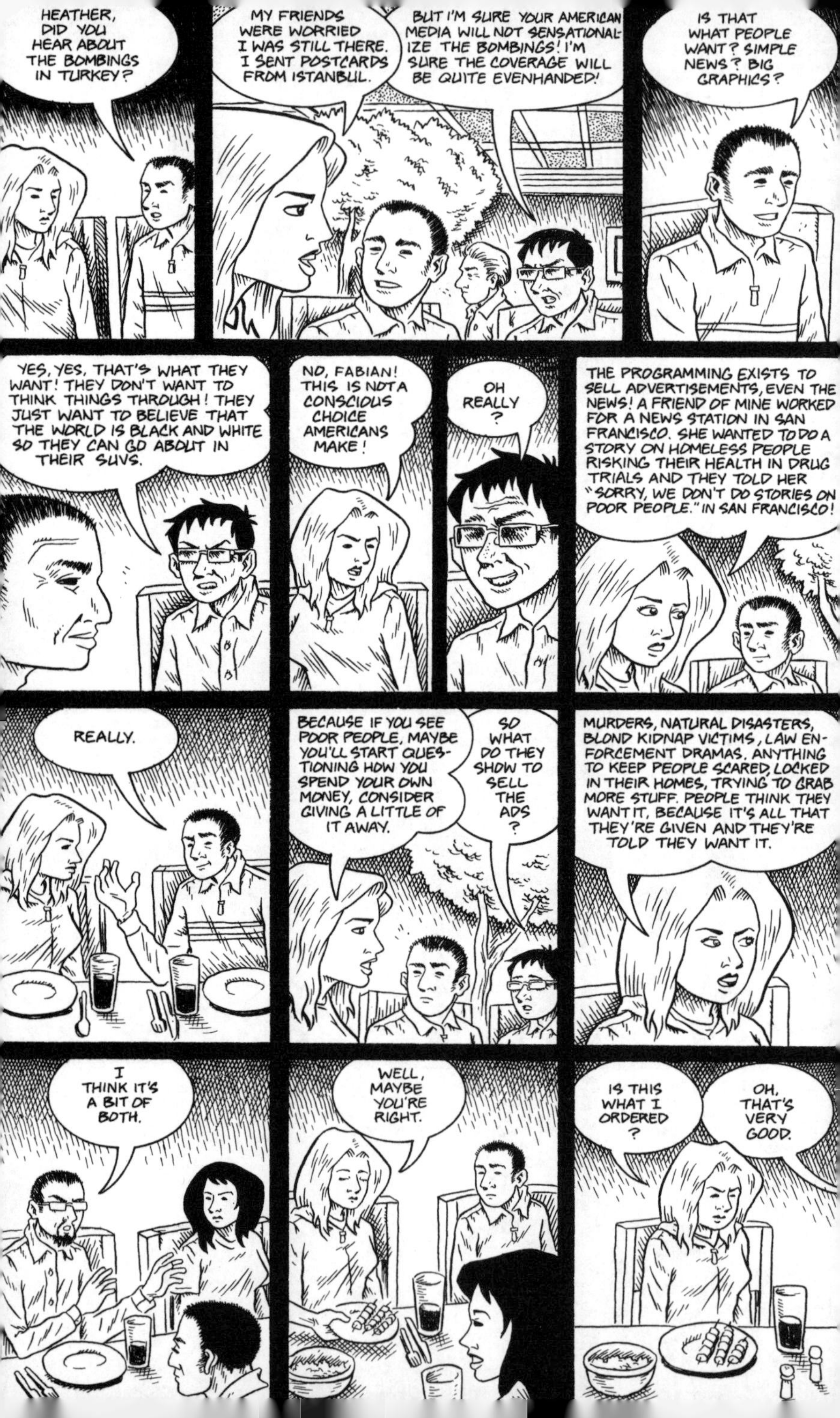
HEATHER, DID YOU HEAR ABOUT THE BOMBINGS IN TURKEY?
MY FRIENDS WERE WORRIED I WAS STILL THERE. I SENT POSTCARDS FROM ISTANBUL.
BUT I'M SURE YOUR AMERICAN MEDIA WILL NOT SENSATIONAL-IZE THE BOMBINGS! I'M SURE THE COVERAGE WILL BE QUITE EVENHANDED!
IS THAT WHAT PEOPLE WANT? SIMPLE NEWS? BIG GRAPHICS?
YES, YES, THAT'S WHAT THEY WANT! THEY DON'T WANT TO THINK THINGS THROUGH! THEY JUST WANT TO BELIEVE THAT THE WORLD IS BLACK AND WHITE SO THEY CAN GO ABOUT IN THEIR SUVS.
NO, FABIAN! THIS IS NOT A CONSCIOUS CHOICE AMERICANS MAKE!
OH REALLY?
THE PROGRAMMING EXISTS TO SELL ADVERTISEMENTS, EVEN THE NEWS! A FRIEND OF MINE WORKED FOR A NEWS STATION IN SAN FRANCISCO. SHE WANTED TO DO A STORY ON HOMELESS PEOPLE RISKING THEIR HEALTH IN DRUG TRIALS AND THEY TOLD HER "SORRY, WE DON'T DO STORIES ON POOR PEOPLE." IN SAN FRANCISCO!
REALLY.
SO WHAT DO THEY SHOW TO SELL THE ADS?
BECAUSE IF YOU SEE POOR PEOPLE, MAYBE YOU'LL START QUES-TIONING HOW YOU SPEND YOUR OWN MONEY, CONSIDER GIVING A LITTLE OF IT AWAY.
MURDERS, NATURAL DISASTERS, BLOND KIDNAP VICTIMS, LAW EN-FORCEMENT DRAMAS. ANYTHING TO KEEP PEOPLE SCARED, LOCKED IN THEIR HOMES, TRYING TO GRAB MORE STUFF. PEOPLE THINK THEY WANT IT, BECAUSE IT'S ALL THAT THEY'RE GIVEN AND THEY'RE TOLD THEY WANT IT.
I THINK IT'S A BIT OF BOTH.
WELL, MAYBE YOU'RE RIGHT.
IS THIS WHAT I ORDERED?
OH, THAT'S VERY GOOD.

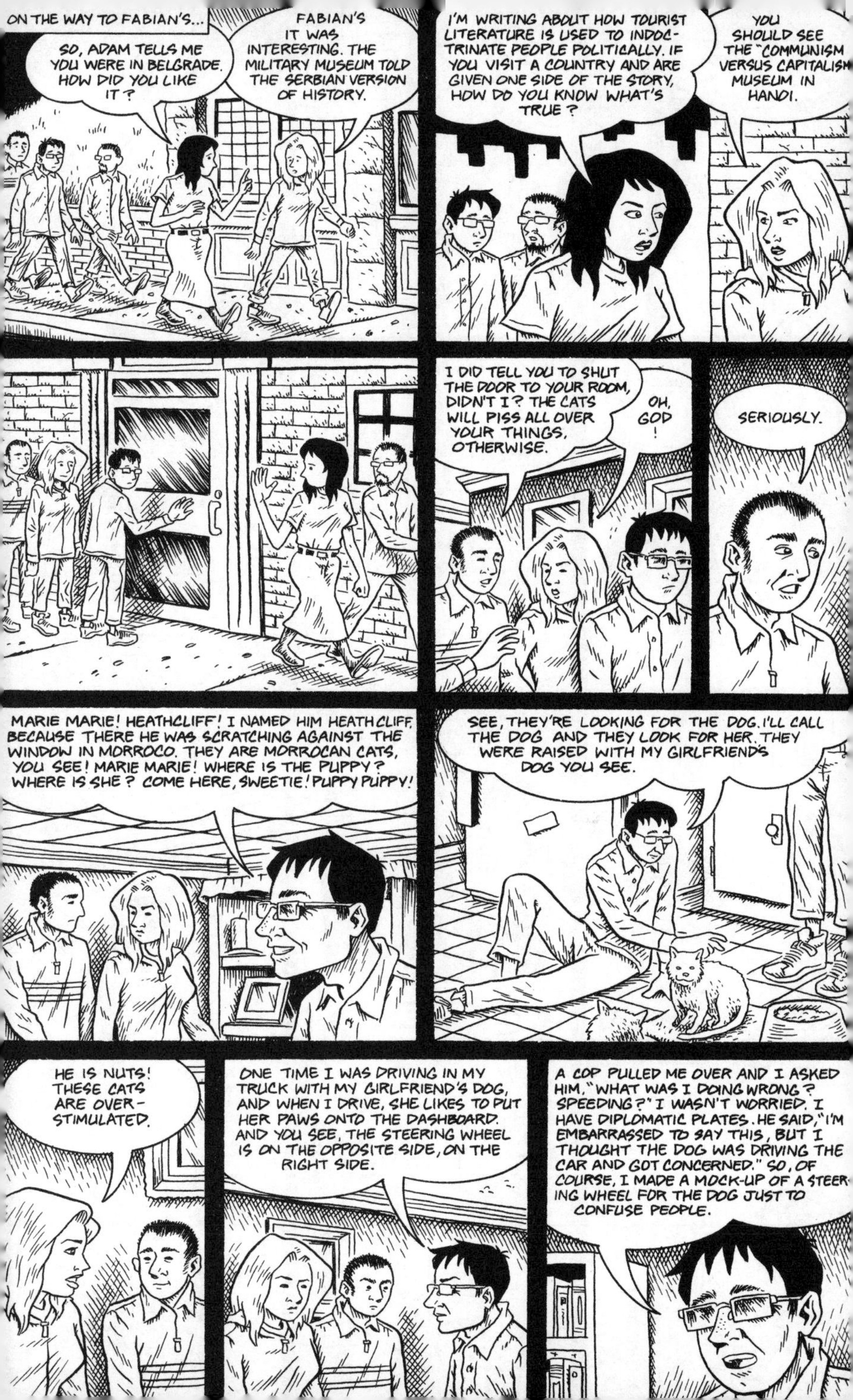
ON THE WAY TO FABIAN'S...
SO, ADAM TELLS ME YOU WERE IN BELGRADE. HOW DID YOU LIKE IT?
FABIAN'S IT WAS INTERESTING. THE MILITARY MUSEUM TOLD THE SERBIAN VERSION OF HISTORY.
I'M WRITING ABOUT HOW TOURIST LITERATURE IS USED TO INDOCTRINATE PEOPLE POLITICALLY. IF YOU VISIT A COUNTRY AND ARE GIVEN ONE SIDE OF THE STORY, HOW DO YOU KNOW WHAT'S TRUE?
YOU SHOULD SEE THE "COMMUNISM VERSUS CAPITALISM" MUSEUM IN HANOI.
I DID TELL YOU TO SHUT THE DOOR TO YOUR ROOM, DIDN'T I? THE CATS WILL PISS ALL OVER YOUR THINGS, OTHERWISE.
OH, GOD!
SERIOUSLY.
MARIE MARIE! HEATHCLIFF! I NAMED HIM HEATHCLIFF, BECAUSE THERE HE WAS SCRATCHING AGAINST THE WINDOW IN MORROCO. THEY ARE MORROCAN CATS, YOU SEE! MARIE MARIE! WHERE IS THE PUPPY? WHERE IS SHE? COME HERE, SWEETIE! PUPPY PUPPY!
SEE, THEY'RE LOOKING FOR THE DOG. I'LL CALL THE DOG AND THEY LOOK FOR HER. THEY WERE RAISED WITH MY GIRLFRIEND'S DOG YOU SEE.
HE IS NUTS! THESE CATS ARE OVER-STIMULATED.
ONE TIME I WAS DRIVING IN MY TRUCK WITH MY GIRLFRIEND'S DOG, AND WHEN I DRIVE, SHE LIKES TO PUT HER PAWS ONTO THE DASHBOARD. AND YOU SEE, THE STEERING WHEEL IS ON THE OPPOSITE SIDE, ON THE RIGHT SIDE.
A COP PULLED ME OVER AND I ASKED HIM, "WHAT WAS I DOING WRONG? SPEEDING?" I WASN'T WORRIED. I HAVE DIPLOMATIC PLATES. HE SAID, "I'M EMBARRASSED TO SAY THIS, BUT I THOUGHT THE DOG WAS DRIVING THE CAR AND GOT CONCERNED." SO, OF COURSE, I MADE A MOCK-UP OF A STEERING WHEEL FOR THE DOG JUST TO CONFUSE PEOPLE.

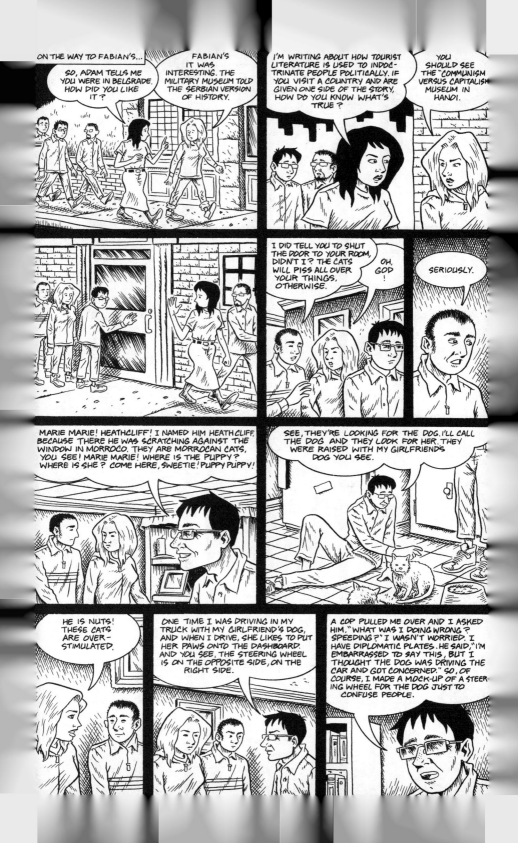

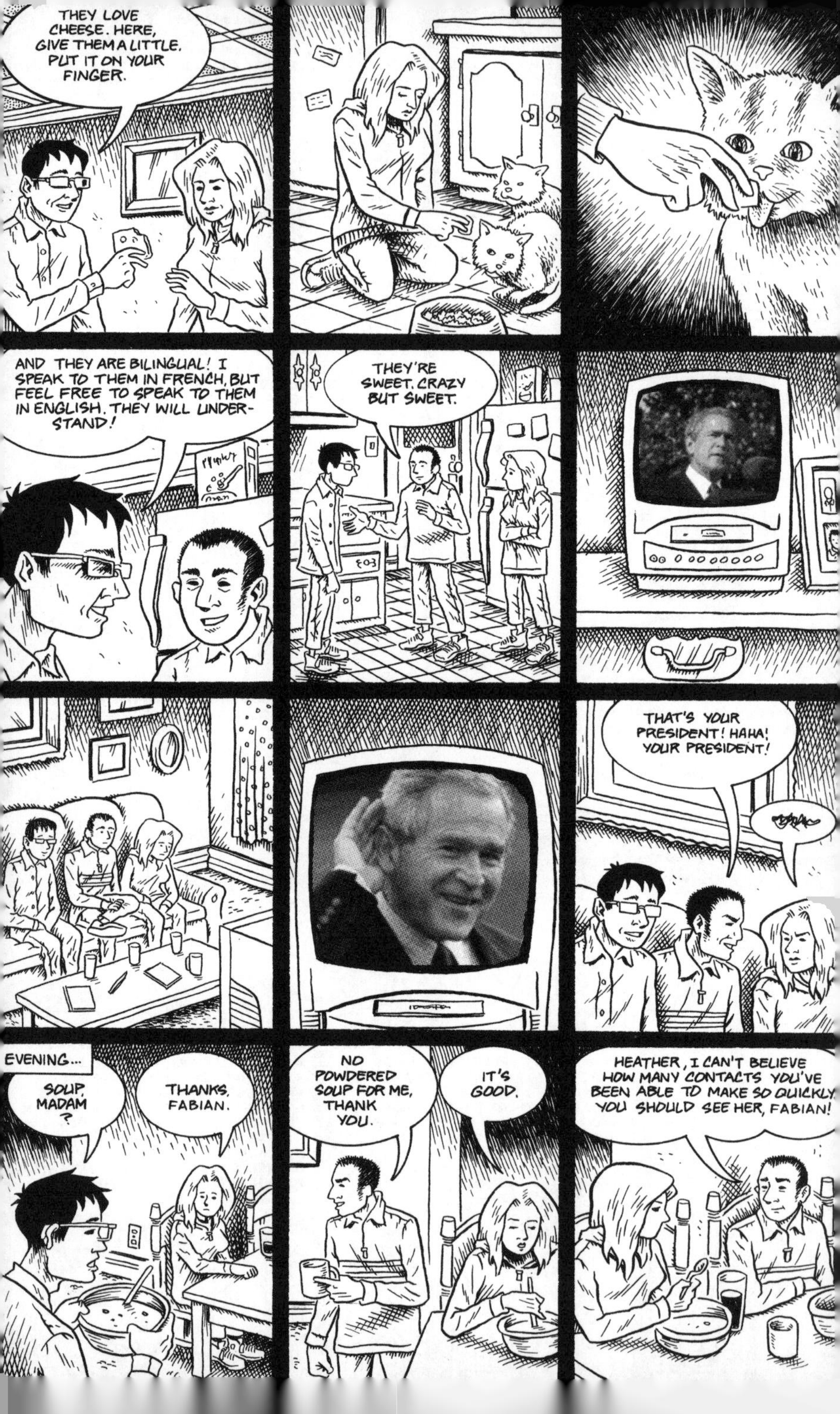
THEY LOVE CHEESE. HERE, GIVE THEM A LITTLE. PUT IT ON YOUR FINGER.
AND THEY ARE BILINGUAL! I SPEAK TO THEM IN FRENCH, BUT FEEL FREE TO SPEAK TO THEM IN ENGLISH. THEY WILL UNDERSTAND!
THEY'RE SWEET. CRAZY BUT SWEET.
THAT'S YOUR PRESIDENT! HAHA! YOUR PRESIDENT!
EVENING...
SOUP, MADAM ?
THANKS, FABIAN.
NO POWDERED SOUP FOR ME, THANK YOU.
IT'S GOOD.
HEATHER, I CAN'T BELIEVE HOW MANY CONTACTS YOU'VE BEEN ABLE TO MAKE SO QUICKLY. YOU SHOULD SEE HER, FABIAN!

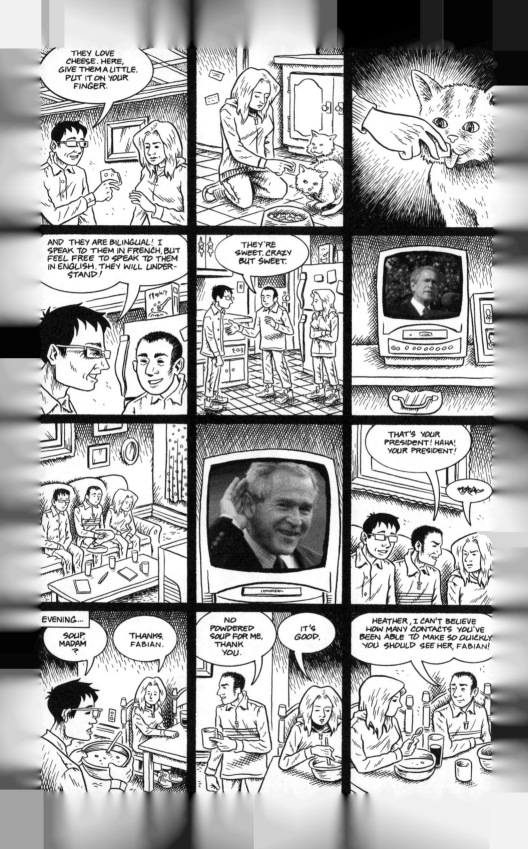

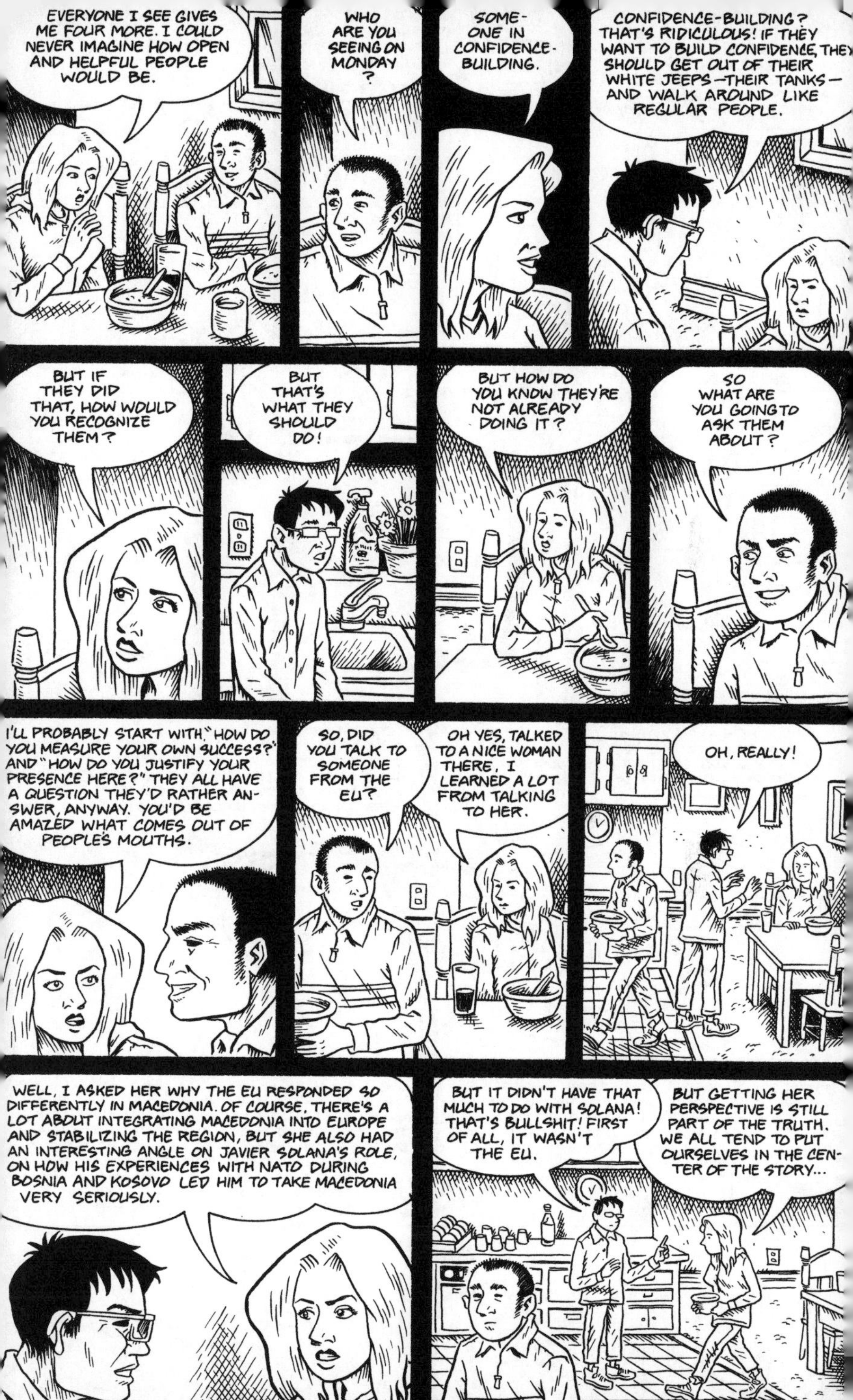
EVERYONE I SEE GIVES ME FOUR MORE. I COULD NEVER IMAGINE HOW OPEN AND HELPFUL PEOPLE WOULD BE.
WHO ARE YOU SEEING ON MONDAY?
SOME-ONE IN CONFIDENCE-BUILDING.
CONFIDENCE-BUILDING? THAT'S RIDICULOUS! IF THEY WANT TO BUILD CONFIDENCE, THEY SHOULD GET OUT OF THEIR WHITE JEEPS—THEIR TANKS—AND WALK AROUND LIKE REGULAR PEOPLE.
BUT IF THEY DID THAT, HOW WOULD YOU RECOGNIZE THEM?
BUT THAT'S WHAT THEY SHOULD DO!
BUT HOW DO YOU KNOW THEY'RE NOT ALREADY DOING IT?
SO WHAT ARE YOU GOING TO ASK THEM ABOUT?
I'LL PROBABLY START WITH "HOW DO YOU MEASURE YOUR OWN SUCCESS?" AND "HOW DO YOU JUSTIFY YOUR PRESENCE HERE?" THEY ALL HAVE A QUESTION THEY'D RATHER ANSWER, ANYWAY. YOU'D BE AMAZED WHAT COMES OUT OF PEOPLE'S MOUTHS.
SO, DID YOU TALK TO SOMEONE FROM THE EU?
OH YES, TALKED TO A NICE WOMAN THERE. I LEARNED A LOT FROM TALKING TO HER.
OH, REALLY!
WELL, I ASKED HER WHY THE EU RESPONDED SO DIFFERENTLY IN MACEDONIA. OF COURSE, THERE'S A LOT ABOUT INTEGRATING MACEDONIA INTO EUROPE AND STABILIZING THE REGION, BUT SHE ALSO HAD AN INTERESTING ANGLE ON JAVIER SOLANA'S ROLE, ON HOW HIS EXPERIENCES WITH NATO DURING BOSNIA AND KOSOVO LED HIM TO TAKE MACEDONIA VERY SERIOUSLY.
BUT IT DIDN'T HAVE THAT MUCH TO DO WITH SOLANA! THAT'S BULLSHIT! FIRST OF ALL, IT WASN'T THE EU.
BUT GETTING HER PERSPECTIVE IS STILL PART OF THE TRUTH. WE ALL TEND TO PUT OURSELVES IN THE CENTER OF THE STORY...

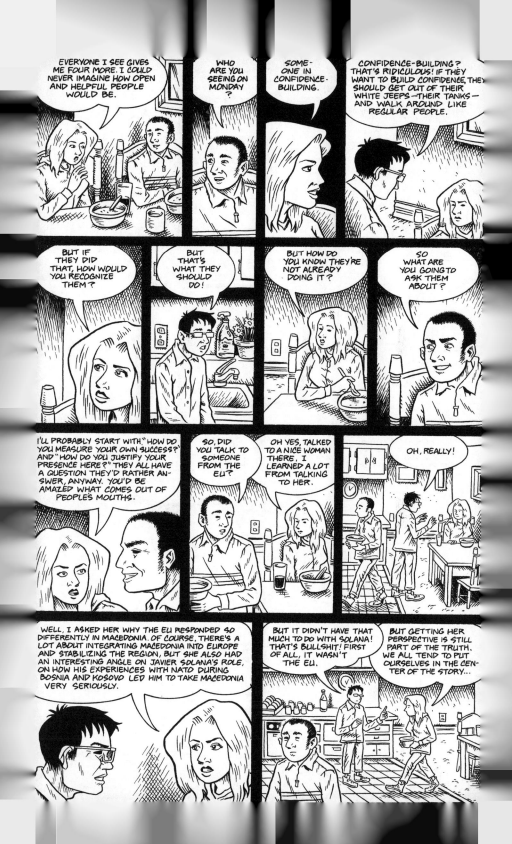

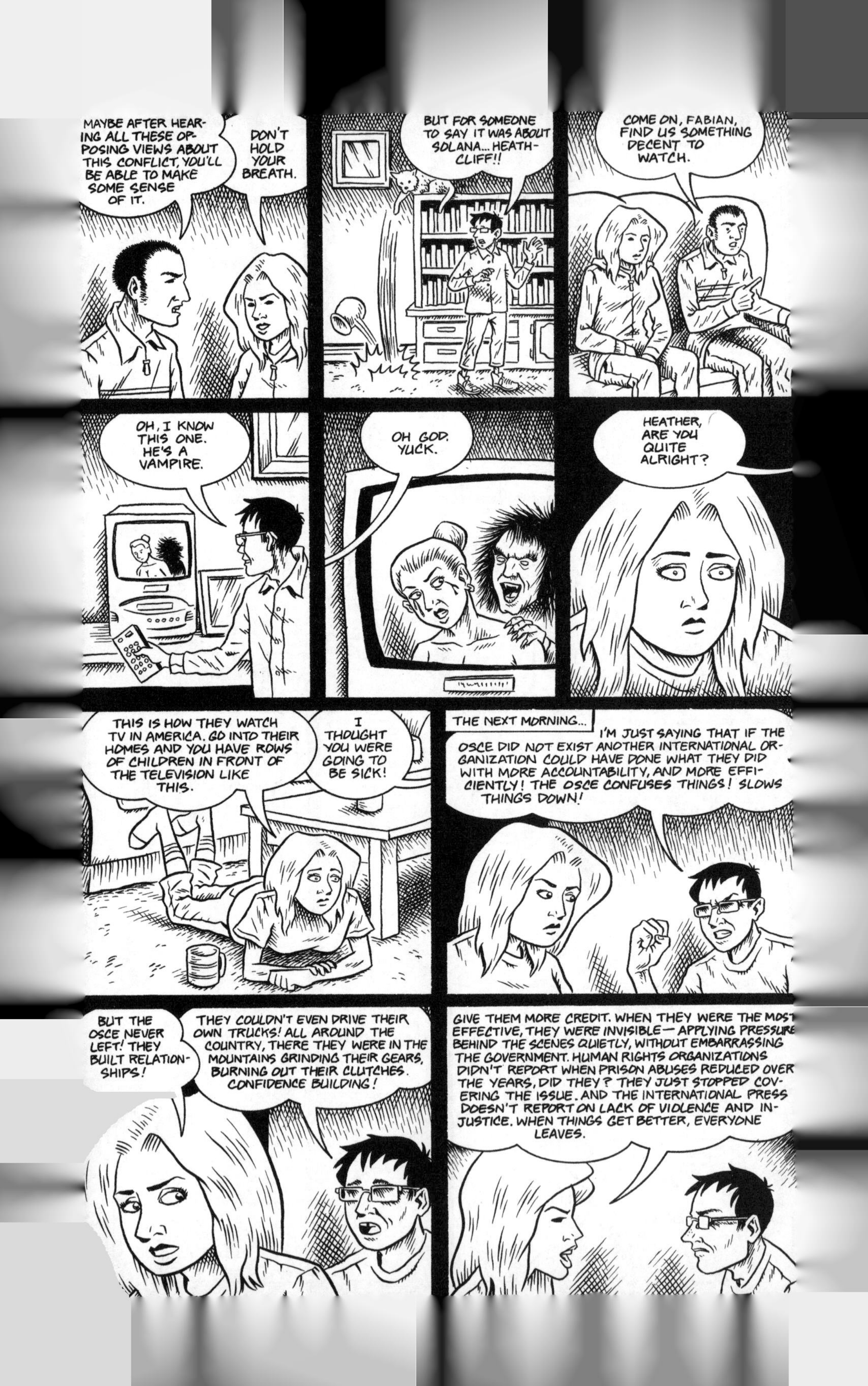
MAYBE AFTER HEARING ALL THESE OPPOSING VIEWS ABOUT THIS CONFLICT, YOU'LL BE ABLE TO MAKE SOME SENSE OF IT.
DON'T HOLD YOUR BREATH.
BUT FOR SOMEONE TO SAY IT WAS ABOUT SOLANA... HEATHCLIFF!!
COME ON, FABIAN, FIND US SOMETHING DECENT TO WATCH.
OH, I KNOW THIS ONE. HE'S A VAMPIRE.
OH GOD. YUCK.
HEATHER, ARE YOU QUITE ALRIGHT?
THIS IS HOW THEY WATCH TV IN AMERICA. GO INTO THEIR HOMES AND YOU HAVE ROWS OF CHILDREN IN FRONT OF THE TELEVISION LIKE THIS.
I THOUGHT YOU WERE GOING TO BE SICK!
THE NEXT MORNING...
I'M JUST SAYING THAT IF THE OSCE DID NOT EXIST ANOTHER INTERNATIONAL ORGANIZATION COULD HAVE DONE WHAT THEY DID WITH MORE ACCOUNTABILITY, AND MORE EFFICIENTLY! THE OSCE CONFUSES THINGS! SLOWS THINGS DOWN!
BUT THE OSCE NEVER LEFT! THEY BUILT RELATIONSHIPS!
THEY COULDN'T EVEN DRIVE THEIR OWN TRUCKS! ALL AROUND THE COUNTRY, THERE THEY WERE IN THE MOUNTAINS GRINDING THEIR GEARS, BURNING OUT THEIR CLUTCHES. CONFIDENCE BUILDING!
GIVE THEM MORE CREDIT. WHEN THEY WERE THE MOST EFFECTIVE, THEY WERE INVISIBLE— APPLYING PRESSURE BEHIND THE SCENES QUIETLY, WITHOUT EMBARRASSING THE GOVERNMENT. HUMAN RIGHTS ORGANIZATIONS DIDN'T REPORT WHEN PRISON ABUSES REDUCED OVER THE YEARS, DID THEY? THEY JUST STOPPED COVERING THE ISSUE. AND THE INTERNATIONAL PRESS DOESN'T REPORT ON LACK OF VIOLENCE AND INJUSTICE. WHEN THINGS GET BETTER, EVERYONE LEAVES.

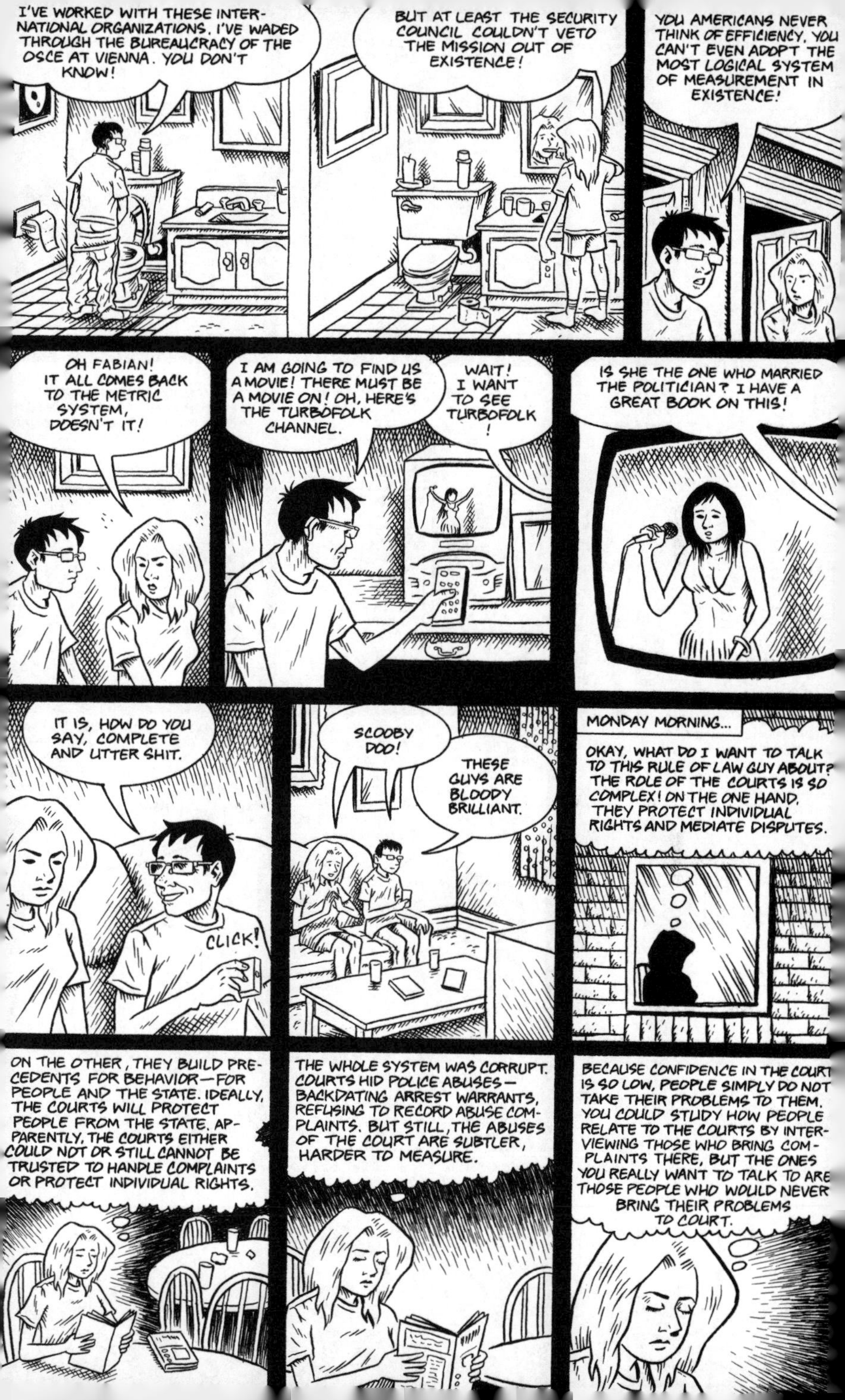
I'VE WORKED WITH THESE INTERNATIONAL ORGANIZATIONS. I'VE WADED THROUGH THE BUREAUCRACY OF THE OSCE AT VIENNA. YOU DON'T KNOW!
BUT AT LEAST THE SECURITY COUNCIL COULDN'T VETO THE MISSION OUT OF EXISTENCE!
YOU AMERICANS NEVER THINK OF EFFICIENCY. YOU CAN'T EVEN ADOPT THE MOST LOGICAL SYSTEM OF MEASUREMENT IN EXISTENCE!
OH FABIAN! IT ALL COMES BACK TO THE METRIC SYSTEM, DOESN'T IT!
I AM GOING TO FIND US A MOVIE! THERE MUST BE A MOVIE ON! OH, HERE'S THE TURBOFOLK CHANNEL.
WAIT! I WANT TO SEE TURBOFOLK!
IS SHE THE ONE WHO MARRIED THE POLITICIAN? I HAVE A GREAT BOOK ON THIS!
IT IS, HOW DO YOU SAY, COMPLETE AND UTTER SHIT.
CLICK!
SCOOBY DOO!
THESE GUYS ARE BLOODY BRILLIANT.
MONDAY MORNING...
OKAY, WHAT DO I WANT TO TALK TO THIS RULE OF LAW GUY ABOUT? THE ROLE OF THE COURTS IS SO COMPLEX! ON THE ONE HAND, THEY PROTECT INDIVIDUAL RIGHTS AND MEDIATE DISPUTES.
ON THE OTHER, THEY BUILD PRECEDENTS FOR BEHAVIOR—FOR PEOPLE AND THE STATE. IDEALLY, THE COURTS WILL PROTECT PEOPLE FROM THE STATE. APPARENTLY, THE COURTS EITHER COULD NOT OR STILL CANNOT BE TRUSTED TO HANDLE COMPLAINTS OR PROTECT INDIVIDUAL RIGHTS.
THE WHOLE SYSTEM WAS CORRUPT. COURTS HID POLICE ABUSES—BACKDATING ARREST WARRANTS, REFUSING TO RECORD ABUSE COMPLAINTS. BUT STILL, THE ABUSES OF THE COURT ARE SUBTLER, HARDER TO MEASURE.
BECAUSE CONFIDENCE IN THE COURT IS SO LOW, PEOPLE SIMPLY DO NOT TAKE THEIR PROBLEMS TO THEM. YOU COULD STUDY HOW PEOPLE RELATE TO THE COURTS BY INTERVIEWING THOSE WHO BRING COMPLAINTS THERE, BUT THE ONES YOU REALLY WANT TO TALK TO ARE THOSE PEOPLE WHO WOULD NEVER BRING THEIR PROBLEMS TO COURT.

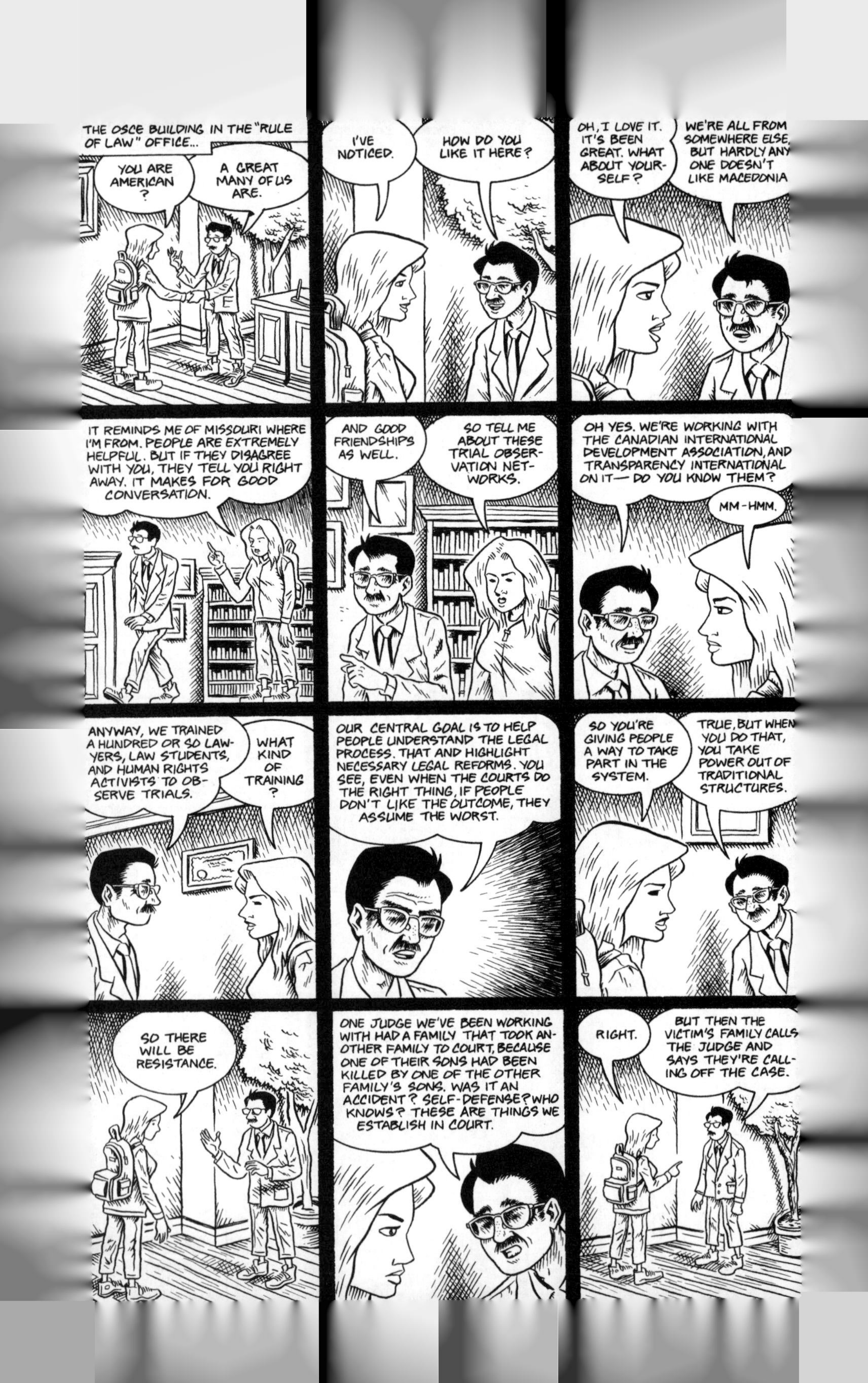
THE OSCE BUILDING IN THE "RULE OF LAW" OFFICE...
YOU ARE AMERICAN ?
A GREAT MANY OF US ARE.
I'VE NOTICED.
HOW DO YOU LIKE IT HERE?
OH, I LOVE IT. IT'S BEEN GREAT. WHAT ABOUT YOURSELF?
WE'RE ALL FROM SOMEWHERE ELSE, BUT HARDLY ANY ONE DOESN'T LIKE MACEDONIA
IT REMINDS ME OF MISSOURI WHERE I'M FROM. PEOPLE ARE EXTREMELY HELPFUL. BUT IF THEY DISAGREE WITH YOU, THEY TELL YOU RIGHT AWAY. IT MAKES FOR GOOD CONVERSATION.
AND GOOD FRIENDSHIPS AS WELL.
SO TELL ME ABOUT THESE TRIAL OBSERVATION NETWORKS.
OH YES. WE'RE WORKING WITH THE CANADIAN INTERNATIONAL DEVELOPMENT ASSOCIATION, AND TRANSPARENCY INTERNATIONAL ON IT— DO YOU KNOW THEM?
MM-HMM.
ANYWAY, WE TRAINED A HUNDRED OR SO LAWYERS, LAW STUDENTS, AND HUMAN RIGHTS ACTIVISTS TO OBSERVE TRIALS.
WHAT KIND OF TRAINING ?
OUR CENTRAL GOAL IS TO HELP PEOPLE UNDERSTAND THE LEGAL PROCESS. THAT AND HIGHLIGHT NECESSARY LEGAL REFORMS. YOU SEE, EVEN WHEN THE COURTS DO THE RIGHT THING, IF PEOPLE DON'T LIKE THE OUTCOME, THEY ASSUME THE WORST.
SO YOU'RE GIVING PEOPLE A WAY TO TAKE PART IN THE SYSTEM.
TRUE, BUT WHEN YOU DO THAT, YOU TAKE POWER OUT OF TRADITIONAL STRUCTURES.
SO THERE WILL BE RESISTANCE.
ONE JUDGE WE'VE BEEN WORKING WITH HAD A FAMILY THAT TOOK ANOTHER FAMILY TO COURT, BECAUSE ONE OF THEIR SONS HAD BEEN KILLED BY ONE OF THE OTHER FAMILY'S SONS. WAS IT AN ACCIDENT? SELF-DEFENSE? WHO KNOWS? THESE ARE THINGS WE ESTABLISH IN COURT.
RIGHT.
BUT THEN THE VICTIM'S FAMILY CALLS THE JUDGE AND SAYS THEY'RE CALLING OFF THE CASE.

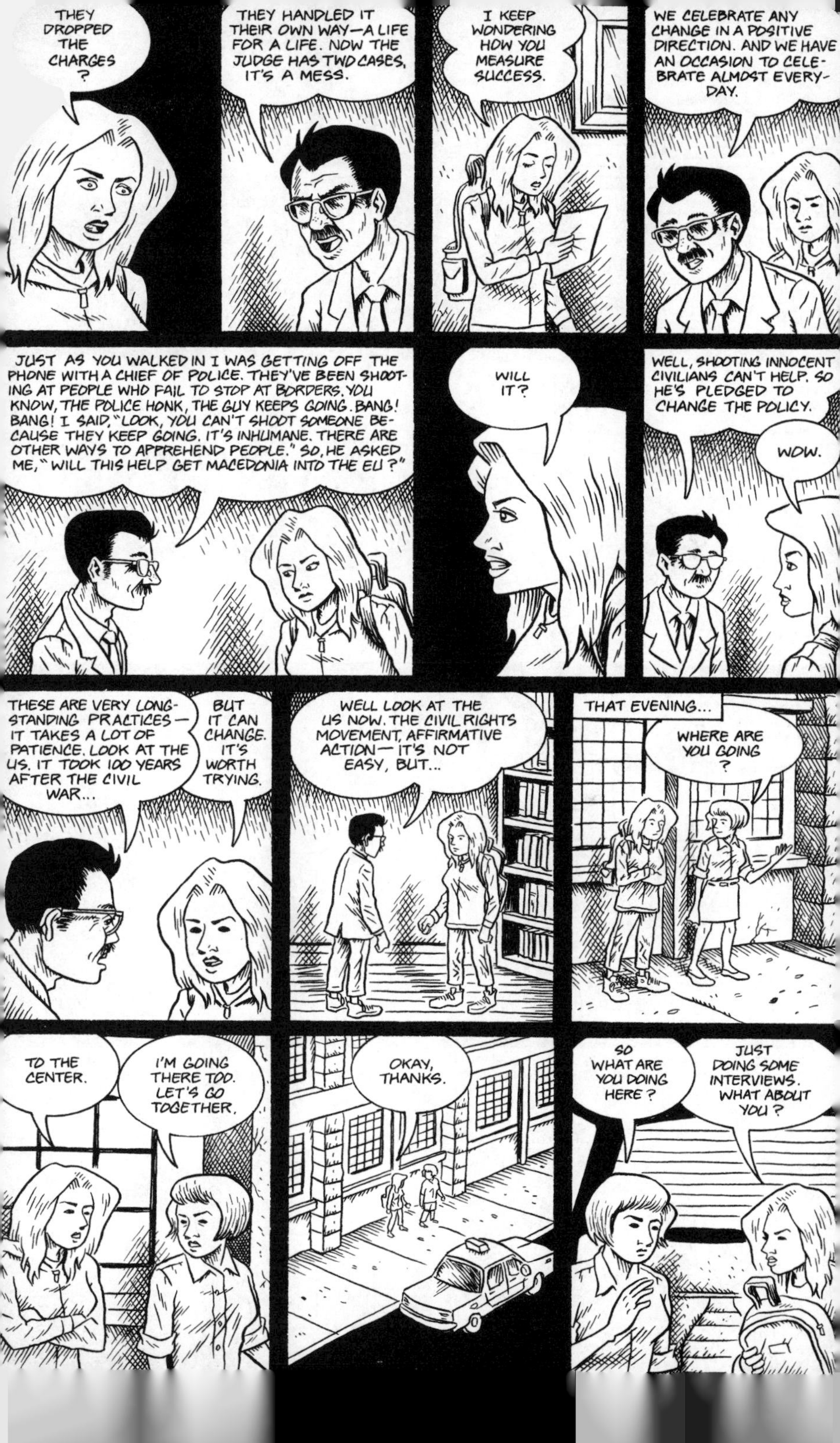
THEY DROPPED THE CHARGES ?
THEY HANDLED IT THEIR OWN WAY—A LIFE FOR A LIFE. NOW THE JUDGE HAS TWO CASES, IT'S A MESS.
I KEEP WONDERING HOW YOU MEASURE SUCCESS.
WE CELEBRATE ANY CHANGE IN A POSITIVE DIRECTION. AND WE HAVE AN OCCASION TO CELEBRATE ALMOST EVERY-DAY.
JUST AS YOU WALKED IN I WAS GETTING OFF THE PHONE WITH A CHIEF OF POLICE. THEY'VE BEEN SHOOTING AT PEOPLE WHO FAIL TO STOP AT BORDERS. YOU KNOW, THE POLICE HONK, THE GUY KEEPS GOING. BANG! BANG! I SAID, "LOOK, YOU CAN'T SHOOT SOMEONE BECAUSE THEY KEEP GOING. IT'S INHUMANE. THERE ARE OTHER WAYS TO APPREHEND PEOPLE." SO, HE ASKED ME, "WILL THIS HELP GET MACEDONIA INTO THE EU ?"
WILL IT ?
WELL, SHOOTING INNOCENT CIVILIANS CAN'T HELP. SO HE'S PLEDGED TO CHANGE THE POLICY.
WOW.
THESE ARE VERY LONG-STANDING PRACTICES— IT TAKES A LOT OF PATIENCE. LOOK AT THE US. IT TOOK 100 YEARS AFTER THE CIVIL WAR...
BUT IT CAN CHANGE. IT'S WORTH TRYING.
WELL LOOK AT THE US NOW. THE CIVIL RIGHTS MOVEMENT, AFFIRMATIVE ACTION— IT'S NOT EASY, BUT...
THAT EVENING...
WHERE ARE YOU GOING ?
TO THE CENTER.
I'M GOING THERE TOO. LET'S GO TOGETHER.
OKAY, THANKS.
SO WHAT ARE YOU DOING HERE ?
JUST DOING SOME INTERVIEWS. WHAT ABOUT YOU ?

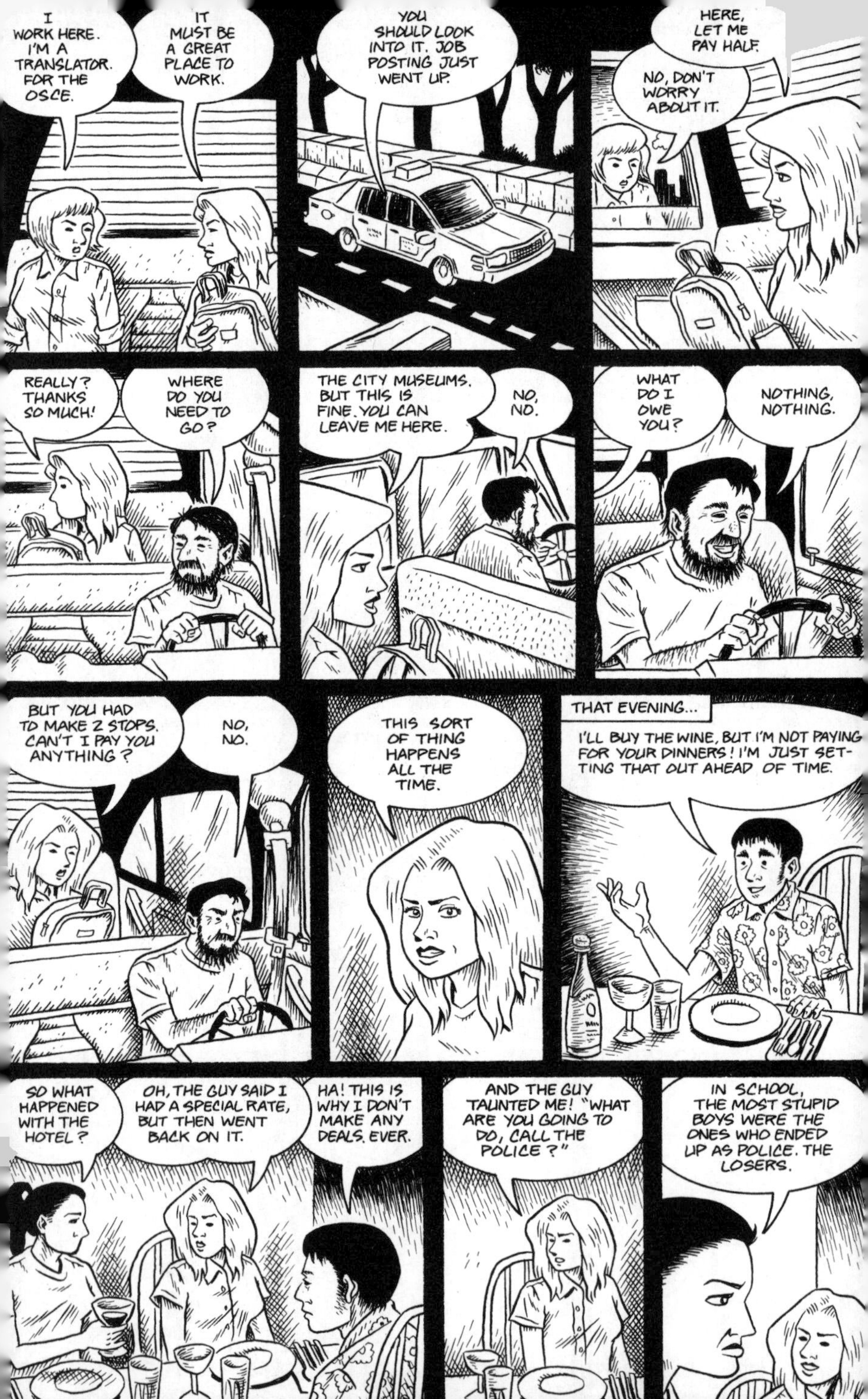
I WORK HERE. I'M A TRANSLATOR. FOR THE OSCE.
IT MUST BE A GREAT PLACE TO WORK.
YOU SHOULD LOOK INTO IT. JOB POSTING JUST WENT UP.
HERE, LET ME PAY HALF.
NO, DON'T WORRY ABOUT IT.
REALLY? THANKS SO MUCH!
WHERE DO YOU NEED TO GO?
THE CITY MUSEUMS. BUT THIS IS FINE. YOU CAN LEAVE ME HERE.
NO, NO.
WHAT DO I OWE YOU?
NOTHING, NOTHING.
BUT YOU HAD TO MAKE 2 STOPS. CAN'T I PAY YOU ANYTHING?
NO, NO.
THIS SORT OF THING HAPPENS ALL THE TIME.
THAT EVENING...
I'LL BUY THE WINE, BUT I'M NOT PAYING FOR YOUR DINNERS! I'M JUST SETTING THAT OUT AHEAD OF TIME.
SO WHAT HAPPENED WITH THE HOTEL?
OH, THE GUY SAID I HAD A SPECIAL RATE, BUT THEN WENT BACK ON IT.
HA! THIS IS WHY I DON'T MAKE ANY DEALS. EVER.
AND THE GUY TAUNTED ME! "WHAT ARE YOU GOING TO DO, CALL THE POLICE?"
IN SCHOOL, THE MOST STUPID BOYS WERE THE ONES WHO ENDED UP AS POLICE. THE LOSERS.

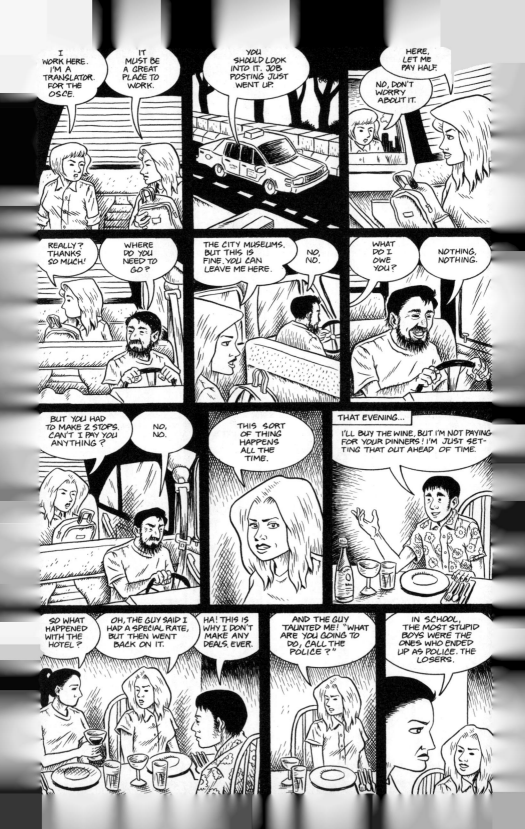

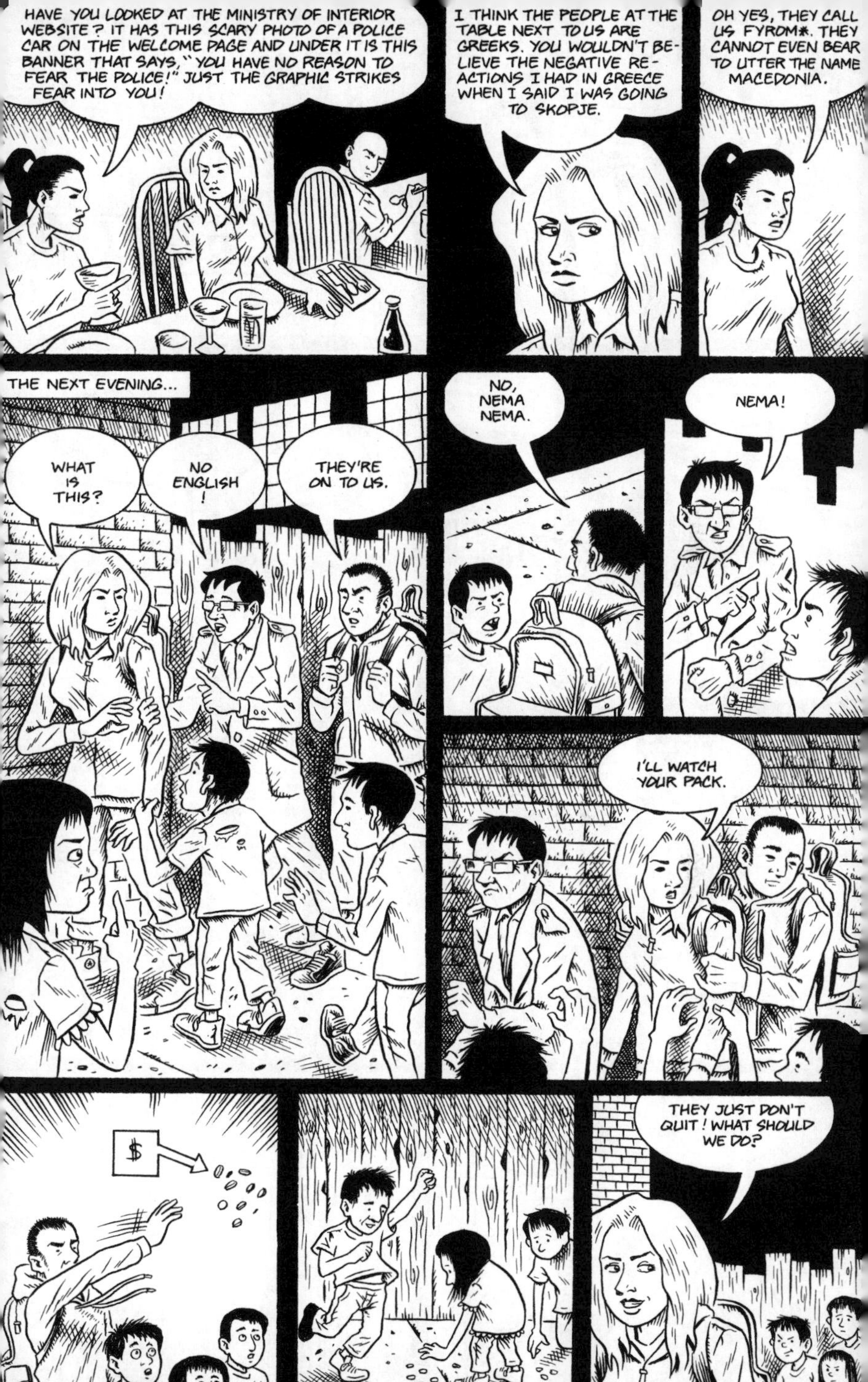
HAVE YOU LOOKED AT THE MINISTRY OF INTERIOR WEBSITE? IT HAS THIS SCARY PHOTO OF A POLICE CAR ON THE WELCOME PAGE AND UNDER IT IS THIS BANNER THAT SAYS, "YOU HAVE NO REASON TO FEAR THE POLICE!" JUST THE GRAPHIC STRIKES FEAR INTO YOU!
I THINK THE PEOPLE AT THE TABLE NEXT TO US ARE GREEKS. YOU WOULDN'T BELIEVE THE NEGATIVE REACTIONS I HAD IN GREECE WHEN I SAID I WAS GOING TO SKOPJE.
OH YES, THEY CALL US FYROM*. THEY CANNOT EVEN BEAR TO UTTER THE NAME MACEDONIA.
THE NEXT EVENING...
WHAT IS THIS?
NO ENGLISH!
THEY'RE ON TO US.
NO, NEMA NEMA.
NEMA!
I'LL WATCH YOUR PACK.
$
THEY JUST DON'T QUIT! WHAT SHOULD WE DO?

* FYROM: FORMER YUGOSLAV REPUBLIC OF MACEDONIA. GREECE HELD UP EU RECOGNITION OF

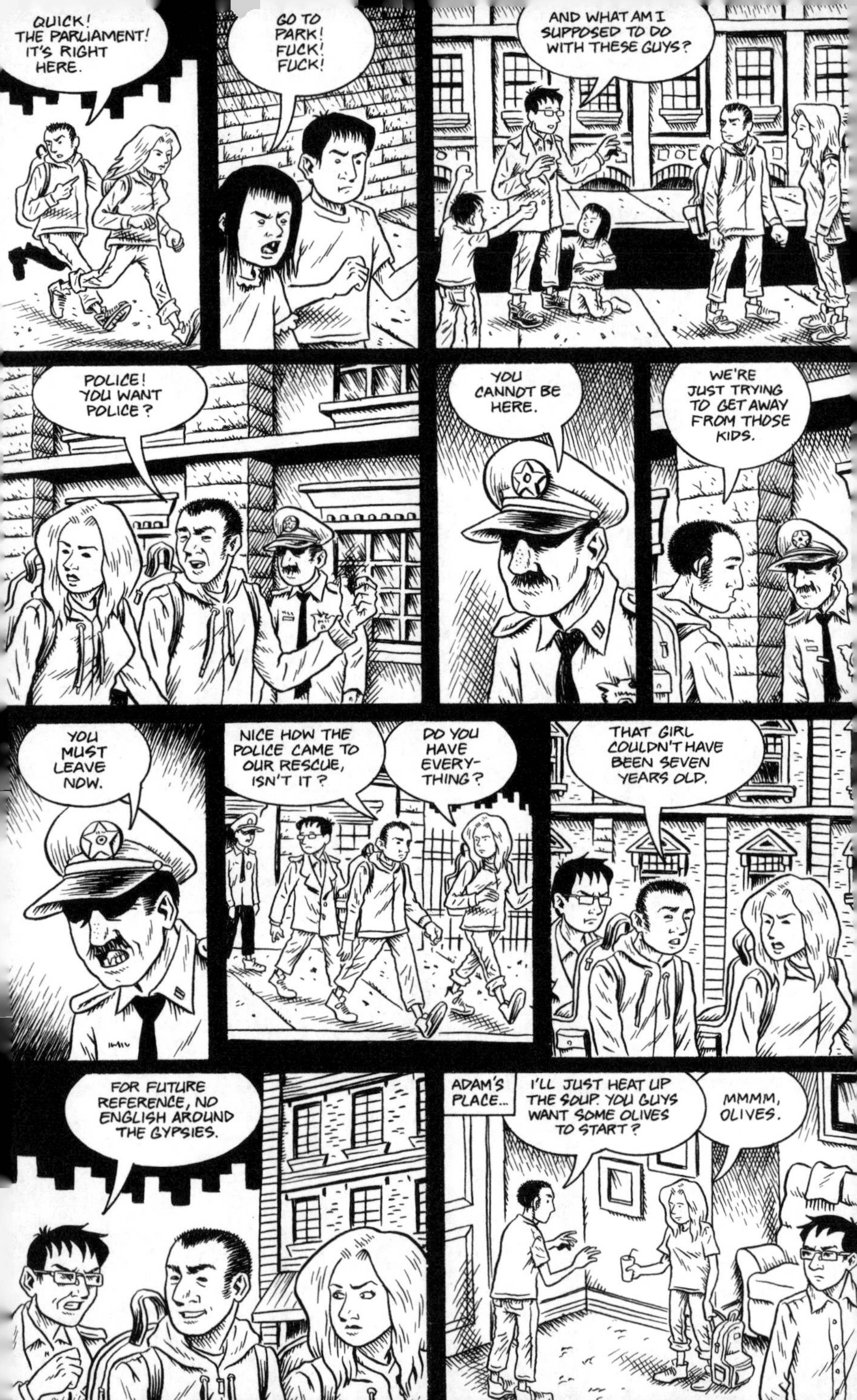
QUICK! THE PARLIAMENT! IT'S RIGHT HERE.
GO TO PARK! FUCK! FUCK!
AND WHAT AM I SUPPOSED TO DO WITH THESE GUYS?
POLICE! YOU WANT POLICE?
YOU CANNOT BE HERE.
WE'RE JUST TRYING TO GET AWAY FROM THOSE KIDS.
YOU MUST LEAVE NOW.
NICE HOW THE POLICE CAME TO OUR RESCUE, ISN'T IT?
DO YOU HAVE EVERYTHING?
THAT GIRL COULDN'T HAVE BEEN SEVEN YEARS OLD.
FOR FUTURE REFERENCE, NO ENGLISH AROUND THE GYPSIES.
ADAM'S PLACE...
I'LL JUST HEAT UP THE SOUP. YOU GUYS WANT SOME OLIVES TO START?
MMMM, OLIVES.

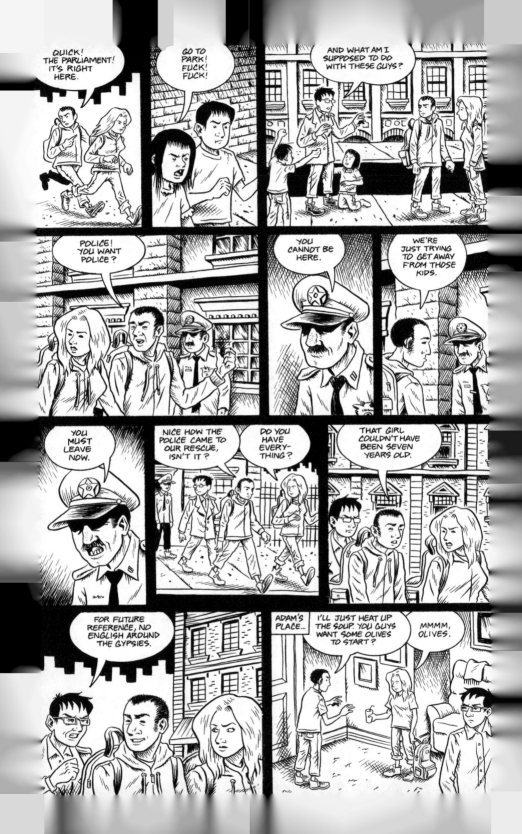

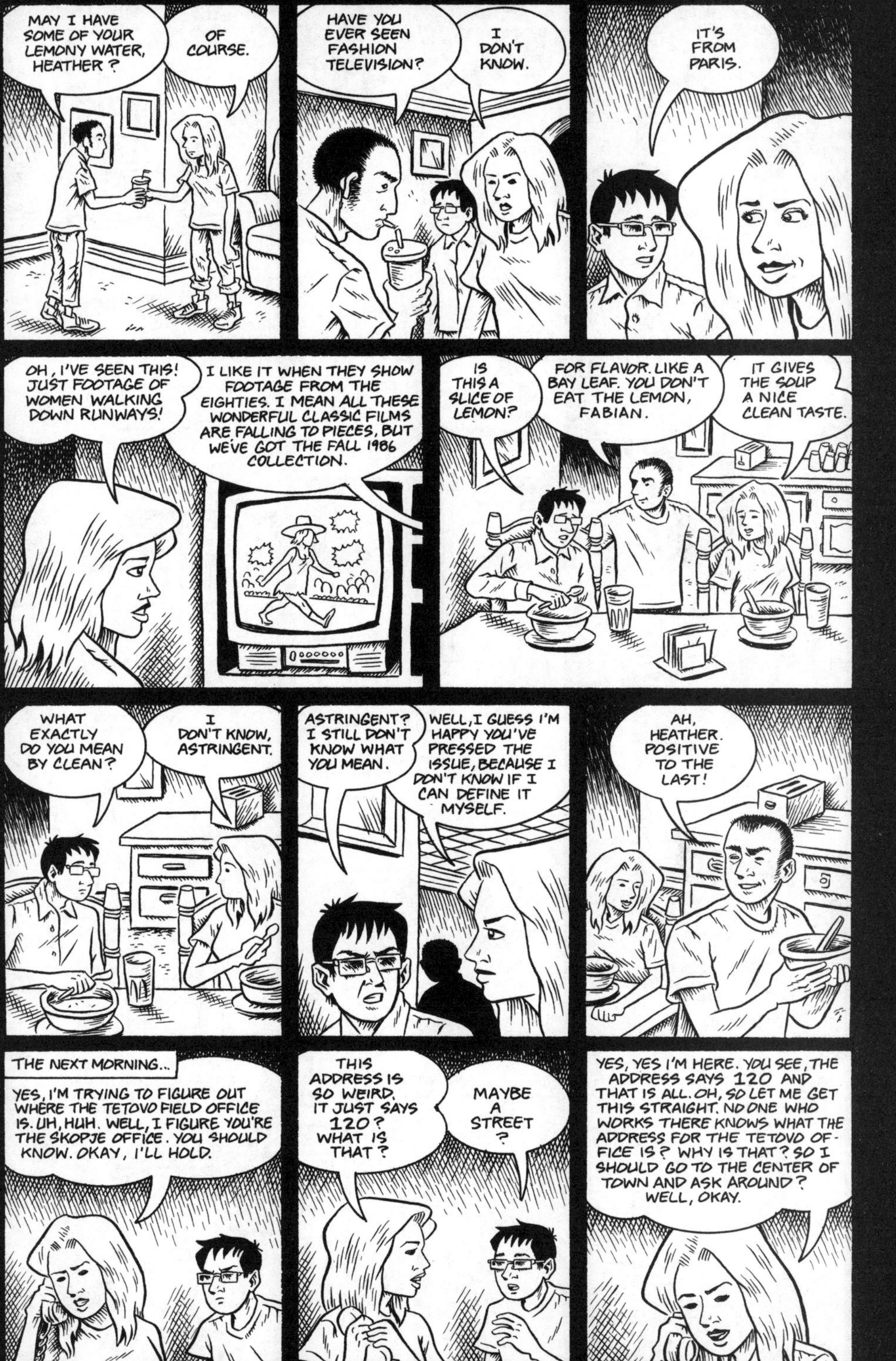
MAY I HAVE SOME OF YOUR LEMONY WATER, HEATHER?
OF COURSE.
HAVE YOU EVER SEEN FASHION TELEVISION?
I DON'T KNOW.
IT'S FROM PARIS.
OH, I'VE SEEN THIS! JUST FOOTAGE OF WOMEN WALKING DOWN RUNWAYS!
I LIKE IT WHEN THEY SHOW FOOTAGE FROM THE EIGHTIES. I MEAN ALL THESE WONDERFUL CLASSIC FILMS ARE FALLING TO PIECES, BUT WE'VE GOT THE FALL 1986 COLLECTION.
IS THIS A SLICE OF LEMON?
FOR FLAVOR. LIKE A BAY LEAF. YOU DON'T EAT THE LEMON, FABIAN.
IT GIVES THE SOUP A NICE CLEAN TASTE.
WHAT EXACTLY DO YOU MEAN BY CLEAN?
I DON'T KNOW, ASTRINGENT.
ASTRINGENT? I STILL DON'T KNOW WHAT YOU MEAN.
WELL, I GUESS I'M HAPPY YOU'VE PRESSED THE ISSUE, BECAUSE I DON'T KNOW IF I CAN DEFINE IT MYSELF.
AH, HEATHER. POSITIVE TO THE LAST!
THE NEXT MORNING...
YES, I'M TRYING TO FIGURE OUT WHERE THE TETOVO FIELD OFFICE IS. UH, HUH. WELL, I FIGURE YOU'RE THE SKOPJE OFFICE. YOU SHOULD KNOW. OKAY, I'LL HOLD.
THIS ADDRESS IS SO WEIRD. IT JUST SAYS 120? WHAT IS THAT?
MAYBE A STREET?
YES, YES I'M HERE. YOU SEE, THE ADDRESS SAYS 120 AND THAT IS ALL. OH, SO LET ME GET THIS STRAIGHT. NO ONE WHO WORKS THERE KNOWS WHAT THE ADDRESS FOR THE TETOVO OF-FICE IS? WHY IS THAT? SO I SHOULD GO TO THE CENTER OF TOWN AND ASK AROUND? WELL, OKAY.

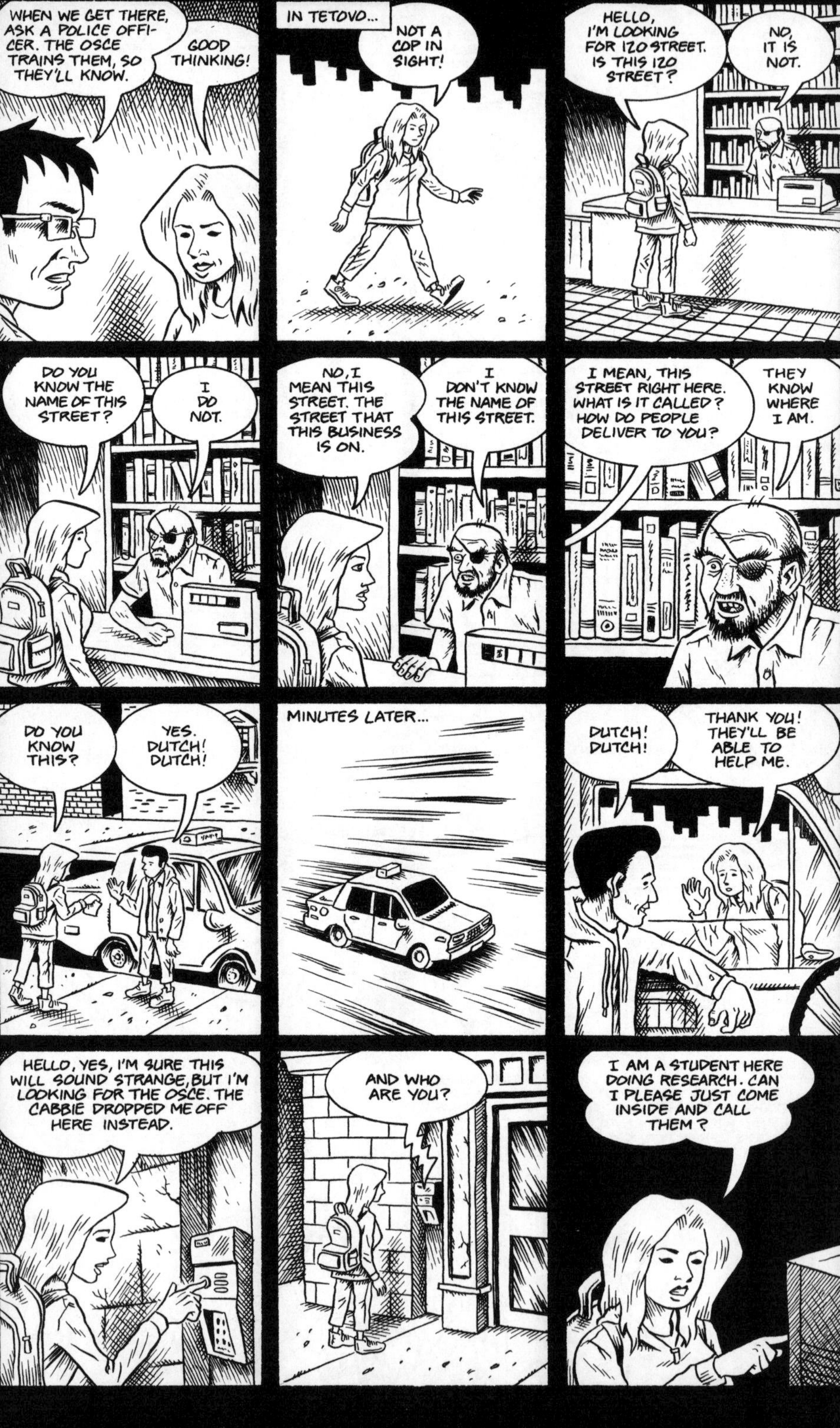
WHEN WE GET THERE, ASK A POLICE OFFICER. THE OSCE TRAINS THEM, SO THEY'LL KNOW.
GOOD THINKING!
IN TETOVO...
NOT A COP IN SIGHT!
HELLO, I'M LOOKING FOR 120 STREET. IS THIS 120 STREET?
NO, IT IS NOT.
DO YOU KNOW THE NAME OF THIS STREET?
I DO NOT.
NO, I MEAN THIS STREET. THE STREET THAT THIS BUSINESS IS ON.
I DON'T KNOW THE NAME OF THIS STREET.
I MEAN, THIS STREET RIGHT HERE. WHAT IS IT CALLED? HOW DO PEOPLE DELIVER TO YOU?
THEY KNOW WHERE I AM.
DO YOU KNOW THIS?
YES. DUTCH! DUTCH!
MINUTES LATER...
DUTCH! DUTCH!
THANK YOU! THEY'LL BE ABLE TO HELP ME.
HELLO, YES, I'M SURE THIS WILL SOUND STRANGE, BUT I'M LOOKING FOR THE OSCE. THE CABBIE DROPPED ME OFF HERE INSTEAD.
AND WHO ARE YOU?
I AM A STUDENT HERE DOING RESEARCH. CAN I PLEASE JUST COME INSIDE AND CALL THEM?

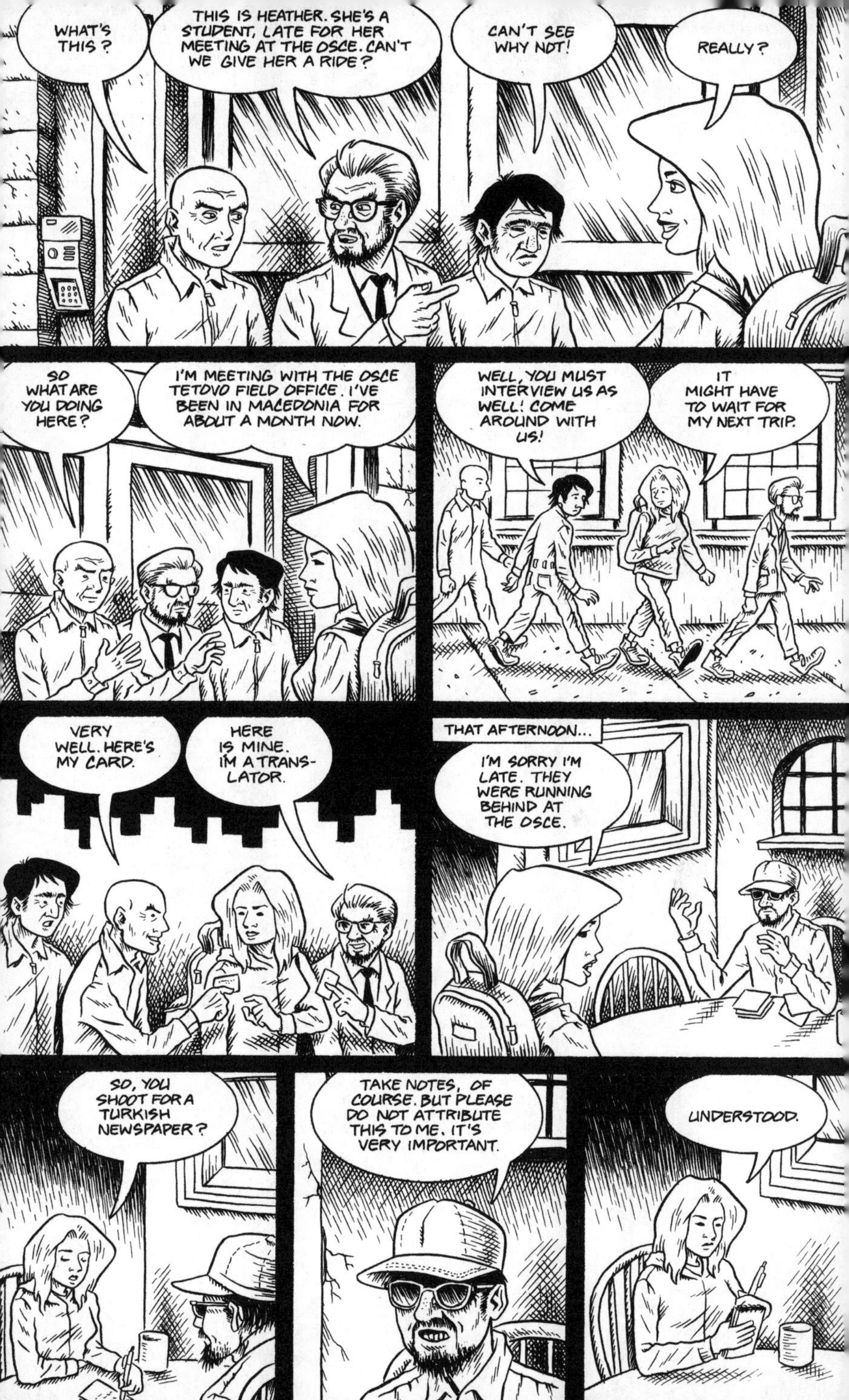
WHAT'S THIS?
THIS IS HEATHER. SHE'S A STUDENT, LATE FOR HER MEETING AT THE OSCE. CAN'T WE GIVE HER A RIDE?
CAN'T SEE WHY NOT!
REALLY?
SO WHAT ARE YOU DOING HERE?
I'M MEETING WITH THE OSCE TETOVO FIELD OFFICE. I'VE BEEN IN MACEDONIA FOR ABOUT A MONTH NOW.
WELL, YOU MUST INTERVIEW US AS WELL! COME AROUND WITH US!
IT MIGHT HAVE TO WAIT FOR MY NEXT TRIP.
VERY WELL. HERE'S MY CARD.
HERE IS MINE. I'M A TRANSLATOR.
THAT AFTERNOON...
I'M SORRY I'M LATE. THEY WERE RUNNING BEHIND AT THE OSCE.
SO, YOU SHOOT FOR A TURKISH NEWSPAPER?
TAKE NOTES, OF COURSE. BUT PLEASE DO NOT ATTRIBUTE THIS TO ME. IT'S VERY IMPORTANT.
UNDERSTOOD.

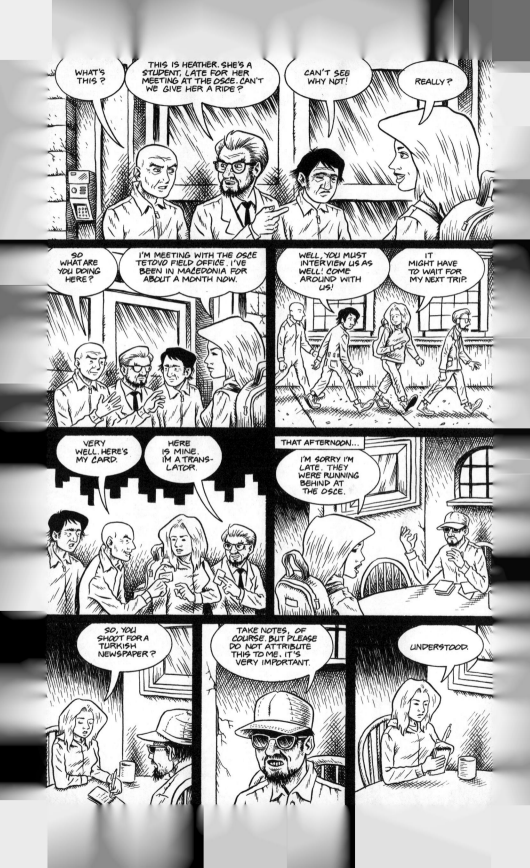

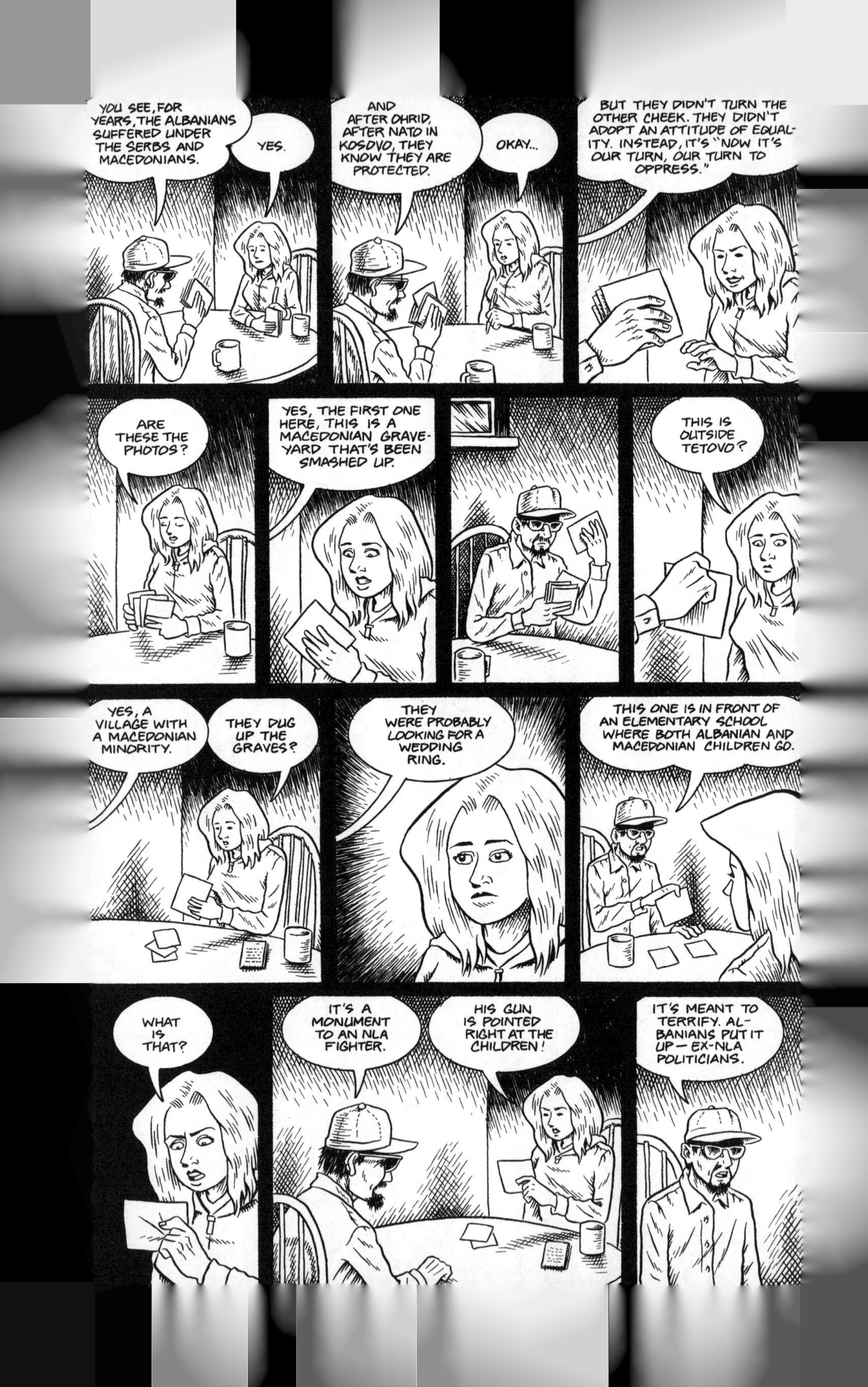
YOU SEE, FOR YEARS, THE ALBANIANS SUFFERED UNDER THE SERBS AND MACEDONIANS.
YES.
AND AFTER OHRID, AFTER NATO IN KOSOVO, THEY KNOW THEY ARE PROTECTED.
OKAY...
BUT THEY DIDN'T TURN THE OTHER CHEEK. THEY DIDN'T ADOPT AN ATTITUDE OF EQUALITY. INSTEAD, IT'S "NOW IT'S OUR TURN, OUR TURN TO OPPRESS."
ARE THESE THE PHOTOS?
YES, THE FIRST ONE HERE, THIS IS A MACEDONIAN GRAVEYARD THAT'S BEEN SMASHED UP.
THIS IS OUTSIDE TETOVO?
YES, A VILLAGE WITH A MACEDONIAN MINORITY.
THEY DUG UP THE GRAVES?
THEY WERE PROBABLY LOOKING FOR A WEDDING RING.
THIS ONE IS IN FRONT OF AN ELEMENTARY SCHOOL WHERE BOTH ALBANIAN AND MACEDONIAN CHILDREN GO.
WHAT IS THAT?
IT'S A MONUMENT TO AN NLA FIGHTER.
HIS GUN IS POINTED RIGHT AT THE CHILDREN!
IT'S MEANT TO TERRIFY. ALBANIANS PUT IT UP—EX-NLA POLITICIANS.

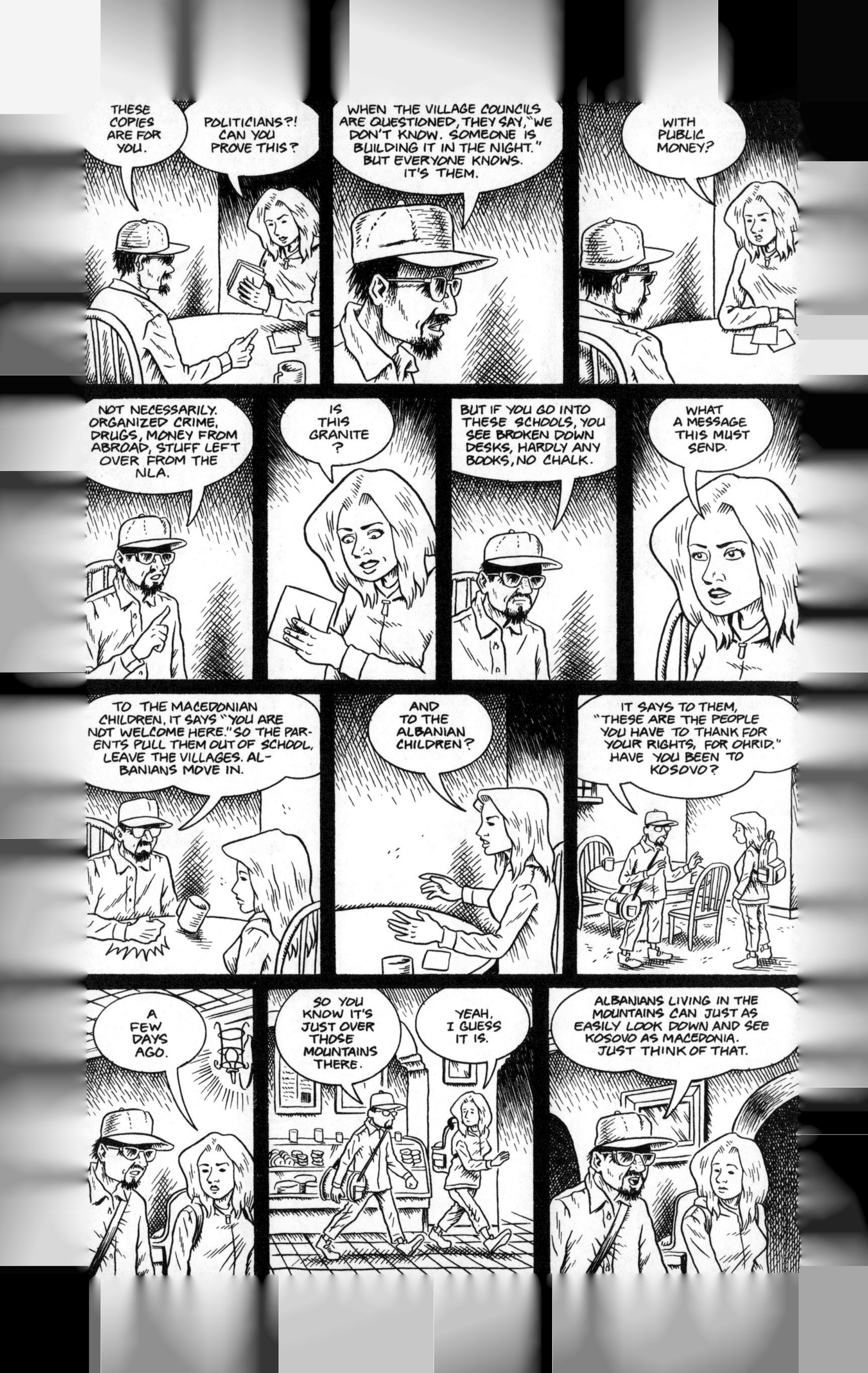
THESE COPIES ARE FOR YOU.
POLITICIANS?! CAN YOU PROVE THIS?
WHEN THE VILLAGE COUNCILS ARE QUESTIONED, THEY SAY, "WE DON'T KNOW. SOMEONE IS BUILDING IT IN THE NIGHT." BUT EVERYONE KNOWS. IT'S THEM.
WITH PUBLIC MONEY?
NOT NECESSARILY. ORGANIZED CRIME, DRUGS, MONEY FROM ABROAD, STUFF LEFT OVER FROM THE NLA.
IS THIS GRANITE?
BUT IF YOU GO INTO THESE SCHOOLS, YOU SEE BROKEN DOWN DESKS, HARDLY ANY BOOKS, NO CHALK.
WHAT A MESSAGE THIS MUST SEND.
TO THE MACEDONIAN CHILDREN, IT SAYS "YOU ARE NOT WELCOME HERE." SO THE PARENTS PULL THEM OUT OF SCHOOL, LEAVE THE VILLAGES. ALBANIANS MOVE IN.
AND TO THE ALBANIAN CHILDREN?
IT SAYS TO THEM, "THESE ARE THE PEOPLE YOU HAVE TO THANK FOR YOUR RIGHTS, FOR OHRID." HAVE YOU BEEN TO KOSOVO?
A FEW DAYS AGO.
SO YOU KNOW IT'S JUST OVER THOSE MOUNTAINS THERE.
YEAH, I GUESS IT IS.
ALBANIANS LIVING IN THE MOUNTAINS CAN JUST AS EASILY LOOK DOWN AND SEE KOSOVO AS MACEDONIA. JUST THINK OF THAT.

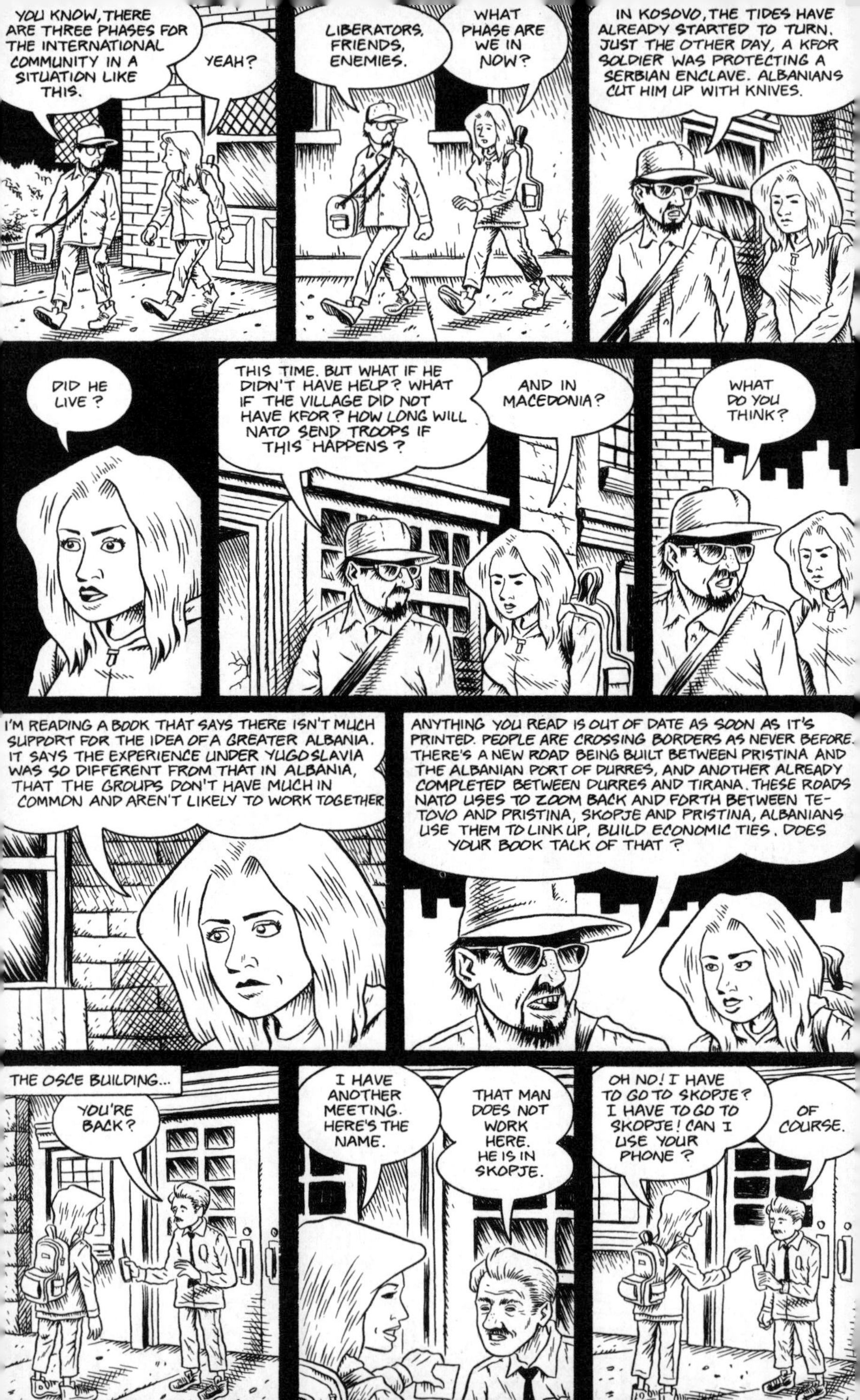
YOU KNOW, THERE ARE THREE PHASES FOR THE INTERNATIONAL COMMUNITY IN A SITUATION LIKE THIS.
YEAH?
LIBERATORS, FRIENDS, ENEMIES.
WHAT PHASE ARE WE IN NOW?
IN KOSOVO, THE TIDES HAVE ALREADY STARTED TO TURN. JUST THE OTHER DAY, A KFOR SOLDIER WAS PROTECTING A SERBIAN ENCLAVE. ALBANIANS CUT HIM UP WITH KNIVES.
DID HE LIVE?
THIS TIME. BUT WHAT IF HE DIDN'T HAVE HELP? WHAT IF THE VILLAGE DID NOT HAVE KFOR? HOW LONG WILL NATO SEND TROOPS IF THIS HAPPENS?
AND IN MACEDONIA?
WHAT DO YOU THINK?
I'M READING A BOOK THAT SAYS THERE ISN'T MUCH SUPPORT FOR THE IDEA OF A GREATER ALBANIA. IT SAYS THE EXPERIENCE UNDER YUGOSLAVIA WAS SO DIFFERENT FROM THAT IN ALBANIA, THAT THE GROUPS DON'T HAVE MUCH IN COMMON AND AREN'T LIKELY TO WORK TOGETHER.
ANYTHING YOU READ IS OUT OF DATE AS SOON AS IT'S PRINTED. PEOPLE ARE CROSSING BORDERS AS NEVER BEFORE. THERE'S A NEW ROAD BEING BUILT BETWEEN PRISTINA AND THE ALBANIAN PORT OF DURRES, AND ANOTHER ALREADY COMPLETED BETWEEN DURRES AND TIRANA. THESE ROADS NATO USES TO ZOOM BACK AND FORTH BETWEEN TETOVO AND PRISTINA, SKOPJE AND PRISTINA, ALBANIANS USE THEM TO LINK UP, BUILD ECONOMIC TIES. DOES YOUR BOOK TALK OF THAT?
THE OSCE BUILDING...
YOU'RE BACK?
I HAVE ANOTHER MEETING. HERE'S THE NAME.
THAT MAN DOES NOT WORK HERE. HE IS IN SKOPJE.
OH NO! I HAVE TO GO TO SKOPJE? I HAVE TO GO TO SKOPJE! CAN I USE YOUR PHONE?
OF COURSE.

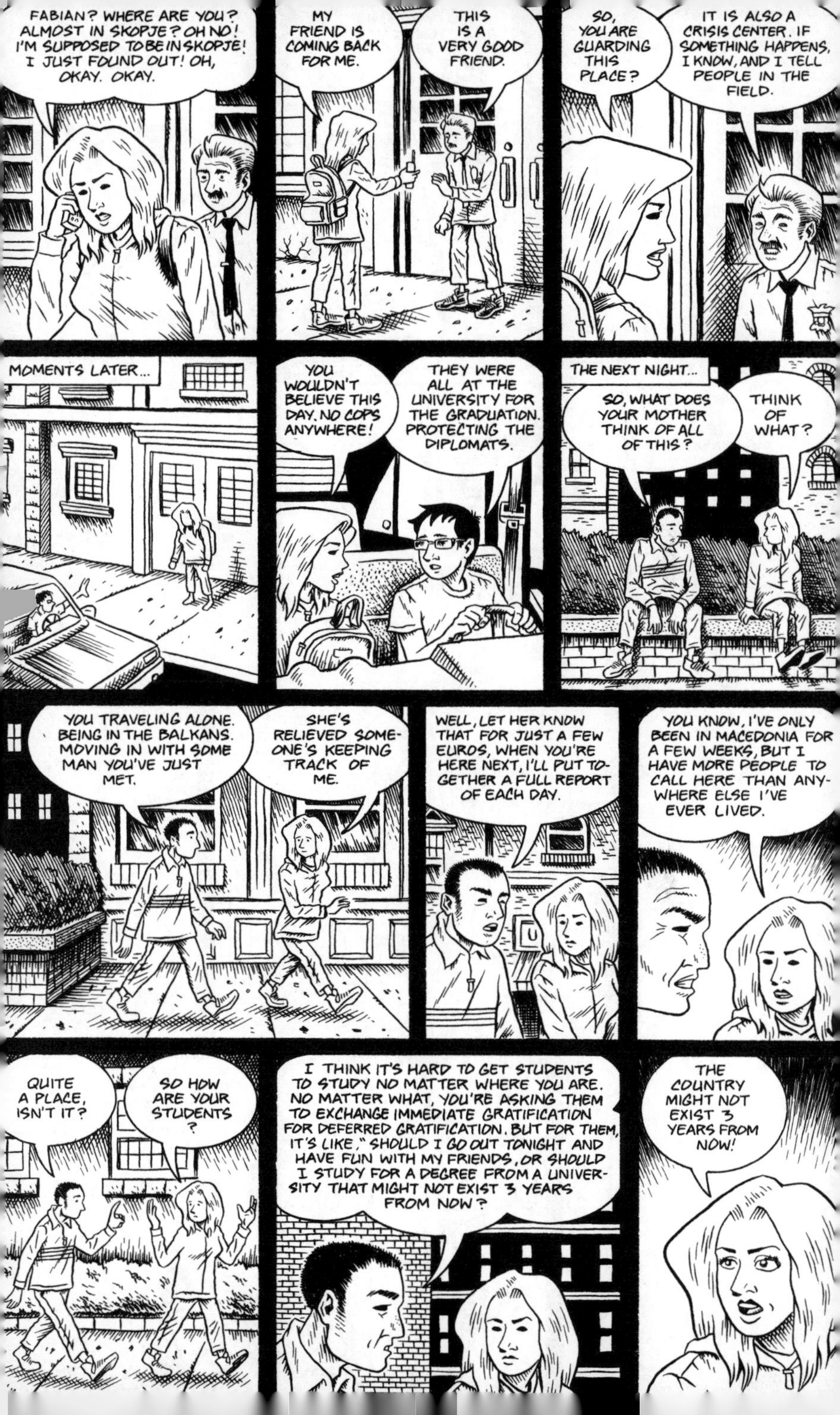
FABIAN? WHERE ARE YOU? ALMOST IN SKOPJE? OH NO! I'M SUPPOSED TO BE IN SKOPJE! I JUST FOUND OUT! OH, OKAY. OKAY.
MY FRIEND IS COMING BACK FOR ME.
THIS IS A VERY GOOD FRIEND.
SO, YOU ARE GUARDING THIS PLACE?
IT IS ALSO A CRISIS CENTER. IF SOMETHING HAPPENS, I KNOW, AND I TELL PEOPLE IN THE FIELD.
MOMENTS LATER...
YOU WOULDN'T BELIEVE THIS DAY. NO COPS ANYWHERE!
THEY WERE ALL AT THE UNIVERSITY FOR THE GRADUATION. PROTECTING THE DIPLOMATS.
THE NEXT NIGHT...
SO, WHAT DOES YOUR MOTHER THINK OF ALL OF THIS?
THINK OF WHAT?
YOU TRAVELING ALONE. BEING IN THE BALKANS. MOVING IN WITH SOME MAN YOU'VE JUST MET.
SHE'S RELIEVED SOME-ONE'S KEEPING TRACK OF ME.
WELL, LET HER KNOW THAT FOR JUST A FEW EUROS, WHEN YOU'RE HERE NEXT, I'LL PUT TO-GETHER A FULL REPORT OF EACH DAY.
YOU KNOW, I'VE ONLY BEEN IN MACEDONIA FOR A FEW WEEKS, BUT I HAVE MORE PEOPLE TO CALL HERE THAN ANY-WHERE ELSE I'VE EVER LIVED.
QUITE A PLACE, ISN'T IT?
SO HOW ARE YOUR STUDENTS?
I THINK IT'S HARD TO GET STUDENTS TO STUDY NO MATTER WHERE YOU ARE. NO MATTER WHAT, YOU'RE ASKING THEM TO EXCHANGE IMMEDIATE GRATIFICATION FOR DEFERRED GRATIFICATION. BUT FOR THEM, IT'S LIKE, "SHOULD I GO OUT TONIGHT AND HAVE FUN WITH MY FRIENDS, OR SHOULD I STUDY FOR A DEGREE FROM A UNIVER-SITY THAT MIGHT NOT EXIST 3 YEARS FROM NOW?
THE COUNTRY MIGHT NOT EXIST 3 YEARS FROM NOW!

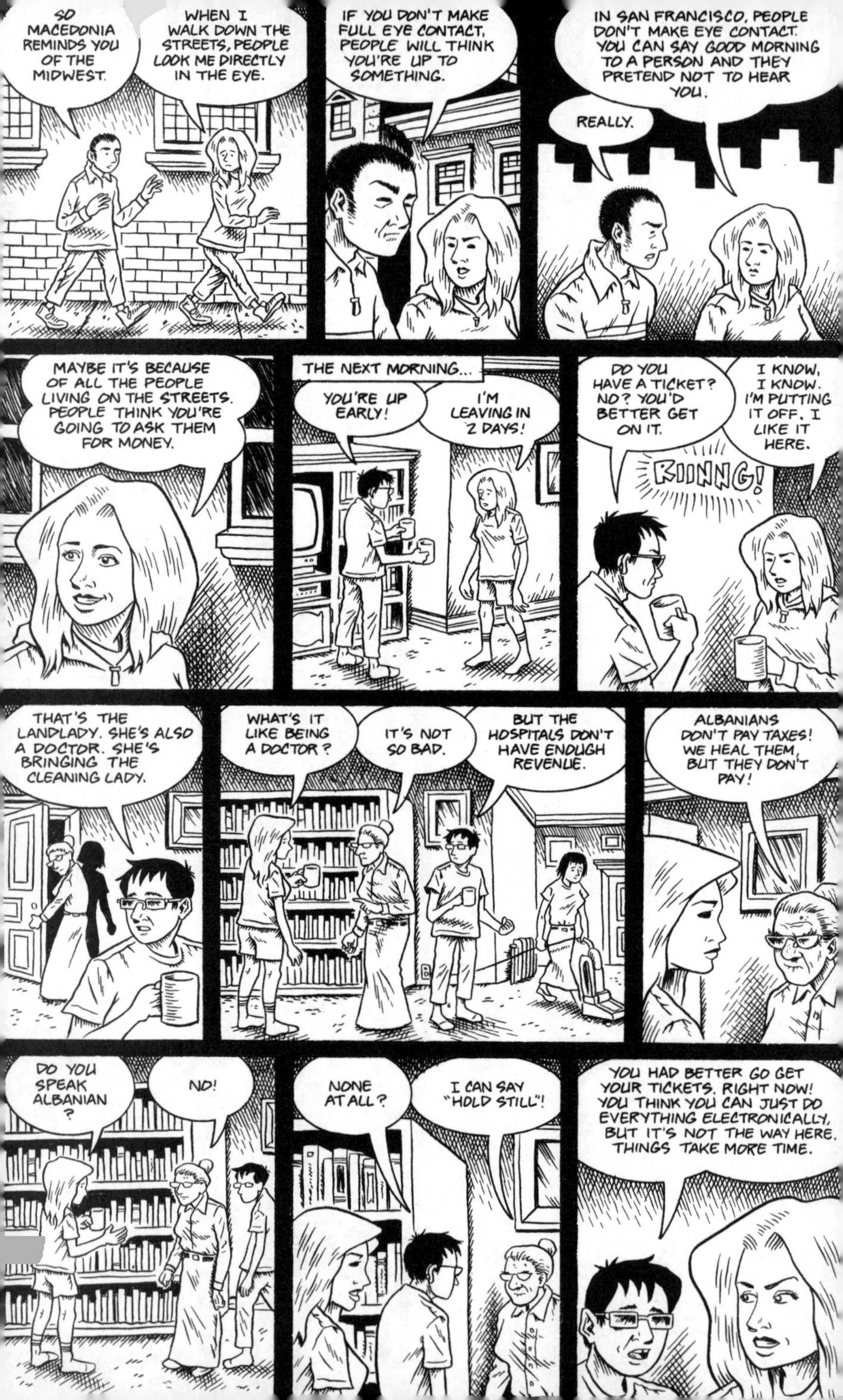
SO MACEDONIA REMINDS YOU OF THE MIDWEST.
WHEN I WALK DOWN THE STREETS, PEOPLE LOOK ME DIRECTLY IN THE EYE.
IF YOU DON'T MAKE FULL EYE CONTACT, PEOPLE WILL THINK YOU'RE UP TO SOMETHING.
IN SAN FRANCISCO, PEOPLE DON'T MAKE EYE CONTACT. YOU CAN SAY GOOD MORNING TO A PERSON AND THEY PRETEND NOT TO HEAR YOU.
REALLY.
MAYBE IT'S BECAUSE OF ALL THE PEOPLE LIVING ON THE STREETS. PEOPLE THINK YOU'RE GOING TO ASK THEM FOR MONEY.
THE NEXT MORNING...
YOU'RE UP EARLY!
I'M LEAVING IN 2 DAYS!
DO YOU HAVE A TICKET? NO? YOU'D BETTER GET ON IT.
I KNOW, I KNOW. I'M PUTTING IT OFF. I LIKE IT HERE.
RIIING!
THAT'S THE LANDLADY. SHE'S ALSO A DOCTOR. SHE'S BRINGING THE CLEANING LADY.
WHAT'S IT LIKE BEING A DOCTOR?
IT'S NOT SO BAD.
BUT THE HOSPITALS DON'T HAVE ENOUGH REVENUE.
ALBANIANS DON'T PAY TAXES! WE HEAL THEM, BUT THEY DON'T PAY!
DO YOU SPEAK ALBANIAN?
NO!
NONE AT ALL?
I CAN SAY "HOLD STILL"!
YOU HAD BETTER GO GET YOUR TICKETS, RIGHT NOW! YOU THINK YOU CAN JUST DO EVERYTHING ELECTRONICALLY, BUT IT'S NOT THE WAY HERE. THINGS TAKE MORE TIME.

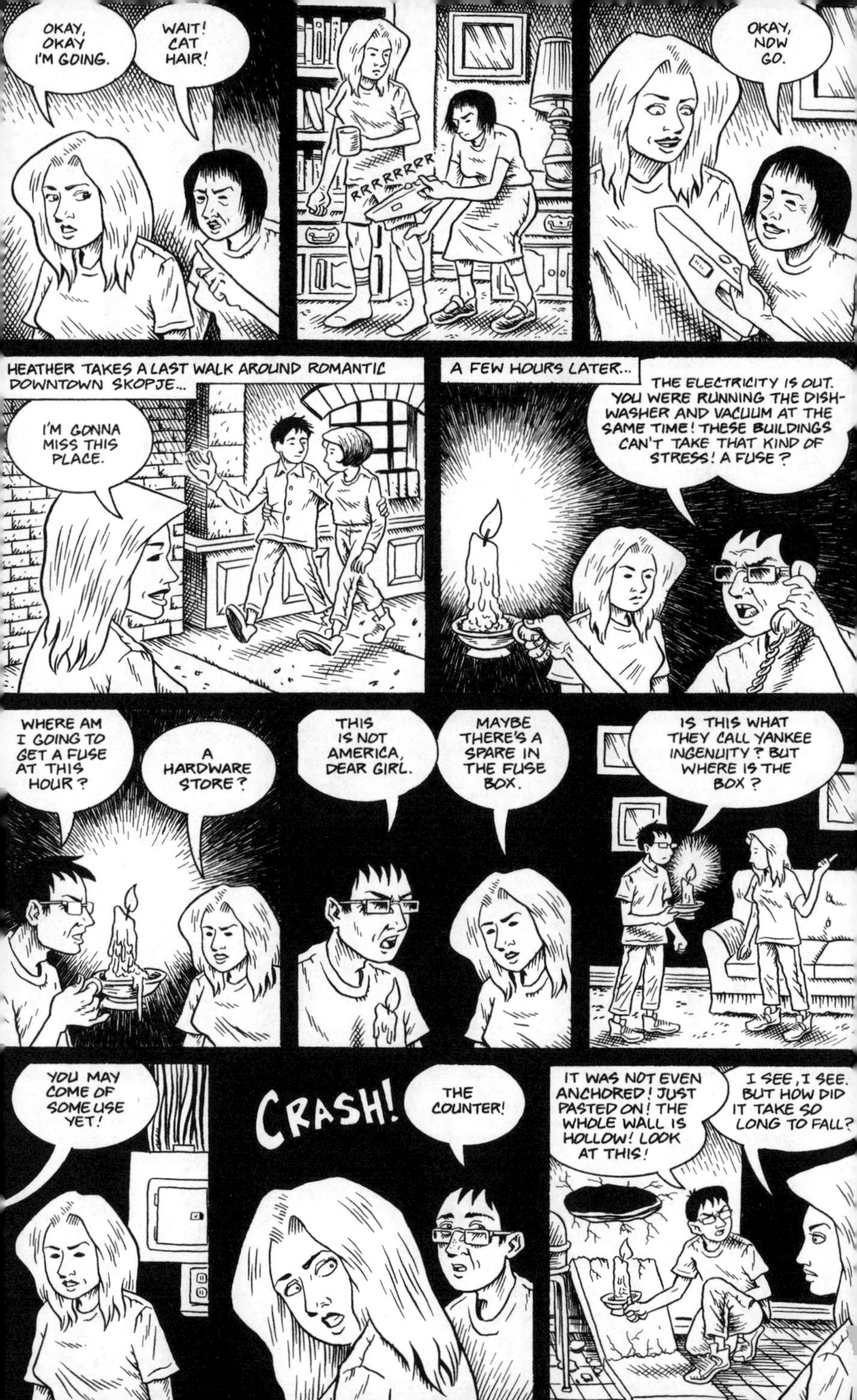

OKAY, OKAY I'M GOING.
WAIT! CAT HAIR!
RRRRRRRRR
OKAY, NOW GO.
HEATHER TAKES A LAST WALK AROUND ROMANTIC DOWNTOWN SKOPJE...
I'M GONNA MISS THIS PLACE.
A FEW HOURS LATER...
THE ELECTRICITY IS OUT. YOU WERE RUNNING THE DISH-WASHER AND VACUUM AT THE SAME TIME! THESE BUILDINGS CAN'T TAKE THAT KIND OF STRESS! A FUSE?
WHERE AM I GOING TO GET A FUSE AT THIS HOUR?
A HARDWARE STORE?
THIS IS NOT AMERICA, DEAR GIRL.
MAYBE THERE'S A SPARE IN THE FUSE BOX.
IS THIS WHAT THEY CALL YANKEE INGENUITY? BUT WHERE IS THE BOX?
YOU MAY COME OF SOME USE YET!
CRASH!
THE COUNTER!
IT WAS NOT EVEN ANCHORED! JUST PASTED ON! THE WHOLE WALL IS HOLLOW! LOOK AT THIS!
I SEE, I SEE. BUT HOW DID IT TAKE SO LONG TO FALL?

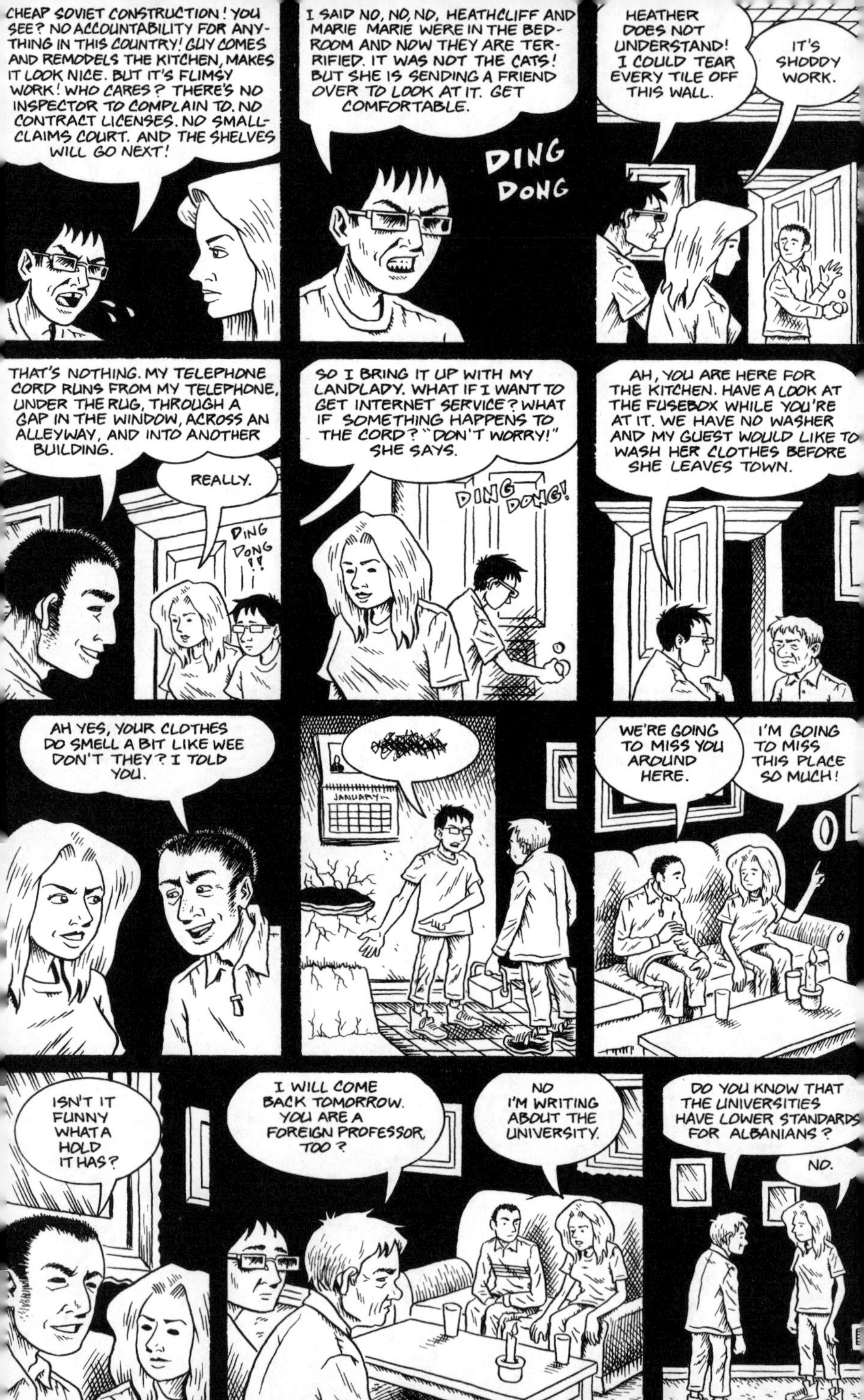
CHEAP SOVIET CONSTRUCTION! YOU SEE? NO ACCOUNTABILITY FOR ANYTHING IN THIS COUNTRY! GUY COMES AND REMODELS THE KITCHEN, MAKES IT LOOK NICE. BUT IT'S FLIMSY WORK! WHO CARES? THERE'S NO INSPECTOR TO COMPLAIN TO. NO CONTRACT LICENSES. NO SMALL-CLAIMS COURT. AND THE SHELVES WILL GO NEXT!
I SAID NO, NO, NO, HEATHCLIFF AND MARIE MARIE WERE IN THE BEDROOM AND NOW THEY ARE TERRIFIED. IT WAS NOT THE CATS! BUT SHE IS SENDING A FRIEND OVER TO LOOK AT IT. GET COMFORTABLE.
DING DONG
HEATHER DOES NOT UNDERSTAND! I COULD TEAR EVERY TILE OFF THIS WALL.
IT'S SHODDY WORK.
THAT'S NOTHING. MY TELEPHONE CORD RUNS FROM MY TELEPHONE, UNDER THE RUG, THROUGH A GAP IN THE WINDOW, ACROSS AN ALLEYWAY, AND INTO ANOTHER BUILDING.
REALLY.
DING DONG !!
SO I BRING IT UP WITH MY LANDLADY. WHAT IF I WANT TO GET INTERNET SERVICE? WHAT IF SOMETHING HAPPENS TO THE CORD? "DON'T WORRY!" SHE SAYS.
DING DONG!
AH, YOU ARE HERE FOR THE KITCHEN. HAVE A LOOK AT THE FUSEBOX WHILE YOU'RE AT IT. WE HAVE NO WASHER AND MY GUEST WOULD LIKE TO WASH HER CLOTHES BEFORE SHE LEAVES TOWN.
AH YES, YOUR CLOTHES DO SMELL A BIT LIKE WEE DON'T THEY? I TOLD YOU.
JANUARY
WE'RE GOING TO MISS YOU AROUND HERE.
I'M GOING TO MISS THIS PLACE SO MUCH!
ISN'T IT FUNNY WHAT A HOLD IT HAS?
I WILL COME BACK TOMORROW. YOU ARE A FOREIGN PROFESSOR, TOO?
NO I'M WRITING ABOUT THE UNIVERSITY.
DO YOU KNOW THAT THE UNIVERSITIES HAVE LOWER STANDARDS FOR ALBANIANS?
NO.

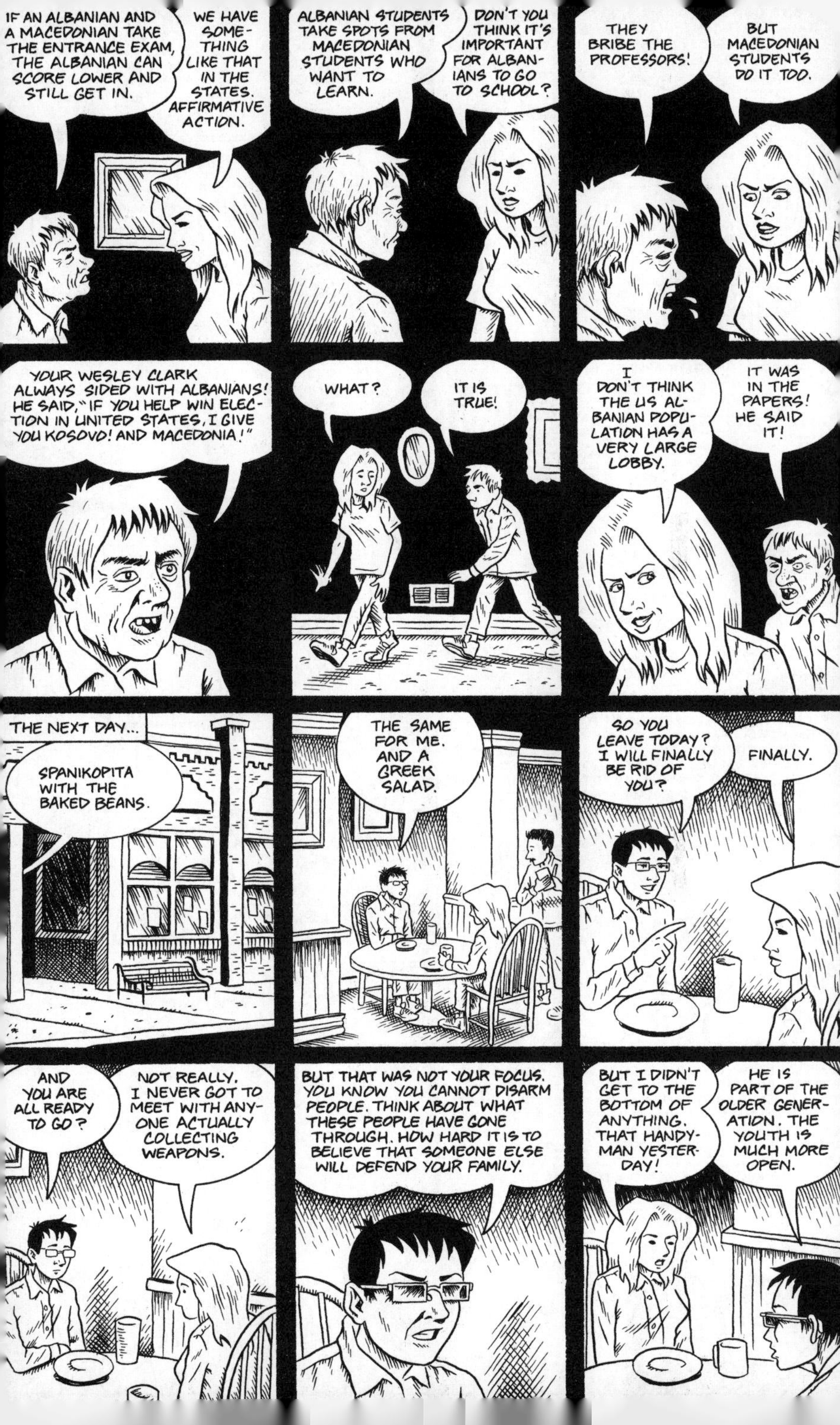
IF AN ALBANIAN AND A MACEDONIAN TAKE THE ENTRANCE EXAM, THE ALBANIAN CAN SCORE LOWER AND STILL GET IN.
WE HAVE SOME-THING LIKE THAT IN THE STATES. AFFIRMATIVE ACTION.
ALBANIAN STUDENTS TAKE SPOTS FROM MACEDONIAN STUDENTS WHO WANT TO LEARN.
DON'T YOU THINK IT'S IMPORTANT FOR ALBAN-IANS TO GO TO SCHOOL?
THEY BRIBE THE PROFESSORS!
BUT MACEDONIAN STUDENTS DO IT TOO.
YOUR WESLEY CLARK ALWAYS SIDED WITH ALBANIANS! HE SAID, "IF YOU HELP WIN ELEC-TION IN UNITED STATES, I GIVE YOU KOSOVO! AND MACEDONIA!"
WHAT?
IT IS TRUE!
I DON'T THINK THE US AL-BANIAN POPU-LATION HAS A VERY LARGE LOBBY.
IT WAS IN THE PAPERS! HE SAID IT!
THE NEXT DAY...
SPANIKOPITA WITH THE BAKED BEANS.
THE SAME FOR ME. AND A GREEK SALAD.
SO YOU LEAVE TODAY? I WILL FINALLY BE RID OF YOU?
FINALLY.
AND YOU ARE ALL READY TO GO?
NOT REALLY. I NEVER GOT TO MEET WITH ANY-ONE ACTUALLY COLLECTING WEAPONS.
BUT THAT WAS NOT YOUR FOCUS. YOU KNOW YOU CANNOT DISARM PEOPLE. THINK ABOUT WHAT THESE PEOPLE HAVE GONE THROUGH. HOW HARD IT IS TO BELIEVE THAT SOMEONE ELSE WILL DEFEND YOUR FAMILY.
BUT I DIDN'T GET TO THE BOTTOM OF ANYTHING. THAT HANDY-MAN YESTER-DAY!
HE IS PART OF THE OLDER GENER-ATION. THE YOUTH IS MUCH MORE OPEN.

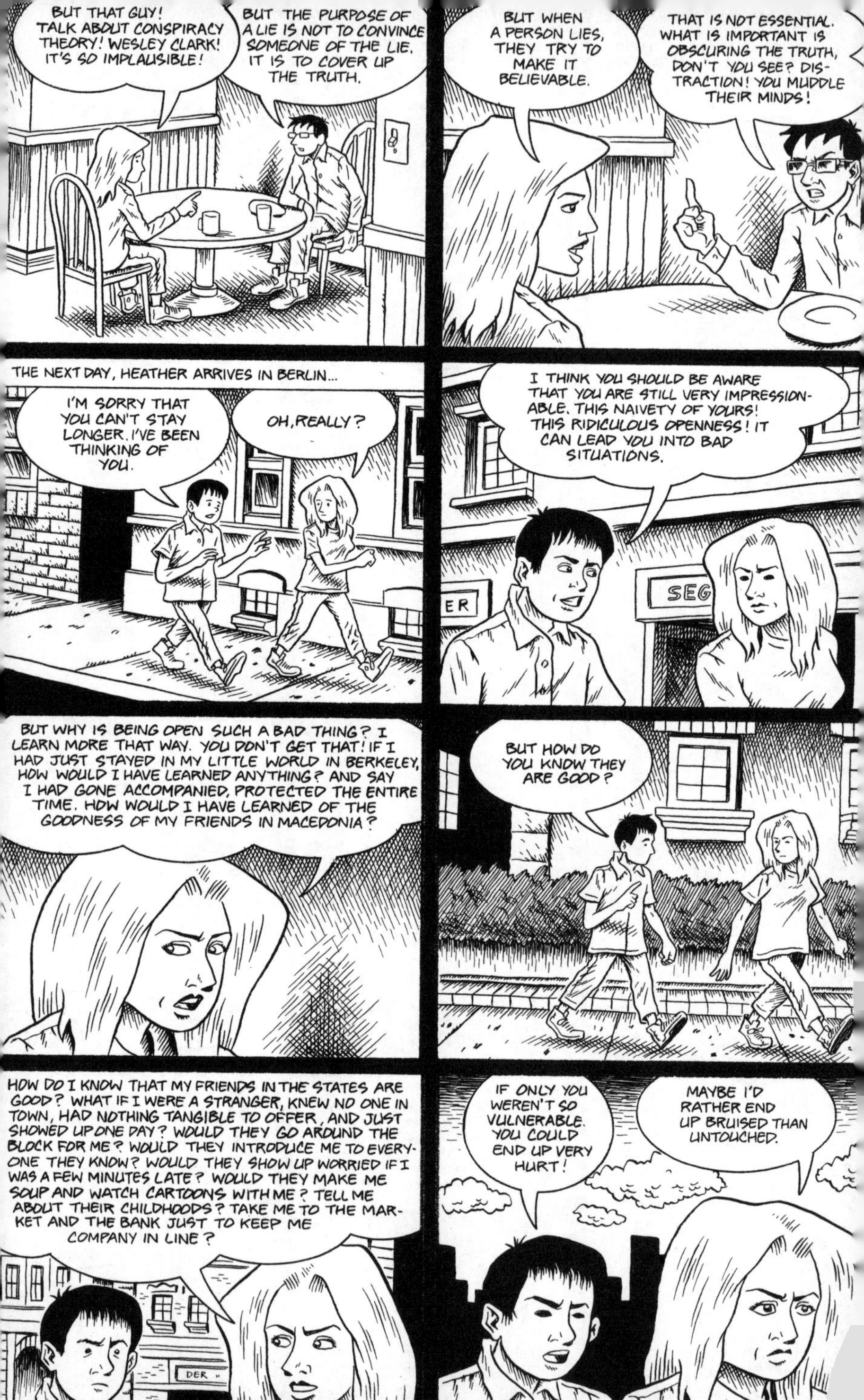
BUT THAT GUY! TALK ABOUT CONSPIRACY THEORY! WESLEY CLARK! IT'S SO IMPLAUSIBLE!
BUT THE PURPOSE OF A LIE IS NOT TO CONVINCE SOMEONE OF THE LIE. IT IS TO COVER UP THE TRUTH.
BUT WHEN A PERSON LIES, THEY TRY TO MAKE IT BELIEVABLE.
THAT IS NOT ESSENTIAL. WHAT IS IMPORTANT IS OBSCURING THE TRUTH, DON'T YOU SEE? DISTRACTION! YOU MUDDLE THEIR MINDS!
THE NEXT DAY, HEATHER ARRIVES IN BERLIN...
I'M SORRY THAT YOU CAN'T STAY LONGER. I'VE BEEN THINKING OF YOU.
OH, REALLY?
I THINK YOU SHOULD BE AWARE THAT YOU ARE STILL VERY IMPRESSIONABLE. THIS NAIVETY OF YOURS! THIS RIDICULOUS OPENNESS! IT CAN LEAD YOU INTO BAD SITUATIONS.
ER
SEG
BUT WHY IS BEING OPEN SUCH A BAD THING? I LEARN MORE THAT WAY. YOU DON'T GET THAT! IF I HAD JUST STAYED IN MY LITTLE WORLD IN BERKELEY, HOW WOULD I HAVE LEARNED ANYTHING? AND SAY I HAD GONE ACCOMPANIED, PROTECTED THE ENTIRE TIME. HOW WOULD I HAVE LEARNED OF THE GOODNESS OF MY FRIENDS IN MACEDONIA?
BUT HOW DO YOU KNOW THEY ARE GOOD?
HOW DO I KNOW THAT MY FRIENDS IN THE STATES ARE GOOD? WHAT IF I WERE A STRANGER, KNEW NO ONE IN TOWN, HAD NOTHING TANGIBLE TO OFFER, AND JUST SHOWED UP ONE DAY? WOULD THEY GO AROUND THE BLOCK FOR ME? WOULD THEY INTRODUCE ME TO EVERYONE THEY KNOW? WOULD THEY SHOW UP WORRIED IF I WAS A FEW MINUTES LATE? WOULD THEY MAKE ME SOUP AND WATCH CARTOONS WITH ME? TELL ME ABOUT THEIR CHILDHOODS? TAKE ME TO THE MARKET AND THE BANK JUST TO KEEP ME COMPANY IN LINE?
DER
IF ONLY YOU WEREN'T SO VULNERABLE. YOU COULD END UP VERY HURT!
MAYBE I'D RATHER END UP BRUISED THAN UNTOUCHED.
FIN!

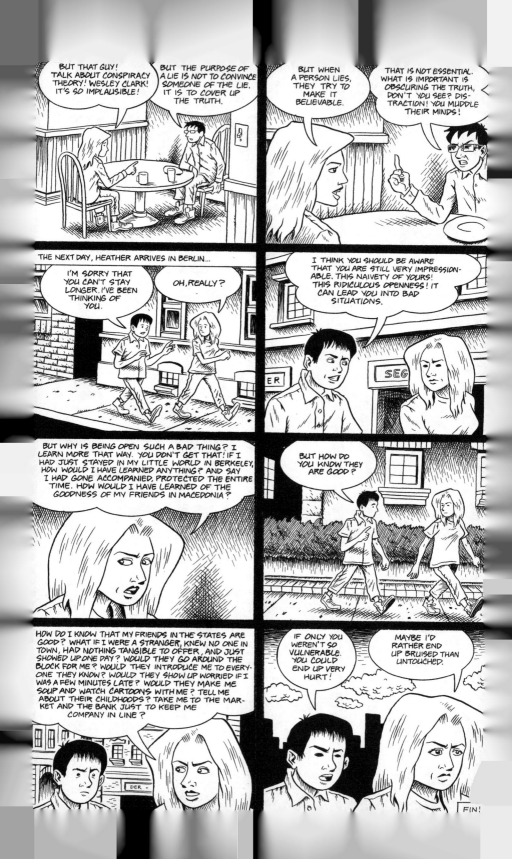

It is not uncommon for world leaders to name peace as their primary ambition. Peace is spoken of as a glorious destination, one that can be reached any number of ways, even through war. What makes Macedonia different is that its leaders and its people have chosen peace as a method. They have chosen to be peaceful in the present so that a future might exist. This has taken no small amount of bravery and sacrifice. To negotiate its way clear of a war of secession with Yugoslavia, Macedonia gave up the army that had always protected it. It took a leap of faith that the international community would help protect its fragile peace. Over the ensuing decade, the people of Macedonia continued to display such bravery, as they expanded—sometimes by great leaps—the social contract of their fledgling democracy.

By engaging early in the project of protecting peace in Macedonia, the international community made steady progress with relatively meager resources. The UN's Macedonia mission was never terribly large—700 troops, 35 military observers, and 26 police monitors—but it arrived quickly, when political will still existed for peace. This made room for a cooperative effort of human-rights monitors, aid agencies, and mediators to delve more deeply into the causes of conflict in Macedonia and to put their conclusions to productive use in 2001.

And yet, even for all its progress, Macedonia remains plagued by nationalism and distrust. Ethnic Macedonians still have trouble believing that Albanians will abide by the law, pay taxes, and lay down their guns. Albanians, on the other hand, still feel excluded from power and tend to think that the Macedonian government is only feigning reform as a way to impress the international community.

As part of the war prevention and democratization process, the US and EU have forced Macedonia to scrap its centralized system, promising that democracy will flourish and radical separatism will diminish as local communities gain access to government. This includes merging smaller municipalities with larger ones and ceding more rights to minorities where demographics demand. However, some fear this will reward fragmentation, as those with little faith in government to reconcile differences gravitate to areas where their group can at least dominate.

The southern Macedonian town of Struga was the loudest in its protest decentralization, when it was shown in November 2004 that under its new boundaries the Struga municipality would become majority Albanian. Struga's leaders announced that, given the considerable differences between Albanian and Macedonian attitudes toward government, it would be impossible to govern Struga. Their only choice, they said, was to secede from Macedonia altogether. Mobs of angry ethnic Macedonians attacked Albanian shops and EU vehicles prompting sympathizers to organize across Macedonia, collecting more than 150,000 signatures to call a vote to repeal the West's decentralization. The furor subsided after the United States' timely decision to recognize Macedonia by its constitutional name, angering Greece and temporarily redirecting Macedonia's nationalist energies.

Nevertheless, Macedonia remains surrounded by intense ethnic nationalism and intolerance. Macedonians believe—and have good reason to believe—that they can only be secure as Macedonians *in Macedonia.* This fear is fueled by the denial and repression of Macedonian minorities in neighboring Greece and Bulgaria, both of which insist that their own populations are almost entirely monoethnic and that the Macedonian people are not really a people at all. As if this were not enough, Macedonian fears are further reinforced by the Kosovo Albanian government's abusive attitudes toward its own Serb minorities. The Albanians of Kosovo and Macedonia, on the other hand, have suffered deeply as minorities among the Slavs and would consider it intolerably naïve to entrust their safety to a newly compassionate majority.

This ideology of ethnic nationalism intensified in the wars of Yugoslav dissolution throughout the 1990s, where, unlike in Macedonia, the international community did not act early to protect minorities, counteract radicalism, and provide alternatives to armed violence. Instead, in Croatia, Bosnia, and Kosovo, it ignored signs of impending war, standing by as radicals rose to power and as thousands were killed, raped, and driven from their homes. In the end, there was little political will left for building multiethnic peace. The wars proved, beyond a shadow of a doubt, that Croats were only safe among Croats, that Serbs were only safe among Serbs, and so on.

When ethnic nationalists rose to power in Croatia, pledging to create a state just for the Croats, this was an obvious threat to peace. After all, Croatia was 12% Serb, and these minority Serbs quite naturally protested the formation of a "de-Serbianized" state and were backed by the Yugoslav army. However, it was a full year after fighting began in Croatia before EU negotiators arrived with promises of economic aid, which by this time fell on deaf ears. Radical nationalists had already solidified power in the Croatian government and in the Serbian paramilitary, and both sides were fully committed to using violence. When UN peacekeepers arrived in Croatia, it was two years after fighting had begun, and the Serbs had already taken a third of Croatia in a violent ethnic-cleansing campaign. The UN could only keep the Serbs and Croats apart, solidifying the ethnic partitions the radicals wanted, allowing them to concentrate their efforts on which parts of Bosnia they would like to have for their future monoethnic states.

The US and EU recognized Bosnia's independence, paying lip service to its multiethnic ideals, but did little to secure it from the increasingly militarized Croats and Serbs, who were coming to carve it into pieces. By the time the UN sent peacekeepers—to hand out humanitarian aid, not to stop the war—the Serbs had taken two-thirds of Bosnia and fighting had heated between the Bosnians and Croat militias. Finally, after the Serbs had killed off most of Bosnia's professional and intellectual class, and after countless people were raped, tortured, and traumatized, the international community rained bombs on the region, trying to beat the Serbs into submission. Even then, international negotiators gave the Serbs half of Bosnia for their monoethnic state, again formalizing the ill-gotten gains of war.

Then, as if it had learned nothing, for eight years the West ignored the nonviolent protests of the Kosovo Albanians suffering under Milošević. Even as Western organizations praised the Albanian leader Ibrahim Rugova for his championing of restraint and patience in the face of such brutality, the international community did not actively engage in resolving this conflict until *after* the violent tactics of the

KLA had gained legitimacy. Indeed, almost two years passed after the violence began between the KLA and Yugoslav security forces before the international community started negotiating, and even then their efforts served mainly as a pretext for NATO's bombing campaign. The bombing caused untold death and destruction, not least because it caused the Yugoslav army to declare war and increase ethnic cleansing, driving hundreds of thousands of Albanians over the border. When the Albanians returned to Kosovo under Western protection, they were too embittered to envision a common future with the Serbs.

The international community expended vast resources trying to put Kosovo back together, turning the province into a de facto international protectorate. However, the governing UN administration has failed to produce a semblance of multiethnic democracy, and NATO's 40,000 troops have, at times, failed to keep the peace. Even under strict international watch, the Kosovo government has not protected its minorities. In 2004, anti-Serb riots saw 19 killed and hundreds of homes destroyed. It seems increasingly unlikely that Kosovo will preserve what remains of its multiethnic character; rather, it will probably be further partitioned and further cleansed.

Unfortunately, the current international setup pretty much guarantees that in the future, Macedonia-style successes will be few, and that failures along the lines of Croatia, Bosnia, and Kosovo will be common. Even though war prevention is obviously easier, more productive, and more humane, the international community is hardly set up to make it standard policy. In fact, the international community hardly exists at all, except as a linguistic crutch used to describe the myriad of international treaty organizations, states, and nongovernmental organizations we hope will cohere into an effective body that can address global challenges.

The international community has no protocol for handling conflict quickly, nor does it appear to have the political will to stick to protocol if one existed. Instead, with each new crisis, the international community seems to reinvent itself. This starts with the UN Security Council, which, contrary to the grave responsibility its name implies, is a collection of states that typically put their own interests before world security. After all, the council's 5 permanent members, who must approve any peacekeeping force, did not rise to their positions because they had a heightened commitment to peace and democracy, but because they won World War II.

Even if the Security Council authorizes action quickly, the UN must still build a peacekeeping force from the ground up, relying on member states to provide troops and equipment. These tend to trickle in slowly and separately, if at all. Then the troops must be trained and a command structure negotiated. Some troops may serve directly under the UN, while others act under a separate mandate and leadership, causing lack of coordination and credibility. At times, the UN cannot find its own troops and must subcontract peace operations to a state or regional organization, but then it risks sponsoring new parties to a conflict.

The Macedonia mission may be the closest we have seen to the UN's true potential if it had—as many have suggested it should—its own standing rapid-reaction force. Because the UN already had an existing peace force on the ground in Croatia and Bosnia, it could send an exploratory mission to Macedonia with less than two weeks of deliberation. Then the UN brought troops in under the existing command, rather than creating an entirely new structure. Most of the troops—from the Nordic states and the US—came equipped and well-trained.

However, for peace to truly take hold in Macedonia, it must continue to work with the international community to increase access to nonviolent processes to handle conflicts, and this presents a central contradiction: while these changes are directed at promoting democracy, they are themselves being imposed from the outside, not emanating up from the people as a truly democratic movement would. It seems unlikely that, if left alone, the Macedonian majority or the Albanian minority would continue to champion multiethnic democracy, and this could lead to a war of ethnic cleansing.

The US and EU have had great success leveraging Macedonian desire for membership in Euro-Atlantic structures into meaningful reform. However, they have hardly proven their own commitment to democracy and the rule of law. The EU was founded as an economic entity and, though it has poured millions into the rule of law and democratization in Macedonia, it appears to be doing so mainly as a means to a profitable future for Europe. It has not, for instance, brought real pressure to bear on affluent, militarily robust Greece to extend equal rights to its Macedonian minorities.

The international community's largest player—the US—preaches democracy and the rule of law, but in practice it has, since the end of the cold war, worked to create an international system based on its own unquestionable dominance. The US seems to want the kind of justice it alone can enforce and to which it and its allies are not accountable. In the wake of September 11, this attitude of exceptionalism hardened. Where there might have been talk of investigation and prosecution, the only words acceptable for use among US leaders seemed to be "Hunt down and kill the terrorists."

Macedonia's leaders took the cue. Two months after the attacks, Interior Minister Boskovski and his police chiefs met to devise ways to prove that Macedonia was a partner in the war on terror. After the meeting, they contracted with a Bulgarian human trafficker, telling him to find a number of economic migrants who "look like mujahideen." He found six Pakistanis and one Indian bound for Germany and convinced them to go with him to Greece instead—via Macedonia.

Once the men were in Skopje, Boskovski told his special police that terrorists had infiltrated Macedonia from Afghanistan and were planning to attack the American embassy. He directed his men to a vineyard outside of town where the seven innocent men waited. His police shot the men point-blank, then planted weapons and uniforms on them. Human-rights organizations insisted that it was a horrible farce. The US only said that it had not known of a threat on its embassy. It was three years later when the new government finally forced the police to come forward to admit what they had done.

The international community promises the Macedonians that, if they put their faith in democracy and the rule of law, these will become tools they can use to improve their lives and gain security at home and abroad. It promises them that, once they breathe life into this system of rights, radical separatists will be marginalized, having less reason to attack the government. In return, the dominant class must only trade in the comforts of unquestionable supremacy for a system that will protect the weak as well as the strong. The minority, which has gained strength through the use of arms, must give them up and trust the law to protect their interests.

Key global players must also look beyond their own dominance to strengthen the international system into something that is more democratic and just. All must work toward a world order based on the mutual recognition of humanity, in which even the weakest can partici-pate and be protected. Surely, this requires great sacrifice on the part of those who dominate, and faith on the part of those who do not. It will be an ongoing adventure, which will be frustrating and scary at times, and which is likely to yield more questions than answers. But the rewards are a world that we may all hold in common and a peace that all are committed to preserving.

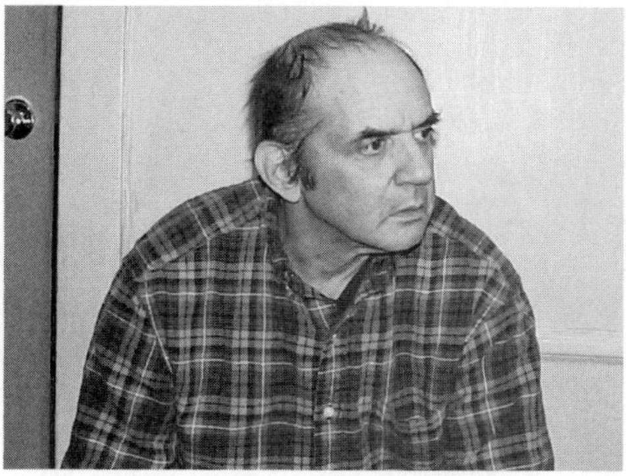

PHOTO: © GARY DUMM

HARVEY PEKAR, a native of Cleveland, is best known for his autobiographical slice-of-life comic book series *American Splendor,* a first-person account of his downtrodden life, which was made into a movie starring Paul Giamatti. He is also the author of *Best of American Splendor* and *American Splendor: Our Movie Year.* He is an omnivorous reader, an obsessive-compulsive collector, and a jazz critic whose reviews have been published in the *Boston Herald, The Austin Chronicle,* and *JazzTimes.* He has done freelance work for the critically acclaimed radio station WKSU and has appeared eight times on *Late Night with David Letterman* and two times on *The Late Show with David Letterman.*